# The Handbook of High-Risk Challenging Behaviors in People with Intellectual and Developmental Disabilities

# The Handbook of
# High-Risk Challenging
# Behaviors in People
# with Intellectual and
# Developmental Disabilities

edited by

**James K. Luiselli, Ed.D., ABPP, BCBA-D**

May Institute
Randolph, Massachusetts

·P·A·U·L·H·
BROOKES
PUBLISHING Cº ®

Baltimore • London • Sydney

**Paul H. Brookes Publishing Co.**
Post Office Box 10624
Baltimore, Maryland 21285-0624
USA

www.brookespublishing.com

Typeset by Spearhead Global, Inc., Bear, Delaware.
Manufactured in the United States of America by
Sheridan Books, Inc., Chelsea, Michigan.

The individuals described in this book are composites or real people whose situations are masked and are based on
the authors' experiences. In all instances, names and identifying details have been changed to protect confidentiality.

The information provided in this book is in no way meant to substitute for a medical or mental health practitioner's
advice or expert opinion. Readers should consult a health or mental health professional if they are interested in
more information. This book is sold without warranties of any kind, express of implied, and the publisher and
authors disclaim any liability, loss, or damage caused by the contents of this book.

**Library of Congress Cataloging-in-Publication Data**

The handbook of high-risk challenging behaviors in people with intellectual and developmental disabilities /
edited by James K. Luiselli.—1st ed.
   p.  cm.
  Includes bibliographical references and index.
  ISBN-13: 978-1-59857-168-4
  ISBN-10: 1-59857-168-0
   1. Developmental disabilities—Handbooks, manuals, etc.  2. Psychology, Pathological—Handbooks, manuals, etc.
3. Behavior disorders in children—Handbooks, manuals, etc.  I. Luiselli, James K.
  RJ506.D47H357 2012
  616.8588—dc23                                                                                                     2011036462

British Library Cataloguing in Publication data are available from the British Library.

| 2015 | 2014 | 2013 | 2012 | 2011 | | | | | |
|------|------|------|------|------|---|---|---|---|---|
| 10 | 9 | 8 | 7 | 6 | 5 | 4 | 3 | 2 | 1 |

# Contents

# About the Editor

**James K. Luiselli, Ed.D., ABPP, BCBA-D,** Clinical Psychologist and Senior Vice President, Applied Research, Clinical Training, and Peer Review, May Institute, 41 Pacella Park Drive, Randolph, Massachusetts 02368

May Institute is a private human services and behavioral health care organization serving children, adolescents, and adults with developmental disabilities, traumatic brain injury, psychiatric disorders, and medically compromised conditions. Dr. Luiselli also maintains a private practice in educational, clinical, and behavioral consultation.

Dr. Luiselli is a licensed psychologist, certified health service provider, diplomate in behavioral psychology from The American Board of Professional Psychology (ABPP), and Board Certified Behavior Analyst (BCBA). He has held academic appointments at Harvard Medical School, Northeastern University, and Indiana State University. Within the May Institute, he is Director of the Predoctoral Internship Program in Clinical Psychology and the Program of Professional Continuing Education.

He is active in clinical treatment, consultation, and research. In 1996 he was ranked by the Association for Advancement of Behavior Therapy (AABT) as one of the top 50 most-published authors in the behavior analysis and therapy literature from 1974 to 1994. The journal *Research in Developmental Disabilities* (2000) listed him as the eighth most-published researcher in the developmental disabilities field from 1979 to 1999. He has authored more than 275 publications, including the books *Behavioral Medicine and Developmental Disabilities* (Springer-Verlag, 1989), *Self-Injurious Behavior: Analysis, Assessment, and Treatment* (Springer-Verlag, 1991), *Antecedent Control: Innovative Approaches to Behavioral Support* (Paul H. Brookes Publishing Co., 1998), *Behavior Psychology in the Schools: Innovations in Evaluation, Support, and Consultation* (The Haworth Press, 2002), *Antecedent Assessment and Intervention: Supporting Children and Adults with Developmental Disabilities in Community Settings* (Paul H. Brookes Publishing Co., 2006), *Effective Practices for Children with Autism: Educational and Behavior Support Interventions that Work* (Oxford University Press, 2011), and *Behavioral Sport Psychology: Evidence-Based Approaches to Performance Enhancement* (Springer, 2011).

Dr. Luiselli has been the senior editor of special-topic journal issues published in *Behavior Modification, Mental Health Aspects of Developmental Disabilities, Child & Family Behavior Therapy, Journal of Developmental and Physical Disabilities,* and *International Journal of Behavioral Consultation & Therapy.* He was a contributing editor to the *Habilitative Mental Healthcare Newsletter* and Associate Editor for *Education and Treatment of Children.* He also is a contributing writer for *The New England Psychologist,* reviews books for *Metapsychology Online Reviews,* and serves on the board of editors of six peer-reviewed journals, including *Journal of Positive Behavior Interventions, Mindulness,* and *Clinical Case Studies.* He has been a national expert consensus panel member for the Treatment of Psychiatric and Behavioral Problems in Mental Retardation for the guideline series published by the *American Journal on Mental Retardation.*

# About the Contributors

· · · · · · · · · · · · · · · · · · · · · · · · · · · · · · · · · · · · · · · · · · · · · · · · · · · · · · · · · · ·

**Michele R. Bishop, Ph.D.,** Research and Development Manager, Center for Autism and Related Disorders, Inc., 1620 North 48th Street, Phoenix, Arizona 85008

Dr. Bishop holds doctorates in philosophy and board-certified behavior analysis. She is currently a research and development manager at the Center for Autism and Related Disorders. She received her doctorate in behavior analysis from the University of Nevada, Reno, and the Behavior Analysis Certification Board, respectively. She has conducted basic and applied behavior analysis research and has worked in schools, home-based treatment programs, and center-based treatment programs with individuals with and without developmental disabilities. Dr. Bishop also teaches graduate-level courses in behavior analysis at Arizona State University.

**Abbey B. Carreau-Webster, M.S., BCBA,** Research Assistant II, Kennedy Krieger Institute, Behavioral Psychology, 707 North Broadway, Baltimore, Maryland 21205

Ms. Carreau-Webster earned her master's degree in applied behavior analysis from Northeastern University, Boston, Massachusetts, and is pursuing her doctorate in applied developmental psychology (with a specialization in behavior analysis) from the University of Maryland, Baltimore. She is currently a research assistant for Dr. Iser DeLeon at the Kennedy Krieger Institute, Baltimore, Maryland, and she also provides in-home board-certified behavior analysis services for children with behavior disorders.

**Travis A. Cos, Ph.D.,** Behavioral Health Consultant/Adjunct Faculty, Public Health Management Corporation/La Salle University, 1900 West Olney Avenue, Philadelphia, Pennsylvania 19141

Dr. Cos is a licensed psychologist with nearly 10 years of experience in the field of intellectual disabilities, particularly focused on applying cognitive behavioral therapy to this population. He currently provides consultative therapy services in a primary care practice, conducts independent psychological assessments for intellectual disability, and teaches and advises counseling psychology graduate students.

**Iser G. DeLeon, Ph.D.,** Associate Professor, Kennedy Krieger Institute and Johns Hopkins University School of Medicine, 707 North Broadway, Baltimore, Maryland 21205

Dr. DeLeon is Director of Research Development for the Department of Behavioral Psychology at the Kennedy Krieger Institute, Baltimore, Maryland, and Associate Professor of Psychiatry and Behavioral Sciences at the Johns Hopkins University School of Medicine, Baltimore. He has over 20 years of clinical and research experience related to the assessment and treatment of behavior disorders in individuals with intellectual and developmental disabilities.

**Richard K. Fleming, Ph.D.,** Associate Professor in Psychiatry, Eunice Kennedy Shriver Center at University of Massachusetts Medical School, 200 Trapelo Road, Waltham, Massachusetts 02452

Dr. Fleming is an associate professor in psychiatry at the Eunice Kennedy Shriver Center, University of Massachusetts Medical School, Waltham. There, he conducts research on lifestyle change and health promotion with people with intellectual and developmental disabilities and their families. He has been the recipient of several National Institutes of Health grants to study obesity and physical activity in this population, including research on a family-based weight loss intervention in youth with Down syndrome, a community-based walking program for adolescents with autism spectrum disorders, and a YMCA-based fitness program with adolescents with Down syndrome.

**Michelle A. Frank-Crawford, M.A., BCBA,** Research Assistant II, Kennedy Krieger Institute, Behavioral Psychology, 707 North Broadway, Baltimore, Maryland 21205

Ms. Frank-Crawford earned her master's degree in applied behavior analysis from the University of Maryland, Baltimore, and is currently pursuing her doctorate in applied developmental psychology (with an emphasis on behavior analysis). In addition, she works at the Kennedy Krieger Institute, Baltimore, as a research assistant for Dr. Iser DeLeon. Her current research interests include the application of behavioral economic principles to the continued refinement of methods for assessing and treating severe behavior disorders.

**William I. Gardner, B.A., M.A., Ph.D.,** Professor (Emeritus), Rehabilitation Psychology Program, University of Wisconsin–Madison, 1000 Bascom Hall, Madison, Wisconsin 53706

William I. Gardner is a clinical psychologist whose academic, research, and clinical activities have focused on assessment and treatment of mental health issues in people with disabilities. He lectures widely in North America and Europe. He currently serves as an expert in a number of litigations concerned with improving mental health services for people with disabilities.

**Mark A. Geren, M.S., BCBA,** Consultant and Trainer, Quality Behavioral Solutions, Inc., Holliston, Massachusetts 01746

Mr. Geren received his master's degree from Northeastern University, Boston, Massachusetts, in applied behavior analysis in 1997. He has directed and consulted in programs serving a full range of populations experiencing challenging behaviors with emphasis on staff training and safe behavior reduction.

**Dorothy M. Griffiths, Ph.D., O.Ont.,** Professor of Child and Youth Studies and Applied Disabilities Studies, Brock University, St. Catharines, Ontario, Canada L2S 3A1

Dr. Griffiths is a Professor in the Child and Youth Studies Department and the Centre for Applied Disabilities Studies and Co-Director of the International Habilitative Mental Health Programme at Brock University in Ontario, Canada. She has published and spoken widely on topics of people with intellectual disabilities and challenging behavior.

**Louis P. Hagopian, Ph.D.,** Program Director and Associate Professor, Kennedy Krieger Institute, Johns Hopkins University School of Medicine, 707 North Broadway, Baltimore, Maryland 21205

Dr. Hagopian is a licensed psychologist and board-certified behavior analyst. He is Program Director of the Neurobehavioral Unit at the Kennedy Krieger Institute and Associate Professor of Psychiatry and Behavioral Sciences at the Johns Hopkins University School of Medicine, both in Baltimore, Maryland. His clinical work and research are focused on the assessment and treatment of problem behavior and anxiety in individuals with intellectual disabilities.

**Jeffery P. Hamelin, M.A.,** Specialist in Applied Behavior Analysis, Graduate Teaching Fellow, Psychology Department, Queens College, The City University of New York, 65-30 Kissena Boulevard, Flushing, New York 11367

Mr. Hamelin is a doctoral student in the Learning Processes and Behavior Analysis subprogram in psychology at the Graduate Center and Queens College, The City University of New York. His work and research experiences have involved the areas of applied behavior analysis, intellectual disabilities, and dual diagnosis.

**Susan Carol Hayes, B.A. (Hons. I), Ph.D.,** Professor of Behavioural Sciences in Medicine, University of Sydney, New South Wales, Australia 2006, Sydney Medical School, Blackburn Building D06

Dr. Hayes is a fellow of the International Association for the Scientific Study of Intellectual Disability, member of the Australian Psychological Society College of Forensic Psychologists, registered psychologist in Australia, and forensic psychologist. Dr. Hayes received the Order of Australia in 1998. She is a nationally and internationally recognized expert in forensic psychology, especially in the field of people with intellectual disabilities in the justice system, and she is the author of many publications.

**Craig H. Kennedy, Ph.D.,** Professor and Associate Dean, Vanderbilt University, 202 Administration Building, Peabody College, Nashville, Tennessee 37212

Dr. Kennedy is the associate dean for research at Peabody College of Vanderbilt University, Nashville, Tennessee, and a professor of special education and pediatrics. Dr. Kennedy's research and development interests focus on students with intellectual and developmental disabilities, including autism spectrum disorders.

**Amy L. Kenzer, Ph.D., BCBA-D,** Manager, Research and Development, Center for Autism and Related Disorders, Inc., 1620 North 48th Street, Phoenix, Arizona 85008

Dr. Kenzer is currently a research and development manager at the Center for Autism and Related Disorders. She received her doctorate in behavior analysis from the University of Nevada, Reno. She has worked in a variety of positions in the field of behavior analysis, including basic and applied research, as well as practical work with individuals with and without developmental disabilities, of all ages. Dr. Kenzer also provides graduate-level training in behavior analysis at Arizona State University, Phoenix.

**Alison M. Kozlowski, M.A.,** Louisiana State University, Department of Psychology, 236 Audubon Hall, Baton Rouge, Louisiana 70803

Ms. Kozlowski is a clinical psychology doctoral student at Louisiana State University. Her current clinical and research interests are the assessment and treatment of individuals with autism spectrum disorders and other developmental disabilities, with a particular emphasis on challenging behaviors and communication training.

**David E. Kuhn, Ph.D., BCBA-D,** Codirector, Assistant Professor, Psychologist, Westchester Institute for Human Development and New York Medical College, Cedarwood Hall, 20 Hospital Oval West, Valhalla, New York 10595

Dr. Kuhn earned his Ph.D. in clinical psychology at Louisiana State University, Baton Rouge, and is a doctoral-level board-certified behavior analyst. He is currently Codirector of the behavioral psychology program at the Westchester Institute for Human Development, Valhalla, New York, where he participates in both clinical and research activities focused on the assessment and treatment of challenging behaviors displayed by individuals diagnosed with developmental disabilities. Dr. Kuhn was previously a member of the faculty at the Kennedy Krieger Institute and Johns Hopkins University School of Medicine, both in Baltimore, Maryland.

**David Lennox, Ph.D.,** CEO of Quality Behavioral Solutions, Holliston, Massachusetts 01746 and Adjunct Professor at Simmons College, Boston, Massachusetts 02115

Dr. Lennox received his Ph.D. from Western Michigan University, Kalamazoo, specializing in applied behavior analysis, in 1984. He has developed, directed, and consulted in programs treating children, adults, and older adults in a variety of settings, including schools, community and group homes, long-term care, academic research programs, day treatment programs, and rehabilitation hospitals.

**Yanerys Leon-Enriquez, M.A.,** Florida Institute of Technology, 150 West University Boulevard, Melbourne, Florida 32901

Ms. Leon-Enriquez received her master's degree in applied behavior analysis from the University of Maryland–Baltimore County while working in the Neurobehavioral Unit at the Kennedy Krieger Institute, Baltimore, Maryland. She is currently working toward her doctoral degree at the Florida Institute of Technology. Her research interests include the assessment and treatment of severe behavior disorders and translational research models to improve interventions for individuals with developmental disabilities.

**William R. Lindsay, B.A., Ph.D.,** Castlebeck, Darlington, United Kingdom; Professor, University of Abertay, 119 Americanmuir Road, Dundee DD3 9AG, Scotland, United Kingdom; Bangor University, Gwynedd, United Kingdom.

Dr. Lindsay has worked with offenders with intellectual disability in community and secure settings for 25 years. He has edited and authored 3 books and published over 250 articles and book chapters.

**Johnny L. Matson, Ph.D.,** Professor, Director of Clinical Training, and Distinguished Research Master, Louisiana State University, Department of Psychology, 236 Audubon Hall, Baton Rouge, Louisiana 70803

Dr. Matson's interests have focused on the development of assessment and treatment methods in the fields of intellectual disabilities and autism spectrum disorders. He has authored over 600 publications, including 38 books on intellectual disabilities, autism, and severe emotional disorders.

**Arthur M. Nezu, Ph.D.,** Distinguished University Professor of Psychology, Drexel University, MS 515, 245 North 15 Street, Philadelphia, Pennsylvania 19102

Dr. Nezu is Distinguished Professor of Psychology, as well as Professor of Medicine and Professor of Public Health at Drexel University, Philadelphia. He is also Special Professor of Forensic Mental Health and Psychiatry at the University of Nottingham in the United Kingdom. He is also currently Editor of the *Journal of Consulting and Clinical Psychology*.

**Christine Maguth Nezu, Ph.D., ABPP,** Professor of Psychology and Medicine, Drexel University, MS 515, 245 North 15th Street, Philadelphia, Pennsylvania 19102, and Clinical Director, Nezu Psychological Associates

Dr. Nezu is Professor of Psychology and medicine at Drexel University in Philadelphia as well as Special Professor of Forensic Mental Health and Psychiatry at the University of Nottingham in the United Kingdom. She is the immediate past president of the American Board of Professional Psychology and Clinical Director of Nezu Psychological Associates.

**J. Gregory Olley, Ph.D.,** Clinical Professor, Psychologist, University of North Carolina at Chapel Hill, Carolina Institute for Developmental Disabilities, CB #7255, University of North Carolina, Chapel Hill, North Carolina 27599-7255

Dr. Olley is a psychologist who has worked in many facets of developmental disabilities, with a focus on significant behavior problems. In recent years he has worked with attorneys and with the Division on Intellectual and Developmental Disabilities of the American Psychological Association toward establishing clearer standards for establishing the diagnosis of intellectual disability in forensic settings.

**Reece L. Peterson, Ph.D.,** Professor, Department of Special Education and Communication Disorders, University of Nebraska–Lincoln, 202A Barkley Center, Lincoln, Nebraska 68583

Dr. Peterson is a professor of special education at the University of Nebraska–Lincoln. His work has focused on identification of and educational programs for students with emotional or behavioral disorders, as well as policy issues including discipline, school violence prevention, and the use of physical restraint and seclusion procedures in schools.

**Jorge R. Reyes, Ph.D., BCBA-D,** Assistant Professor, Psychology Department, 577 Western Avenue, Westfield State University, Westfield, Massachusetts 01085

Dr. Reyes is a board-certified behavior analyst and an assistant professor at Westfield State University, Westfield, Massachusetts, where he is the graduate advisor for the master's degree program in applied behavior analysis. His research has primarily focused on the assessment and treatment of sexual offenders with developmental disabilities.

**Johannes Rojahn, Ph.D.,** Professor, George Mason University, Department of Psychology, 10340 Democracy Lane, Suite 202, Fairfax, Virginia 22030

Dr. Rojahn has published over 150 scientific articles and book chapters and 2 books. He currently serves as Editor-in-Chief of the *Journal of Mental Health Research in Intellectual Disabilities* and as Associate Editor for *Research in Developmental Disabilities*. In addition, he is on the editorial board of several other peer-reviewed journals in the area of intellectual and developmental disabilities.

**Natalie U. Rolider, B.A., Ph.D.,** Senior Behavior Analyst, Neurobehavioral Unit, Kennedy Krieger Institute, 707 North Broadway, Baltimore, Maryland 21205

Dr. Rolider received her Ph.D. in applied behavior analysis from University of Florida, Gainesville. She is currently a senior behavior analyst in the Neurobehavioral Unit at the Kennedy Krieger Institute, Baltimore, Maryland. Her research interests include extensions to functional analysis methodology, antecedent interventions, and data collection training.

**Griffin W. Rooker, B.A., M.S., Ph.D.,** Postdoctoral Fellow, Kennedy Krieger Institute, Johns Hopkins University School of Medicine, Neurobehavioral Unit, 707 North Broadway, Baltimore, Maryland 21205

Dr. Rooker earned his master's degree at Northeastern University, Boston, Massachusetts, and his doctoral degree at the University of Florida, Gainesville, in applied behavior analysis. Currently, he is a postdoctoral fellow at Johns Hopkins University School of Medicine, Baltimore, Maryland. His research interests include functional assessment and function-based treatment of problem behavior and applications of economic principles to the treatment of severe problem behavior.

**David Rourke, M.S.,** Senior Consultant/Trainer, Quality Behavioral Solutions, Holliston, Massachusetts 01746

After earning his bachelor's degree at the University of Pennsylvania, Philadelphia, and his master's at Villanova University, Villanova, Pennsylvania, over the last 20-plus years Mr. Rourke has worked to behavioral support to adults and children with a wide range of diagnoses, including developmental disabilities, autism, brain injury, and psychiatric disorders. He has served as the director of several treatment programs and has experience in community, residential, school, and inpatient settings. Since 2007 he has worked as a consultant and trainer at Quality Behavioral Solutions, primarily in developing and teaching the use of the Safety-Care™ Behavioral Safety Training program.

**Joseph B. Ryan, Ph.D.,** Associate Professor, Special Education Programs, Clemson University, 227 Holtzendorff Hall, Clemson, South Carolina 29634

Dr. Ryan is an associate professor of special education at Clemson University, Clemson, South Carolina, and has taught students with behavioral disorders from kindergarten through grade 12 across a variety of educational settings, including resource and self-contained classrooms, special day schools, and a residential treatment center. He has published over 30 journal articles and book chapters and frequently consults and speaks at national and international professional conferences regarding behavior management, seclusion, and restraint policies for schools, psychotropic medications, therapeutic recreation, and postsecondary transition services.

**Frank J. Symons, B.A., M.Ed., Ph.D.,** Professor of Special Education and Educational Psychology, Department of Educational Psychology, University of Minnesota, Education Sciences Building, 56 River Road, Minneapolis, Minnesota 55455

Dr. Symons's research interests include the development, assessment, and treatment of severe behavior problems among individuals with intellectual and developmental disabilities. His work also focuses on the assessment and treatment of health problems, including pain, in relation to behavior problems among individuals with intellectual and developmental disabilities.

**Jonathan Tarbox, Ph.D., BCBA-D,** Director of Research and Development, Center for Autism and Related Disorders, 19019 Ventura Blvd, Third Floor, Tarzana, California 91356

Dr. Tarbox is currently Director of Research and Development at the Center for Autism and Related Disorders. Dr. Tarbox received his Ph.D. in behavior analysis from Dr. Linda J. Parrott Hayes at the University of Nevada, Reno. Dr. Tarbox has served on the editorial boards of the *Journal of Applied Behavior Analysis, Behavior Analysis in Practice*, and *The Analysis of Verbal Behavior*, and his research interests include autism, challenging behaviors, and behavioral approaches to assessing and treating complex language and cognition.

**Timothy R. Vollmer, Ph.D.,** Professor of Psychology, Psychology Department, University of Florida, Gainesville, Florida 32622

Dr. Vollmer received his Ph.D. in psychology from the University of Florida, Gainesville, in 1992. He was on the psychology faculty in at Louisiana State University, Baton Rouge, from 1992 to 1996; he was on the faculty in Pediatrics at the University of Pennsylvania from 1996 to 1998; and he returned to the University of Florida in 1998.

**Stephen F. Walker, B.S., M.S.,** Graduate Research Assistant, Department of Psychology, University of Florida, Room 114, Psychology Building, Gainesville, Florida 32611-2250

Mr. Walker received his master's degree in behavior analysis from the University of North Texas, Denton, and is currently a doctoral student in the Department of Psychology at the University of Florida, Gainesville. His research interests are in applied behavior analysis, assessment and treatment of severe behavior disorders, and assessment and treatment of sex offenders with intellectual disabilities.

# Foreword

· · · · · · · · · · · · · · · · · · · · · · · · · · · · · · · · · · · · · · · · · · · · · · · · · · · · · ·

High-risk challenging behaviors thwart the lives of many people with intellectual and developmental disabilities (IDD), their families, staff, and peers. When we encounter a child with IDD excluded repeatedly from general and special educational settings or an adult with IDD who lives in a locked setting with intrusive staffing and multiple restrictive management practices, we see lives that are greatly diminished because of a lifetime history of high-risk challenging behavior. As professionals we often see treatment strategies that are inappropriate and/or unimplemented. As taxpayers we see expensive services that seem to return little or nothing for the public dollar.

Thirty years ago, deinstitutionalization was accelerating. Many naively hoped that institutions were the cause of these problems and mere placement in a community setting might reverse or eliminate existing problems and prevent these problems from developing. As we look around us today, however, these old problems continue. Preschool children with IDD, who self-injure or who are aggressive, are restrained by their parents and staff. Schools exclude children with IDD from mainstream settings and use restrictive staffing and other intrusive management strategies. Some adults with high-risk challenging behavior, having spent much of their development in ineffective educational services, live a restricted life in prison or in forensic or psychiatric settings. Some services, rather than develop responsive services themselves, contract out the services away from their clients' regular setting: Too often, out of sight is out of mind, even if the bill is high.

I believe that many such children and adults with IDD and high-risk behaviors could benefit significantly from effective treatment. Jim Luiselli's excellent book provides vital information about what is most likely to work for the most common high-risk behaviors. Self-injurious behavior, aggression, inappropriate sexual behavior, health-threatening eating disorders, and forensic issues are widely recognized as some of the most common high-risk behaviors that are potentially treatment responsive. The final section of the book on safe management of restraint also provides a model for the safe management of other restrictive practices that services should strive to eliminate. Thus, this volume addresses some of the key issues in the lives of people with IDD and high-risk challenging behaviors. The chapters in this volume are of uniformly high quality and written by internationally recognized practitioners and researchers and thus provide all of us with vital information. If we learn the lessons from *The Handbook of High-Risk Challenging*

*Behaviors in People with Intellectual and Developmental Disabilities* and effectively and accurately implement the treatments described in this volume, the lives of people with IDD and high-risk challenging behaviors will be greatly improved.

*Peter Sturmey, Ph.D.*
*Professor of Psychology*
*The Graduate Center and Queens College*
*The City University of New York*
*Flushing, New York*

# Preface

∙ ∙ ∙ ∙ ∙ ∙ ∙ ∙ ∙ ∙ ∙ ∙ ∙ ∙ ∙ ∙ ∙ ∙ ∙ ∙ ∙ ∙ ∙ ∙ ∙ ∙ ∙ ∙ ∙ ∙ ∙ ∙ ∙ ∙ ∙ ∙ ∙ ∙ ∙ ∙ ∙ ∙ ∙ ∙ ∙ ∙ ∙ ∙ ∙ ∙ ∙ ∙ ∙ ∙ ∙ ∙ ∙ ∙ ∙

Many children, adolescents, and adults with intellectual and developmental disabilities (IDD) demonstrate high-risk challenging behaviors. For example, a problem such as self-injury causes tissue damage, bodily harm, and resulting medical complications. Other behaviors, like aggression and destruction, pose a threat to peers and caregivers as well as the physical environment. Several eating disorders, notably pica, ruminative vomiting, and obesity, also are health threatening. Additional high-risk behaviors include sexual offending, fire setting, theft, and similar criminal acts.

The seriousness of high-risk challenging behaviors often requires intervention within restrictive settings but, just as frequently, in more normative environments such as schools, homes, vocational programs, and community group residences. Also, practitioners sometimes resort to invasive and controversial procedures when treating these behaviors. Of critical concern is how to intervene effectively with high-risk challenging behaviors in different settings using procedures that are socially acceptable and consistent with evidence-based and empirically supported practices.

*The Handbook of High-Risk Challenging Behaviors in People with Intellectual and Developmental Disabilities* is comprised of 6 sections and 16 chapters. Each chapter aims to provide the reader with a "state-of-the art" review of the respective topical area based on available research information and the clinical acumen of the authors. The chapters focus on recommending how to improve intervention practices, therapeutic outcomes, and quality of life. More specifically, the chapters consider person-specific, biological, social, and systems-level influences on high-risk challenging behaviors and the best evidence-based and empirically supported practices for preventing and treating them. The book is geared toward effective interventions that can be implemented in the least restrictive settings that provide habilitation services to people who have IDD and high-risk challenging behaviors.

Section I, *Self-Injurious Behavior*, has 3 chapters that discuss biological influences on self-injury, function-based assessment, and behavioral intervention. Section II, *Aggressive Behavior*, examines chapters devoted to environmental (learning) etiologies and a biopsychosocial approach to assessment and therapy. In Section III, *Sexual Offending Behavior*, 3 chapters address risk assessment, behavioral intervention, and problem-solving treatment. The 3 chapters in Section IV, *Health-Threatening Eating Disorders*, consider pica, ruminative vomiting, and obesity. Section V, *Criminal*

*Behavior*, consists of a chapter about people with IDD in the criminal justice system and one chapter about the death penalty and related legal concerns. Finally, the topic of Section VI is not a specific high-risk challenging behavior but, instead, the controversial area of therapeutic (physical) restraint. This section was included because the professional community continues to debate the merits and limitations of restraint, restraint procedures are applied for many of the identified high-risk challenging behaviors, and the research evidence for and against restraint demands detailed explication. The 3 chapters found in Section VI, *Therapeutic (Physical) Restraint*, deal with implementation practices, regulatory guidelines, and staff training and supervision.

The book addresses topics that are conspicuously represented in the contemporary clinical and research literature. Furthermore, many practitioners in the field of IDD are confronted by these high-risk challenging behaviors and many intervention alternatives. Some chapters in the book, for example, in Sections III and V, focus exclusively on adolescents and adults. The sections that concern self-injury, aggression, eating-related disorders, and therapeutic (physical restraint) also consider child populations because they have been and continue to be heavily researched. Each chapter author is an experienced clinician and researcher who is highly visible in the professional community.

*The Handbook of High-Risk Challenging Behaviors in People with Intellectual and Developmental Disabilities* is intended as a resource book for human services professionals from the disciplines of education, psychology, psychiatry, social work, medicine, and behavior analysis. However, it is anticipated that the book will reach other IDD professional groups such as educators, behavior analysts, and administrators of habilitation settings. In this capacity it will serve as a practitioner's guide for implementing assessment, intervention, and evaluation practices. The book also can be used as a text for university students at the advanced undergraduate and graduate school level, internship trainees, and early career professionals receiving postdoctoral training. The types of courses and seminars suited for this purpose would be treatment applications in developmental disabilities, topics in applied behavior analysis, forensic psychology, and criminal justice and behavior.

I wish to thank the staff at Paul H. Brookes Publishing Co. for their guidance from start to finish. The authors who wrote for the book have my highest praise and admiration. So, too, I am indebted to many mentors and colleagues along the way for shaping my thinking about how to improve the lives of people who pose high-risk concerns. Finally, as I have done in every book I have published, I dedicate this one to my family—Tracy, Gabrielle, and Thomas—with love and devotion.

# Self-Injurious Behavior

**I**

SECTION

# Biological Perspectives on Self-Injury Among People with Intellectual and Neurodevelopmental Disabilities

**CHAPTER 1**

*Frank J. Symons and Craig H. Kennedy*

Our starting point is an assertion that in the field of self-injurious behavior (SIB) and intellectual and neurodevelopmental disabilities (IDD), the field too often confuses causation with treatment outcome and efficacious therapy with etiology (Novak, 2003; Barrera, Violo, & Graver, 2007). Said another way, because the field can show treatment effects for a given intervention, it does not necessarily mean the field understands understand the cause(s) of the behavior. The current state-of-the-science approach to behavioral treatment for SIB among individuals with IDD relies on some form of functional behavioral assessment (FBA) (i.e., interview, descriptive, experimental) in which information is gathered or generated about the possible behavioral mechanism(s) regulating SIB (i.e., it is differentially sensitive to one or more classes of reinforcement contingency). Finding out whether SIB is mediated by reinforcement mechanisms is important because it can directly inform the development of an intervention. At the same time, discovering that an individual's SIB is more or less sensitive to, or regulated by, different classes of social reinforcement does not logically lead to the following conclusions: 1) SIB is socially reinforced; therefore, biology is irrelevant or 2) social reinforcement mechanisms are operating to maintain SIB; therefore, reinforcement mechanisms are how SIB developed. Because a positive FBA outcome neither eliminates biological influences on SIB nor identifies a reinforcement contingency etiology for the behavior, the field needs to expand its conceptualization of SIB mechanisms to account fully for these behaviors.

Funding for this work was provided, in part, by the Eunice Kennedy Shriver NICHD Grant Nos. 44763 and 447201 and U.S. Department of Education Grant No. H325D050102. This chapter is dedicated to the memory of Edward G. Carr, who provided much of the theoretical and empirical inspiration for our own work.

SIB is one of the most disturbing and destructive forms of behavior problems among individuals with IDD (Schroeder, Oster-Granite, & Thompson, 2002). SIB is a heterogeneous disorder and, like other behaviorally defined disorders, it is reasonable to assume that SIB can be the consequence of a variety of etiologies which, in turn, involve a variety of environment–brain–behavior relations. This chapter selectively reviews the evidence for the biological bases of SIB among individuals with IDD. We begin by outlining some conceptual issues and problems with the current logic underlying assessment and treatment approaches to studying SIB. Next, we describe and discuss different health and neurobiological variables associated with SIB in preclinical models and clinical populations. Finally, we suggest that thinking about risk models in which the notion of predisposing vulnerabilities that confer differential vulnerability to SIB among individuals with IDD is important and has been ignored. Although none of the precise mechanisms regulating underlying genetic vulnerabilities and the way in which they interact with environmental risk factors—including adverse environments—to potentiate the development of SIB is well understood, we think it is worth considering such a conceptual framework to move the field forward beyond its current status.

## BEHAVIOR AND BIOLOGY

In the mid-1980s, biologist Susan Oyama noted that "nature is the product of nurture" (Midgley & Morris, 1992; Oyama, 2000). More recently, Travis Thompson (2007) pointed out that there are several levels of behavioral, environmental, neurobiological, and genetic determinants of responding and that these levels are consistent among themselves and potentially integratable. All of these observations pay service to the death of the "nature versus nurture" dichotomy that was for too long a dictum of psychological thinking. In this paradigm past, researchers relegated causality to either biological or environmental determinants of behavior and focused their experimental and theoretical efforts on determining which of the two held in any particular instance of responding. The result, some have observed (Kennedy, 2004; Oyama, 2000), was the forcing of richly complex causes of behavior into a binary system that rarely did justice to the phenomenon being analyzed.

An evolution away from nature versus nurture to nature and nurture has taken place in the behavioral analysis of SIB and other problematic behaviors. Carr (1977), in his classic conceptual paper on the motivation of SIB, identified reinforcement contingencies and biological causes as potential determinants of behavior, suggesting that they may even be interrelated in some instances. Similarly, in the original description of what went on to become the standard experimental FBA procedure, Iwata et al. (1982) stated that the purpose of the technique was not to address the issue of environmental versus physiological determinants of self-injury in regard to etiology or maintenance. Instead, the authors suggested that using analogue functional analyses might be helpful in reducing the effects of environmental variance in biobehavioral investigations of self-injury, even in cases where the maintenance of SIB appeared to be largely biological. This work has been extended by Thompson and colleagues (Kennedy & Thompson, 2000; Symons,

Davis, & Thompson, 1998) to specific instances in which biological variables and reinforcement contingencies interact to regulate SIB. Thus, the precursors to an integrative account of SIB reflecting possible biological and environmental determinants exist in the behavior–analytic literature.

Perhaps a parsimonious approach to conceptualizing environmental and biological determinants of SIB is to acknowledge a continuum of causal mechanisms. Figure 1.1 displays such an arrangement. On the far left-hand side of the graphic are instances of SIB that are almost exclusively a function of reinforcement contingencies with little to no known biological influence. An example of this might be an individual whose SIB is maintained by positive social reinforcement in the form attention from adults. The behavior would be maintained by positive reinforcement contingencies for SIB that exists in the social environment. On the far right-hand side of the figure are occurrences of SIB that are a function almost exclusively of biological factors. The classic example of this is Lesch–Nyhan syndrome (Lesch & Nyhan, 1964), which is an inherited X-chromosome linked disorder caused by a deficiency of the enzyme *hypoxanthine-guanine phosphoribosyltransferase* (Henderson, 1968). A defining characteristic of this genetically based enzymatic disorder is the presence of SIB in the form of finger and lip biting. Even in this scenario, however, there is evidence that environmental contingencies can affect the rate of SIB (Bergen, Holborn, & Scott-Huyghebaert, 2002). The careful reader will note that even with these examples, the authors have "slipped" into potentially confusing etiology with maintenance. In neither example do the authors really understand why SIB started, but using an FBA approach helps

## Contributions to Self-Injurious Behavior

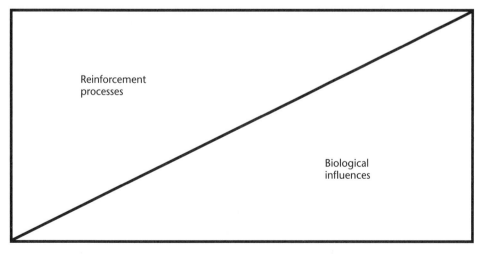

**Figure 1.1.** Contributions to self-injurious behavior (SIB). On the far left-hand side of the figure are instances of SIB that may be primarily a function of reinforcement contingencies without biological influence. On the far right-hand side of the figure are occurrences of SIB that are primarily a function of biological factors. What is of most interest are the relative interactions between behavior and biology along this continuum where both sets of variables can contribute to the etiology and maintenance of SIB.

to provide clues about the relative strength or likelihood of reinforcement contingencies operating as a maintaining variable.

What is of most scientific interest to us in this chapter is the interaction between behavioral (i.e., reinforcement contingencies) and biological variables and their relation to the etiology *and* maintenance of SIB. From a clinical perspective, knowing the relative contribution between behavior and biology in relation to maintenance could be used effectively in an algorithm-based approach to treatment resource allocation. Beyond intervention, however, we are willing to assume, for the sake of pushing the frontier of our knowledge of SIB forward, that improving the understanding of behavior–biology relations may eventually lead to more informed approaches for recognizing distinctive risk factors that could be converted to preventative approaches. In the remainder of this chapter, based on the existing research literature, we make the case that these biological-reinforcement inter-actions occur and may be more likely than many researchers and clinicians treating SIB may appreciate.

## EVIDENCE FOR THE BIOLOGICAL BASIS OF SELF-INJURIOUS BEHAVIOR

There are a variety of models—preclinical and clinical—that have direct relevance to improving our understanding of the biological bases of SIB. Although not all models are set up to fully reflect complete systems, each of the models reviewed briefly below provide some form of evidence that we think is relevant for under-standing the role of different biological substrates directly or indirectly influencing the expression of SIB. The evidence generated from different model systems, however, ranges from highly controlled laboratory-based experiments to detailed clinical observations. Thus, there are different degrees of inference warranted with respect to the causal role of different biological systems. However, one of the primary points of our argument is that the issue is not to parse out whether it is "biology" versus "behavior," as no system operates in isolation. The point here and in the following sections is to find out what kinds of evidence exist for the role that different biological systems may play in influencing SIB.

## EARLY DEPRIVATION/ENRICHMENT MODELS AND SELF-INJURIOUS BEHAVIOR

There are numerous ways to induce repetitive stereotyped movement including SIB in animal models including exposure to a variety of pharmacologic agents, specific central nervous system (CNS) insults, and a range of perturbations in the parameters related to early social deprivation and environmental restriction (Lewis, Tanimura, Lee, & Bodfish, 2007). Although pharmacological challenge models (see following) provide information specific to particular neurotransmitters and their receptors, they are often conducted in highly controlled conditions and do not necessarily provide insight into the role early environment may play in the etiology of SIB. We still know very little about the early developmental course of SIB, its relation to naturally occurring early rhythmic or repetitive behavior, or its relation to any forms of early aberrant repetitive behavior such as motor stereotypies (Symons, Sperry, Dropik, & Bodfish, 2005). Richman and Lindauer (2005), in a review of the early development of SIB, extended a behavioral model outlined by Guess and Carr (1991) in which specific features of the social context can acquire discriminative, reinforcing, and evocative functions supporting and shaping early forms of SIB and, perhaps, the evolution of early repetitive behavior into SIB (Kennedy, 2002a). Although behavioral mechanisms appear to provide a parsimonious model for why some forms of SIB persist, they do not necessarily adequately account for the initial emergence of SIB.

In contrast to models relying on some form of specific neurological insult or pharmacological challenge, Lewis and colleagues developed and characterized a model of *spontaneous* early aberrant repetitive behavior using deer mice (*Peromyscus maniculatus*) (Lewis et al., 2007; Powell, Newman, Pendergast, & Lewis, 1999). The model system is important because it does not require social isolation, specific environmental cues, pharmaceutics, or any form of CNS injury to induce repetitive behavior (in the form of repetitive vertical jumping and/or backward somersaulting). The behaviors develop early and persist across the lifespan. These characteristics (spontaneous, early onset, lifespan persistent) make Lewis' model novel and an important tool in understanding the etiology of repetitive behavior with relevance for SIB in IDD populations given the high proportion of SIB and related repetitive behavior problems that seem to share the same characteristics occurring among a number of neurodevelopmental disorders (Lewis & Bodfish, 1998). Equally important, there are individual differences apparent in the model. Not all mice are spontaneous "jumpers." This observation provides a unique scientific opportunity to more fully explore biobehavioral parameters related to individual differences and context effects in the expression of early repetitive behavior.

With regard to early environmental context, Lewis' model has produced a number of important findings. Mice reared in more complex environments express less stereotyped behavior than standard cage–reared controls. The observed "enrichment effects" (reduced repetitive behavior) hold for both young and adult animals. Moreover, there are protective effects possible such that mice exposed early to enriched or complex environments and then placed in standard cage housing are less likely to engage in repetitive behavior. The neurobiological substrate mediating the behavioral effects of complex environments has also been studied (Turner & Lewis, 2003; Turner Yang, & Lewis, 2002). Complex environment exposed mice that did not develop repetitive behavior show greater neuronal metabolic activity and dendritic spine densities in the motor cortex as well as elevated levels of striatal brain-derived neurotrophin factor. In contrast, complex environment exposed mice that did develop stereotyped behavior do not show the same level of neurobiological change (although they have greater gains than standard cage–reared mice). One conclusion to draw from these data sets is that mice that display early stereotypy are failing to engage with the environment in ways that are sufficient to drive changes in the brain. Despite the environmental complexity afforded them, the mice were unable to "take advantage" of the effects. Such findings are extremely important with regard to the notion of how "resistant" to intervention repetitive behavior, including SIB, may be. From a dynamical systems perspective, aberrant repetitive behavior may be likened to a "dynamic disease" process (Newell & Bodfish, 2007). Behavior in systems that is less complex and periodic (contrasted with healthy behavior that is complex and variable) is often associated with the most severe pathological conditions and highly resistant to change (Glass & Mackey, 1988). These observations argue for improving our understanding as completely as possible about the origins of SIB and the importance of early intervention.

Early development and environmental effects have also been studied in other nonhuman species, the majority focused on primates. It is beyond the scope of our chapter, however, to review in detail the range of studies using primate models of SIB, but several findings are worth noting. There are common factors across many of the models which can be grouped into categories related to adverse early rearing, adult isolation, and repeated experimentation (Dellinger-Ness & Handler, 2006). In each of these categories, there are studies showing that the likelihood of SIB increases for the majority of the sample (typically rhesus monkeys) as a function of early experience within each category. There is an important conditional probability distinction to note here, that likely extends to the human phenomenon as well. The probability of SIB in a given population given an adverse early rearing environment, history of isolation as an adolescent or adult, or repeated experimentation is relatively low. But, given some form of chronic SIB, the probability is relatively high that there will be a positive history of some form of adverse early rearing environment, history of adolescent/adult isolation, or repeated experimentation.

There are several parameters related to the three categories noted previously that should be briefly noted and that may be equally important for improving our understanding of the emergence of SIB among individuals with severe neurodevelopmental disorders. There may be "dosage" effects related to the length of isolation such that there is an increasing probability of SIB among animals that have spent longer time periods in isolation (Platt, Kinsey, Jorgensen, & Novak, 1996). Similarly, there are apparent timing effects with the likelihood of SIB emerging related to earlier ages of individual (i.e., isolate) housing (Platt et al., 1996, cited in Dellinger-Ness & Handler, 2006). Collectively, the early experience of abnormal rearing along with the timing and duration of isolation are robust risk predictors for the later expression of SIB (Lutz, Well, & Novak, 2003). Similarly, a history of repeated experimentation has been linked with the emergence of SIB (Novak, 2003). As we suggested, not all individual animals exposed to any or all of these conditions go on to develop SIB, suggesting there are as-of-yet unknown risk and protective factors operating to mediate the environmental effects. Adopting a similar stance with respect to the understanding of the emergence of SIB among individuals with IDD may be helpful. Not all individuals with severe IDD go on to develop SIB. Parsing out factors—environmental and biological—that may confer protection or elevate risk remains relatively uncharted territory.

## AUTONOMIC AROUSAL AND SELF-INJURIOUS BEHAVIOR

The observed persistence and severity of SIB has led to questions about whether the normal homeostatic mechanisms regulating autonomic arousal may be disrupted or disordered. The conventional wisdom regarding arousal physiology and SIB among individuals with IDD centers on the autonomic nervous system and arousal. For over 40 years, autonomic arousal has been hypothesized to account for a variety of aberrant (i.e., stereotyped) and destructive (i.e., self-injurious) forms of behavior among individuals with IDD (Berkson, 1967; Graveling & Brooke, 1978; Maisto, Baumeister, & Maisto, 1978). The core theoretical premise is a homeostatic metaphor in which aberrant forms of behavior such as self-injury regulate chronic over- or underarousal (Graveling & Brooke, 1978; Guess & Carr, 1991). From this perspective, SIB is considered a response to an internal state (i.e., "over-underaroused") or, alternatively, as a response regulating the internal state (i.e., reduce/increase arousal level) (Berkson, 1967). Despite long-standing speculations, there have been few empirical studies directly examining autonomic arousal in relation to SIB among individuals with significant IDD.

Two studies to date that were 1) specific to IDD and 2) directly measured SIB produced contradictory findings. Freeman, Horner, and Reichle (1999) found that arousal (as measured by heart rate [HR]) increased following SIB, whereas Barrera et al. (2007) found the opposite with arousal (i.e., HR) increasing prior to SIB. The methodologies for the two studies were different which make it very difficult to directly compare. In the Freeman et al. study, HR data were collected in beats per minute (BPM) during naturally occurring daily routines for two adult individuals with developmental disabilities. The authors then tested whether increased HR preceded or followed episodes of destructive behavior (SIB, aggression). HR did not reliably increase before SIB, but SIB was significantly more likely to be followed by HR increase for both participants. Although the sample included only two participants and was limited by a fairly "rough" time scale of HR measurement, the study illustrates the use of HR monitoring during naturalistic observations of SIB and related behavior problems.

The Barrera et al. (2007) study provides a model of integrating HR monitoring into single-subject experimental designs. HR was monitored during functional behavioral analyses with three adults with SIB and developmental disabilities. The results were examined using visual inspection of raw HR data streams and plots of problem behavior. HR increased prior to SIB for each of the cases. The importance of the Barrera study is that it provides a heuristic model to integrate HR and problem behavior within a single case experimental design. One of the limitations of the study itself is that it lacked replicable statistical analysis of HR or quantification of the sequential dependencies between HR changes and SIB. Because results were based on visual examination of plots, the methods did not necessarily account for the possibility of chance co-occurrence between HR and SIB change.

Overall, the biological evidence for arousal and SIB among individuals with IDD remains limited. It is worth noting, however, there is an emerging evidence base from studies of individuals without IDD but with SIB or "nonsuicidal self-injury" (NSSI). Using a group comparison design (adolescents with and without NSSI), Nock and Mendes (2008) showed that the NSSI group had higher levels of physiological reactivity (indexed by skin conductance) during a distressing task, more difficulties tolerating task-related distress, and social problem-solving deficits. These findings are important because they provide a direct examination of physiological arousal among individuals with and without NSSI and complement prior work demonstrating that imagining engaging in NSSI leads to decreased physiological arousal (Haines, Williams, Brain, & Wilson, 1995). Similar work directly investigating autonomic arousal and tics associated with Tourette syndrome has been conducted. Using galvanic skin response (GSR; considered to be a sensitive index of sympathetic nervous system activity) with individuals meeting *DSM-IV* criteria for Tourette syndrome, Nagai, Cavanna, and Critchley (2009) showed that tic frequency was positively correlated with sympathetic arousal during arousal sessions. Moreover, biofeedback-enhanced relaxation sessions that directly decreased sympathetic arousal also produced lower rates of tics.

Taken together, despite the limited database *directly* related to SIB and IDD, the emerging evidence from other clinical populations with SIB (NSSI, Tourette syndrome), as well as preclinical animal models of SIB (HR in rhesus monkeys with SIB increases *prior* to SIB and then decreases—as previously described; Novak, 2003) suggests that the role of autonomic arousal in relation to SIB should be more fully explored. None of the evidence sets speak directly to the role arousal or, perhaps more specifically the neural systems regulating it, may play in the etiology of SIB. To put it another way, whether altered neural regulation of arousal is a cause, consequence, or correlate of SIB is not altogether clear. The experimental treatment evidence from Nagai et al. (2009), in which reducing arousal resulted in reduced tics, suggests a mediating relation. In a more general sense, from a functional perspective, SIB may function for some individuals as a form of "affect regulation" (Nock & Prinstein, 2004; Symons, 2002) mediated by the autonomic nervous system. Although not a "new" idea (see Sourfe, Stuecher, & Stutzer, 1973), perhaps the new evidence is catching up with an old idea.

## SENSORY VARIABLES AND SELF-INJURIOUS BEHAVIOR

SIB that occurs at high rates over long time periods with tissue damage can result in irreversible mutilation, blindness, or brain injury, suggesting that the normal sensory mechanisms for perceiving and responding to painful stimuli are disrupted. Little is known about the sensory and nociceptive neurobiological basis of such behavior, and, in many cases, chronic SIB that has no apparent social function is often treatment refractory. In behavioral models of SIB, self-injury that occurs either primarily during an "alone" (nonsocial) analysis condition, or indiscriminately across multiple differing social contexts is often presumed by default to involve altered sensory processes. However, there is little in the way of direct evidence linking SIB to sensory variables, and the mechanisms regulating sensory behavior and their relation to biological variables have not been delineated. In this context, a useful bridge between behavior and biology may be found in the mechanisms regulating peripheral and central sensory transmission of painful or noxious stimuli.

Pain is a sensory experience normally generated by activation of a specific subset of high-threshold peripheral sensory neurons, the nociceptors (nociception is the detection of noxious or tissue-damaging stimuli). After repeated injury, however, dramatic alterations in the somatosensory system can occur, amplifying responses and increasing sensitivity to peripheral stimuli so that pain can be activated by normally nonnoxious or low-intensity stimuli. In models of sensory dysfunction associated with chronic and neuropathic pain (i.e., pain induced by injury or dysfunction in the nervous system) the behavioral parameters used to indicate pain include allodynia (i.e., increased sensitivity to normally nonnoxious stimuli), hyperalgesia (i.e., increased pain sensitivity to noxious stimuli) and auto-tomy (i.e., self-injury). The exact mechanisms regulating sensory dysfunction are unclear, but it appears to depend in part, or at least in some cases, on desensitization of afferent sensory fibers involving structural changes in the epidermal nerve fibers mediated, in part, by substance P such that sensory dysfunction results from degeneration of intracutaneous nerve fibers. Whether similar consequences are associated with chronic tissue-damaging SIB among individuals with develop-mental disorders is unknown, but recent evidence suggests that some individuals with IDD and chronic SIB have altered peripheral innervation consistent with this hypothesis (Symons et al. 2008, 2009). Knowing whether chronic SIB is associated with altered pain thresholds would suggest treatment specific to mechanisms of analgesia and pain regulation.

Of the existing neurochemical models of SIB (reviewed briefly earlier), the opioid model explicitly addresses the clinical puzzle of why SIB is not regulated by its painful consequences. In this model, people with SIB are presumed to have either a congenital or acute dysfunction in endogenous opioid production that results in elevated pain thresholds (i.e., hypoalgesia) (Sandman, 1988). Support for the opioid model has come from preclinical studies that have demonstrated altered beta-endorphin levels in people with SIB (Sandman, Barron, Chicz-DeMet, & DeMet, 1991), and from controlled treatment trials of the opiate antagonist medication naltrexone (Buzan, Dubovsky & Treadway, & Thomas, 1995; Sandman, Spence, & Smith,1999; Symons, Fox, & Thompson, 1998). Despite this evidence, multiple cases of naltrexone nonresponse have been documented in controlled trials (Bodfish, McCuller, Madison, Register, Mailman, & Lewis, 1994), and even in responders the magnitude and breadth of the clinical effects of naltrexone have been questioned (Barrera, Teodoro, Selmeci, & Madappuli, 1994). Although clinical interest in naltrexone seems to have waned (Symons, Thompson, & Rodriguez, 2004), the likelihood that people with severe SIB have altered pain sensitivity remains. Analysis of beta-endorphin activity and naltrexone response, however, represents only a partial or preliminary analysis of the role of pain circuitry in the mediation of SIB. To date, despite the face validity of the opioid model with respect to the presumed link between SIB and altered pain thresholds, there have been limited direct tests of the notion that people with SIB have significantly altered pain sensitivity (but see Barrera et al., 1994; reviewed in detail as follows).

The definition of pain includes both emotional and sensory components, which are difficult to assess in subgroups of individuals with IDD who are non-verbal or experience language and cognitive impairment. In other nonverbal or similarly compromised populations (e.g., neonates, infants, older adults with medical frailty or cognitive impairment), objective measurement strategies have been used to identify pain based on facial coding of expression during known painful events such as vaccination, blood draw, or minor invasive procedures (Grunau & Craig, 1987; 1990). This work draws upon the large body of empirical evidence for objective, nonverbal signs of emotional expression based on changes in facial action units (Ekman & Friesen, 1978). Facial action units are anatomically based configurations of facial musculature that can be directly observed and reliably coded. Faces are highly plastic and can configure into a wide range of different displays in very short time spans. Work with facial action coding has identified reliable configurations of facial muscles that correspond to discrete emotional states and includes a "pain face" configuration of facial action units (Craig, Prkachin, & Grunau, 1992). In studies of individuals with IDD, facial action coding has been used to identify painful experiences during invasive procedures (LaChapelle, Hadjistavropoulos T., & Craig, 1999; Oberlander, Gilbert, Chambers, O'Donnell, & Craig, 1999). Results showed that facial actions associated with acute vaccine and venipuncture-related pain among nonverbal individuals with IDD corresponded to timing of injection. The studies demonstrated that the magnitude of pain expression in nonverbal people with severe intellectual disabilities can be reliably quantified.

Accordingly, some limited research has applied measurement strategies for quantifying pain expression to the problem of SIB (Breau, Camfield, Symons, Bodfish, MacKay, Finley, & McGrath, 2003; Symons & Danov, 2005). In a single-case "proof of concept" study, Symons and Danov (2005) collected prospective data from daily direct observations of pain expression examined in relation to the presence and absence of SIB for a 6-year-old boy with severe self-injury. Pain behavior was measured using the Non-Communicating Children's Pain Checklist–Revised (NCCPC-R; Breau, McGrath, Camfield, & Finley, 2002; Breau et al., 2003) and SIB was measured using the Self-Injury Trauma Scale (SITS; Iwata, Pace, Kissel, Nau, & Farber, 1990). Substantive analyses were performed by first plotting successive time intervals for visual analysis of directly rated behavior. Time intervals with elevated ratings of SIB were associated with elevated pain ratings. Similarly, a cross-sectional study with caregivers of 101 nonverbal children (some with SIB, some without) ages 3–18 years (55% boys) completed the NCCPC-R for a pain episode observed at home (Breau et al., 2003). Children with severe intellectual impairments with SIB did not have reduced pain expression relative to matched controls and chronic pain was associated with altered structural features of SIB (frequency, location). These findings—specifically intact (cf. blunted) pain expression—from a group of children with IDD and SIB were subsequently replicated among an adult group with similar findings (SIB group > pain expression than non-SIB group; Symons, Harper, Breau, McGrath, & Bodfish, 2009).

In addition to evaluating pain expression, some work has been performed to assess sensory function more directly among samples of individuals with IDD and

SIB. Barrera et al. (1994) used algometers to test sensory thresholds during a trial of naltrexone (an opioid antagonist) to treat SIB for four individuals with severe IDD. Results specific to the sensory findings in relation to SIB were mixed—some individuals showed decreased sensory sensitivity during different conditions of the study whereas others showed increased sensory sensitivity. Examining the individual-level results in detail shows that in the majority of the conditions, in fact, the individual response pattern could be described as "algesic" (more pain, or reactivity, not less), reflecting reduced thresholds and increased mechanical sensitivity. This finding, although interpreted at the time as contrary to the "endorphin theory" of SIB, is consistent with more recent work on pain expression (described previously) and sensory sensitivity (described as follows) among individuals with chronic SIB and IDD.

In a test of sensory sensitivity to an array of calibrated stimuli, Symons, Shinde, Clary, Harper, and Bodfish (2010) investigated a sham-controlled (to guard against observer bias) sensory testing protocol with a sample of adults with IDD with and without SIB. The facial behavior of the participants before, during, and after five sensory stimulation modalities (pin prick, light touch, deep pressure, coolness, warmth) was coded by three raters using the Facial Action Coding System (FACS). Importantly, observers were blinded to active vs. sham stimulation status. FACS scores increased significantly during active sensory trials compared with sham trials, providing some evidence that the sensory testing protocol was valid (i.e., distinguished between active versus sham stimulation). There were also significant effects for the presence of SIB with individuals having SIB more expressive than individuals without SIB, thus providing additional evidence as that reviewed above for the "pain expression" studies.

Collectively, the foregoing reviewed findings suggest that perhaps pain among individuals with IDD and chronic SIB is not blunted, at least among a subgroup, and, in fact, some individuals may be hyperalgesic, not hypoalgesic. The overall relevance here is that the components of the sensory neurobiology systems regulating sensory and pain transmission appear to be intact—in some but perhaps not all individuals with SIB—and for a subgroup of individuals, some components of the sensory system may be enhancing or amplifying pain, but it is not clear whether this is a central problem related to ascending or descending pathways or whether there may also be a peripheral component related to the SIB severity and of the tissue damage produced by chronic SIB. Clarifying these issues may lead to novel treatment approaches informed by the state of the science in pain and its management.

## HEALTH CONDITIONS AND SELF-INJURIOUS BEHAVIOR

The observation that SIB can be cyclical has long been reported but poorly understood (Fisher, Piazza, & Roane, 2002). Over the past two decades, there has been increased attention focused on intermittent patterns of SIB in order to identify environmental correlates of this variability. These efforts led to the identification of several distinct types of health care conditions that were idiosyncratically associated with bouts of self-injury. These observations, which were theoretically predicted by Carr (1977) and conceptualized as organic or biological influences on SIB, have become an area of frequent study by behavior analysts.

The accumulated literature has identified a number of health conditions, that when present, are associated with increased rates of SIB in people with IDD (Carr & Smith, 1995; Kennedy & Becker, 2006). Frequently noted conditions include allergies, asthma, constipation, dysmenorrhea, gastroesophageal reflux disease (GERD), otitis media, and sleep disruption. Typically, the onset of one of these health conditions is associated with an increase in the occurrence of SIB or a worsening of its intensity. When the condition is alleviated by medication or the health condition resolves, there can be a corresponding decrease in the intensity or frequency of self-injury. It has been observed that a common mechanism among these health conditions is that each produces some level of discomfort or pain (Kennedy & O'Reilly, 2006). Although much of this evidence comes from sub-jective and correlative reports, there is also accumulating evidence from animal models that discomfort can exacerbate the noxious properties of stimuli. This has led to the hypothesis that health conditions can serve as establishing operations for negative reinforcers, the net result being an increase in negatively reinforced SIB. For the remainder of this section, we briefly review evidence relating to one health condition that exemplifies this observation: sleep disruption.

## Sleep Disruption

Problems with sleep include a broad array of instances in which disruptions in sleep quality or duration occur. Among people with IDD, the most prevalent sleep problems include psychotropic medication side effects, sleep apnea, restless legs syndrome, difficulty falling asleep, and night awakenings. Many of these sleep disruptions manifest themselves in a cyclical pattern that can very from day to day, week to week, or in idiosyncratic patterns, influencing behavioral problems in an intermittent manner. Prevalence estimates for sleep disruption varies across disability types, but anywhere from 35%–90% of people with IDD have identified sleep disruptions (Clements, Wing, & Dunn, 1986; Robinson & Richdale, 2004). Although very common among people with IDD, similar sleep problems are prevalent across a range of psychiatric conditions and it is currently unclear whether these are results of the underlying disorder and/or byproducts of medical treat-ment (Wulff, Gatti, Wettstein, & Foster, 2010). Symons, Davis, and Thompson (2000) found evidence of altered sleep (reductions) associated with chronic daytime SIB among an adult sample of individuals with IDD.

An experimental example of how sleep disruption can influence SIB was provided by Kennedy and Meyer (1996). They analyzed the SIB and related problem behavior of a man who had comorbid sleep problems. Kennedy and Meyer documented the sleep patterns of the person while concurrently conducting daily analogue functional analyses to assess the operant functions the behaviors served. When the individual had slept 5 or more hours at night, SIB was infrequent. When the man slept < 5 hours, SIB was frequent during the analogue functional analyses, but only under negative reinforcement contingencies. No other types of operant contingencies were affected by the disrupted sleep. The identification of negatively reinforced behavior being increased by sleep disruptions has been frequently documented in the research literature (O'Reilly, 1995; O'Reilly & Lancioni, 2000; Piazza & Fisher, 1991; Reed, Dolezal, Cooper-Brown, & Wacker, 2005).

Research using rodent models has shown that negatively reinforced responding is increased by REM sleep deprivation (Harvey, Smith, May, Caruso, Roberts, Patterson, Valdovinos, & Kennedy, 2004; Kennedy, Meyer, Werts, & Cushing, 2000). The biological mechanisms associated with an increase in avoidance responding following REM sleep deprivation appear to be increased nociceptive sensitivity (Harvey, Kline, Roberts, May, Valdovinos, Wiley, & Kennedy, 2010; May, Harvey, Valdovinos, Kline, Wiley & Kennedy, 2005). This increased sensitivity to pain may involve alterations in aminergic neurotransmitter circuits, particularly serotonergic pathways (Harvey et al., 2004; Wei, Wang, & Pertovaara, 2008). From a behavior analytic perspective, sleep deprivation acts as a motivating operation to increase the noxious properties of negatively reinforcing stimuli, resulting in increased rates of avoidance responding (Laraway, Snycerski, Michael, & Poling, 2003). REM sleep deprivation appears to have the opposite effect on rates of a positively reinforced response, decreasing these behaviors particularly at high levels of sleep disruption (Kennedy, 2002b; Kirby & Kennedy, 2003). In these instances, access to sleep may become a higher valiance reinforcer than the established positive reinforcement contingency, resulting in response allocation shifting toward access to sleep (Kennedy, 2002b).

Sleep disruption can produce changes in SIB that the present literature summarizes as increases in rate or duration of responding. Because sleep problems tend to be intermittent, their motivational effects on negative and positive reinforcers is similarly episodic (making them more challenging to detect). The rapidly developing research base on the neurobiology of sleep is beginning to suggest what mechanisms might underlie the behavioral processes that are now well documented. Such an evidence base strongly suggests that biological variables are involved in sleep deprivation effects on SIB.

## IMPLICATIONS AND CONCLUSIONS

We have shown that SIB has a significant biological basis. In some instances biological contributions predominate in the control of behavior (e.g., Lesch–Nyhan syndrome). In many other instances there is an interaction between biological and environmental factors of SIB (e.g., sleep deprivation and negatively reinforced behavior). This observation stands in contrast to the standard behavioral model of SIB that dominates current assessment and intervention practices in psychology (i.e., socially mediated reinforcement). Although future behavioral-biological-epidemiological studies of SIB will determine the extent to which biology and environment interact in individual cases of self-injury, it is likely that current estimations of biological contributions to SIB substantially underestimate their occurrence (e.g., Iwata et al., 1994).

Consideration of this more complex causal model will require revisions to existing approaches for assessment and treatment of SIB. Although the field's current approaches to assessing and treating SIB based on social reinforcement processes will undoubtedly remain core tools, an elaboration of processes and variables seems inevitable. First, assessment practices need to be broadened. Health care professionals need to be incorporated into assessments of SIB with the knowledge that medical conditions and biological variables can contribute to self-injury. This incorporation of health professionals may include health status exams, psychotropic medication reviews, establishing drug side effect profiles, and completion of genetic and neurological workups. This information—which may note neuropathic contributors to pain sensitivity, health conditions produced by psychoactive medicines, and so on—will also need to be closely integrated with behavioral-environmental assessment information. Identifying the various contributing variables to self-injury and how the constituent elements interact may reveal a much more complex causal pattern of SIB.

Similarly, interventions will require a broadening of approaches. If biomedical information determines organic contributions to the occurrence of SIB, then a large array of health professionals may also be involved in treating the behavioral disorder including disciplines like genetics, internal medicine, neurology, nursing, nutrition, otolaryngology, ophthalmology, pediatrics, and psychiatry, to name only a few. Obviously, such a broad range of potential contributors will call for a much more robust approach to individual case management than is currently best practice. It may be that behavior analysts serve this coordination role, but it may also lead to behavior analysis being viewed as a specialty area contributing to a larger intervention panoply that is best overseen by another profession. In either scenario, it is likely that medical treatments will be more prevalent and more integrated into SIB treatment programs.

How should the field move forward with this broadened vision of SIB causality and treatment? Perhaps the best path forward is to take the existing strengths, which are largely behavior-analytic in nature, and evolve them. Current FBA approaches are powerful tools for identifying social reinforcers contributing to SIB, but these approaches tend to rely on clinical intuition and, at times, serendipity to identify biological contributors to self-injury (Hartmann, Gilles, Danov, McComas, & Symons, 2008). A more robust and organized approach will need to be developed from initial identification through to long-term treatment. The path along which this process will unfold will entail a reorienting of existing approaches and the expectations they are based on to achieve a more robust and effective approach to understanding and resolving SIB.

## REFERENCES

Barrera, F.J., Teodoro, J.M., Selmeci, T., & Madappuli, A. (1994). Self-injury, pain, and the endorphin theory. *Journal of Developmental and Physical Disabilities, 6,* 169–192.

Barrera, F.J., Violo, R.A., & Graver, E.E. (2007). On the form and function of severe self-injurious behavior. *Behavioral Interventions, 22,* 5–33.

Bergen, A.E., Holborn, S.W., & Scott-Huyghebaert, V.C. (2002). Functional analysis of self-injurious behavior in an adult with Lesch-Nyhan syndrome. *Behavior Modification, 26,* 187–204.

Berkson, G. (1967). Abnormal stereotyped motor acts. *Proceedings of the annual meeting of the American Psychopathological Association, 55,* 76–94.

Bodfish, J.W., McCuller, W.R., Madison, J.M., Register, M., Mailman, R.B., & Lewis, M.H. (1994). Placebo, double-blind evaluation of long-term naltrexone treatment effects for adults with mental retardation and self-injury. *Journal of Developmental and Physical Disabilities, 9,* 135–151.

Breau L.M., Camfield C.S., Symons F.J., Bodfish J.W., MacKay A., Finley G.A., et al. (2003). Relation between pain and self-injurious behavior in nonverbal children with severe cognitive impairments. *Journal of Pediatrics, 142,* 498–503.

Breau L.M., McGrath P.J., Camfield C.S., Finley G.A. (2002). Psychometric properties of the noncommunicating children's pain checklist-revised. *Pain, 99,* 349–357.

Buzan, R.D., Dubovsky, S.L., Treadway, J.T., & Thomas, M. (1995). Opiate antagonists for recurrent self-injurious behavior in three mentally retarded adults. *Psychiatric Services, 46,* 511–512.

Carr, E.G. (1977). The motivation for self-injurious behavior: A review of some hypotheses. *Psychological Bulletin, 84,* 800–816.

Carr, E.G., & Smith, C.E. (1995). Biological setting events for self-injury. *Mental Retardation and Developmental Disabilities Research Reviews, 1,* 94–98.

Clements, J., Wing, L., & Dunn, G. (1986). Sleep problems in handicapped children: A preliminary study. *Journal of Child Psychology and Psychiatry, 27,* 399–407.

Craig, K.D., Prkachin, K.M., Grunau, R.V.E. (1992). The facial expression of pain. In D.C. Turk & R. Melzack (Eds.), *Handbook of pain assessment* (pp. 257–276). New York: Guilford Press.

Dellinger-Ness, L.A., & Handler, L. (2006). Self-injurious behavior in human and nonhuman primates. *Clinical Psychology Review, 26,* 503–514.

Ekman, P., & Friesen, W.V. (1978). *Investigator's guide to the Facial Action Coding System.* Palo Alto: Consulting Psychologists Press.

Fisher, W.W., Piazza, C.C., & Roane, H.S. (2002). Sleep and cyclical variables related to self-injurious and other destructive behavior. In S.R. Schroeder, M. Oster-Granite, & T. Thompson (Eds.), *Self-injurious behavior: Gene-brain-behavior relationships* (pp. 205–221). Washington DC: American Psychological Association.

Freeman, R., Horner, R., & Reichle, J. (1999). Relation between heart rate and problem behaviors. *American Journal on Mental Retardation, 104,* 330–345.

Glass, L., & Mackey, M.C. (1988). *From clocks to chaos: The rhythms of life.* Oxford: Clarendon Press.

Graveling, R.A., & Brooke, J.D. (1978). Hormonal and cardiac response of autistic children to changes in environmental stimulation. *Journal of Autism and Childhood Schizophrenia, 8,* 441–455.

Grunau, R.V.E., & Craig, K.D. (1987). Pain expression in neonates: Facial action and cry. *Pain, 28,* 395–410.

Grunau, R.V.E., & Craig, K.D. (1990). Facial activity as a measure of neonatal pain expression. In D.C. Tyler & E.J. Crane (Eds.). *Advances in pain research and therapy, Vol. 15.* (pp. 147–156). New York: Raven Press.

Guess, D., & Carr, E.G. (1991). Emergence and maintenance of stereotypy and self-injury. *American Journal on Mental Retardation, 96,* 299–319.

Haines, J., Williams, C.L., Brain, K.L., & Wilson, G.V. (1995). The psychophysiology of self-mutilation. *Journal of Abnormal Psychology, 104,* 471–489.

Hartmann, E., Gilles, E., Danov, S., McComas, J.J., & Symons, F.J. (2008). Self-injurious behavior correlated with changes in intracranial pressure associated with congenital hydrocephalus. *Journal of Child Neurology, 23,* 1062–1065.

Harvey, M.T., Kline, R., Roberts, C., May, M.E., Valdovinos, M.G., Wiley, R.G., et al. (2010). Parametric analysis of thermal place preference following sleep deprivation in the rat. *Neuroscience Letters, 485,* 98–101.

Harvey, M.T., Smith, R.L., May, M.E., Caruso, M., Roberts, C., Patterson, T.G., et al. (2004). Possible role for the 5-HT1A receptor in the effects of REM sleep deprivation on avoidance responding in rats. *Psychopharmacology (Berl), 176,* 123–128.

Henderson, J.F. (1968). Possible functions of hypoxanthine-guanine phosphoribosyltransferase and their relation to the biochemical pathology of the Lesch-Nyhan syndrome. *Federal Proceedings, 27,* 1075–1077.

Iwata, B.A., Dorsey, M.F., Slifer, K.J., Bauman, K.E., & Richman, G.S. (1982). Toward a functional analysis of self-injury. *Analysis and Intervention in Developmental Disabilities, 2,* 3–20.

Iwata, B.A., Pace, G.M., Dorsey, M.F., Zarcone, J.R., Vollmer, T.R., Smith, R.G., et al. (1994). The functions of self-injurious behavior: An experimental-epidemiological analysis. *Journal of Applied Behavior Analysis, 27,* 215–240.

Iwata B.A., Pace G.M., Kissel R.C., Nau P.A., & Farber J.M. (1990). The self-injury trauma (SIT) scale: A method for quantifying surface tissue damage caused by self-injurious behavior. *Journal of Applied Behavior Analysis, 23,* 99–110.

Kennedy, C.H. (2002a). Evolution of stereotypy into self-injury. In S.R. Schroeder, M. Oster-Granite, & T. Thompson (Eds.), *Self-injurious behavior: Gene-brain-behavior relationships* (pp. 105–118). Washington DC: American Psychological Association.

Kennedy, C.H. (2002b). Effects of REM sleep deprivation on FI and FR schedules of positive reinforcement. *Behavioural Brain Research, 128,* 205–214.

Kennedy, C.H. (2004). Facts, interpretations, and explanations: A review of Evelyn Fox Keller's *Making Sense of Life. Journal of Applied Behavior Analysis, 37,* 539–553.

Kennedy, C.H., & Becker, A. (2006). Health conditions in antecedent assessment and intervention of problem behavior. In J.K. Luiselli (Ed.), *Antecedent assessment and intervention: Supporting children and adults with developmental disabilities in community settings* (pp. 73–97). Baltimore: Paul H. Brookes Publishing Co.

Kennedy, C.H., & Meyer, K.A. (1996). Sleep deprivation, allergy symptoms, and negatively reinforced problem behavior. *Journal of Applied Behavior Analysis, 29,* 133–135.

Kennedy, C.H., Meyer, K.A., Werts, M.G., & Cushing, L.S. (2000). Effects of sleep deprivation on free-operant avoidance. *Journal of the Experimental Analysis of Behavior, 73,* 333–345.

Kennedy, C.H., & O'Reilly, M.E. (2006). Pain, health conditions, and problem behavior in people with developmental disabilities. In T.F. Oberlander & F. J. Symons (Eds.), *Pain in children and adults with developmental disabilities* (pp. 121–138) Baltimore: Paul H. Brookes Publishing Co.

Kennedy, C.H., & Thompson, T. (2000). Health conditions contributing to problem behavior among people with mental retardation and developmental disabilities. In M. Wehmeyer & J. Patten (Eds.), *Mental retardation in the 21st century* (pp. 211–231). Austin, TX: ProEd.

Kirby, M., & Kennedy, C.H. (2003). Variable-interval reinforcement schedule value influences responding following REM sleep deprivation. *Journal of the Experimental Analysis of Behavior, 80,* 253–260.

LaChapelle D.L., Hadjistavropoulos T., & Craig K.D. (1999). Pain measurement in persons with intellectual disabilities. *Clinical Journal of Pain, 15,* 13–23.

Laraway, S., Snycerski, S., Michael, J., & Poling, A. (2003). Motivating operations and terms to describe them: Some further refinements. *Journal of Applied Behavior Analysis, 36,* 407–414.

Lesch, M., & Nyhan, W.L. (1964). A familial disorder of uric acid metabolism and central nervous system function. *American Journal of Medicine, 36,* 561–570.

Lewis, M.H. & Bodfish, J.W. (1998). Repetitive behavior disorders in autism. *Mental Retardation and Developmental Disabilities Research Reviews, 4,* 80–89.

Lewis, M.H., Tanimura, Y., Lee, L., & Bodfish, J.W. (2007). Animal models of restricted repetitive behavior in autism. *Behavioural Brain Research, 176,* 66–74.

Lutz, C.K., Well, A., & Novak, M. (2003). Stereotypic and self-injurious behavior in rhesus macaques: A survey and retrospective analysis of environment and early experience. *American Journal of Primatology, 60,* 1–15.

Maisto, C., Baumeister, A., & Maisto, A. (1978). An analysis of variables related to self-injurious behavior among institutionalized retarded persons. *Journal of Mental Deficiency Research, 22,* 27–36.

May, M.E., Harvey, M.T., Valdovinos, M., Kline, R.J., Wiley, R.G., & Kennedy, C.H. (2005). Nociceptor and age-specific effects of REM sleep deprivation induced hyperalgesia. *Behavioural Brain Research, 159,* 89–94.

Midgley, B.D., & Morris, E.K. (1992). Nature = *f*(nurture). A review of Oyama's *The Ontogeny of Information: Developmental Systems and Evolution. Journal of the Experimental Analysis of Behavior, 58,* 229–240.

Nagai, Y., Cavanna, A., & Critchley, H.D. (2009). Influence of sympathetic autonomic arousal on tics: Implications for a therapeutic behavioral intervention for Tourette syndrome. *Journal of Psychosomatic Research, 67,* 599–605.

Newell, K.M., & Bodfish, J.W. (2007). Dynamical origins of stereotypy: Relation of postural movements during sitting to stereotyped movements during body-rocking. *American Journal on Mental Retardation, 112,* 66–75.

Nock, M.K., & Mendes, W.B. (2008). Physiological arousal, distress tolerance, and social problem-solving deficits among adolescent self-injurers. *Journal of Consulting and Clinical Psychology, 76,* 28–28.

Nock, M.K., & Prinstein, M.J. (2004). A functional approach to the assessment of self-mutilative behavior. *Journal of Consulting and Clinical Psychology, 72,* 885–890.

Novak, M. (2003). Self-injurious behavior in rhesus monkeys: New insights into it etiology, physiology, and treatment. *American Journal of Primatology, 59,* 3–19.

Oberlander T.F., Gilbert C.A., Chambers C.T., O'Donnell M.E., & Craig K.D. (1999). Biobehavioral responses to acute pain in adolescents with a significant neurologic impairment. *Clinical Journal of Pain, 15,* 201–209.

O'Reilly, M.F. (1995). Functional analysis and treatment of escape-maintained aggression correlated with sleep deprivation. *Journal of Applied Behavior Analysis, 28,* 225–226.

O'Reilly, M.F., & Lancioni, G. (2000). Response covariation of escape-maintained aberrant behavior correlated with sleep deprivation. *Research in Developmental Disabilities, 21,* 125–136.

Oyama, S. (2000). *The ontogeny of information: Developmental systems and evolution.* Durham, NC: Duke University Press.

Piazza, C.C., & Fisher, W. (1991). A faded bedtime with response cost protocol for treatment of multiple sleep problems in children. *Journal of Applied Behavior Analysis, 24,* 129–140.

Platt, D.M., Kinsey, J.H., Jorgensen, M.J., & Novak, M.A. (1996). Factors affecting the expression of self-injurious behavior in rhesus monkey (*Macaca mulatta*). *ISP/ASP Congress Abstracts* (pp. 768).

Powell, S.B., Newman, H.A., Pendergast, J.F., & Lewis, M.H. (1999). A rodent model of spontaneous stereotypy: Initial characterization of developmental, environmental, and neurobiological factors. *Physiology and Behavior, 66,* 355–363.

Reed, G.K., Dolezal, D.N., Cooper-Brown, L.J., & Wacker, D.P. (2005). The effects of sleep disruption on the treatment of a feeding disorder. *Journal of Applied Behavior Analysis, 38,* 243–245.

Richman, D.M., & Lindauer, S.E. (2005). Longitudinal assessment of stereotypic, proto-injurious, and self-injurious behavior exhibited by young children with developmental delays. *American Journal on Mental Retardation, 110,* 439–450.

Robinson, A.M., & Richdale, A.L. (2004). Sleep problems in children with intellectual disability: Parental perceptions, sleep problems, and views of treatment effectiveness. *Child Care and Health Development, 30,* 139–150.

Sandman, C.A. (1988). Beta-endorphin dysregulation in autistic and self-injurious behavior: A neuro-developmental hypothesis. *Synapse, 2,* 193–199.

Sandman, C.A., Barron, J.L, Chicz-DeMet, A. & DeMet, E.M. (1991). Plasma B-endorphin levels in patients with self-injurious behavior and stereotypy. *American Journal on Mental Retardation, 95,* 84–92.

Sandman, C.A., Spence, M.A., & Smith, M. (1999). Proopiomelanocortin (POMC) disregulation and response to opiate blockers. *Mental Retardation and Developmental Disabilities Research Reviews, 5,* 314–321.

Schroeder, S.R., Oster-Granite, M.L., & Thompson, T. (2002). *Self-injurious behavior: Gene-brain-behavior relationships.* Washington, DC: American Psychological Association.

Sourfe, L.A., Stuecher, H.U., & Stutzer, W. (1973). The functional significance of autistic behaviors for the psychotic child. *Journal of Abnormal Child Psychology, 1,* 225–240.

Symons, F.J. (2002). Pain and self-injury: Mechanisms and models. In S. Schroeder, M.L. Oster-Granite, & T. Thompson. *Self-injurious behavior: Genes, brain, and behavior* (pp. 223–234). Washington DC: American Psychological Association.

Symons, F.J., & Danov, S. (2005). A prospective clinical analysis of pain behavior and self-injurious behavior. *Pain 117,* 473–477.

Symons, F.J., Davis, M.L., & Thompson, T. (2000). Self-injurious behavior and sleep disturbance in adults with developmental disabilities. *Research in Developmental Disabilities, 21,* 115–223.

Symons, F.J., Fox, N.D., & Thompson, T. (1998). Functional communication training and naltrexone treatment of self-injurious behavior: An experimental case report. *Journal of Applied Research in Intellectual Disabilities, 11,* 273–292.

Symons, F.J., Harper, V.H., Breau, L., McGrath, P.J., & Bodfish, J.W. (2009). Evidence of increased nonverbal behavioral signs of pain in adults with neurodevelopmental disorders and chronic self-injury. *Research in Developmental Disabilities, 30,* 521–528.

Symons, F.J., Shinde, S., Clary, J., Harper, V., & Bodfish, J.W. (2010). A sham-controlled sensory testing protocol for nonverbal individuals with intellectual and developmental disabilities: Self-injury and gender effects. *The Journal of Pain, 11,* 773–781.

Symons, F.J., Sperry, L.A., Dropik, P., & Bodfish, J.W. (2005). The early development of stereotypy and self-injury in developmental disabilities: A review of research methods. *Journal of Intellectual Disability Research, 49,* 144–158.

Symons, F.J., Thompson, A., & Rodriguez, M.R. (2004). Self-injurious behavior and the efficacy of naltrexone treatment: A quantitative review. *Mental Retardation and Developmental Disabilities Research Reviews, 10,* 193–200.

Symons, F.J., Wendelschafer-Crabb, G., Kennedy, W., & Bodfish, J.W. (2009). Degranulated mast cells in the skin of adults with self-injurious behavior and neurodevelopmental disorders. *Brain, Behavior, & Immunity, 23*, 365–370.

Symons, F.J., Wendelschafer-Crabb, G., Kennedy, W., Hardrict, R., Dahl, N., & Bodfish, J.W. (2008). Evidence of altered epidermal nerve fiber morphology in adults with self-injurious behavior and neurodevelopmental disorders. *Pain, 134*, 232–237.

Thompson, T. (2007). Relations among functional systems in behavior analysis. *Journal of the Experimental Analysis of Behavior, 87,* 423–440.

Turner, C.A., & Lewis, M.H. (2003). Environmental enrichment: Effects on stereotyped behavior and neurotrophin levels. *Physiology and Behavior, 80*, 259–266.

Turner, C.A., Lewis, M.H., & King, M.A. (2003). Environmental enrichment: Effects on stereotyped behavior and dendritic morphology. *Developmental Psychobiology, 43*, 20–27.

Turner, C.A., Yang, M.C., & Lewis, M.H. (2002). Environmental enrichment: Effects on stereotyped behavior and regional neuronal metabolic activity. *Brain Research, 938*, 15–21.

Wei, H., Ma, A., Wang, Y.X., & Pertovaara, A. (2008). Role of spinal 5-HT receptors in cutaneous hypersensitivity induced by REM sleep deprivation. *Pharmacology Research, 57,* 469–7045.

Wulff, K., Gatti, S., Wettstein, J.G., & Foster, R.G. (2010). Sleep and circadian rhythm disruption in psychiatric and neurodegenerative disease. *Nature Reviews Neuroscience, 11,* 589–599.

# Functional Behavioral Assessment and Functional Analysis of Self-Injury

CHAPTER 2

*David E. Kuhn*

Self-injurious behavior, or SIB, is one of the most interesting and perplexing problem behaviors to assess and treat. SIB is characterized by the physical effect it has on the individual. In other words, a behavior will be classified as self-injurious if it causes tissue damage (Ballinger, 1971; Bodfish, Crawford, Powell, Parker, Golden, & Lewis, 1995; Tate & Baroff, 1966). Although SIB is not a disorder in and of itself, the *Diagnostic and Statistical Manual of Mental Disorders* (*DSM-IV-TR*; American Psychiatric Association, 2000) recognizes SIB within the diagnosis of Stereotypic Movement Disorder. This is helpful insofar as diagnostic codes are often necessary to allow an individual to access professional services. However, to some extent this diagnosis supposes that SIB is a form of stereotypic behavior and consequently infers behavioral function. That is, the diagnostic criteria state that the behavior occurs in a repetitive manner and persists because of the sensory consequences it produces. Therefore, it is important to make the distinction between these two classes of behavior, SIB and stereotypic behavior, as the functions may not be the same. Beyond the function of the behavior(s), the effects the behaviors have on the individual are also distinct, where stereotypic behavior alone does not produce any physical injury, whereas SIB does.

Like other categories of challenging behavior, SIB does not assume one form. Some research has found that the majority of cases of SIB take the form of head banging (e.g., striking head onto hard surfaces) or hand to head (e.g., hitting side of head with a closed fist) (Iwata et al., 1994c; Lowe et al., 2007); however, there are numerous variations within these forms as well as many other topographies, such as knee to head, eye poking, skin scratching, and arm biting.

Upon reading or hearing about SIB, two inevitable questions arise: who would engage in this type of behavior and why? The answer to the first question is a little easier to answer. The majority of individuals who engage in SIB have an intellectual and developmental disability (IDD) (Borthwick-Duffy, 1994; Lowe et al., 2007). To a small degree, SIB is demonstrated by typically developing individuals. For example, MacLean and Symons (2002) report that 5%–19% of typically developing infants and toddlers will engage in SIB in the form of head banging; however, the course of these behaviors is generally short lived. Some typically developing adolescents and adults engage in behaviors such as pulling their own hair out (i.e., trichotillomania) or cutting themselves. Although likely sensitive to social and nonsocial contingencies, these types of behaviors are generally considered distinct from SIB. Within the population of individuals who have IDD, there are several genetic syndromes where the presence of SIB is considered to be a diagnostic feature/symptom of the disorder. For example, close to 100% of individuals diagnosed with Lesch–Nyhan syndrome engage in SIB involving the lips, tongue, and/or fingers (Nyhan, 2002), and individuals diagnosed with Smith–Magenis syndrome display head banging SIB in 55% of cases (Finucane, Dirrigl, & Simon, 2001).

The answer to the second question is a little more complex and troubling. One cannot help but wonder why someone would continue to engage in a behavior that causes him or her significant harm. Common sense says that it must be something outside of his or her control—similar to a reflex or involuntary tic. However, this is not the case. Although SIB may occur in a highly repetitive fashion, research has overwhelmingly shown that these behaviors are learned and remain under the control of the individual (i.e., operant) (Carr, Newsom, & Binkoff, 1976; Iwata et al., 1994c; Lovaas, Freitag, Gold, & Kassorla, 1965). In other words, SIB adheres to the same three-term contingency as other operant behaviors. The three-term contingency consists of 1) an antecedent event—which can both set the occasion for the SIB to occur and signal that reinforcement is available following engagement in SIB (i.e., discriminative stimulus), 2) the behavior (e.g., SIB), and 3) the consequent event—which reinforces or supports the behavior. Furthermore, these behaviors have been shown to be sensitive to the same social contingencies as other challenging (and socially appropriate) behaviors—that is, social positive reinforcement (i.e., access to attention, access to preferred items/activities) and social negative reinforcement (i.e., avoidance or escape from instruction or nonpreferred activities). In 1994, Iwata and colleagues reviewed the functional analysis outcomes of 152 cases of SIB and found that in at least 67.1% of the cases the SIB persisted because of the social consequences it produced (note: this percentage does not include individuals whose SIB was maintained by both social and nonsocial consequences). They found further that 38.1% engaged in SIB to avoid or produce a break from instructional situations, and 26.3% engaged in SIB to access attention, preferred items, or food. These data have been supported by other research demonstrating high levels of socially mediated SIB (Kahng, Iwata, & Lewin, 2002).

Another finding within this body of research is that in approximately 25.7% of cases, SIB persists independent of social consequences (Iwata et al., 1994c; Kahng et al., 2002). In effect, SIB is maintained because of some desirable sensory consequence produced by the behavior itself. In many ways, this latter behavior–consequence relation is unique to SIB. This relation between the behavior and sensory consequence is often termed automatic reinforcement (Vollmer, 1994). Similar to social reinforcement, automatic reinforcement can be conceptualized as either positive reinforcement (i.e., SIB produces a pleasurable sensory experience) or negative reinforcement (i.e., SIB results in the termination or attenuation of an undesirable sensory experience). Despite the connotation associated with the word "automatic," the act of engaging in the behavior remains under the control of the individual.

## ASSESSING THE FUNCTION OF SELF-INJURIOUS BEHAVIOR

Anyone who has observed the occurrence of SIB recognizes the need for intervention. The question becomes, is it necessary to understand why this behavior is occurring or is it simply necessary to stop it from occurring? The answer to this question is yes (to both). A good analogy to this predicament is something most people have faced at one point or another—determining whether or not to go to the physician's office with a sore throat. If I am simply interested in ending the pain associated with the sore throat, I can take some pain-relief medication such as ibuprofen, knowing that I am not treating the problem but merely addressing a symptom. However, if I am interested in knowing why I am experiencing this pain, and potentially receiving a specific treatment to fix the problem (e.g., an antibiotic), I will likely go the physician's office and subject myself to a strep test. A positive result of the test would suggest that my sore throat could be treated with antibiotics, whereas a negative test may suggest a viral infection that would be insensitive to such treatment. Regardless of the outcome, the best approach may be to both treat the symptom and assess the cause (i.e., diagnose the problem). This would eliminate the discomfort and ensure that that the problem is fixed. To make the leap back to SIB, in many cases when treating SIB clinicians must both attempt to minimize or prevent the symptom and conduct assessments/analyses to understand why the symptom is occurring—so that a specific treatment can be developed.

Understanding why the behavior occurs is critical to the development of an effective and sustaining behavioral (or in some cases pharmacological) intervention (Didden, Duker, & Korzilius, 1997). Given the various social and nonsocial contingencies (described previously) that may be responsible for maintaining an individual's SIB, it is impractical to think that one intervention could successfully treat all SIB. Therefore, gaining an understanding of the variables maintaining an individual's SIB before attempting to treat the problem is essential. *Functional behavioral assessment* (FBA) is a term used to describe a group of procedures for understanding why challenging behaviors occur. In concept, it was derived from a set of procedures developed to directly assess the relation between SIB and environmental/social variables. Iwata, Dorsey, Slifer, Bauman, and Richman (1994) described what is referred to as a (experimental) functional analysis. Using these procedures Iwata and colleagues directly manipulated and evaluated the relation between environmental events (antecedents and consequences) and SIB. Since then, researchers and clinicians have adapted these procedures and developed various other procedures to gather information and formulate hypotheses about the variables responsible for behavioral maintenance. Generally speaking, these procedures can be subdivided into three main categories of assessment: 1) indirect, 2) descriptive, and 3) experimental analysis. These approaches vary across several dimensions including, but not limited to, the level of inference associated with the findings, the amount of time required to complete the assessment, and the level of training required by the assessment administrator(s).

Prior to attempting to outline the steps necessary to conduct a thorough FBA, it is necessary to obtain a greater understanding of the various approaches to assessment so that one can see how they fit together. *Indirect assessment* is often the most attractive assessment method to use when dealing with SIB. An indirect assessment can be completed in a short period of time and does not require the direct observation of the behavior, relying entirely on the reports of others (Sturmey, 1994). Because many people seek immediate intervention for SIB, indirect assessment is viewed as desirable in that clinicians do not need to take time to observe the behavior or allow it to persist in order to assess behavioral function.

There are two types of indirect assessment, open ended and closed ended. An open-ended assessment, such as the Functional Analysis Interview Form (O'Neill et al., 1997) asks about the conditions under which the SIB is more or less likely to occur, such as which times of the day the behaviors are most and least probable and after which activities the behaviors are more or less likely to occur. In addition, this assessment provides scenarios for the caregiver to respond to, such as the impact on the person's behavior if he or she is asked to do a difficult task. This type of indirect assessment yields information about the individual's SIB and the specific conditions under which it occurs (or does not occur), allowing for respondents to describe individual events and circumstances. The information gathered can subsequently be collapsed into summary statements such as, "When person X is asked to complete a difficult task, she will bang her head on the desk in order to escape from completing the task."

The closed-ended indirect assessments ask questions about specific relations between the SIB and antecedent and consequent events. For example, both the Motivation Assessment Scale (MAS; Durand & Crimmins, 1988) and Questions About Behavioral Function (QABF; Matson & Vollmer, 1995) ask questions about the extent to which an antecedent or consequence likely precedes or follows the SIB such as whether the behavior happens after the person is asked to do a difficult task. Informants are required to respond to these questions using a Likert-type scale. The Functional Analysis Screening Tool (Iwata & DeLeon, 1996) asks similar questions but requires a "yes," "no," or "N/A" response from informants. Responses to each of the questions get categorized under different reinforcement categories (e.g., social positive, social negative, automatic). Behavioral function hypotheses are derived from categories with one or more endorsements. Collectively, indirect assessments have several advantages. First, completion of an indirect assessment is the quickest and easiest of the assessment methods. That is, within a few minutes a clinician can gather information that may suggest a functional relation between the SIB and environmental events. Although preferred, it is not essential that the clinician administering the assessment have extensive training in conducting FBAs. Also, an indirect assessment may be advantageous when assessing a very dangerous behavior like SIB where one would want to limit the occurrence(s) of the behavior. Thus an indirect assessment allows clinicians to assess the SIB without observing it directly. This may prove to be both an advantage and a disadvantage. That is, with an indirect measure the clinician is relying on the accuracy and subjective interpretations of someone else's observations. This variable is likely responsible for the inconsistent psychometrics associated with these measures (Shogren & Rojahn, 2003; Zarcone, Rodgers, Iwata, Rourke, & Dorsey, 1991). A benefit of the closed-ended assessment is that it forces informants to think about the SIB in relation to antecedents and consequences; however, it is also limited in that the questions/scenarios are not individualized and require informants to make judgments about behavioral function. An open-ended assessment has this limitation as well but facilitates more of a discussion and description of the SIB and related variables. Ultimately, it is the specific and individualized information gathered within the assessment that is the most useful to clinicians, especially as they navigate the FBA process.

*Descriptive assessment* is distinct from indirect assessment in that it requires the clinician to directly observe SIB. The purpose of the descriptive assessment is to observe behavior under the conditions it occurs in the natural environment (Bijou, Peterson, & Ault, 1968; Iwata, Kahng, Wallace, & Lindberg, 2000; Lerman & Iwata, 1993). By observing behavior in the natural environment, clinicians can attempt to identify the specific conditions that control the behavior, including the setting, antecedent, and consequent events (described previously). Hence, the goal of the assessment is to observe, record, and identify common situations where the SIB is likely to occur (e.g., school, day program, bus), events that reliably precede the SIB (e.g., instructions, removal of attention) as well as events/responses that reliably follow the occurrence of SIB (e.g., termination of instructions, peer attention). If/when clinicians are able to gather a sufficient amount of data, hypotheses can be generated regarding how these events interact and influence behavior. For example, if a clinician records that an adult, Scott, frequently engages in SIB during snack time at his day program if/when another client receives snack before he does, followed by staff immediately giving Scott his snack, then it may be possible to formulate the hypothesis that Scott engages in SIB to receive food. Unfortunately, gathering descriptive data is not always easy because there may be multiple antecedent and consequent events occurring simultaneously. The specific events controlling the behavior may not be easily recognized by the observer or the behavior may not occur during the time(s) of observation. Two methods of descriptive assessment, also open ended and closed ended, can be considered. The closed-ended method of assessment provides clinicians with a fixed number of antecedent and consequent events to choose from (e.g., see Closed-Ended Descriptive Assessment form on the next page) and clinicians are required to force an observation into a category at the time of observation. For example, if antecedent and consequence options include those depicted in the Closed-Ended Descriptive Assessment form and if clinician observes the SIB occurring during the completion of activities of daily living (e.g., hair brushing), he or she may endorse the antecedent event as being "demand presentation." If the occurrence of the SIB results in the delivery of a verbal reprimand along with the postponement of task completion, he or she may then endorse the consequence as being "attention" and "task avoidance." Data collected within this format allows clinicians to look for recurring patterns regarding antecedent and consequent events (e.g., demand presentation→SIB→task avoidance).

## Closed-Ended Descriptive Assessment

| Time | Antecedent | Behavior | Consequence |
|---|---|---|---|
| | 1  2  3  4  5 | 1  2  3  4 | 1  2  3  4  5 |
| | 1  2  3  4  5 | 1  2  3  4 | 1  2  3  4  5 |
| | 1  2  3  4  5 | 1  2  3  4 | 1  2  3  4  5 |

**Antecedents**

1 = Demand

2 = Transition

3 = Low/diverted attention

4 = Removal of preferred item

5 = No clear antecedent

**Behaviors**

1 = Hand to head

2 = Head banging

3 = Arm biting

4 = Eye poking

**Consequences**

1 = Escape

2 = Attention

3 = Tangible

4 = Edible

5 = Ignore

An open-ended descriptive assessment is similar to the closed ended insofar as clinicians observe and record various antecedent and consequent events. However, within an open-ended assessment there are no preidentified events from which to choose (e.g., see Open-Ended Descriptive Assessment form on the next page). This approach is more flexible since the clinician records the specific events they observe as they occur and do not interpret the events by forcing them into categories. The data gathered read more like a brief narrative of what was observed. Once the data have been collected, patterns within the data are examined. At this time, clinicians can group common events into categories. For example, if one antecedent event was described as, "while client was watching TV the staff turned the channel" and an antecedent in another situation was described as, "while client was watching TV, staff told him it was time to go to take a shower," the clinician may group these two events together under the category of "termination of preferred activity." This grouping technique is also applied towards descriptions of consequences.

An *experimental (or analog) functional analysis* (EFA) is similar to a structured descriptive assessment in that the behaviors are directly observed under specific conditions. However, in an EFA the clinician arranges the antecedent condition and prescribes the consequence(s) for the SIB. Loosely speaking, an EFA involves placing the client in a variety of different situations that have been shown to elicit SIB (as well as a situation where SIB is less likely to occur) and then responding to the SIB in ways that "common sense" often dictates. A standard set of procedures were developed by Iwata, Dorsey, et al., (1994) and his colleagues (1982/1994a) for testing relations between antecedent and consequent events and the occurrence of SIB. This analysis consists of three test conditions testing for positive, negative, and automatic reinforcement contingencies, as well as one control condition. Although subsequent studies have evaluated additional conditions and modifications (e.g., Adelinis, Piazza, Fisher, & Hanley, 1997; Fisher, Kuhn, & Thompson, 1998; Northup et al., 1995), the framework of arranging a specific antecedent condition and prescribing a consequence has remained the same (see Hanley, Iwata, & McCord, 2003, for a review).

The three test conditions of the original study (Iwata, Dorsey, et al., 1994) include an attention condition wherein the antecedent manipulation is characterized by low or diverted attention from the experimenter and the consequence for SIB is the delivery of attention. SIB occurring and persisting under these conditions is thought to be maintained by positive reinforcement in the form of access to attention. In the second condition, the antecedent condition consists of the experimenter delivering instructions/demands and the consequence for SIB is the termination of the instruction along with a brief break. SIB occurring and persisting under these conditions is said to be maintained by negative reinforcement in the form of escape from demands. The third test condition tests the hypothesis that the behavior is maintained independent of any social consequences (i.e., automatic reinforcement). In this condition, the participant remains in a room alone without access to other sources of stimulation (e.g., no toys). The last condition is the toy play condition, which serves as the control condition to which the other conditions are compared. This condition is characterized by access to high levels of stimulation (i.e.,

# Open-Ended Descriptive Assessment

| Time | Antecedent (what happened prior to SIB) | Behavior (which behavior) | Consequence (how did people respond to SIB) |
|---|---|---|---|
|  |  |  |  |
|  |  |  |  |
|  |  |  |  |
|  |  |  |  |

Key: SIB, self-injurious behavior.

preferred activities, social praise) and no instructions. Under these conditions one would not expect to observe any SIB. After completion of an EFA, a clinician visually inspects the data to compare the relative rates of SIB across conditions. A condition associated with elevated levels of SIB compared to the control condition and or the other test conditions indicates the presence of a functional relation (see Hagopian et al., 1997, and Iwata, Dorsey, et al., 1994, for reviews of different patterns of responding and associated interpretations).

Although the experimental functional analysis provides the clearest demonstration of a functional relation between environmental events and SIB, this approach has raised ethical concerns because these dangerous behaviors are allowed to occur and persist within the analysis (Neef & Peterson, 2007). To minimize and potentially avoid the risks of injury associated with a direct functional analysis of SIB, several accommodations have been described in the literature. Some researchers have examined whether or not a functional analysis of SIB is possible to complete while using protective equipment (e.g., padded helmet). In three studies (Borrero, Vollmer, Wright, Lerman, & Kelley, 2002; Le & Smith, 2002; Moore, Fisher, & Pennington, 2004), experimenters found that the application of protective equipment resulted in near or total suppression of SIB during experimental functional analyses, limiting any demonstration of a behavioral function. Each of these studies concluded that SIB persisted because of the sensory consequences it produced. In addition, the protective equipment interrupted the response–reinforcer relation (i.e., sensory extinction) resulting in little to no responding. Conversely, Contrucci Kuhn and Triggs (2009) found that the application of protective equipment was instrumental in identifying a social behavioral function of SIB (i.e., SIB maintained in part by positive reinforcement in the form of access to attention). Patterns of responding in the initial functional analysis suggested the SIB was maintained by automatic reinforcement, but responding with the use of protective equipment revealed the presence of a social behavioral function. As mentioned above (Iwata, Pace, et al., 1994) a significant percent of functional analyses conducted on SIB have identified a social behavioral function. Therefore, in spite of the results and conclusions obtained from the Borrero, Moore, and Le studies, it is possible that other individuals will respond in ways similar to the participant in the Contrucci Kuhn study.

Another approach clinicians and researchers have evaluated in an attempt to assess behavioral function while avoiding/preventing injury is the analysis of precursor behaviors (Smith & Churchill, 2002). A precursor behavior is one that reliably precedes another behavior. It is believed that the SIB and precursor behavior are members of the same functional response class, that is, both behaviors are maintained by the same consequence(s). Therefore, it may be possible to apply the prescribed contingencies within a functional analysis to the precursor behavior(s) such that the reinforcer is delivered following the precursor and prior to the participant engaging in the SIB. By doing this, clinicians can identify a behavioral function without requiring the individual to self-injure. Smith and Churchill (2002) applied this procedure with four individuals who engaged in SIB and compared the results to functional analysis outcomes where the prescribed consequences were delivered only following SIB. Both analyses revealed identical results suggesting that a functional analysis of precursor behaviors can be a viable alternative to directly assessing the behavioral function of SIB. Similar studies by Najdowski, Wallace, Ellsworth, MacAleese, and Cleveland (2008) and Borrero and Borrero (2008) confirmed that functional analysis of precursor behaviors could (indirectly) identify the function of SIB. Unfortunately, as is clearly described by Borrero and Borrero (2008), it can be difficult to identify behavior that reliably precedes SIB. In determining whether or not a behavior is indeed a precursor, it may be necessary to first determine the probability of the behavior occurring independent of SIB and compare it to the probability of the behavior occurring immediately prior to SIB.

In recent years, some researchers have evaluated other methods to indirectly assess behavioral function within an experimental analysis. In 2007 Berg and colleagues described and evaluated a concurrent-operants assessment wherein participants were provided the opportunity to choose between two environments—an arrangement similar to a paired-choice preference assessment (Fisher et al., 1992). However, in this assessment, each choice is associated with exposure to distinct antecedent events (e.g., task demands, attention, toys, nothing). This analysis provides information about preference for certain situations relative to others. For example, a participant could be presented with a choice between two conditions such as an environment where he is provided with attention while prompted to complete academic tasks and an environment with nothing to do. If the participant chooses the environment associated with work and attention, we may determine that he prefers an environment where attention is available. However, if he chooses to be in the environment with nothing to do, we may hypothesize that he either prefers to be alone or is avoiding an environment associated with demands. Hypotheses about behavioral function may be that behavior is maintained by access to attention or behavior is maintained by escape from instructions, respectively. Within the Berg et al. (2007) study, similar hypotheses of behavioral function were developed for three or four participants across experimental functional analyses and concurrent-operants assessments. Despite these promising data and the benefits of measuring a nondangerous behavior (i.e., choice), it is important to recognize that this type of assessment only yields information about conditions that a participant prefers (or possibly avoids) and does not confirm whether or not he would engage in SIB in order to access (or avoid) the environment.

Based on the information described above, it is evident that there are multiple approaches to assess the behavioral function of SIB. It is clear that there are additional factors a clinician must consider when assessing SIB (e.g., severity of physical injury) that may not be present when assessing other behaviors (e.g., screaming). Therefore, it is essential that the process of completing a functional behavior assessment of SIB be overseen by a professional with extensive experience and understanding of applied behavior analysis, particularly within the area of developmental disabilities and challenging behaviors. Consistent with best practice, as well as state and federal laws (described at greater length below), a comprehensive functional behavior assessment should include information gathered from multiple approaches/sources. Therefore, an approach toward thoroughly assessing behavioral function of SIB can be achieved by systematically applying aspects of each of the aforementioned assessment approaches such that appropriate and sufficient information is gathered, hypotheses are tested, and a behavioral function is identified. A functional assessment is neither complete nor sufficient following only an indirect or descriptive assessment. A functional assessment of SIB should include, in some form, a direct analysis of the effects of environmental events on the behavior. Following is a proposed set of procedures and guidelines for completing a functional behavior assessment of SIB. These procedures can and should be applied across settings (i.e., school, home, day program). That is, each procedure is sufficiently flexible to be implemented in all settings. Keep in mind that these procedural recommendations (and the decisions made within) are written to be somewhat vague in order to ensure that decisions are made based on the individual being served and not according to an instructional manual.

## A MODEL FOR CONDUCTING FUNCTIONAL BEHAVIORAL ASSESSMENTS OF SELF-INJURIOUS BEHAVIOR

The first step in conducting a functional behavioral assessment of SIB is to clearly identify and define the target behavior. This can and should be accomplished by a combination of both direct and indirect methods. Using an open-ended indirect functional assessment described earlier (e.g., Functional Analysis Interview Form; O'Neill et al., 1997) a clinician interviews people familiar with the client. Within this interview the clinician will clarify what the behavior looks like (i.e., the form of the behavior) in order to develop an operational or topography-based definition (Cooper, Heron, & Heward, 2007). The definition must be specific such that observers can easily recognize the behavior when it occurs. The definition should be sensitive so that observers can distinguish between occurrences and nonoccurrences of the behavior. A direct observation of the behavior by the clinician should follow in order to confirm the accuracy and completeness of the definition. A good operational definition is crucial towards ensuring that all assessments are addressing the exact same behavior(s) and accurate data can be collected.

Once the behavior has been identified, a decision must be made whether or not to immediately introduce protective equipment to ensure the safety of the individual, or whether some other measures are necessary (e.g., response blocking). Regardless of the decision, assessment should then proceed in the same general manner. Consistent with all behavior analytic approaches, appropriate measurement of the SIB is essential. It is important to determine how the SIB will be measured and evaluated. The determination may be that measurement will be of the behavior itself, a precursor behavior, or possibly an artifact of the behavior (i.e., permanent product) if the behavior occurs in a covert manner and is not readily observable (Grace, Thompson, & Fisher, 1996). The appropriate dimension to measure must be determined. For example, a clinician working with an individual who mouths his hand needs to determine whether it is better to measure the number of times mouthing occurs, the duration per occurrence, or both.

Beyond informing the clinician about what the SIB looks like, the open-ended indirect assessment can and should provide information about variables that may influence the behavior. These variables are not restricted to only social consequences but also variables such as time of day, people present, and sleep patterns. This assessment can help ascertain other relevant information including situations in which the behavior is less likely to occur. Gathering this information allows the clinician to begin generating hypotheses about the variables supporting the SIB. Equally important is that the information allows the clinician to narrow down the situations under which he or she can subsequently observe the behavior. For example, if results of the indirect assessment suggests that the SIB is mostly likely to occur during seated work tasks, particularly when a specific staff member is present, then the clinician can arrange the descriptive assessment at those times. Similarly, if the indirect assessment finds that the SIB is more likely to occur during the morning, the clinician could conduct the descriptive assessment at that time, thereby increasing the likelihood of observing the SIB. As one example, McCord, Thomson, and Iwata (2001) learned through staff report and interviews that the SIB of two participants was most likely to occur during transitions between activities, which allowed the experimenters to conduct structure observations and formulate hypotheses about behavioral function.

Thus, the information from indirect assessment should be used to structure the descriptive assessment(s). As described in the examples above, the information will inform the clinician about when to observe the client, possibly eliminating the need to conduct extended (nonproductive) observations. Once the clinician has identified the conditions for observation, he should initiate a descriptive assessment. Although the closed-ended descriptive assessment provides relevant information and can be easier to use, an open-ended descriptive assessment is more likely to yield the information necessary to proceed onto the experimental analysis. That is, a goal of the descriptive assessment is to identify idiosyncratic features of the variables influencing behavior. For example, if the indirect assessment indicated that SIB was likely to occur during low interaction, unstructured times, the descriptive assessment may confirm that the occurrence of SIB is likely during those activities, and may reveal that the SIB is often followed by staff attention (e.g., "Don't hit your head.") along with redirection to an appropriate activity (e.g., "Let's play with these blocks.").

Based on direct observations of parent-child and staff-child interactions, Thompson, Fisher, Piazza, and Kuhn (1998) were able to develop, and subsequently test, a hypothesis that a behavior previously characterized as aggression (i.e., chin grinding) was likely maintained by automatic reinforcement based on the conditions surrounding the occurrence of the behavior. Thus, information gathered via descriptive assessment can be used to test specific hypotheses about behavioral function (described as follows). By conducting an open-ended descriptive assessment a clinician may be able to document the occurrence of other behaviors (e.g., screaming) that reliably precede the SIB (i.e., precursor behaviors). Again, this information informs the experimental analysis of the SIB. Finally, by conducting these direct observations of SIB under the conditions where it occurs, a clinician can obtain an accurate measurement of the frequency and/or duration of the behavior. This result is extremely useful, as it provides a baseline measure of the behavior prior to intervention against which changes can be compared. In the event that protective equipment is introduced, clinicians can observe the SIB and limit the opportunity for injuries by arranging brief targeted observations without the protective equipment during activities/times identified through the indirect assessment. Further, clinicians can observe the individual under these same conditions with the protective equipment in place. Persistent SIB under this condition may support the use of protective equipment during experimental analyses.

Using the information obtained from the indirect and descriptive assessments, a clinician can formulate hypotheses about the variables supporting the SIB, for example, "Billy's SIB may be maintained by escape from demands involving physical guidance." Based on the assessment data collected, hypotheses should be identified for all possible determinants of the SIB (e.g., social positive reinforcement, social negative reinforcement, automatic reinforcement). In many, if not most, cases clinicians should also identify conditions under which SIB is not likely or less likely to occur. This latter condition is important for the purpose of identifying a condition to which the test conditions are compared and may also be helpful in guiding treatment development. If the clinician has a sufficient amount of resources and training, she should conduct an experimental functional analysis using procedures similar to those described by Iwata et al. (1982/1994), but only including those conditions indicated by the indirect and descriptive assessments. Furthermore, clinicians should individualize the analysis such that the antecedents and consequences replicate those observed during the descriptive assessments. For example, instead of delivering a verbal statement of disapproval during the attention condition, observations during the descriptive assessment may indicate that the verbal statement be paired with physical attention. In a designated "therapy" space the clinician would expose the client to each of the test and control conditions for 10 minutes at a time, (randomly) alternating between the conditions while measuring the levels of SIB. As mentioned before, clinicians should apply visual inspection techniques to interpret the data. Also, if levels of SIB were observed during descriptive assessments with protective equipment in place, exposing the client to functional analysis conditions with the protective equipment on would be indicated and the analysis could proceed as described.

Experimental functional analyses can also be arranged to test specific reinforcement hypotheses under more "naturalistic" conditions. The clinician must first identify which variables to test based on the findings of the descriptive assessment. Although multiple hypotheses can be tested, it may be easier to compare one test condition to the control in what is termed a "pair-wise design" (Iwata, Duncan, Zarcone, Lerman, & Shore, 1994). This type of analysis is feasible to do in school, home, or day programs. In order to do this successfully, the conditions must be arranged such that only one variable is manipulated at a time. In doing so, it is necessary to have a staff member or caregiver implement the condition accurately. For example, if the hypothesis to be tested is that the SIB is maintained by adult attention, then the clinician may alternate between periods of time (e.g., 10 minutes) where attention is provided independent of SIB (i.e., control condition) and where adult attention is only provided contingent on SIB (i.e., test condition). Similarly, if the hypothesis to be tested is that the SIB is maintained by escape from instruction, the clinician can alternate between periods of time in which there is no instruction (i.e., control) and periods in which instructions are delivered and SIB results in a brief termination of instruction. Again, elevated levels of SIB in test conditions when compared to control conditions would confirm the reinforcement hypothesis. This procedure can be applied to test each hypothesized behavioral function (e.g., access to preferred activities, automatic reinforcement). For individuals requiring protective equipment, these analyses can be conducted if the behavior persists at some level with the equipment on. However, if the behavior is suppressed when equipment is worn, it may be possible to remove the equipment for brief periods of time (e.g., 5–10 minutes) in order to expose the client to these conditions and measure the occurrence (or nonoccurrence) of SIB.

If wearing protective equipment inhibits all SIB and if it is unsafe for the individual to engage in any unprotected SIB, it may be necessary to indirectly assess behavioral function using some of the approaches described previously. Identification of a precursor behavior through the descriptive assessment would permit the clinician to proceed with a functional analysis of that behavior. In doing this, the clinician would arrange the conditions as described above but deliver the prescribed consequences following the precursor behavior and not the SIB. Given the high correspondence in behavioral function between the precursor and the SIB (Borrero & Borrero, 2008), an analysis of the behavioral function of the precursor may be sufficient. The prevalence of precursor behaviors is not known, yet it is unlikely that an alternative behavior reliably precede SIB in all cases. Therefore, if a precursor behavior is not identified clinicians may consider proceeding to a concurrent operants assessment (Berg et al., 2007) for the purpose of identifying preferred and nonpreferred conditions. Since there is no manipulation of con-sequences, this type of assessment does not provide a direct demonstration of behavioral function so clinicians must be cautious when interpreting the results. Still, if the hypothesis is that the SIB functions to access adult attention, it may be supported if the client reliably chooses an environment where attention is available. This information can also help develop an intervention, although the intervention would not (necessarily) be considered a function-based intervention.

The above approach towards completing a thorough functional behavioral assessment makes a few assumptions: 1) the SIB occurs at times when it can be observed, and 2) the SIB occurs often enough under certain conditions to allow repeated measurements of the behavior. Violation of these assumptions does not necessarily mean that the same methodology cannot be applied; however, extra steps or modifications may be necessary. For example, in assessing an individual's covert SIB, Grace, Thompson, and Fisher (1996) used procedures similar to Berg et al. (2007) by assessing preferences for different social reinforcers using a concurrent operants assessment. An interesting feature of this study was to evaluate a preference for different qualitative features of the social reinforcers (i.e., who was delivering the attention), which was obtained through descriptive assessments. Also, extending the length of observations across each functional analysis condition may be necessary to demonstrate a functional relation with individuals who engage in very low-rate SIB (Kahng, Abt, & Schonbachler, 2001).

## CONSIDERATIONS AND FUTURE DIRECTIONS

Among individuals with IDD, SIB is not specific to one age group and, consequently, functional behavioral assessment is not age-specific. Although there is no law entitling non-school-age individuals who exhibit challenging behaviors to receive an FBA, federal and state laws require that an FBA be completed for school-aged people who engage in challenging behavior. Specifically, according to, the Individuals with Disabilities Education Improvement Act of 2004 (PL 108–446), "A child with a disability who is removed from the child's current placement (irrespective of whether the behavior is determined to be a manifestation of the child's disability)…shall—receive, as appropriate, a functional behavioral assessment…." Or if "relevant members of the IEP (individualized education program) team make the determination that the conduct was a manifestation of the child's disability, the IEP team shall…conduct a functional behavioral assessment…." Although federal law does not outline what should be included within an FBA, state laws generally provide more specific guidelines. For example, the New York State Education Department defines an FBA as "the process of determining why the student engages in behaviors that impede learning and how the student's behavior relates to the environment." In describing how to conduct an FBA, the law further states that an FBA "shall include, but is not limited to, the identification of the problem behavior, the definition of the behavior in concrete terms, the identification of the contextual factors that contribute to the behavior…and the formulation of a hypothesis regarding the general conditions under which a behavior usually occurs and probable consequences that serve to maintain it." Furthermore, hypotheses about behavioral function should be based on "multiple sources of data including, but not limited to, information obtained from direct observation of the student, information from the student, the student's teacher(s) and/or related service provider(s), a review of available data and information from the student's record and other sources including any relevant information provided by the student's parent. The FBA shall not be based solely on the student's history of presenting problem behaviors" (New York State Education Law, §200.1, 200.22, 200.4, and 201.3). Even with these guidelines in place there is little consensus or consistency across schools or districts about the exact method(s) for completing these assessments.

The set of procedures outlined within this chapter are consistent with the guidelines stated within New York State law. Within the proposed model all steps "funnel down" to an experimental demonstration of a functional relation. Some have argued that sufficient information can be gathered through indirect or descriptive assessments alone. Although the results of nonexperimental analysis match those of the experimental analysis in some cases, this is not always true.

What is true is the overwhelming evidence that empirical demonstrations of functional relation are instrumental in developing effective and sustaining behavioral interventions (Iwata et al., 1994c; Kahng et al., 2002). Given the severe risks (often) associated with SIB, clinicians should do whatever possible to diagnose the problem correctly. Clearly, this approach requires more time and effort than other approaches. However, the confidence associated with making the correct determination of behavioral function and identification of the exact features of the reinforcer increases the likelihood of developing an effective and sustaining intervention. The time and costs associated with incorrectly identifying the true behavioral function or implementing an intervention based on incomplete information would likely exceed those associated with conducting a thorough assessment initially.

Our understanding of SIB and the conditions under which it is likely to occur has significantly increased over the last two plus decades. That these behaviors are, in fact, learned and represent a means of communicating desires to access or avoid environmental conditions in the majority of cases suggests that proactively teaching appropriate alternative forms of communication to access these same conditions may decrease the emergence of this dangerous behavior in many individuals. Still, for those individuals who engage in SIB, the need for careful assessment of the variables maintaining this behavior remains. Despite the clear benefits of conducting a thorough functional behavioral assessment of SIB, the process can be lengthy at times and result in a (necessary) delay of treatment. Future research should continue to examine ways to make the process more efficient without sacrificing quality. Researchers should also continue to look for ways to experimentally assess the function of high-severity SIB while preventing the behavior and resulting injury from occurring.

## REFERENCES

Adelinis, J.D., Piazza, C.C., Fisher, W.W., & Hanley, G.P. (1997). The establishing effects of client location on self-injurious behavior. *Research in Developmental Disabilities, 18,* 383–391.

American Psychiatric Association. (2000). *Diagnostic and statistical manual of mental disorders.* (4th ed. rev.) Washington, DC: Author.

Ballinger B.R. (1971). Minor self-injury. *British Journal of Psychiatry, 118,* 535–538.

Berg, W.K., Wacker, D.P., Cigrand, K., Merkle, S., Wade, J., Henry, K., & Wang, Y-C. (2007). Comparing functional analysis and paired-choice assessment results in classroom settings. *Journal of Applied Behavior Analysis, 40,* 545–552.

Bijou, S.W., Peterson, R.F., & Ault, M.H. (1968). A method to integrate descriptive and experimental field studies at the level of data and empirical concepts. *Journal of Applied Behavior Analysis, 1,* 175–191.

Bodfish, J.W., Crawford, T.W., Powell, S.B., Parker, D.E., Golden, R.N., & Lewis, M.H. (1995). Compulsions in adults with mental retardation: Prevalence, phenomenology, and comorbidity with stereotypy and self-injury. *American Journal of Mental Retardation, 100,* 183–192.

Borrero C.S.W., & Borrero, J.C. (2008). Descriptive and experimental analyses of potential precursors to problem behavior. *Journal of Applied Behavior Analysis, 41,* 83–96.

Borrero, J.C., Vollmer, T.R., Wright, C.S., Lerman, D.C., & Kelley, M.E. (2002). Further evaluation of the role of protective equipment in the functional analysis of self-injurious behavior. *Journal of Applied Behavior Analysis, 35,* 69–72.

Borthwick-Duffy, S. (1994). Prevalence of destructive behaviors: A study of aggression, SIB and property destruction. In T. Thompson, & D. B. Gray (Eds.), *Destructive behavior in developmental disabilities: Diagnosis and treatment* (pp. 3–23). London: Sage Publications, Inc.

Carr, E.G., Newsom, C.D., & Binkoff, J.A. (1976). Stimulus control of self-destructive behavior in a psychotic child. *Journal of Abnormal Child Psychology, 4,* 139–153.

Contrucci Kuhn, S.A., & Triggs, M. (2009). Analysis of social variables when an initial functional analysis indicates automatic reinforcement as the maintaining variable for self-injurious behavior. *Journal of Applied Behavior Analysis, 42*, 679–683.

Cooper, J.O., Heron, T.E., & Heward, W.L. (2007). Selecting, defining, and measuring behavior. In J.O. Cooper, T.E. Heron, & W.L. Heward (Eds.). *Applied behavior analysis.* 2nd ed. (pp. 47–71). Upper Saddle River, NJ: Pearson Education, Inc.

Didden, R., Duker, P.C., & Korzilius, H. (1997). Meta-analytic study on treatment effectiveness for problem behaviors with individuals who have mental retardation. *American Journal on Mental Retardation, 101*, 387–399.

Durand, V.M., & Crimmins, D.B. (1988). Identifying the variables maintaining self-injurious behavior. *Journal of Autism and Developmental Disorders, 18*, 99–117.

Finucane, B., Dirrigl, K.H., & Simon, E.W. (2001). Characterization of self-injurious behavior in children and adults with Smith-Magenis syndrome. *American Journal on Mental Retardation, 106*, 52–58.

Fisher, W.W., Kuhn, D.E., & Thompson, R.H. (1998). Establishing discriminative control of responding using functional and alternative reinforcers during functional communication training. *Journal of Applied Behavior Analysis, 31*, 543–560.

Fisher, W.W., Piazza, C.C., Bowman, L.G., Hagopian, L.P., Owens, J.C., Slevin, I. (1992). A comparison of two approaches for identifying reinforcers for persons with severe and profound disabilities. *Journal of Applied Behavior Analysis, 25*, 491–498.

Grace, N.C., Thompson, R., & Fisher, W.W. (1996). The treatment of covert self-injury through contingencies on response products. *Journal of Applied Behavior Analysis, 29*, 239–242.

Hagopian, L.P., Fisher, W.W., Thompson, R.H., Owen-DeSchryver, J., Iwata, B.A., & Wacker, D.P. (1997). Toward the development of structured criteria for interpretation of functional analysis data. *Journal of Applied Behavior Analysis, 30*, 313–326.

Hanley, G.P., Iwata, B.A., & McCord, B.E. (2003). Functional analysis of problem behavior: A review. *Journal of Applied Behavior Analysis, 36*, 147–185.

Individuals with Disabilities Education Improvement Act. (2004). 20 USC 1400. Retrieved from http://idea.ed.gov/

Iwata, B.A., & DeLeon, I.G. (1996). Functional Analysis Screening Tool (FAST). Gainesville, Florida Center on Self-Injury, University of Florida.

Iwata, B.A., Dorsey, M.F., Slifer, K.J., Bauman, K.E., & Richman, G.S. (1994). Toward a functional analysis of self-injury. *Journal of Applied Behavior Analysis, 27*, 197–209. (Reprinted from *Analysis and Intervention in Developmental Disabilities, 2*, 3–20, 1982).

Iwata, B.A., Duncan, B.A., Zarcone, J.R., Lerman, D.C., & Shore, B.A. (1994). A sequential, test-control methodology for conducting functional analyses of self-injurious behavior. *Behavior Modification, 18*, 289–306.

Iwata, B.A., Kahng, S.W., Wallace, M.D., & Lindberg, J.S. (2000). The functional analysis model of behavioral assessment. In J. E. Carr, & J. Austin (Eds.). *Handbook of applied behavior analysis* (pp. 91–112). Reno, NV: Context Press.

Iwata, B.A., Pace, G.M., Dorsey, M.F., Zarcone, J.R., Vollmer, T.R., Smith, R.G., et al. (1994). The functions of self-injurious behavior: An experimental-epidemiological analysis. *Journal of Applied Behavior Analysis, 27*, 215–240.

Kahng, S., Abt, K.A., & Schonbachler, H.E. (2001). Assessment and treatment of low-rate high-intensity problem behavior. *Journal of Applied Behavior Analysis, 34*, 225–228.

Kahng, S., Iwata, B.A., & Lewin, A.B. (2002). The impact of functional assessment on the treatment of self-injurious behavior. In S.R. Schroeder, M.L. Oster-Granite, & T. Thompson (Eds.), *Self-injurious behavior: Gene-brain-behavior relations* (pp. 119–132). Washington, DC: American Psychological Association.

Le, D.D., & Smith, R.G. (2002). Functional analysis of self-injury with and without protective equipment. *Journal of Developmental and Physical Disabilities, 14*, 277–290.

Lerman, D.C., & Iwata, B.A. (1993). Descriptive and experimental analysis of variables maintaining self-injurious behavior. *Journal of Applied Behavior Analysis, 26*, 293–319.

Lovaas, O.I., Freitag, G., Gold, V.J., & Kassorla, I.C. (1965). Experimental studies in childhood schizophrenia: Analysis of self-destructive behavior. *Journal of Experimental Child Psychology, 2*, 67–84.

Lowe, K., Allen, D., Jones, E., Brophy, S., Moore, K., & James, W. (2007). Challenging behaviors: Prevalence and topographies. *Journal of Intellectual Disability Research, 51*, 625–636.

MacLean, W.E., & Symons, F. (2002). Self-injurious behavior in infancy and young childhood. *Infants and Young Children, 14*, 31–41.

Matson, J.L., & Vollmer, T.R. (1995). *User's guide: Questions about behavioral function (QABF).* Baton Rouge, LA: Scientific Publishers.

McCord, B.E., Thomson, R.J.,& Iwata, B.A. (2001). Functional analysis and treatment of self-injury associated with transitions. *Journal of Applied Behavior Analysis*, *34*, 195–210.

Moore, J.W., Fisher, W.W., & Pennington A. (2004). Systematic application and removal of protective equipment in the assessment of multiple topographies of self-injury. *Journal of Applied Behavior Analysis*, *37*, 73–77.

Najdowski, A.C., Wallace, M.D., Ellsworth, C.L., MacAleese, A.N., & Cleveland. J.M. (2008). Functional analyses and treatment of precursor behavior. *Journal of Applied Behavior Analysis*, *41*, 97–105.

Neef, N.A., & Peterson, S.M. (2007). Functional behavior assessment. In J.O. Cooper, T.E. Heron, & W.L. Heward (Eds.). *Applied behavior analysis*. 2nd ed. (pp. 500–524). Upper Saddle River, NJ: Pearson Education, Inc.

New York State Education Law. (2011). Students with Disabilities, §200.1, 200.22, 200.4, and 201.3 Retrieved from http://www.p12.nysed.gov/specialed/lawsregs/

Northup, J., Broussard, C., Jones, K., George, T., Vollmer, T.R., & Herring, M. (1995). The differential effects of teacher and peer attention on the disruptive classroom behavior of three children with a diagnosis of attention deficit hyperactivity disorder. *Journal of Applied Behavior Analysis*, *28*, 227–228.

Nyhan, W.I. (2002). Lessons from Lesch-Nyhan syndrome. In S.R. Schroeder, M.L. Oster-Granite, & T. Thompson (Eds.), *Self-injurious behavior: Gene-brain-behavior relations* (pp. 251–267). Washington, DC: American Psychological Association

O'Neill, R.E., Horner, R.H., Albin, R.W., Sprague, J.R., Storey, K., & Newton (1997). *Functional assessment and program development for problem behavior: A practical handbook*. Pacific Grove, CA: Brooks/Cole.

Shogren, K.A., & Rojahn, J. (2003). Convergent reliability and validity of the Questions About Behavioral Function and the Motivation Assessment Scale: A replication study. *Journal of Developmental and Physical Disabilities*, *15*, 367–375.

Smith, R.G., & Churchill, R.M. (2002). Identification of environmental determinants of behavior disorders through functional analysis of precursor behaviors. *Journal of Applied Behavior Analysis*, *35*, 125–136.

Sturmey, P. (1994). Assessing functions of aberrant behaviors: A review of psychometric instruments. *Journal of Autism and Developmental Disorders*, *24*, 293–304.

Tate, B.G., & Baroff, A.S. (1966) Aversive control of self-injurious behavior in a psychotic boy. *Behaviour Research and Therapy*, *4*, 281–287.

Thompson, R.H., Fisher, W.W., Piazza, C.C., & Kuhn, D.E. (1998). The evaluation and treatment of aggression maintained by attention and automatic reinforcement. *Journal of Applied Behavior Analysis*, *31*, 103–116.

Vollmer, T.R. (1994). The concept of automatic reinforcement: Implications for behavioral research in developmental disabilities, *Research in Developmental Disabilities*, *15*, 187–207.

Zarcone, J.R., Rodgers, T.A., Iwata, B.A., Rourke, D.A., & Dorsey, M.F. (1991). Reliability analysis of the Motivation Assessment Scale: A failure to replicate. *Research in Developmental Disabilities*, *12*, 349–362.

# Function-Based Behavioral Intervention for Self-Injury

*Johannes Rojahn, Iser G. DeLeon,*
*Griffin W. Rooker, Michelle A. Frank-Crawford,*
*Abbey B. Carreau-Webster, and Yanerys Leon-Enriquez*

Prevalence studies estimate that 10%–40% of individuals with intellectual and developmental disabilities (IDD) exhibit significant degrees of destructive behavior (Borthwick-Duffy, 1994; Meador & Osborn, 1992; Rojahn, Schroeder, & Hoch, 2008). The most extreme cases involve people with serious self-injury (Luiselli, 2009). The prevalence of self-injurious behavior (SIB) in individuals diagnosed with IDD has been estimated to be around 15% (Kahng, Iwata, & Lewin, 2002), but estimates have varied widely as a function of several variables including level of cognitive functioning and specific comorbid disorders (Rojahn & Esbensen, 2002).

Although less prevalent than other severe behavior problems displayed by individuals with IDD, SIB has perhaps received a disproportionate attention in the treatment literature. SIB, defined by its potential to cause harm to the individual (Tate & Baroff, 1966), is more likely to put the individual at risk and lead to serious subsequent impairments in the person's overall health (e.g., blinding through a detached retina). In addition, SIB can lead to diminished psychological and social development, social isolation, and other clear detriments to quality of life (Rojahn & Esbensen, 2002).

Applied behavior analysis has emerged as the dominant psychological paradigm for assessing and treating the destructive behavior of individuals with IDD. Within a behavior analytic framework, problem behaviors are viewed as learned responses that occur because they have historically resulted in the delivery or production of valuable consequences, or reinforcers. SIB has been repeatedly demonstrated to be a learned function of these behavior-environment relations (see Chapter 2, this volume; Hanley, Iwata, & McCord, 2003, for reviews). The first crucial step in function-based intervention for SIB is, therefore, conducting a functional behavioral assessment to suggest hypotheses regarding the nature of specific environment-behavior relations that give rise to and maintain SIB. Common maintaining reinforcers include access to positive reinforcement (in the form of attention or material items), negative reinforcement (in the form of escape from aversive contexts), and automatic reinforcement (often cast as a form of self-stimulation or termination of stimulation). Large-scale analyses suggest that these variables accounted for the maintenance SIB in the majority of individuals exposed to functional assessments (Iwata et al., 1994). The reader is referred to Chapter 2 of this book for more detailed consideration of functional assessment methods and the impact of this process on the ability to treat SIB effectively.

Functional assessment is, in essence, a method of reinforcement identification. Armed with knowledge about the relevant reinforcer(s) for SIB, the clinician is then better prepared to execute operations to reduce the target behavior (e.g., extinction—withholding the putative reinforcer following instances of SIB, differential reinforcement—using the reinforcer to establish/strengthen alternative responses). In the following, we briefly describe these operations as executed for each of the common behavioral functions of SIB: positive reinforcement, negative reinforcement, and automatic reinforcement. Thereafter, we consider a variety of factors that clinicians need to take into account when selecting among these alternatives.

## TREATMENT OF SELF-INJURIOUS BEHAVIOR MAINTAINED BY POSITIVE REINFORCEMENT

### Extinction

Extinction involves terminating the reinforcement contingency that maintains a behavior. Advances in functional analysis methodology have facilitated the use of extinction in clinical settings in that sources of reinforcement can be clearly and efficiently identified (Lerman & Iwata, 1996). Procedurally, extinction of SIB maintained by positive reinforcement (i.e., caregiver attention, material reinforcers) involves withholding the reinforcer following the occurrence of SIB. For example, if SIB is maintained by adult attention, extinction would require that the caregiver withhold attention following all occurrences of SIB (Iwata, Pace, Cowdery, & Miltenberger, 1994). High-integrity implementation of extinction is a crucial component in many interventions for SIB (e.g., Fisher et al., 1993; Mazaleski, Iwata, Vollmer, Zarcone, & Smith, 1993; Shirley, Iwata, Kahng, Mazaleski, & Lerman, 1997).

### Differential Reinforcement Procedures

Generally, differential reinforcement involves withholding reinforcers for one response class while reinforcing behavior in another response class (Cooper, Heron, & Heward, 2007), but it comes in varying forms. Differential reinforcement of other behavior (DRO) involves delivering reinforcers contingent on the *nonoccurrence* of a target response following a predetermined time interval (a reinforcement component) while eliminating the contingency between SIB and its maintaining consequence (an extinction component). That is, a specified time interval is set (e.g.,

30 seconds) and reinforcers are delivered following intervals in which the target response does not occur. In DRO contingencies, intervals can be either fixed, in which interval duration is held constant, or variable, in which interval duration varies around a mean value (Vollmer & Iwata, 1992).

DRO contingencies often involve a resetting feature (Mazaleski et al., 1993). In a resetting DRO, occurrences of the target behavior restart the DRO interval. For example, if a DRO interval is set for 30 seconds and an individual emits the target response 15 seconds into the interval, the interval is reset to 0 seconds and the individual must not emit the target response for 30 consecutive seconds to earn the reinforcer. DRO intervals can also be nonresetting. In this case, a target behavior that occurs within an interval cancels reinforcement for that interval. Reinforcers cannot be earned until that interval as well as the next interval time out (Catania, 1998). Nonresetting DRO schedules are perhaps easier to arrange, as they do not require constant resetting of timing instruments, but they may also arrange periods in which there is no consequence of further instances of the problem behavior. Once the reinforcer has been forfeited for a given interval, there is no further contingency in operation to impact SIB until the next scheduled interval has begun.

Further variations of the DRO contingency involve manipulations of the omission contingency. The most common variation is whole-interval DRO in which reinforcers are only delivered if the target behavior did not occur at any time during the interval. An alternative is a momentary DRO in which reinforcers are delivered if the target response does not occur at the *end* of a prespecified interval, regardless of whether or not it occurred *during* the interval (Repp, Barton, & Brulle, 1983). Whole-interval DRO has been proven to be a more effective treatment for reducing SIB than momentary DRO; however, momentary DRO is an effective treatment when implemented following whole-interval DRO as a maintenance procedure (Barton, Brulle, & Repp, 1986). In addition, Lindberg, Iwata, Kahng, and DeLeon (1999) found that both variable-interval and variable-momentary DRO were effective procedures for reducing the SIB of three individuals. Momentary DRO may be preferred in some cases because the therapist does not have to constantly monitor problem behavior.

Although DRO contingencies often incorporate the consequence that maintains problem behavior as the reinforcer for response omission, this need not be the case for an effective DRO intervention. The reinforcer delivered at the end of the DRO interval can be the functional reinforcer or an "arbitrary" reinforcer (i.e., not responsible for behavioral maintenance). Mazaleski et al. (1993) treated three participants whose SIB was maintained by adult attention by arranging DRO schedules in which an arbitrary reinforcer (music) was delivered following intervals in which problem behavior did not occur. Clinically significant reductions in SIB were achieved for all participants. However, Mazaleski et al. also examined a condition in which the reinforcement component of the DRO contingency was in place while SIB continued to produce the functional reinforcer. This condition did not result in decreases in SIB relative to baseline. Results of Mazaleski et al. suggest that decreases in problem behavior that result from exposure to DRO contingencies are largely attributed to the extinction component.

A differential reinforcement of alternative behavior (DRA) contingency involves systematically reinforcing a specific alternative response to displace SIB. Unlike DRO, DRA contingencies establish or promote a specific functional response. A common variation of DRA has been termed functional communication training (FCT; Carr & Durand, 1985). Generally, FCT consists of delivering the functional reinforcer contingent on an appropriate, socially acceptable communicative response while withholding the reinforcer following problem behavior. An individual whose SIB is maintained by access to tangible items might be taught to emit the phrase "toys please," generally in combination with extinction. Fisher, Kuhn, and Thompson (1998) treated the SIB of one participant whose SIB was sensitive to positive reinforcement in the form of attention and tangible items. The participant was taught to emit the phrases "Excuse me please" and "I want my toys please" to access 30 seconds of attention or tangibles, respectively. The intervention resulted in near elimination of the participant's SIB as well as increases in appropriate rates of the alternative response. Treatment effects following the implementation of FCT for positively reinforced SIB have been robust and are abundantly described in the literature (e.g., Fisher et al., 1993; Hanley, Iwata, Thompson, 2001; Worsdell, Iwata, Hanley, Thompson, & Kahng, 2000).

## Noncontingent Reinforcement

Although differential reinforcement procedures have been widely used to treat SIB, they can be unwieldy to implement in that they often involve continuous monitoring of the individual. In addition, differential reinforcement procedures can potentially result in relatively low rates of reinforcement if the individual continues to engage in problem behavior or rarely meets the omission requirements of a DRO. Alternatively, noncontingent reinforcement (NCR) is response-independent or time-based delivery of the reinforcer (i.e., according to a predetermined schedule *independent* of the individual's behavior; Vollmer, Iwata, Zarcone, Smith, & Mazaleski, 1993). NCR has been demonstrated to be an effective treatment for reducing SIB maintained by attention (e.g., Derby, Fisher, & Piazza, 1996; Hagopian, Crockett, van Stone, DeLeon, & Bowman, 2000; Hagopian, Fisher, & Legacy, 1994; Kahng, Iwata, DeLeon, & Worsdell, 1997) and tangible items (e.g., Lalli, Casey, & Kates, 1997; Marcus & Vollmer, 1996).

NCR for positively reinforced SIB typically involves three components: reinforcer delivery (i.e., attention, tangibles) on a continuous or relatively dense, fixed-time schedule, extinction for problem behavior, and schedule thinning. For example, Vollmer et al. (1993) treated the positively reinforced SIB of three adult females by implementing a NCR procedure. Interactions between the therapist and participants lasted 10 seconds and attention deliveries were initially scheduled 6 times per minute (i.e., attention was continuous). Attention delivery was then systematically thinned to a rate of 0.2 per minute (i.e., one every 5 minutes). Hagopian et al. (1994) compared the effects of initial dense and lean schedules of NCR on the positively-reinforced problem behavior (including SIB) of four identical quadruplets. The dense schedule was identical to the initial schedule described by Vollmer et al. (i.e., continuous) while the lean schedule was identical to the terminal schedule described by Vollmer et al. (i.e., one every 5 minutes). Results of Hagopian et al. demonstrated that the dense schedule reduced SIB to a greater extent than the lean schedule when both were implemented as the initial schedule. However, results corroborated those of Vollmer et al. in that SIB remained low at increasingly leaner schedule values when the initial value was dense and the schedule of reinforcement was systematically thinned. Several methods have been suggested for determining an appropriate initial schedule in the use of NCR. Lalli et al. (1997) suggested using the latency to the first occurrence of problem behavior as the initial interval, while Kahng, Iwata, DeLeon and Wallace (2000) suggested using the mean inter-response time (IRT) from baseline as the initial interval. Additionally, stimuli signaling the NCR schedule may enhance the suppressive effects of NCR (Ringdahl, Call, Christensen, & Boelter, 2010).

The previously described NCR studies all involved delivery of the functional reinforcer according to a time-base schedule to reduce the occurrence of SIB. In addition, the aforementioned studies also implemented extinction for SIB in addition to NCR. However, high-integrity implementation of extinction may be difficult to achieve outside of controlled clinical settings. Time-based delivery of arbitrary stimuli may have therapeutic effects on SIB even when problem behavior continues to be reinforced. For example, Fischer, Iwata, and Mazaleski (1997) treated the positively-reinforced SIB of two individuals by delivering arbitrary reinforcers (i.e., reinforcers not indicated in behavioral maintenance). Clinically significant results were achieved for both participants as a result of implementation of the arbitrary NCR procedure even though the problem behavior continued to produce reinforcement. Fisher, O'Connor, Kurtz, DeLeon, and Gotjen (2000) described a procedure to evaluate the effects of noncontingent availability of arbitrary stimuli on the SIB of an individual with developmental disabilities. Each stimulus was presented 5 times during 30-second trials and problem behavior continued to result in attention. Item engagement and problem behavior were measured within each 30-second trial. Stimuli that resulted in high levels of item engagement and low rates of problem behavior were identified as competing stimuli. The items that were identified to compete and not compete with SIB, respectively, were then compared in a treatment evaluation. Results indicated that only the arbitrary stimuli that were identified as competing stimuli (i.e., those stimuli that resulted in high levels of engagement and low rates of SIB) resulted in clinically significant decreases in SIB when problem behavior continued to be reinforced.

## TREATMENT OF SELF-INJURIOUS BEHAVIOR MAINTAINED BY NEGATIVE REINFORCEMENT

Several function-based treatment approaches have been used to decrease SIB that is sensitive to negative reinforcement. These interventions generally attempt to decrease SIB by altering the consequences associated with problem behavior (i.e., extinguishing the response-reinforcer contingency between SIB and access to escape or avoidance of the aversive stimulus) and/or weakening the establishing operation associated with negatively reinforced SIB (e.g., teaching alternative ways to access escape, providing noncontingent access to escape, or altering specific aspects of the demand context).

## Extinction

Like positively reinforced SIB, many of the interventions targeting SIB sensitive to negative reinforcement typically employ extinction as a treatment component. There are several procedural variations of extinction for negatively reinforced SIB. If problem behavior is sensitive to escape from demands (e.g., academic demands, daily living demands, or demands to comply with medical procedures), extinction would involve the continued presentation of the demands and may also include physically guiding the individual to complete the task (Iwata et al., 1994; Iwata, Pace, Kalsher, Cowdery, & Cataldo, 1990; Mace, Lalli, & Lalli, 1991). If SIB functions to escape or avoid social interactions, extinction would consist of continued engagement with the individual in the presence of SIB (Hagopian, Wilson, & Wilder, 2001). Regardless of the exact form it takes, it is important to note that functionally, extinction of negatively reinforced SIB involves disruption of the escape or avoidance contingency associated with SIB (i.e., no longer allowing escape or avoidance of the aversive stimulus contingent on the occurrence of SIB).

## Differential Reinforcement Procedures

Differential negative reinforcement of alternative behavior (DNRA) procedures typically consist of the provision of escape from, or avoidance of, the aversive stimulus contingent on an appropriate alternative response often while simultaneously withholding escape or avoidance following the occurrence of problem behavior. Under these conditions, responding should be allocated toward the alternative response rather than problem behavior as the schedule of reinforcement favors appropriate responding. DNRA can take several forms. For example, a break from demand situations may be provided following an appropriate communicative response to terminate the aversive stimulus (FCT; Lalli, Casey, & Kates, 1995; Steege et al., 1990) or contingent on compliance with demands (e.g., Piazza, Moes, & Fisher, 1996; Roberts, Mace, & Daggett, 1995).

   FCT for negatively reinforced SIB is similar to that of FCT for SIB sensitive to positive reinforcement in that an appropriate communicative response is selected and taught to the individual and the functional reinforcer is only provided contingent on the alternative response. However, in cases in which SIB is maintained by negative reinforcement, the communicative response usually takes the form of a request for a break or termination of the aversive stimulus (e.g., "Break please"). Alternatively, other communicative responses may be taught that function to weaken the establishing operation by requesting assistance with the demand thereby minimizing the aversiveness of the noxious stimulus (e.g., "I don't understand"; Carr & Durand, 1985; Durand & Carr, 1991). Communication training for negatively reinforced SIB can be conducted using a discrete trial training format. This procedure requires the initial presentation of the aversive stimulus (e.g., an academic demand), followed by prompts for the individual to engage in the target mand (e.g., touch the break card or vocally request a break), and then terminating the aversive stimulus contingent on the appropriate communicative response (Cipani & Spooner, 1997). Both least-to-most (e.g., Shirley et al., 1997) and most-to-least (e.g., Fisher et al., 1993) prompting techniques have been used to teach alternative responses. Shirley et al. used least-to-most prompting by waiting 5 seconds following the delivery of a demand to provide an opportunity for the alternative response to occur independently. If the participant did not communicate independently, the therapist prompted the correct response. Most-to-least prompting was used in a study conducted by Fisher et al. and involved the presentation of the aversive stimulus followed by immediate physical guidance to emit the targeted communicative response. Physical guidance was then faded until the participant communicated independently. Another method for teaching the communicative response includes imbedding training trials during naturally occurring aversive situations (e.g., during morning routines or academics). See Tiger, Hanley, and Bruzek (2008) for a review of other considerations for conducting functional communication training (e.g., selection of response topography, who should implement FCT, strategies for promoting generalization of the alternative response).

Several other studies have examined the effects of reinforcing compliance with a break from demand situations. Contingent on compliance with a predetermined number of demands or within a specified amount of time from the presentation of the demand, the individual may receive a brief break from instruction (e.g., Butler & Luiselli, 2007; Roberts et al., 1995; Vollmer, Roane, Ringdahl, & Marcus, 1999). Vollmer et al. assessed the effectiveness of full and partial implementation of a DNRA procedure on the negatively reinforced SIB of two individuals with ID. During the full implementation of the DNRA procedure, compliance always resulted in a 30-seconds break from instructions and problem behavior was placed on extinction. During partial implementation of DNRA, various combinations of treatment integrity failures were examined (e.g., the partial and/or full implementation of reinforcement of compliance and/or extinction). Results indicated that SIB remained low under conditions in which the schedule of reinforcement favored compliance. An alternative strategy is to terminate the entire session once the response requirement has been met. The number of demands the individual must comply with before the session is terminated is then gradually increased across sessions (e.g., Piazza et al., 1996).

Positive reinforcement has also been demonstrated to effectively reduce negatively reinforced SIB (DeLeon, Neidert, Anders, & Rodriguez-Catter, 2001; Fisher et al., 2005; Lalli et al., 1999; Piazza et al., 1997). Results of several studies have further suggested that positive reinforcement may result in lower levels of SIB relative to the use of negative reinforcement (DeLeon et al.; Lalli et al.) and that when given a choice of positive or negative reinforcement, some individuals show preference for positive reinforcement, at least under low schedule requirements (DeLeon et al., 2001; Fisher et al., 2005). Two possible explanations have been given as to why the use of positive reinforcement is effective in reducing problem behavior. First, the value of the negative reinforcer can be momentarily overridden by the value of the positive reinforcer. An alternative is that the presentation of the positive reinforcer momentarily alters the value of escape as a reinforcer, thus decreasing the likelihood of problem behavior (Lalli et al., 1999; Fisher et al., 2005).

Another differential reinforcement variation is providing the functional reinforcer contingent on the absence of SIB for a specified amount of time (differential negative reinforcement of other behavior, or DNRO). Fewer studies have evaluated the effectiveness of DNRO for SIB sensitive to negative reinforcement. One compared the effectiveness of DNRA and DNRO in the treatment of SIB maintained by escape from tooth brushing and bathing tasks (Roberts et al., 1995). During the DNRA procedure, a 15-second break was provided following compliance within 3 seconds of the presentation of a demand. This was compared to a DNRO procedure in which a break was given contingent on the absence of SIB for 20 consecutive seconds. Although both treatments decreased SIB relative to baseline levels, the DNRA procedure resulted in the largest decreases in problem behavior.

## Antecedent-Based Interventions

Several antecedent interventions have also been evaluated for negatively reinforced SIB, including noncontingent escape (NCE) from demands, demand or instructional fading, and curricular and instructional revision (Luiselli, 2008). During NCE, escape or a break from the aversive stimulus is provided on a time-based schedule independent of responding. Initially, escape is provided according to a relatively dense schedule of reinforcement. As problem behavior remains low, the time between noncontingent reinforcer deliveries is increased until some target reinforcement schedule is reached. There are several ways one can determine the changing schedule of reinforcement. For example, Vollmer, Marcus, and Ringdahl (1995) evaluated the use of NCE to reduce SIB for two individuals with ID. A different method was used for each participant to determine the schedules of reinforcement. Initially, a continuous break from the aversive stimulus was provided for both participants. Then, for one participant, the fixed-time (FT) interval for a 30-second break from walking was increased across sessions by adding 10 seconds to the interval (or adding 1 minute to the interval once the FT schedule reached 1 minutes) until 10 minutes elapsed between reinforcer deliveries. For the second participant, the FT interval for a 20-second break from instructional tasks was determined by calculating the mean interresponse time (IRT) from the preceding five sessions. This continued until a FT 2.5-minute schedule of reinforcement was reached. For the second participant only, the effectiveness of the NCE procedure was compared to a resetting DNRO procedure in which a 20-second break was provided contingent on the absence of SIB for a prespecified amount of time. Like the NCE interval, the DNRO interval was calculated by determining the mean IRT from the preceding 5 sessions. Although both the NCE and DNRO procedures successfully decreased SIB, the terminal goal of a FT 2.5-minute interval was reached in fewer sessions using the NCE procedure.

Demand fading (also known as instructional or stimulus fading) has also been used to decrease SIB maintained by negative reinforcement. During demand fading, the aversive stimulus is completely removed and then gradually reintroduced contingent on low levels of problem behavior (Geiger, Carr, & LeBlanc, 2010). Several studies have evaluated the effectiveness of extinction, both with and without the use of demand fading (Pace, Iwata, Cowdery, Andree, & McIntyre, 1993; Zarcone et al., 1993). Pace et al. evaluated whether the inclusion of a demand fading procedure in conjunction with extinction would decrease the likelihood of the occurrence of extinction bursts. Initially, no instructional demands were presented. This was followed by the gradual reintroduction of instructional tasks. Extinction with demand fading produced immediate and sustained decreases in SIB. Alternatively, high and variable rates of problem behavior were observed when extinction alone was evaluated for one participant. Zarcone et al. extended this line of research by comparing extinction alone and extinction combined with demand fading in a multielement format for three individuals whose SIB was maintained by escape from demands. Results indicated that although extinction alone effectively reduced SIB to criterion levels more rapidly than did extinction with demand fading, extinction alone was associated with extinction bursts for two of the three participants.

During curricular (or instructional) revision, one initially attempts to identify the specific aspects of the aversive stimulus that occasion problem behavior and then makes alterations in an attempt to minimize or eliminate these aversive properties (Geiger et al., 2010; Reed, Luiselli, Morizio, & Child, 2010). The goal is to reduce motivation to engage in SIB by decreasing the aversiveness of the demand context. By modifying certain aspects of the demand condition of the functional analysis, Smith, Iwata, Goh, and Shore (1995) identified three potential motivating variables for SIB maintained by escape, including task novelty, duration of session, and rate of task presentation. Others have suggested that the presentation of difficult (Ebanks & Fisher, 2003; Geiger et al; Reed et al., 2010) or nonpreferred demands (Clarke et al., 1995) may differentially occasion problem behavior.

Several modifications can be made to the instructional sequence to weaken the motivation to escape the demand context. For example, if duration of task presentation is problematic, interventions could include several brief tasks rather than one or more longer tasks (Kern, Childs, Dunlap, Clarke, & Falk, 1994). Activity choice and task interspersal have also been used to address SIB occasioned by the presentation of difficult, novel, or non-preferred demands. Dyer, Dunlap, and Winterling (1990) evaluated the effects of task choice and reinforcement for compliance on the escape-maintained SIB of three individuals with IDD. Percent of intervals with problem behavior was lower when the children were allowed to select the order in which the tasks were presented relative to when no choice was presented. Ebanks and Fisher (2003) demonstrated that the interspersal of easy and difficult tasks combined with the presentation of corrective prompting the next time a previously failed item was presented effectively reduced escape-maintained SIB for one individual with IDD. Tasks interspersed with play time have also been demonstrated to effectively reduce SIB that is sensitive to negative reinforcement (Asmus et al., 1999).

## TREATMENT OF AUTOMATICALLY
## REINFORCED SELF-INJURIOUS BEHAVIOR

The automatic reinforcement of SIB might be best considered a default function. It implies that some product of the response itself, independent of social consequences, reinforces the response. The nature of that product is subject to debate, but many have suggested some form of sensory stimulation is the controlling influence, thus evoking terms such as sensory reinforcement or self-stimulatory behavior. As a result, treatments developed over the years have attempted to directly target the presumed form of stimulation (Favell, McGimsey, & Schell, 1982; Goh et al., 1995; Kennedy & Souza, 1995; MacDonald, Wilder, & Dempsey, 2002). Approaches to identifying the specific form of sensory consequences have often involved the continuous and noncontingent access to items thought to mimic the putative sensory consequences derived from the self-injurious response (Ladd, Luiselli, & Baker, 2009; O'Reilly, Murray, Lancioni, Sigafoos, & Lacey, 2003). For example, Goh et al. (1995) posited that self-injurious hand mouthing could be maintained by stimulation to the hand or stimulation to the mouth. They arranged conditions in which mouth stimulation or hand stimulation was provided in a noncontingent fashion and found that hand stimulation was the critical form for each of five participants. Armed with information from this sort of analysis, clinicians are then in a better position to develop interventions that specifically target the presumed critical form of stimulation.

### Sensory Extinction

The rationale behind sensory extinction is that the sensory products of the self-injurious response could be removed or attenuated even when the behavior occurs, thus disrupting the response–reinforcer contingency. Sensory extinction is sometimes executed through the use of protective equipment (Luiselli, 1988; 1991; 1992; Moore, Fisher, & Pennington, 2004). For example, padding parts of the body to which SIB is directed has the putative effects of 1) permitting the response to occur but 2) preventing the response from producing the presumed form of stimulation. Note, however, that the mechanism underlying the effects of protective equipment may sometimes be related to, or additionally supplemented by, a punitive process (Mazaleski, Iwata, Rodgers, Vollmer, & Zarcone, 1994). For example, placing a hard-shell helmet on the patient's head may prevent the sort of direct hand-to-head contact that produces to presumed critical form of stimulation, but striking a hard shell helmet with one's hands may also be more painful than striking one's head with one's hand (Kuhn, DeLeon, Fisher, & Wilke, 1999).

Other instances of sensory extinction for SIB have involved response blocking. Generally, this requires the therapist to manually prevent the self-injurious response from producing the putative outcome. Reid, Parsons, Phillips, and Green (1993) decreased self-injurious hand mouthing by permitting the two individuals in the study to bring their hand up to their mouth, but manually preventing the hand from entering the mouth through placement of the therapist's palm in front of the mouth. In this sense, attempts at hand mouthing could still occur, but if actual contact with the mouth is the putative reinforcer, the response-reinforcer contingency was disrupted. Luiselli (1998) also found a similar intervention to be effective with a child who had multiple disabilities and self-injurious hand mouthing.

Response blocking as a form of extinction is difficult to implement with great fidelity (Tarbox, Wallace, & Tarbox, 2002) and, unfortunately, in some cases substantive decreases in SIB (or attempts at SIB) are not produced unless the response is blocked continuously (e.g. each time it is emitted). Smith, Russo, and Le (1999) observed that although continuous response blocking resulted in clear decreases in the eye poking of the participant in their study, intermittent blocking during which only half or two-thirds of the responses were blocked resulted in levels of eye poking that were indistinguishable from baseline levels. When intermittent response blocking is effective, the likely operative mechanism is punishment rather than extinction (Lerman & Iwata, 1996).

When the form of SIB seems specific to stimulation of circumscribed body parts, sensory extinction has also been executed through the use of agents that desensitize the specific area. For example, Kern, Bailin, and Mauk (2003) applied topical anesthetic to exposed skin to decrease the self-slapping of a 12-year-old boy, resulting in moderate decreases in SIB relative to periods in which the anesthetic was not applied. These investigators suggested that the anesthetic served to remove the maintaining stimulation.

## Competing Stimuli

Often, SIB can be decreased by providing continuous access to items and activities that are said to "compete" with the products of the response (Humenik, Curren, Luiselli, & Child, 2008). This is typically carried out as a two-part procedure. The first is what has often been termed a competing stimulus assessment (DeLeon, Toole, Gutshall, & Bowman, 2005; Piazza, Fisher, Hanley, Hilker, & Derby, 1996). This is a variant of preference assessment in which the patient is given continuous free access to a variety of stimuli, usually one at a time for a specified period of time, while the therapists measures 1) the patient's engagement (i.e., contact) with the item and 2) levels of SIB in the presence of each item (Humenik et al.). Those items associated with the highest levels of engagement and the lowest levels of SIB are said to best compete with the response product(s) of SIB. The items that best compete are then provided continuously for longer periods of time to reduce SIB.

The reductive effects of stimuli identified in such an assessment may not persist over extended periods of time. In such cases, it has been useful to provide simultaneous access to multiple competing stimuli and/or to systematically rotate access (i.e., the first stimulus is provided for 10 minutes, then replaced by another effective stimulus for 10 minutes, and so forth). Such procedures have sometime been found to extend the effects of treatment across time (DeLeon, Anders, Rodriguez-Catter, & Neidert, 2000; Rosales, Worsdell, & Trahan, 2010). Still, these studies have generally examined effects over fairly brief periods of time (e.g., 30 minutes to 2 hours). Further research is needed to determine how best to arrange such interventions across even greater times spans.

## Differential Reinforcement Procedures

Differential reinforcement works a bit differently with automatically reinforced SIB, relative to other functions, because the exact form of the maintaining outcome is unknown. One cannot, with certainty, arrange to deliver the maintaining reinforcer contingent upon an appropriate response. As such, differential reinforcement has largely taken the form of delivering a known reinforcer that is sufficiently potent to overcome the putative reinforcer for problem behavior in an arrangement in which the two kinds of reinforcement are currently available (i.e., no extinction component; Shore, Iwata, DeLeon, Kahng, & Smith, 1997). Most typically, this has meant delivery of the reinforcer in a DRO arrangement, a procedure that has been shown effective in a handful of studies on SIB (Cowdery, Iwata, & Pace, 1990; Repp, Deitz, & Deitz, 1976; Tiger, Fisher, & Bouxsein, 2009). Generally, this has involved 1) identifying a preferred stimulus through something akin to a stimulus preference assessment, 2) delivering that stimulus contingent upon an initially brief period of omission of the automatically reinforced responses, and 3) gradually extending the temporal parameters of the DRO schedule. Cowdery et al., for example, were able to thin out successful DRO treatment effects for up to 30 minutes.

Note, however, that the treatment literature also contains several instances of unsuccessful use of DRO schedules for the treatment of automatically reinforced SIB and other "stereotypic" responses (Harris & Wolchik, 1979; Piazza et al., 1996; Shore et al., 1997). Several possible reasons have been offered for such failures. One is related to the relativity of reinforcers. In essence, this suggests that reinforcers that support one response or level of response effort may not necessarily support other classes of behavior or responses of greater effort. In both the Piazza et al. and Shore et al. studies, the reinforcers used during the DRO schedules had previously been found to displace the SIB in question during the sort of competing stimulus evaluations describe above. Thus, those reinforcers seemed preferred over the response products of SIB when the reinforcers were continuously available and their procurement required no effort. However, DRO schedules may be viewed as a sort of "cost," in terms of delay to reinforcement. That is, in cases where the critical form of reinforcement is unknown and uncontrolled, as is often the case with automatically reinforced SIB, preferred stimuli may compete well with those response products when both are equally available with little effort, but less so if one has to wait for the alternative reinforcer on the DRO schedule. From the patient's perspective, they can engage in SIB and produce those response products immediately or wait and receive the alternative reinforcer after a delay. Thus, the additional cost of waiting may be sufficient to offset the preference for the alternative reinforcer.

In this light, DRO might be best combined with other procedures (sensory extinction, response blocking) that devalue the response products, thus permitting the stimulus delivered on the DRO schedule to compete with a reinforcer that is not quite as strong or consistent. Although not arranged in a DRO contingency, such an effect was demonstrated by Zhou, Goff, and Iwata (2000) who observed that preferred items did not compete well with self-injurious hand mouthing until the response products of hand mouthing were made more effortful to procure by making elbow flexion more difficult through the use of flexible arm sleeves.

Alternatively, DRO contingencies may be considered less discriminable than other forms of differential reinforcement insofar as there is no specific response requirement. It may be difficult for individuals with limited cognitive abilities to accurately discern the parameters of the contingency (loosely, what it is they "cannot do" as opposed to what they have to do to produce reinforcement). Piazza et al. (1996) therefore suggested that DRO schedules may be contraindicated for individuals with low intellectual abilities that are unable to discriminate the DRO schedule contingencies. Future investigations may be needed to determine whether the addition of signaling stimuli, used to clearly indicate the mechanics of the DRO schedule to the patient, could enhance the efficacy of DRO arrangement for individuals with low intellectual abilities.

## TREATMENT OF MULTIPLY CONTROLLED SELF-INJURIOUS BEHAVIOR

Few examples of SIB maintained by multiple sources of reinforcement have been demonstrated in the literature. Hanley, Iwata, and McCord (2003) found that in 14.6% of published FAs, multiple maintaining contingencies were maintaining problem behavior. Treatment of multiply controlled SIB may be particularly difficult when it requires competing contingencies. For example, if SIB is maintained by both escape from demands and access to attention, treatments based on extinction are at cross purposes. The extinction of escape maintained responding requires the continued presentation of attention (a reinforcing variables for SIB) and the extinction of attention-maintained responding requires ignoring the individual (a reinforcing variable for SIB). Because of the complexity of treating multiply controlled SIB, several unique forms of treatment have been developed.

One strategy is to treat the behavior in one context, while minimizing the motivation to engage in the behavior for the other reinforcer. Smith, Iwata, Vollmer, and Zarcone (1993), assessed and treated the SIB of three individuals with developmental disabilities who engaged in multiply controlled problem behavior. For one participant (Marc), SIB was maintained by both access to attention and automatic reinforcement. The authors arranged a DRO schedule for behavior maintained by positive reinforcement and noncontingent access to toys for behavior maintained by automatic reinforcement. The authors demonstrated that treatment was effective only when both treatment components were in place. Smith et al. also examined demand fading and NCR. For another participant (Laura), the authors found that SIB was maintained by escape from demands and automatic reinforcement. To treat SIB, the authors conducted demand fading for SIB maintained by escape into a context where noncontingent access to toys was available for SIB maintained by automatic reinforcement.

## PRACTICAL IMPLICATIONS FOR TREATMENT SELECTION

In this concluding section of the chapter we highlight and discuss several factors that impact the selection and implementation of function-based treatments for self-injury. Table 3.1 provides a summary of common behavioral interventions for SIB along with potential advantages and disadvantages to consider when selecting among treatment options.

**Table 3.1.** Common behavioral interventions for SIB and advantages and disadvantages of each

| Treatment | Contingency description | Strengths | Weaknesses or risks |
|---|---|---|---|
| Extinction of SR+ | Nondelivery or termination of attention or tangible item | Highly effective | 1. Potential for behavior to get worse before it gets better<br>2. Restricts access to SR+<br>3. High-level integrity required but may be difficult |
| DRO for SR+ | Delivery of attention or tangible item for the absence of responding | 1. EXT component<br>2. SR+ component | 1. No functional replacement skills taught<br>2. High-level integrity required |
| DRA for SR+ | Delivery of attention or tangible item for appropriate alternative response | Functional alternative to SIB | High-level integrity required |
| NCR for SR+ | Delivery of attention or tangible item independent of SIB | Ease of implementation | No functional replacement skills taught |
| Extinction of SR– | Continuation of demands or social interaction | Highly effective | 1. Potential for behavior to get worse before it gets better<br>2. Restricts access to SR–<br>3. High-level integrity required |
| DNRO | Delivery of escape for not engaging in SIB | 1. EXT component<br>2. SR– component | 1. No functional replacement skills taught<br>2. High-level integrity required |
| DNRA | Delivery of escape for appropriate behavior (compliance or request) | Functional alternative to SIB | High-level integrity required |
| NCR for SR– | Delivery of escape independent of SIB | Ease of implementation | Loss of time engaged in academic learning |
| Demand fading | Systematic increase in the number of demands | 1. Immediate and sustained decrease in SIB<br>2. Larger number of demand can be required | 1. May be ineffective without EXT<br>2. Lengthy procedure |
| Curricular revision | Altering EO to decrease the aversiveness of the demand context | 1. No changes to the consequences for SIB required<br>2. May be a more socially accepted modification | May require extensive assessment to determine required manipulations |
| Sensory extinction | Sensory reinforcement blocked or mitigated | Highly effective | May be difficult or impossible to implement |
| Competing stimuli | Items that decrease the occurrence of SIB are freely provided | May create appropriate alternative skill | Required multiple assessments to implement |
| DRO for automatic SR | Delivery of reinforcers for not engaging in SIB | May identify items that are preferred to SIB | 1. Extinction cannot be implemented<br>2. No functional replacement skills taught |
| DRA for automatic SR | Reinforcement for alternative behavior (toy play) provide | Trains appropriate alternative skill | 1. Extinction cannot be implemented<br>2. May be difficult to train appropriate alternative |

*Key:* DRA, differential reinforcement of alternative behavior; DRO, differential of other behavior; EO, establishing operations; EXT, extinction; DNRA, negative reinforcement of alternative behavior; DNRO, differential negative reinforcement of other behavior; NCR, noncontingent reinforcement; SIB, self-injurious behavior; SR+, positive reinforcement; SR–, negative reinforcement.

52

## The Severity and Frequency of Self-Injurious Behavior

One goal of function-based treatment is to diminish the risk of injury to the individual who engages in SIB. Therefore, the amount of behavior that can occur during treatment prior to suppression is an important consideration. For example, one limitation to the use of extinction to treat SIB is the potential for an extinction burst (Lerman & Iwata 1996; Lerman, Iwata, & Wallace, 1999). If problem behavior is particularly severe, the use of extinction alone would not be recommend as it may put the individual or others in significant danger. In this case, antecedent manipulations that abolish or diminish the motivation for SIB would be recommended because SIB should be less likely to occur in the first place. If the motivational manipulation can be maintained (as in the case of curriculum revision) this could be the final treatment. The use of dense NCR/NCE schedules suppresses all behavior because there is no motivation to engage in problem behavior; however, dense schedules of NCR/NCE (continuous attention/no demands) are impracticable in most environments. Therefore, fading of very dense schedules of NCR/NCE is often necessary until acceptable levels of attention delivery or demands are present. In addition, the inclusion of highly preferred leisure items may reduce the aversive nature of the demand context or periods in which attention is not available and could be used during fading. For example, Long, Hagopian, DeLeon, Marhefka, and Resau (2005) examined the effects of providing a highly preferred leisure item during a demand routine that occasioned problem behavior. For three individuals, the researchers found decreases in problem behavior when the leisure item was present in the demand context. Similarly, Hagopian, Contrucci Kuhn, Long, and Rush (2005) supplemented an FCT procedure by including competing items and found that this procedure produced more stable reductions in problem behavior than a similar procedure without competing items.

However, in cases where motivational manipulation is insufficient, supplements to extinction are required, for example, requiring response omission (DRO/DNRO) or alternative responses (DRA/DNRA) to obtain reinforcement. In this case, the potential side effects of extinction may be diminished by providing access to the reinforcer that maintains SIB, either for the absence of responding (DRO) or for an alternative response (DRA). This is because some reinforcement can be obtained, unlike the use of extinction alone. Combining reinforcement-based procedures with extinction lessens the likelihood of extinction bursts (Lerman & Iwata, 1995).

## Resources Necessary to Implement Treatment

Another concern when selecting treatment is the extent of resources required for implementation. For example, implementing escape extinction is at times associated with aggression and bursts in behavior (Lerman & Iwata, 1996). If sufficient staff are not available to deal with these potential side-effects, extinction will not be implemented with full integrity. In addition, many treatments require continuous observation of the individual to appropriately deliver consequences and maintain the integrity of the treatment. Extinction, DRA, and DRO (with the exception of momentary DRO) all require that a therapist be present to monitor whether or not behavior occurred and implement the appropriate procedure (e.g., escape extinc-tion) or provide reinforcement, whereas treatments such as NCR or momentary DRO do not require continuous observation. In general, it seems prudent to evaluate, and deem ineffective, interventions that could be carried out with fewer resources before moving to those that are more labor intensive. Antecedent manipulations that decrease motivation should probably be considered in the first line of intervention.

## Functioning Level of the Individual

The functioning level of the individual is a practical consideration when imple-menting treatment. For example, FCT demands that an alternative response can be trained efficiently. Although there have been cases where nonverbal individuals have been taught to emit verbal responses to access reinforcement, treatments that incorporate communication forms with which individuals are most proficient with are more desirable (Horner & Day, 1991). For example, Ringdahl et al. (2009) evaluated two FCT procedures with different forms of communication (card, sign, and switch) for three participants who engaged in SIB and aggression. The authors found that communication increased and problem behavior decreased in conditions where individuals were highly proficient with the form of communication. In addition to the proficiency with an alternative response, Tiger, Hanley, and Bruzek (2008) provided guidelines for selecting an appropriate alternative behavior. These include the amount of effort to engage in the response, the degree to which others will be able to recognize the response, and the speed of acquisition.

A further consideration, as already noted, is the discriminability of the treatment contingency. Interventions such as DRO that provide few signals and require no discrete response on the part of the individual may be less successful with individuals with limited cognitive abilities.

## Treatment Generalization and Maintenance

Because the goal of treatment is to decrease problem behavior, appropriate attention must be paid to the environment in which treatment will be implemented. Therefore, fading naturally occurring stimuli into the therapeutic environment will make the effects of treatment more generalizable and promote maintenance of the treatment. Shore, Iwata, Lerman, and Shirley (1994) demonstrated that implementing treatment contingencies across multiple stimulus parameters (e.g., different therapists, settings, and tasks) was an important factor in treatment of SIB for three individuals. In addition, the authors found that the stimulus parameters that were important to train were idiosyncratic to the individual.

## Adapting Function-Based Treatment to Clinical Settings

Treatment efficacy is necessarily related to the degree to which that treatment can be implemented in the clinical environment and produces meaningful changes in everyday life (Kazdin, 2008). Therefore, function-based treatments must be designed to match the resources available in that environment. Because of this, schedule thinning in treatment is often necessary. However, because thinning decreases the number of reinforcers obtained, it is possible that problem behavior may reemerge due to the deprivation from the reinforcer. One possible reason for the reemergence of problem behavior is treatment degradation due to rapid fading. A significant amount of research has examined thinning of reinforcement schedules. Empirical evidence supports three procedures in particular: multiple schedule fading (e.g., Tiger & Hanley, 2004), delay-to-reinforcement fading (e.g., Hagopian, Fisher, Sullivan, Acquisto, & LeBlanc, 1998), and chain schedule fading for escape maintained problem behavior (e.g., Lalli et al., 1995).

Multiple schedule fading is typically used in FCT with extinction. In this type of fading, a discriminative stimulus (SD) is correlated with the availability of reinforcement, on an FR1 schedule, and another stimulus (S-delta) is correlated with extinction, or the unavailability of the reinforcer. Initially, the SD is available for the majority of time and is systematically faded as problem behavior remains at low levels. Recent research in multiple schedule fading involves the necessary stimulus arrangements (signal for reinforcement only, signal for extinction only, signal for both) for the schedule (Jarmolowicz, DeLeon, & Contrucci Kuhn, 2009), as well as the inclusion of naturally occurring stimuli (e.g, brief verbalizations) serving as the SD (Tiger, Hanley, & Larsen, 2008).

Delay-to-reinforcement fading is typically used in DRA (or FCT) and NCR/NCE. In this type of fading, the delay to reinforcement is systematically increased across sessions as problem behavior is maintained at low level. For example, if the individual asks for a break from tasks, initially, the break is provided. Following a series of sessions with low levels of problem behavior, the fading continues. For example, the individual asks for a break from tasks, and the break is provided after 5 s. This fading continues until a more practical value is achieved (e.g., 10 minutes). Similarly, the fading of an NCR schedule is conducted by increasing the amount of time between deliveries of reinforcers across sessions. If problem behavior remains low across sessions, the fading continues until a practical value is achieved. Several procedures may facilitate the delay-to-reinforcement training. For example, Fisher, Thompson, Hagopian, Bowman, and Krug (2000) examined two additional procedures (punishment and an alternative activity) that may facilitate delay-to-reinforcement procedures for three individuals. The authors found that although delay-to-reinforcement fading may be sufficient to maintain low levels of problem behavior, both punishment and alternative activities can also prevent treatment degradation during this type of fading.

Chain schedule fading, for escape maintained problem behavior, is typically used for FCT or DRA of escape-maintained SIB. In this type of fading, the number of demands completed prior to negative reinforcement is systematically increased. For example, the individual must complete one demand to gain access to reinforcement. Following a series of sessions with low levels of problem behavior the individual must then complete two demands in order to gain access to reinforcement. The fading continues until a practical level of demands is reached. For example, DeLeon, Neidert, Anders, and Rodriguez-Catter (2001) treated the escape–maintained problem behavior of one child through DRA (for compliance) plus extinction. Initially the authors introduced extinction for problem behavior and provided a choice between either the food or break contingent on each instance of compliance. They then systematically increased the number of responses required to obtain the choice until the child complied 10 times prior to gaining access to reinforcement.

## Change of Behavioral Functions

Although a significant amount of research has addressed avoiding treatment degradation based on the speed with which reinforcement schedules are faded, a number of other factors may be responsible for the reemergence of problem behavior over extended treatment. These include satiation to the reinforcement stimulus or habituation to the punishment stimulus. In these cases, relatively minor changes in the treatment may be sufficient to reinstate the treatment's effectiveness. However, if the consequence that maintains problem behavior transfers to another function, more dramatic changes to the treatment are required. Lerman, Iwata, Smith, Zarcone, and Vollmer (1994) found that the SIB of three (of four) individuals referred back for treatment after several months following initial treatment had transferred functions. In cases of transfer, treatment is ineffective not for procedural reasons (lack of integrity, speed of fading, habituation to consequences), but because the treatment is no longer targeting the appropriate contingency. Functional assessment of SIB is not only a procedure, it is a process; assessment of behavioral function should therefore be considered an ongoing activity.

## REFERENCES

Asmus, J.M., Wacker, D. P., Harding, J., Berg, W.K., Derby, K.M., & Kocis, E. (1999). Evaluation of antecedent stimulus parameters for the treatment of escape-maintained aberrant behavior. *Journal of Applied Behavior Analysis, 32*, 495–513.

Barton, L.E., Brulle, A.R., & Repp, A.C. (1986). Maintenance of therapeutic change by momentary DRO. *Journal of Applied Behavior Analysis, 19*, 277–282.

Borthwick-Duffy, S.A. (1994). Prevalence of destructive behaviors: A study of aggression, self-injury, and property destruction. In T. Thompson, & D.B. Gray (Eds.), *Destructive behavior in developmental disabilities: Diagnosis and treatment* (pp. 3–23). Thousand Oaks, CA: Sage Publications.

Butler, L.R., & Luiselli, J.K. (2007). Escape maintained problem behavior in a child with autism: Antecedent functional analysis and intervention evaluation of noncontingent escape (NCE) and instructional fading. *Journal of Positive Behavior Interventions, 9*, 195–202.

Carr, E.G., & Durand, V.M. (1985). Reducing behavior problems through functional communication training. *Journal of Applied Behavior Analysis, 18*, 111–126.

Catania, A.C. (1998). *Learning* (4th ed.). Upper Saddle River, NJ: Prentice Hall.

Cipani, E., & Spooner, F. (1997). Treating problem behaviors maintained by negative reinforcement. *Research in Developmental Disabilities, 18*, 329–342.

Clarke, S., Dunlap, G., Foster-Johnson, L., Childs, K.E., Wilson, D., White, R., & Vera, A. (1995). Improving the *conduct* of students with behavioral disorders by incorporating students interests into curricular activities. *Behavioral Disorders, 20*, 221–237.

Cooper, J.O., Heron, T.H., & Heward, W.L. (2007). *Applied Behavior Analysis* (2nd ed.). Columbus, OH: Prentice Hall.

Cowdery, G.E., Iwata, B.A., & Pace, G.M. (1990). Effects and side effects of DRO as treatment for self-injurious behavior. *Journal of Applied Behavior Analysis, 23*, 497–506.

DeLeon, I.G., Anders, B.M., Rodriguez-Catter, V., & Neidert, P.L. (2000). The effects of noncontingent access to single- versus multiple-stimulus sets on self-injurious behavior. *Journal of Applied Behavior Analysis, 33*, 623–626.

DeLeon, I.G., Neidert, P.L., Anders, M.M., & Rodriguez-Catter, V. (2001). Choices between positive and negative reinforcement during treatment for escape-maintained behavior. *Journal of Applied Behavior Analysis, 34,* 521–525.

DeLeon, I.G., Toole, L.M., Gutshall, K.A., & Bowman, L.G. (2005). Individualized sampling parameters for behavioral observations: Enhancing the predictive validity of competing stimulus assessments. *Research in Developmental Disabilities, 26,* 440–455.

Derby, K.M., Fisher, W.W., & Piazza, C.C. (1996). The effects of contingent and noncontingent attention on self-injury and self-restraint. *Journal of Applied Behavior Analysis, 29,* 107–110.

Durand, V.M., & Carr, E.G. (1991). Functional communication training to reduce challenging behavior: Maintenance and application in new setting. *Journal of Applied Behavior Analysis, 24,* 251–264.

Dyer, K., Dunlap, G., & Winterling, V. (1990). Effects of choice making on the serious problem behaviors of students with severe handicaps. *Journal of Applied Behavior Analysis, 23,* 515–524.

Ebanks, M.E., & Fisher, W.W. (2003). Altering the timing of academic prompts to treat destructive behavior maintained by escape. *Journal of Applied Behavior Analysis, 36,* 355–359.

Favell, J.E., McGimsey, J.F., & Schell, R.M. (1982). Treatment of self-injury by providing alternate sensory activities. *Analysis and Intervention in Developmental Disabilities, 2,* 83–104.

Fischer, S.M., Iwata, B.A., & Mazaleski, J.L. (1997). Noncontingent delivery of arbitrary reinforcers as treatment for self-injurious behavior. *Journal of Applied Behavior Analysis, 30,* 239–249.

Fisher, W.W., Adelinis, J.D., Volkert, V.M., Keeney, K.M., Neidert, P.L., & Hovanetz, A. (2005). Assessing preferences for positive and negative reinforcement during treatment of destructive behavior with functional communication training. *Research in Developmental Disabilities, 26,* 153–168.

Fisher, W.W., Kuhn, D.E., & Thompson, R.H. (1998). Establishing discriminative control of responding using functional and alternative reinforcers during functional communication training. *Journal of Applied Behavior Analysis, 31,* 543–560.

Fisher, W.W., O'Connor, J.T., Kurtz, P.F., DeLeon, I.G., & Gotjen, D.L. (2000). The effects of non-contingent delivery of high- and low-preference stimuli on attention-maintained destructive behavior. *Journal of Applied Behavior Analysis, 33,* 79–83.

Fisher, W., Piazza, C., Cataldo, M., Harrel, R., Jefferson, G., & Conner, R. (1993). Functional communication training with and without extinction and punishment. *Journal of Applied Behavior Analysis, 26,* 23–26.

Fisher W.W., Thompson R.H., Hagopian L.P., Bowman L.G., & Krug A. (2000). Facilitating tolerance of delayed reinforcement during functional communication training. *Behavior Modification, 24,* 3–29.

Geiger, K.B., Carr, J.E., & LeBlanc, L.A. (2010). Function-based treatments for escape-maintained problem behavior: A treatment-selection model for practicing behavior analysts. *Behavior Analysis in Practice, 3,* 22–32.

Goh, H., Iwata, B.A., Shore, B.A., DeLeon, I.G., Lerman, D.C., Ulrich, S.M., & Smith R.G. (1995). An analysis of the reinforcing properties of hand mouthing. *Journal of Applied Behavior Analysis, 28,* 269–283.

Hagopian, L.P., Contrucci Kuhn, S.A., Long, E.S., & Rush, K.S. (2005). Schedule thinning following communication training: Using competing stimuli to enhance tolerance to decrements in reinforcer density. *Journal of Applied Behavior Analysis, 38,* 177–193.

Hagopian, L.P., Crockett, J.L., van Stone, M., DeLeon, I.G., & Bowman, L.G. (2000). Effects of noncontingent reinforcement on problem behavior and stimulus engagement: The role of satiation, extinction, and alternative reinforcement. *Journal of Applied Behavior Analysis, 33,* 433–449.

Hagopian, L.P., Fisher, W.W., & Legacy, S.M. (1994). Schedule effects of noncontingent reinforcement on attention-maintained destructive behavior. *Journal of Applied Behavior Analysis, 27,* 317–325.

Hagopian, L.P., Fisher, W.W., Sullivan, M.T., Acquisto, J., & LeBlanc, L.A. (1998). Effectiveness of functional communication training with and without extinction and punishment: A summary of 21 inpatient cases. *Journal of Applied Behavior Analysis, 31,* 211–235.

Hagopian, L.P., Wilson, D.M., & Wilder, D.A. (2001). Assessment and treatment of problem behavior maintained by escape from attention and access to tangible items. *Journal of Applied Behavior Analysis, 34,* 229–232.

Hanley, G.P., Iwata, B.A., & McCord, B.E. (2003). Functional analysis of behavior problem: A review. *Journal of Applied Behavior Analysis, 36,* 147–185.

Hanley, G.P., Iwata, B.A., & Thompson, R.H. (2001). Reinforcement schedule thinning following treatment with functional communication training. *Journal of Applied Behavior Analysis, 34,* 17–38.

Harris, S.L., & Wolchik, S.A. (1979). Suppression of self-stimulation: Three alternative strategies. *Journal of Applied Behavior Analysis, 12,* 199–210.

Horner, R.H., & Day, H.M. (1991). The effects of response efficiency on functionally equivalent competing behaviors. *Journal of Applied Behavior Analysis, 24,* 719–732.

Humenik, A.L., Curran, J., Luiselli, J.K., & Child, S.N. (2008). Intervention for self-injury in a child with autism: Effects of choice and continuous access to preferred stimuli. *Behavioral Development Bulletin, 3,* 17–22.

Iwata, B.A., Pace, G.M., Cowdery, G.E., & Miltenberger, R.G. (1994). What makes extinction work: An analysis of procedural form and function. *Journal of Applied Behavior Analysis, 27,* 131–144.

Iwata, B.A., Pace, G.M., Dorsey, M.F., Zarcone, J.R., Vollmer, T.R., Smith, R.G., et al. (1994). The functions of self-injurious behavior: An experimental-epidemiological analysis. *Journal of Applied Behavior Analysis, 27,* 215–240.

Iwata, B.A., Pace, G.M., Kalsher, M.J., Cowdery, G.E., & Cataldo, M.F. (1990). Experimental analysis and extinction of self-injurious escape behavior. *Journal of Applied Behavior Analysis, 23,* 11–27.

Jarmolowicz, D.P., DeLeon, I.G., & Contrucci Kuhn, S.A. (2009). *Behavioral Interventions, 24,* 265–273.

Kahng, S., Iwata, B.A., DeLeon, I.G., & Wallace, M.D. (2000). A comparison of procedures for programming noncontingent reinforcement schedules. *Journal of Applied Behavior Analysis, 33,* 223–231.

Kahng, S., Iwata, B.A., DeLeon, I.G., & Worsdell, A. (1997). Evaluation of the "control over reinforcement" component in functional communication training. *Journal of Applied Behavior Analysis, 30,* 267–277.

Kahng, S., Iwata, B., & Lewin, A. (2002). Behavioral treatment of self-injury, 1964 to 2000. *American Journal on Mental Retardation, 107,* 212–221.

Kazdin, A. (2008). Evidence-based treatment and practice: New opportunities to bridge clinical research and practice, enhance the knowledge base, and improve patient care. *American Psychologist, 63,* 146–159.

Kennedy, C.H., & Souza, G. (1995). Functional analysis and treatment of eye poking. *Journal of Applied Behavior Analysis, 28,* 27–37.

Kern, L., Bailin, D., & Mauk, J.E. (2003). Effects of a topical anesthetic on non-socially maintained self-injurious behavior. *Developmental Medicine and Child Neurology, 45,* 769–771.

Kern, L., Childs, K.E., Dunlap, G., Clarke, S., & Falk, G.D. (1994). Using assessment-based curricular interventions to improve the classroom behavior of a student with emotional and behavioral challenges. *Journal of Applied Behavior Analysis, 27,* 7–19.

Kuhn, D.E., DeLeon, I.G., Fisher, W.W., & Wilke, A.E. (1999). Clarifying an ambiguous functional analysis with matched and mismatched extinction procedures. *Journal of Applied Behavior Analysis, 32,* 99–102.

Ladd, M.V., Luiselli, J.K., & Baker, L. (2009). Continuous access to competing stimulation as intervention for self-injurious skin picking in a child with autism. *Child & Family Behavior Therapy, 31,* 54–60.

Lalli, J.S., Casey, S., & Kates, K. (1995). Reducing escape behavior and increasing task completion with functional communication training, extinction, and response chaining. *Journal of Applied Behavior Analysis, 28,* 261–268.

Lalli, J.S., Casey, S.D., & Kates, K. (1997). Noncontingent reinforcement as treatment for severe problem behavior: Some procedural variations. *Journal of Applied Behavior Analysis, 30,* 127–137.

Lalli, J.S., Vollmer, T.R., Progar, P.R., Wright, C., Borrero, J., Daniel, D. et al. (1999). Competition between positive and negative reinforcement in the treatment of escape behavior. *Journal of Applied Behavior Analysis, 32,* 285–296.

Lerman, D.C., & Iwata, B.A. (1995). Prevalence of the extinction burst and its attenuation during treatment. *Journal of Applied Behavior Analysis, 28,* 93–94.

Lerman, D.C., & Iwata, B.A. (1996). Developing a technology for the use of operant extinction in clinical settings: An examination of basic and applied research. *Journal of Applied Behavior Analysis, 29,* 345–382.

Lerman, D.C., Iwata, B.A., Smith, R.G., Zarcone, J.R., & Vollmer, T.R. (1994). Transfer of behavioral function as a contributing factor in treatment relapse. *Journal of Applied Behavior Analysis, 27,* 357–370.

Lerman, D.C., Iwata, B.A., & Wallace, M.D. (1999). Side effects of extinction: Prevalence of bursting and aggression during the treatment of self-injurious behavior. *Journal of Applied Behavior Analysis, 32,* 1–8.

Lindberg, J.S., Iwata, B.A., Kahng, S., & DeLeon, I.G. (1999). DRO contingencies: An analysis of variable-momentary schedules. *Journal of Applied Behavior Analysis, 32,* 123–136.

Long, E.S., Hagopian, L.P., DeLeon, I.G., Marhefka, J.M., & Resau, D. (2005). Competing stimuli in the treatment of multiply controlled problem behavior during hygiene routines. *Research in Developmental Disabilities, 26,* 57–69.

Luiselli, J.K. (1988). Comparative analysis of sensory extinction treatments for self-injury. *Education and Treatment of Children, 11,* 149–156.

Luiselli, J.K. (1991). Functional assessment and treatment of self-injury in a pediatric, nursing care resident. *Behavioral Residential Treatment, 6,* 311–320.

Luiselli, J.K. (1992). Protective equipment. In J.K. Luiselli, J.L. Matson & N.N. Singh (Eds.), *Self-injury: Analysis, assessment and treatment* (pp. 201–233). New York: Springer-Verlag, Inc.

Luiselli, J.K. (1998). Treatment of self-injurious hand-mouthing in a child with multiple disabilities. *Journal of Developmental and Physical Disabilities, 10,* 167–174.

Luiselli, J.K. (2008). Antecedent (preventive) intervention. In J.K. Luiselli, S. Wilczynski, D.C. Russo, & W.P. Christian. *Effective practices for children with autism: Educational and behavior support interventions that work* (pp. 393–412). New York, NY: Oxford University Press.

Luiselli, J.K. (2009). Non-suicidal self-injury among people with developmental disabilities. In M.K. Nock (Ed.), *Understanding non-suicidal self-injury: Current science and practice* (pp. 157–179). Washington, DC: American Psychological Association Press.

MacDonald, J.E., Wilder, D.A., & Dempsey, C. (2002). Brief functional analysis and treatment of eye poking. *Behavioral Interventions, 17,* 261–270.

Mace, F.C., Lalli, J.S., & Lalli, E.P. (1991). Functional analysis and treatment of aberrant behavior. *Research in Developmental Disabilities, 12,* 155–180.

Marcus, B.A., & Vollmer, T.R. (1996). Combining noncontingent reinforcement and differential reinforcement schedules as treatment for aberrant behavior. *Journal of Applied Behavior Analysis, 29,* 43–51.

Mazaleski, J.L., Iwata, B.A., Rodgers, T.A., Vollmer, T.R., & Zarcone, J.R. (1994). Protective equipment as treatment for stereotypic hand mouthing: Sensory extinction or punishment effects? *Journal of Applied Behavior Analysis, 27,* 345–355.

Mazaleski, J.L., Iwata, B.A., Vollmer, T.R., Zarcone, J.R., & Smith, R.G. (1993). Analysis of the reinforcement and extinction components in DRO contingencies with self-injury. *Journal of Applied Behavior Analysis, 26,* 143–156.

Meador, D.M., & Osborn, R.G. (1992). Prevalence of severe behavior disorders in persons with mental retardation and treatment procedures used in community and institutional settings. *Behavioral Residential Treatment, 7,* 299–314.

Moore, J.W., Fisher, W.W., & Pennington, A. (2004). Systematic application and removal of protective equipment in the assessment of multiple topographies of self-injury. *Journal of Applied Behavior Analysis, 37,* 73–77.

O'Reilly, M.F., Murray, N., Lancioni, G.E., Sigafoos, J., & Lacey, C. (2003). Functional analysis and intervention to reduce self-injurious and agitated behavior when removing equipment for brief time periods. *Behavior Modification, 27,* 538–559.

Pace, G.M,. Iwata, B.A., Cowdery, G.E., Adree, P.J., & McIntyre, T. (1993). Stimulus (instructional) fading during extinction of self-injurious escape behavior. *Journal of Applied Behavior Analysis, 26,* 205–212.

Piazza, C.C., Fisher, W.W., Hanley, G.P., Hilker, K., & Derby, K.M. (1996). A preliminary procedure for predicting the positive and negative effects of reinforcement-based procedures. *Journal of Applied Behavior Analysis, 29,* 137–152.

Piazza, C.C., Fisher, W.W., Hanley, G.P., Remick, M.L., Contrucci, S.A., & Aitken, T.L. (1997). The use of positive and negative reinforcement in the treatment of escape-maintained destructive behavior. *Journal of Applied Behavior Analysis, 30,* 279–298.

Piazza, C.C., Moes, D.R., & Fisher, W.W. (1996). Differential reinforcement of alternative behavior and demand fading in the treatment of escape-maintained destructive behavior. *Journal of Applied Behavior Analysis, 29,* 569–572.

Reed, D.D., Luiselli, J.K., Morizio, L.C., & Child, S.N. (2010). Sequential modification and the identification of instructional components occasioning self-injurious behavior. *Child & Family Behavior Therapy, 32,* 1–16.

Reid, D.H., Parsons, M.B., Phillips, J.F., & Green, C.W. (1993). Reduction of self-injurious hand mouthing using response blocking. *Journal of Applied Behavior Analysis, 26,* 139–140.

Repp, A.C., Barton, L.E., & Brulle, A.R. (1983). A comparison of two procedures for programming the differential reinforcement of other behaviors. *Journal of Applied Behavior Analysis, 16,* 435–445.

Repp, A.C., Deitz, S.M., & Deitz, D.E.D. (1976). Reducing inappropriate behaviors in classrooms and in individual sessions through DRO schedules of reinforcement. *Mental Retardation, 14,* 11–15.

Ringdahl, J.E., Call, N.A., Christensen, T., & Boelter, E.W. (2010). Brief report: Signals enhance the suppressive effects of noncontingent reinforcement. *Journal of Autism and Developmental Disorders, 40,* 378–382.

Ringdahl, J.E., Falcomata, T.S., Christensen, T.J., Bass-Ringdahl, S.M., Lentz, A., Dutt, A., et al. (2009). Evaluation of a pretreatment assessment to select mand topographies for functional communication training. *Research in Developmental Disabilities, 30,* 330–341.

Roberts, M.L., Mace, F.C., & Daggett, J.A. (1995). Preliminary comparison of two negative reinforcement schedules to reduce self-injury. *Journal of Applied Behavior Analysis, 28,* 579–580.

Rojahn, J., & Esbensen, A.J. (2002). Epidemiology of self-injurious behavior in mental retardation: A review. In S.R. Schroeder, M.L. Oster-Granite, & T. Thompson (Eds.), *Self-injurious behavior: Gene-brain-behavior relationships* (pp. 41–77). Washington, DC: American Psychological Association.

Rojahn, J., Schroeder, S. R., & Hoch, T. A. (2008). *Self-injurious behavior in intellectual disabilities.* New York: Elsevier.

Rosales, R., Worsdell, A., & Trahan, M. (2010). Comparison of methods for varying item presentation during noncontingent reinforcement. *Research in Autism Spectrum Disorders, 4,* 367–376.

Shirley, M.J., Iwata, B.A., Kahng, S., Mazaleski, J.L., & Lerman, D.C. (1997). Does functional communication training compete with ongoing contingencies of reinforcement? An analysis during response acquisition and maintenance. *Journal of Applied Behavior Analysis, 30,* 93–104.

Shore, B.A., Iwata, B.A., DeLeon, I.G., Kahng, S., & Smith, R.G. (1997). An analysis of reinforcer substitutability using object manipulation and self-injury as competing responses. *Journal of Applied Behavior Analysis, 30,* 21–41.

Shore, B.A., Iwata, B.A., Lerman, D.C., & Shirley, M.J. (1994). Assessing and programming generalized behavioral reduction across multiple stimulus parameters. *Journal of Applied Behavior Analysis, 27,* 371–384.

Smith, R.G., Iwata, B.A., Goh, H., & Shore, B.A. (1995). Analysis of establishing operations for self-injury maintained by escape. *Journal of Applied Behavior Analysis, 28,* 515–535.

Smith, R.G., Iwata, B.A., Vollmer, T.R., & Zarcone, J.R. (1993). Experimental analysis and treatment of multiply controlled self-injury. *Journal of Applied Behavior Analysis, 26,* 183–196.

Smith, R.G., Russo, L., & Le, D.D. (1999). Distinguishing between extinction and punishment effects of response blocking: A replication. *Journal of Applied Behavior Analysis, 32,* 367–370.

Steege, M.W., Wacker, D.P., Cigrand, K.C., Berg, W.K., Novak, C.G., Reimers, T.M., et al. (1990). Use of negative reinforcement in the treatment of self-injurious behavior. *Journal of Applied Behavior Analysis, 23,* 459–467.

Tarbox, J., Wallace, M.D., & Tarbox, R.S.F. (2002). Successive generalized parent training and failed schedule thinning of response blocking for automatically maintained object mouthing. *Behavioral Interventions, 17,* 169–178.

Tate, B.G., & Baroff, G.A. (1966). Aversive control of self-injurious behavior in a psychotic boy. *Behaviour Research and Therapy, 4,* 281–287.

Tiger, J.H., Fisher, W.W., & Bouxsein, K.J. (2009). Therapist- and self-monitored DRO contingencies as a treatment for the self-injurious skin picking of a young man with Asperger syndrome. *Journal of Applied Behavior Analysis, 42,* 315–319.

Tiger, J.H., & Hanley, G.P. (2004). Developing stimulus control of preschooler mands: An analysis of schedule-correlated and contingency-specifying stimuli. *Journal of Applied Behavior Analysis, 37,* 517–521.

Tiger, J.H., Hanley, G.P., & Bruzek, J. (2008). Functional communication training: A review and practical guide. *Behavior Analysis in Practice, 1,* 10–23.

Tiger, J.H., Hanley, G.P., & Larsen, K.M. (2008). An evaluation of intraverbal training and listener training for teaching categorization skills. *Journal of Applied Behavior Analysis, 41,* 125–130.

Vollmer, T.R., & Iwata, B.A. (1992). Differential reinforcement as treatment for behavior disorders: Procedural and functional variations. *Research in Developmental Disabilities, 13,* 393–417.

Vollmer, T.R., Iwata, B.A., Zarcone, J.R., Smith, R.G., & Mazaleski, J.L. (1993). The role of attention in the treatment of attention-maintained self-injurious behavior: Noncontingent reinforcement and differential reinforcement of other behavior. *Journal of Applied Behavior Analysis, 26,* 9–21.

Vollmer, T.R., Marcus, B.A., & Ringdahl, J.E. (1995). Noncontingent escape as treatment for self-injurious behavior maintained by negative reinforcement. *Journal of Applied Behavior Analysis, 28,* 15–26.

Vollmer, T.R., Roane, H.S., Ringdahl, J.E., & Marcus, B.A. (1999). Evaluating treatment challenges with differential reinforcement of alternative behavior. *Journal of Applied Behavior Analysis, 32,* 9–23.

Worsdell, A.S., Iwata, B.A., Hanley, G.P., Thompson, R.H., & Kahng, S. (2000). Effects of continuous and intermittent reinforcement for problem behavior during functional communication training. *Journal of Applied Behavior Analysis, 33,* 167–179.

Zarcone, J.R., Iwata, B.A., Vollmer, T.R., Jagtiani, S., Smith, R.G., & Mazaleski, J.L. (1993). Extinction of self-injurious escape behavior with and without instructional fading. *Journal of Applied Behavior Analysis, 26,* 353–360.

Zhou, L., Goff, G.A., & Iwata, B.A. (2000). Effects of increased response effort on self-injury and object manipulation as competing responses. *Journal of Applied Behavior Analysis, 33,* 29–40.

# SECTION II

# Aggressive Behavior

CHAPTER **4**

# Environmental Determinants of Aggressive Behavior

*Johnny L. Matson and*
*Alison M. Kozlowski*

Aggressive behavior is one of the most common challenging behaviors to occur within the intellectual and developmental disabilities (IDD) population, as well as one that can have many severe consequences. Unfortunately, the definition of aggressive behavior is quite variable given the possible inclusion and exclusion of different topographies, leaving its operational definition inconclusive (Allen, 2000; Crocker et al., 2006). The most commonly referred to form of aggressive behavior is physical aggression, which involves an individual attempting to or successfully injuring another person through physical means (e.g., hitting, kicking, scratching, biting). However, several other topographies can be included under the heading of aggressive behavior, including but not limited to verbal aggression (e.g., threatening others, yelling at others, bullying), sexual aggression (e.g., fondling others), property aggression (e.g., throwing objects, defacing property), and even self-directed aggression, more commonly referred to as self-injurious behavior (SIB) (Crocker et al., 2006; Montes & Halterman, 2007).

Due to the variability in the definition of aggressive behavior, the exact prevalence of aggressive behavior within the IDD population is difficult to estimate. However, many researchers have sought to determine the prevalence rate of such behaviors within this population and have estimated 9.8%–51.8% of individuals across a variety of IDD to engage in some form of aggressive behavior (Cooper et al., 2009; Crocker et al., 2006; Hartley, Sikora, & McCoy, 2008; Matson, Wilkins, & Macken, 2009; Montes & Halterman, 2007; Tenneij & Koot, 2008; Tyrer et al., 2006). Although this is a large range and is no doubt directly affected by differing definitions of aggressive behavior, it is evident that aggressive behavior presents itself relatively frequently within the IDD population.

Similar to many other challenging behaviors evinced by individuals with IDD, aggressive behavior can have a number of severe consequences. These behaviors place significant hardship on families, teachers, and other service providers. Aggressive behaviors involving physical contact can cause injury to others and may even provoke others to inflict physical injury upon the individual him/herself. Incidents of aggressive behavior can interfere with the individual's involvement in educational and social activities, thus infringing upon his or her success in these areas. Social opportunities may also be limited due to the possibility of harming others or the fear that others may feel in the presence of individuals known to exhibit aggressive behaviors (Emerson, 2005; Luiselli & Slocumb, 1983). Furthermore, severe aggressive behaviors often result in institutionalization (Antonacci, Manuel, & Davis, 2008) or can lead to loss of community placement (Gardner & Moffatt, 1990). Unfortunately, individuals who exhibit challenging behaviors are also at increased risk of being abused or neglected (Mudford et al., 2008).

In addition to the numerous consequences of aggressive behavior mentioned hitherto, aggressive behavior is also a major risk factor for restraint and psychotropic medication use (Antonacci et al., 2008; Mudford et al., 2008). Physical and/or mechanical restraints may be used following aggressive behavior incidents as a means of protecting both the individual and others around him/her. Additionally, although the use of psychotropic medication in the IDD population is exceptionally controversial, its use has increased drastically over the past few decades (Provenzano & Mantia, 2008). Those individuals evincing aggression, among other challenging behaviors, are the most likely recipients of these medications despite a lack of empirical support for the use of such medications in these situations (Matson & Neal, 2009; Tyrer et al., 2008). These medications are deemed extremely restrictive and also have a number of side effects including tardive dyskinesia, irritability, sedation, and weight gain which may lead to more serious medical issues later in life (Campbell, Schopler, Cueva, & Hallin, 1996; Matson, Fodstad, Neal, Dempsey, & Rivet, 2010; Posey, Stigler, Erickson, & McDougle, 2008).

## SETTING AND MAINTAINING AGGRESSIVE BEHAVIOR

### Overview of Maintaining Variables

Due to the detrimental effects aggressive behavior can have on the individual evincing the behavior as well as those around him or her, referrals for treatment for these types of issues are often deemed necessary within the IDD population and are, in fact, among the most common reasons for referrals (Mudford et al., 2008). In order to be able to treat these behaviors effectively, the maintaining variable or function of the aggressive behavior needs to be determined. The maintaining variable or function of a challenging behavior is the environmental or other factor that is perpetuating the specific behavior. Many variables could be responsible for the continuing presence of target behaviors including receiving attention or tangibles during or immediately following engaging in the behavior, being allowed to escape demands or situations by engaging in the behavior, or by receiving automatic reinforcement due to performance of the behavior eliciting its own reinforcement. Because maintaining variables may differ across individuals, situations, and challenging behaviors and will directly affect treatment strategies contrived, these variables warrant attention. Therefore, a functional behavioral assessment (FBA) is often completed prior to implementing treatment in order to guide what components should be included in the treatment plan.

## Functional Behavioral Assessment

Determining the maintaining variables of aggressive behavior, as well as an assortment of other challenging behaviors, can be accomplished using one or more of a variety of different methodologies. Typically considered to be the standard method of FBA, experimental functional analysis (EFA) seeks to determine the maintaining variables of challenging behavior through experimental manipulation of antecedents and/or consequences that are potentially maintaining the challenging behavior (Didden, 2007; Iwata, Dorsey, Slifer, Bauman, & Richman, 1982; Martin, Gaffan, & Williams, 1999; Matson & Minshawi, 2007; Sturmey, Seiverling, & Ward-Horner, 2008). This can be accomplished by selecting a single event hypothesized to perpetuate the challenging behavior, or more commonly by randomizing a series of antecedents and/or consequences and comparing the frequency and duration of the challenging behavior across conditions. Despite its status as the most popular form of FBA, psychometric data for EFA is sparse. Available data are variable, with some authors indicating good to excellent validity and reliability, whereas others do not (Calloway & Simpson, 1998; Martin et al., 1999; Toogood & Timlin, 1996). Furthermore, the procedure requires specialized personnel, specific materials, and can also be quite time-consuming (Matson & Minshawi, 2007).

Due to some of the drawbacks of EFA, alternate forms of FBA have been developed using indirect methods and direct observational approaches. The key difference with respect to these assessment modalities in comparison to EFA is that manipulation of antecedents and/or consequences of behavior do not occur. Indirect assessment methods have predominantly focused on the use of checklists such as the Motivation Assessment Scale (MAS; Durand & Crimmins, 1992), Questions About Behavioral Function (QABF; Matson & Vollmer, 1995), and Functional Assessment for multiple CausaliTy (FACT; Matson et al., 2003), among others.

The MAS was the first attempt at using a checklist to determine the maintaining variables of challenging behaviors and consists of 16 items that are rated on a scale from 0 (never) to 6 (always) (Durand & Crimmins, 1988, 1992). Results of the assessment indicate whether the behavior serves an escape, attention, tangible, or sensory function. Although the authors of the MAS reported good internal consistency, interrater reliability, test–retest reliability, and construct validity, others have failed to replicate these psychometric properties with respect to interrater reliability and construct validity (Duker & Sigafoos, 1998; Joosten & Bundy, 2008; Shogren & Rojahn, 2003; Sigafoos, Kerr, & Roberts, 1994; Zarcone, Rodgers, Iwata, Rourke, & Dorsey, 1991) and found inconsistencies with respect to internal consistency (Duker & Sigafoos, 1998; Newton & Sturmey, 1991; Shogren & Rojahn, 2003). However, efforts at replicating test–retest reliability have been successful (Shogren & Rojahn, 2003). Because no additional research has been conducted that counters the failures to replicate some of the authors' original findings, it is not recommended that the MAS be used at this time unless done so in conjunction with other validated and reliable assessments.

Similar to the MAS, the QABF was later developed and consists of 25 statements describing situations in which attention, escape, tangible, physical, and nonsocial functions could be maintained (Paclawskyj, Matson, Rush, Smalls, & Vollmer, 2000). These items are also administered to a caregiver or other person that knows the individual in question well and are rated on a scale with 0, indicating not at all, up to 3, indicating often. Much research has been conducted on the QABF demonstrating that the measure possesses sound psychometric properties with respect to interrater reliability, test–retest reliability, internal consistency, convergent validity, and construct validity (Matson, Bamburg, Cherry, & Paclawskyj, 1999; Nicholson, Konstantinidi, & Furniss, 2006; Paclawskyj et al., 2000; Paclawskyj, Matson, Rush, Smalls, & Vollmer, 2001; Shogren & Rojahn, 2003). More recently, Singh and colleagues (2009) have revised the original QABF in order to shorten the assessment to 15 statements as opposed to 25. Initial evaluation suggests that this shortened measure also possesses good validity and reliability. However, future research still needs to be conducted. Therefore, given the consistent favorable findings for the original QABF, the QABF appears to be the indirect assessment method of choice at this time.

When multiple maintaining variables may be identified for a specific target behavior, FACT was created to assist in determining the primary maintaining variable by requiring a forced choice between functions (Matson et al., 2003). The antecedents and consequences assessed through administration of this measure are identical to those assessed with the QABF. However, FACT is still in its infancy, and although the authors reported good internal consistency, future research needs to be completed on additional psychometric properties. Therefore, it is suggested that FACT be used with caution and in conjunction with other FBAs.

Another form of FBA frequently used requires direct observation of the individual within his or her natural environment so that antecedents and consequences of the target behavior can be examined. This objective is most commonly achieved through the use of scatterplot analyses or antecedent–behavior–consequence (ABC) recordings. In both instances, information is gathered in the presence of the individual. When completing a scatterplot analysis, behavior data are collected by denoting whether or not the specific target behavior occurred during a predetermined time interval (Touchette, MacDonald, & Langer, 1985). These time intervals are decided prior to data collection, and it is recommended that they represent different activities throughout the day to allow for easier interpretation. Although Touchette and colleagues reported excellent interrater reliability, additional studies on psychometric properties have been scant with little evidence to support the reliability, validity, and utility of scatterplots (Furniss, 2009).

However, ABC recordings may also be used in order to establish the maintaining variable of a target behavior. In fact, ABC recordings were among the first FBA strategies employed in applied settings (Bijou, Peterson, & Ault, 1968). ABC recordings can be completed by creating a document with columns designated for the date, time, antecedent event, target behavior, and consequent events with the possible inclusion of other categories possessing factors that may pertain to the target behavior, such as the location where the behavior occurred and other individuals present (Rojahn, Schroeder, & Hoch, 2008). These columns can then either be filled out during the observation, or prespecified antecedents, behaviors, and consequences can be checked off when witnessed (Tarbox et al., 2009). Unfortunately, a major criticism of ABC recordings is that irrelevant factors may correlate with the target behavior but not necessarily serve as its function (Furniss, 2009; Tarbox et al., 2009; Vollmer, Borrero, Wright, Van Camp, & Lalli, 2001). Furthermore, as with scatterplots, very little research has been conducted to date in support of the validity and reliability of ABC recordings. Therefore, it is recommended that this assessment method be used with caution and in conjunction with other FBA strategies.

## Maintaining Variables of Aggressive Behaviors

Although challenging behaviors in individuals with IDD can be maintained by an array of factors, there are a few maintaining variables that have been found time and time again to maintain and strengthen aggressive behaviors. In fact, aggressive behaviors are more likely than most other challenging behaviors to bring about social consequences (Embregts, Didden, Schreuder, Huitink, & van Nieuvenhuijzen, 2009; Matson et al., 1999; Thompson & Iwata, 2001), most probably due to the aggressive behavior being directed toward another individual which will likely produce a reaction. As a result, it appears that most aggressive behaviors are maintained through social consequences, predominantly positive and negative reinforcement (Marcus, Vollmer, Swanson, Roane, & Ringdahl, 2001; Ringdahl, Call, Mews, Boelter, & Christensen, 2008). The most frequently derived maintaining variables of aggressive behavior for individuals with IDD then are those serving attention, escape, and tangible functions (Braithewaite & Richdale, 2000; Didden, 2007; Johnson, McComas, Thompson, & Symons, 2004; Marcus et al., 2001).

### *Attention*

Understandably, attention is a common consequence of aggressive behavior. Therefore, it is not unusual for aggressive behavior to emerge in an effort to gain attention from others. Although this attention is generally given in a negative form, such as verbal reprimands, receiving the attention positively reinforces the aggressive behavior. For example, if a teacher is attending to another student so that the individual in question is not receiving any attention, this may serve as an antecedent to aggression. The individual may aggress toward the teacher in an attempt to gain the teacher's attention, albeit negative attention. In most circumstances, the teacher will react to the aggression by redirecting his or her attention from the peer student to the individual exhibiting the aggressive behavior. As such, the aggressor has successfully fulfilled his or her intended purpose, thereby reinforcing the misbehavior.

However, although attention certainly serves as a consequence to aggressive behavior in the majority of cases, it is important to note that delivery of a specific consequence does not necessarily mean that the behavior has been exhibited for that purpose (Thompson & Iwata, 2001). Aggressive behavior is commonly known to elicit attention from others; yet this attention may also be accompanied by other consequences as well. Unless highly trained staff is working with the individual exhibiting the aggressive behavior, it is likely that the victim of aggressive behavior or witnesses to the incident would display some facial and/or verbal response. This is especially true when taking into consideration that aggressive behaviors may be directed toward peers as opposed to staff. Therefore, although attention may serve as the dominant maintaining variable of aggression, it is also necessary to consider other maintaining factors that may be occurring in tandem with attention.

### Escape

Many individuals engage in aggression when attempting to escape demands, situations, or people. The behavior occurs as a response to these antecedents, which will often allow the individual to escape from undesirable situations. Even if the individual is not permitted to completely escape the demand, situation, or person, the aggressive behavior will typically bring about a delay in the less preferred event due to the need to manage the aggressive behavior. Therefore, the aggressive behavior is negatively reinforced via escape. For example, if a caregiver asks an individual to complete an undesired task (e.g., brushing his/her teeth), the individual may attack the caregiver thus discontinuing the task. Aggression is, as a result, reinforced. The individual learns that engaging in that behavior results in avoidance of brushing his or her teeth.

### Tangible

Tangibles are preferred items, edibles, or activities. In these circumstances, the individual is either not permitted to access a preferred tangible when desired or access to a preferred tangible is discontinued. At this point the individual may become aggressive, which can result in someone providing the individual with access to the preferred tangible desired as a means of ameliorating the misbehavior. Delivery of the preferred item, edible, or activity contingent on aggressive behavior will then reinforce this negative behavior, thus causing it to continue in the future. For example, a child who is playing with toys, such as cars, may attack another child if that peer child approached and attempted to also play with the cars or take them away. The peer child would likely then abandon his or her attempt to engage with the toys, thus reinforcing the other child's aggressive behavior. Now the child has learned that becoming aggressive when preferred items are taken away will result in the items being returned.

Although aggression may serve a tangible function, it is important to note that removal of a preferred tangible resulting in aggressive behavior may serve a dual function with escape dependant on the situation. In the situation just described, if a supervising adult had requested the child to discontinue playing with the cars while directing him or her to another, less preferred activity, the aggressive behavior then could have been in response to either the removal of the tangible, presentation of the demand, or both. This example highlights the importance of accurately assessing the maintaining variables of aggression when tailoring interventions. Thus, FBA has the value of providing useful information on the design of treatment methods.

## Maintaining Variables of Aggression

In a sample of 36 institutionalized adults who were diagnosed with IDD, the functions of aggression, SIB, and stereotypies were assessed through administration of the QABF (Dawson, Matson, & Cherry, 1998). The maintaining variables receiving the greatest endorsement for aggressive behaviors were attention and tangible, which were both significantly higher than the other possible functions assessed through administration of this FBA scale (i.e., escape, physical, nonsocial). Therefore, it appears as though these adults' aggressive behaviors were perpetuated by them receiving positive reinforcement, whether it was in the form of attention or preferred items, edibles, or activities, specifically.

In a much larger study, 417 individuals with severe and profound IDD who resided at developmental centers were studied. Applegate, Matson, and Cherry (1999) assessed the function of several different challenging behaviors through administration of the QABF. Of the total sample, 123 adults engaged in aggression. The maintaining variable with the greatest endorsement for aggressive behavior was escape. In fact, the most frequently endorsed items on the QABF by individuals engaging in aggression were two items found along the escape subscale—that the individual seemed to be saying "leave me alone" or "stop asking me to do this" when engaging in aggression, and that the individual engaged in the behavior to try to get people to leave him or her alone. As such, aggression was negatively reinforced. The tangible and attention subscales were also elevated, suggesting that numerous social consequences were responsible for the presence of aggressive behaviors. These authors also make an interesting point that aggression, being a low-frequency and high-intensity behavior, is more likely than other behaviors to serve social functions whereas high frequency behaviors (e.g., SIB, pica) are commonly maintained by nonsocial functions.

In a validity study on the QABF, Matson et al. (1999) assessed the maintaining variables of aggression in 83 adults residing in a developmental center who had diagnoses of severe or profound IDD. Of these individuals, a clear function was found for 74% of the sample through administration of the QABF. Attention served as the primary function of aggressive behavior in 38.7% of residents and escape in 35.3%. Therefore, similar to the studies already mentioned, positive and negative reinforcement played a fundamental role in the reoccurrence of aggressive behaviors.

A similar study was conducted by Embregts et al. (2009) in which the function of aggressive behavior of 87 children and adults with moderate to borderline IDD residing in several residential facilities was assessed using the QABF. The authors concluded that social consequences (attention, tangible, and escape) most frequently brought about aggressive behavior with 78.2% of clients having one of these three functions as their primary maintaining variable. More specifically, with respect to the primary maintaining variables of aggression, a tangible function was identified for 42.5% of clients, escape in 34.5%, and attention in 28.7%. Physical discomfort was identified as the predominant maintaining variable in slightly fewer residents (19.5%), and self-stimulation was rarely identified as the primary maintaining variable of aggression (2.3%).

In a much smaller study, the maintaining variables of destructive behavior were assessed in two young children who had diagnoses of IDD through the use of an EFA (Piazza, Hanley, Fisher, Ruyter, & Gulotta, 1998). Although destructive behavior was not operationally defined to solely include aggressive behavior, such behaviors were incorporated into the definition. For one child the EFA initially revealed that the destructive behaviors functioned as a means of gaining attention because the child engaged in destructive behavior significantly more frequently during attention conditions as opposed to tangible, demand (e.g., escape), and toy play (e.g., nonsocial) conditions. However, the authors note that the behaviors may have also been maintained by escape and tangible functions. Because the attention condition allotted for only a few seconds of reinforcement following engagement in the destructive behavior, as the verbal reprimand was brief in duration, there was more opportunity to gain access to the reinforcer during this condition. In the tangible and escape conditions, the child received either a preferred item or escape from a demand for 30 seconds—a significantly longer time period. Thus, the authors concluded that all three social consequences served as maintaining variables for the child's destructive behavior. Similarly, the other child was found to engage in destructive behaviors for many reasons including receiving attention, access to tangibles, and escape from demands. Although the first child also engaged in destructive behavior more frequently in the attention condition, the rationale put forth for the other child's maintaining variables may be extended to this child as well.

Marcus, Vollmer, Swanson, Roane, and Ringdahl (2001) examined the aggressive behavior of seven children with developmental disabilities and other related conditions using an EFA. Results of the EFA suggested that four of the seven children engaged in aggression as a means of gaining access to tangibles. These children commonly elicited aggressive behaviors when they were denied access to preferred items or activities. The remaining three children engaged in aggressive behaviors to escape instructional demands. In this specific situation, academic demands were made every 30 seconds and were removed if the child exhibited aggressive behavior. As such, the child was negatively reinforced for exhibiting aggression by being able to escape less preferred or relatively difficult tasks.

O'Reilly (1995) conducted a case study with a 31-year-old man who had a diagnosis of IDD and engaged in aggressive behavior. The maladaptive behavior was hypothesized to serve either an attention or escape function, which was then tested through an EFA using only these two conditions. The man only engaged in aggressive behavior during demand conditions, thus providing evidence that his aggression was negatively reinforced by the ability to escape difficult tasks.

## GUIDING INTERVENTION PLANNING

Once the maintaining variable of the aggressive behavior has been discovered, this function should guide treatment options. Although this is a critical element in the treatment of aggression, as well as other challenging behaviors, it is also a difficult concept for most individuals formulating intervention plans. Teaching adaptive skills is a critical part of any behavior plan; simply suppressing aggression will not suffice in most cases because the individual needs to acquire skills to use in place of aggression. Therefore, based on the ascribed function, a replacement behavior should be identified. This replacement behavior will serve as an appropriate competing behavior to fulfill the same function that had previously maintained the aggression. In order to increase the likelihood of the individual relying on this behavior to maintain the designated function as opposed to aggression, the replacement behavior should result in easier and quicker access to the predetermined variable(s) maintaining aggression. In addition, aggression should no longer retain the same reinforcer quality. For example, an individual who had been exhibiting aggression as a means of receiving attention from others should be ignored as much as possible when engaging in this behavior during treatment.

## Reinforcement Procedures

Although teaching a replacement behavior that is compatible with the function of aggression is a critical component of a treatment plan, proper reinforcement is also an integral part of a treatment plan and should be implemented along with replacement behaviors. A variety of reinforcement procedures are commonly used to reduce aggression including noncontingent reinforcement and differential reinforcement. Following a FBA, the variable found to maintain the behavior is then selected as the reinforcement to be delivered. For example, if the aggression is found to be maintained by attention, the individual will receive attention as his or her reinforced her reinforcement during the selected reinforcement procedure. Although reinforcement procedures can be incorporated into an individual's treatment plan in the absence of a FBA, conducting such an assessment increases the effectiveness of the procedure by ensuring that the appropriate reinforcement is being given. Conducting a FBA also ensures that the reinforcement previously delivered for aggression is now withheld during and immediately following these situations, also known as placing the behavior on extinction. Although reinforcement procedures clearly all rely on the delivery of reinforcement, the timing and contingencies of this reinforcement may vary between procedures. As was previously referenced, it is important that the individual is also taught a replacement behavior in conjunction with any reinforcement program.

### *Noncontingent Reinforcement*

When implementing a noncontingent reinforcement (NCR) program, the predetermined reinforcer is delivered at a specified time interval whether or not aggression is exhibited. Deciding at which time interval to begin delivering reinforcement will depend on the baseline frequency of the aggressive behavior. Ideally, the reinforcement time interval should be approximately half of the time interval between aggressive behaviors and can increase systematically as the individual's aggressive behaviors become less frequent. To illustrate, if an individual engages in aggressive behavior an average of once every 10 minutes, reinforcement should begin at 5-minute intervals. This formula ensures that the individual receives the desired reinforcer, which he or she historically received by engaging in aggression, prior to exhibition of the behavior. As a result, it is expected that the individual will no longer exhibit the behavior since he or she will have already accessed the reinforcer. Gradually, with a documented reduction in aggressive behavior, the reinforcement time interval can be increased so that reinforcement is delivered after longer time periods, a procedure called "schedule thinning" (Carr et al., 2000). Clearly, FBA is needed to determine what reinforcement will be delivered. Without this information the aggression may persist, as the NCR will not satisfactorily be reinforcing the individual unless multiple forms of reinforcement are delivered, which may be difficult or even impossible in certain situations.

In general, the effectiveness of NCR procedures has been shown with respect to many challenging behaviors, including aggression (Carr et al., 2000; Carr, Severtson, & Lepper, 2009). However, not all NCR procedures operate in exactly the same manner, which may alter the effectiveness of the program. For example, although the standard NCR program incorporates a fixed-time interval (i.e., the individual receives reinforcement after the specified time has elapsed), variations to this method exist such as variable-time (VT) schedules (Van Camp, Lerman, Kelley, Contrucci, & Vorndran, 2000). Using a VT schedule accommodates situations in which a fixed-time interval cannot be followed exactly, such as in group homes and other residential facilities where the individual is not receiving one-on-one attention throughout the day. Although there is a set time interval, a buffer is incorporated surrounding that time period so that the reinforcement can be delivered at anytime during that time period, thus increasing treatment consistency. In a meta-analysis conducted by Carr, Severtson, and Lepper (2009), NCR on a fixed-time interval schedule with the inclusion of extinction and schedule thinning was determined to be a well-established treatment. Both NCR on a fixed-time interval schedule and on a VT interval schedule with extinction, but no schedule thinning was found to be probably efficacious.

An important aspect to note with NCR is that the individual is not receiving reinforcement in the absence of aggression. Although a reduction in aggression is the goal, individuals are still scheduled to receive reinforcement regardless of their behaviors. As such, NCR is not without limitations. If the individual engages in aggression moments before the individual's current time interval has concluded, the individual will still receive the reinforcement. Inadvertently then, the aggressive behavior has been reinforced. However, some NCR programs choose to incorporate a stimulus–delay feature in which the reinforcer is not delivered as scheduled if the individual engages in the aggressive behavior within a specified time of the scheduled reinforcement; in these cases the individual is required to wait a predetermined time interval with an absence of aggressive behavior prior to receiving the reinforcement (Britton, Carr, Kellum, Dozier, & Weil, 2000).

### Differential Reinforcement

In contrast to NCR procedures, differential reinforcement programs reinforce the absence or suppression of targeted challenging behaviors with the potential to also reinforce appropriate behaviors depending on the exact protocol undertaken. There are several differential reinforcement procedures that can be used such as differential reinforcement of other (DRO), alternative (DRA), incompatible (DRI), and low-rate (DRL) behavior. The difference among these procedures is the behavior that is being reinforced. For example, DRO only requires that the individual refrain from engaging in the targeted behavior during the selected time period. Anyother behavior will be reinforced. Similarly, for DRL, reinforcement is delivered when the individual displays maladaptive behavior below a predetermined frequency. However, DRA and DRI have more specific contingencies. They require the individual to practice a specific skill in order to receive reinforcement. DRA seeks to teach the individual to engage in a more appropriate behavior that will compete with the challenging behavior by fulfilling the same function through an easier means, thereby tying a replacement behavior into the reinforcement program. Conversely, DRI requires the individual to engage in a behavior that would be incompatible with the aggressive behavior (e.g., sitting with one's hands folded). Although this is a more appropriate behavior, it does not require the level of specificity for DRA. In the former case, the new behavior does not fulfill the same function as the aggressive behavior. Instead, DRI prohibits the individual from engaging in aggression due to the fact that both behaviors cannot occur simultaneously. As with NCR, differential reinforcement procedures have shown repeatedly to be effective in reducing aggression and other challenging behaviors in the IDD population (Luiselli & Slocumb, 1983; Petscher, Rey, & Bailey, 2009; Vollmer, Iwata, Smith, & Rodgers, 1992).

Although there are many differences between NCR and differential reinforcement programs, there are also similarities. Much like a NCR program, a FBA is recommended to guide the differential reinforcement program by identifying the specific reinforcer or reinforcers to be delivered. Additionally, differential reinforcement time intervals can be systematically increased or decreased depending on the individual's progress with their reduction in aggression. An advantage that differential reinforcement has over NCR is the prevention of inadvertent reinforcement of the aggressive behavior. The absence or suppression of aggressive behavior is being rewarded so that engagement in the aberrant behavior will not result in delivery of the reinforcer. A disadvantage in comparison to NCR programs is that programs implementing the differential reinforcement program need to observe the client consistently in order to determine when the reinforcer is to be delivered (Britton et al., 2000).

## Examples of Common Replacement Behaviors

### Functional Communication Training

Functional communication training (FCT) is an increasingly common replacement behavior taught to individuals who have IDD and challenging behaviors (Carr & Durand, 1985). The rationale behind these techniques is that individuals frequently have difficulty communicating their wants and needs, which may precipitate challenging behaviors that function as communication. FCT teaches individuals to appropriately communicate requests for attention, escape, or tangibles that previously were obtained through challenging behavior. Depending on the communicative abilities of the individual, different modes of communication may be taught including verbalizations, a picture exchange communication system, sign language, pointing/gesturing, and utilization of augmentative communication electronic devices. To increase the effectiveness of FCT, it is often suggested that a lower-level communicative ability is taught for the purposes of decreasing the challenging behavior (Johnson, 2002). Therefore, although an individual may present with minimal verbalization skills, this may not be the communicative ability chosen for FCT. The goal of FCT is to decrease challenging behaviors through increasing appropriate communication; choosing a more difficult mode of communication may hinder progress.

The exact skill to be taught through FCT will rely on the results from the FBA. For aggressive behavior maintained by an attention function, communications to be taught may consist of raising one's hand to get attention, tapping someone on the shoulder, verbally saying "Excuse me," or exchanging a picture icon to request a social activity. If the aggressive behavior is maintained by escape, other communications can be taught such as using a sign to indicate that the individual is done with the current task, touching a break icon, or verbally asking for a break. Finally, in situations in which the aggression has a tangible function, ways of communicating a desire to access specific items or activities can be the focus of the FCT. For example, the individual can learn to exchange a picture of an item for the actual item, verbally ask for an item, or gesture to preferred items within view.

### Social Skills Training

In some circumstances, individuals may engage in aggressive behavior because they lack the ability to interact appropriately with others in social situations. A variety of methods currently exist to increase appropriate social skills of individuals with IDD as a means of replacing aggressive behavior. One strategy that has become exceedingly popular incorporates Social Stories into the individuals' daily routines (Gray, 1994, 2000; Gray & Garand, 1993). Social Stories are short narratives that are tailored to each individual child or adult to provide the scenario of the social situation the individual will be experiencing. The stories may contain either words alone or a combination of words and pictures depending on the individual's developmental level. However, the authors recommend that the individual function minimally at the moderate level of IDD to benefit from FCT. The emphasis of the Social Stories is on describing the social situation to be encountered rather than on instructing the child throughout the situation. These stories can be used to increase a variety of social behaviors and have also received support in decreasing aggressive behavior (Gray, 1994; Swaggart & Gagnon, 1995).

### Behavioral Momentum

When aggression serves an escape function, behavioral momentum can be an effective procedure. Behavioral momentum involves delivering a planned sequence of requests or commands that the individual is likely to comply with based on personal history (i.e., high-probability commands) followed by a request or command that the individual frequently refuses to comply with (i.e., low-probability command). When implemented in this manner, individuals are likely to experience a momentum effect in which they continue to comply with the requests so that individuals are eventually completing tasks with which they had previously been noncompliant. For example, a high-probability command might be requesting an individual to "give me five" whereas a low-probability command might request the individual to "throw away" an item. This strategy is limited in that the requests or demands should only require a minimal amount of time to complete (e.g., 30 seconds). For example, short tasks such as picking up a piece of paper or completing a discrete trial in an academic program are ideal. If the target behavior is to have the individual complete a lengthier task (e.g., brushing teeth), it is likely that the steps will need to be broken down in order to maintain momentum.

Although this strategy primarily targets general noncompliance (i.e., refusing to follow a request or demand), it is based on an escape function and can therefore be applied to aggressive behaviors that are demonstrated within the scope of noncompliance with demands or requests (Mace et al., 1988; Romano & Roll, 2000). In fact, treatment of general noncompliance often results in concomitant reductions in aggression as well as in other challenging behaviors (Cataldo, Ward, Russo, Riordan, & Bennett, 1986; Ellison, 1997; Parrish, Cataldo, Kolko, Neef, & Egel, 1986). This is understandable, especially in situations where aggression is commonly preceded by general noncompliance.

## WHEN A CLEAR FUNCTION CANNOT BE IDENTIFIED

When no maintaining variable for aggression can be identified, or when there are multiple functions, several steps can be taken to increase successful treatment. First, it is important to note when continuing a FBA is no longer helpful and may, in fact, become hurtful to the individual's success in reducing aggressive behavior. This is especially important to consider when using an EFA, as these assessments have the potential to last up to several months. During this time period, treatment of the aggressive behavior is commonly put on hold while attempts are made to identify its maintaining variable. Therefore, criteria need to be agreed upon when a FBA should cease if a maintaining variable is not clearly identified. Aspects of the aggressive behavior, such as frequency and intensity, should be monitored throughout the assessment and may play a significant role in the time at which a FBA will no longer be pursued. For example, if an individual's aggressive behavior is less frequent, it may be necessary to continue a FBA for an extended period of time in order to have ample opportunity to assess the maintaining variables. At the same time, an EFA may not be the best assessment method to use for less frequent behaviors as the likelihood of witnessing such behaviors during the analysis may remain low despite manipulation of the environment. Furthermore, if the aggressive behavior is severe in intensity and the FBA is not providing clear results, continuation of such an assessment may prove unprofitable.

However, despite the stress on importance of FBA and the integral role it plays in the process of treatment planning, it is important to note that behavioral interventions can still be used when one specific maintaining variable is unrecognizable. This method should only be implemented after a FBA has been attempted. Failure to identify a clear environmental determinant of aggressive behavior may be indicative of two different circumstances; either the aggressive behavior is being reinforced automatically (i.e., the aggressive behavior itself is reinforcing to the individual) or the aggressive behavior is not being properly exposed to or observed within the antecedent and consequent conditions maintaining the behavior (Marcus et al., 2001; Ringdahl et al., 2008). Although automatic reinforcement is extremely rare, some researchers have identified it as the form of reinforcement to perpetuate aggressive behavior, or at least failed to successfully determine a social function (O'Reilly et al., 2010; Ringdahl et al., 2008; Thompson, Fisher, Piazza, & Kuhn, 1998). If a social function cannot be identified after repeated assessment, behavioral treatment strategies, such as differential reinforcement, have still been documented to reduce aggressive behavior (Ringdahl et al., 2008; Thompson et al., 1998). Furthermore, when social variables are hypo-thesized to maintain aggressive behavior despite a single function being known, behavioral strategies continue to be the evidence-based treatment of choice. In these cases, an overall FCT program is likely to be the best starting point in terms of a replacement behavior to teach the individual appropriate communication skills in order to access these social variables. The individual can be taught appropriate communication to gain access to the hypothesized social variables (i.e., attention, tangible, escape) in different situations to reduce the aggressive behavior in those situations (Braithewaite & Richdale, 2000; Day, Horner, & O'Neill, 1994).

An added concern when a social function cannot be identified may be the presence of comorbid psychopathology. The symptoms of a comorbid disorder may be able to account for the presence of aggression. Many individuals with IDD also present with symptoms of various psychopathologies including, but not limited to, anxiety, conduct disorder, eating disorders, obsessive compulsive disorder, depression, phobia, psychosis, attention deficit/hyperactivity disorder, and impulse control disorder (Al-Salehi, Al-Hifthy, & Ghaziuddin, 2009; Ghaziuddin, Ghaziuddin, & Greden, 2002; Ghaziuddin, Tsai, & Alessi, 1992; Ghaziuddin & Zafar, 2008; Newman & Ghaziuddin, 2008; Reaven, 2009). Many of these disorders may exacerbate the presence of aggression and complicate the process of determining the purpose of aggression. Furthermore, a comorbid diagnosis of intellectual disability and an autism spectrum disorder is commonly known to be related to increased rates of challenging behaviors, including aggression (Matson & Rivet, 2008). Given this information, it is imperative that comorbid psychopathology be assessed in individuals with IDD to ensure that the best treatment procedures are put in place. A variety of diagnostic tools and screeners exist to identify IDD individuals who may be at risk for or possess a comorbid psychiatric disorder, including the Diagnostic Assessment for the Severely Handicapped-II (DASH-II; Matson, 1995), Assessment of Dual Diagnosis (ADD; Matson, 1997), Autism Spectrum Disorders-Comorbidity-Adult Version (ASD-AC; Matson, Terlonge, & González, 2006), Autism Spectrum Disorders-Comorbidity-Child Version (ASD-CC; Matson & González, 2007), Baby and Infant Screen for Children with aUtIsm Traits (BISCUIT)-Part 2 (Matson, Boisjoli, & Wilkins, 2007), Child Behavior Checklist (CBCL; Achenbach, 1991), and the Behavioral Assessment System for Children, Second Edition (BASC-2; Reynolds & Kamphaus, 1992). Based on the results of these assessments, treatment may require incorporating interventions to directly target symptoms of psychopathology in conjunction with function-based treatments.

## CONCLUDING REMARKS

Aggressive behaviors are reported frequently in the IDD population and often require treatment due to the many serious consequences that may arise. This set of behaviors is regularly maintained by social consequences providing positive and/or negative reinforcement. Mainly, the ability to obtain attention, escape less desirable tasks or individuals, and gain or retain access to tangibles perpetuates aggressive behavior in this population. Interventions to reduce aggression and increase adaptive skills are necessary and require that the function of the aggression is deduced so that treatment can target the behavior adequately. FBA has been researched extensively, and it is now an accepted method as well as one that has received extensive support (Campbell, 2003).

Despite evidence supporting the use of FBAs to guide treatment planning in the IDD population, future research is needed with respect to different assessment strategies. There are numerous protocols available for conducting a FBA to establish the maintaining variable(s) of aggression. When choosing which specific FBA method to use, clinicians may need to take into account several components of aggression (e.g., frequency, intensity) as well as pragmatic issues that may affect implementation of assessment (e.g., time, cost, resources). Furthermore, the psychometrics of each method need to be researched further to determine which assessment provides the most accurate results. Vollmer, Marcus, Ringdahl, and Roane (1995) suggest progressing from using brief FBAs to more time-consuming labor-intensive assessments as needed to differentiate the function of the challenging behavior. This method, at present, provides the most parsimonious way of establishing maintaining variables.

## REFERENCES

Achenbach, T. (1991). *Manual for the Child Behavior Checklist and Revised Child Behavior Profile.* Burlington, VT: University Associates in Psychiatry.

Allen, D. (2000). Recent research on physical aggression in persons with intellectual disability: An overview. *Journal of Intellectual and Developmental Disability, 25,* 41–57.

Al-Salehi, S.M., Al-Hifthy, E.H., & Ghaziuddin, M. (2009). Autism in Saudi Arabia: Presentation, clinical correlates and comorbidity. *Transcultural Psychiatry, 46,* 340–347.

Antonacci, D.J., Manuel, C., & Davis, E. (2008). Diagnosis and treatment of aggression in individuals with developmental disabilities. *Psychiatric Quarterly, 79,* 225–247.

Applegate, H., Matson, J.L., & Cherry, K.E. (1999). An evaluation of functional variables affecting severe problem behaviors in adults with mental retardation by using the Questions about Behavioral Function scale (QABF). *Research in Developmental Disabilities, 20,* 229–237.

Bijou, S.W., Peterson, R.F., & Ault, M.H. (1968). A method to integrate descriptive and experimental field studies at the level of data and empirical concepts. *Journal of Applied Behavior Analysis, 1,* 175–191.

Braithewaite, K.L., & Richdale, A.L. (2000). Functional communication training to replace challenging behaviors across two behavioral outcomes. *Behavioral Interventions, 15,* 21–36.

Britton, L.N., Carr, J.E., Kellum, K.K., Dozier, C.L., & Weil, T.M. (2000). A variation of noncontingent reinforcement in the treatment of aberrant behavior. *Research in Developmental Disabilities, 21,* 425–435.

Calloway, C.J., & Simpson, R.L. (1998). Decisions regarding functions of behavior: Scientific versus informal analyses. *Focus on Autism and Other Developmental Disabilities, 13,* 167–175.

Campbell, J.M. (2003). Efficacy of behavioral interventions for reducing problem behavior in persons with autism: A quantitative synthesis of single-subject research. *Research in Developmental Disabilities, 24,* 120–138.

Campbell, M., Schopler, E., Cueva, J.E., & Hallin, A. (1996). Treatment of autistic disorder. *Journal of the American Academy of Child and Adolescent Psychiatry, 35,* 134–143.

Carr, E.G., Coriaty, S., Wilder, D.A., Gaunt, B.T., Dozier, C.L., Britton, L.A., et al. (2000). A review of "noncontingent" reinforcement as treatment for the aberrant behavior of individuals with developmental disabilities. *Research in Developmental Disabilities, 21,* 377–391.

Carr, E.G., & Durand, V.M. (1985). Reducing behavior problems through functional communication training. *Journal of Applied Behavior Analysis, 18,* 111–126.

Carr, E.G., Severtson, J.M., & Lepper, T.L. (2009). Noncontingent reinforcement is an empirically supported treatment for problem behavior exhibited by individuals with developmental disabilities. *Research in Developmental Disabilities, 30,* 44–57.

Cataldo, M.F., Ward, E.M., Russo, D.C., Riordan, M., & Bennett, D. (1986). Compliance and correlated problem behavior in children: Effects of contingent and noncontingent reinforcement. *Analysis and Intervention in Developmental Disabilities, 6,* 265–282.

Cooper, S.-A., Smiley, E., Jackson, A., Finlayson, J., Allan, L., Mantry, D., et al. (2009). Adults with intellectual disabilities: prevalence, incidence and remission of aggressive behaviour and related factors. *Journal of Intellectual Disability Research, 53,* 217–232.

Crocker, A.G., Mercier, C., Lachapelle, Y., Brunet, A., Morin, D., & Roy, M.-E. (2006). Prevalence and types of aggressive behaviour among adults with intellectual disabilities. *Journal of Intellectual Disability Research, 50,* 652–661.

Dawson, J.E., Matson, J.L., & Cherry, K.E. (1998). An analysis of maladaptive behaviors in persons with autism, PDD-NOS, and mental retardation. *Research in Developmental Disabilities, 19,* 439–448.

Day, H.M., Horner, R.H., & O'Neill, R.E. (1994). Multiple functions of problem behaviors: Assessment and intervention. *Journal of Applied Behavior Analysis, 27,* 279–289.

Didden, R. (2007). Functional analysis methodology in developmental disabilities. In P. Sturmey (Ed.), *Functional analysis in clinical treatment* (pp. 65–86). Burlington, MA: Academic Press.

Duker, P.C., & Sigafoos, J. (1998). The Motivation Assessment Scale: Reliability and construct validity across three topographies of behavior. *Research in Developmental Disabilities, 19,* 131–141.

Durand, V.M., & Crimmins, D.B. (1988). Identifying the variables maintaining self-injurious behavior. *Journal of Autism and Developmental Disorders, 18,* 99–117.

Durand, V.M., & Crimmins, D.B. (1992). *The Motivation Assessment Scale administrative guide.* Topeka, KS: Monaco & Associates.

Ellison, D.M. (1997). Compliance training decreases maladaptive behaviors in two people with developmental disabilities: Report of five years' treatment. *Behavioral Interventions, 12,* 183–194.

Embregts, P.J.C.M., Didden, R., Schreuder, N., Huitink, C., & van Nieuwenhuijzen. (2009). Aggressive behavior in individuals with moderate to borderline intellectual disabilities who live in a residential facility: An evaluation of functional variables. *Research in Developmental Disabilities, 30,* 682–688.

Emerson, E. (2005). *Challenging behaviour: Analysis and intervention with people with learning difficulties.* Cambridge: Cambridge University Press.

Furniss, F. (2009). Assessment methods. In J.L. Matson (Ed.), *Practitioner's guide to applied behavior analysis for children with autism spectrum disorders.* New York: Springer.

Gardner, W.I., & Moffatt, C.W. (1990). Aggressive behaviour: Definition, assessment, treatment. *International Review of Psychiatry, 2,* 91–100.

Ghaziuddin, M., Ghaziuddin, N., & Greden, J. (2002). Depression in persons with autism: Implications for research and clinical care. *Journal of Autism and Developmental Disorders, 32,* 299–306.

Ghaziuddin, M., Tsai, L., & Alessi, N. (1992). ADHD and PDD. *Journal of the American Academy of Child and Adolescent Psychiatry, 31,* 567.

Ghaziuddin, M., & Zafar, S. (2008). Psychiatric comorbidity of adults with autism spectrum disorders. *Clinical Neuropsychiatry: Journal of Treatment Evaluation, 5,* 9–12.

Gray, C. (1994). *The new Social Story book.* Arlington, TX: Future Horizons.

Gray, C. (2000). *Writing Social Stories with Carol Gray.* Arlington, TX: Future Horizons.

Gray, C., & Garand, J. (1993). Social Stories: Improving responses of students with autism with accurate social information. *Focus on Autistic Behavior, 8,* 1–10.

Hartley, S.L., Sikora, D.M., & McCoy, R. (2008). Prevalence and risk factors of maladaptive behaviour in young children with autistic disorder. *Journal of Intellectual Disability Research, 52,* 819–829.

Iwata, B.A., Dorsey, M.F., Slifer, K.J., Bauman, K.E., & Richman, G.S. (1982). Toward a functional analysis of self-injury. *Analysis and Intervention in Developmental Disabilities, 2,* 3–20.

Johnson, C.R. (2002). Functional communication training. In M. Hersen & W. Sledge (Eds.), *Encyclopedia of psychotherapy* (pp. 847–852). New York: Academic Press.

Johnson, L., McComas, J., Thompson, A., & Symons, F.J. (2004). Obtained versus programmed reinforcement: Practical considerations in the treatment of escape-reinforced aggression. *Journal of Applied Behavior Analysis, 37,* 239–242.

Joosten, A.V., & Bundy, A.C. (2008). The motivation of stereotypic and repetitive behavior: Examination of construct validity of the Motivation Assessment Scale. *Journal of Autism and Developmental Disorders, 38,* 1341–1348.

Luiselli, J.K., & Slocumb, P.R. (1983). Management of multiple aggressive behaviors by differential reinforcement. *Journal of Behavior Therapy and Experimental Psychiatry, 14,* 343–347.

Mace, F.C., Hock, M.L., Lalli, J.S., West, B.J., Belfiore, P., Pinter, E., & Brown, D.K. (1988). Behavioral momentum in the treatment of noncompliance. *Journal of Applied Behavior Analysis, 21,* 123–141.

Marcus, B.A., Vollmer, T.R., Swanson, V., Roane, H.R., & Ringdahl, J.E. (2001). An experimental analysis of aggression. *Behavior Modification, 25,* 189–213.

Martin, N.T., Gaffan, E.A., & Williams, T. (1999). Experimental functional analyses for challenging behavior: A study of validity and reliability. *Research in Developmental Disabilities, 20,* 125–146.

Matson, J.L. (1995). *Diagnostic Assessment for the Severely Handicapped-II (DASH-II).* Baton Rouge, LA: Disability Consultants, LLC.

Matson, J.L. (1997). *Assessment of Dual Diagnosis (ADD).* Baton Rouge, LA: Disability Consultants, LLC.

Matson, J.L., Bamburg, J.W., Cherry, K.E., & Paclawskyj, T.R. (1999). A validity study on the Questions about Behavioral Function (QABF) scale: Predicting treatment success for self-injury, aggression, and stereotypies. *Research in Developmental Disabilities, 20,* 163–176.

Matson, J.L., Boisjoli, J., & Wilkins, J. (2007). *Baby and Infant Screen for Children with Autism Traits (BISCUIT).* Baton Rouge, LA: Disability Consultants, LLC.

Matson, J.L., Fodstad, J.C., Neal, D., Dempsey, T., & Rivet, T.T. (2010). Risk factors for tardive dyskinesia in adults with intellectual disability, comorbid psychopathology, and long-term psychotropic use. *Research in Developmental Disabilities, 31,* 108–116.

Matson, J.L., & González, M.L. (2007). *Autism Spectrum Disorders-Comorbidity-Child Version.* Baton Rouge, LA: Disability Consultants, LLC.

Matson, J.L., Kuhn, D.E., Dixon, D.R., Mayville, S.B., Laud, R.B., Cooper, C.L., et al. (2003). The development and factor structure of the Functional Assessment for multiple CausaliTy (FACT). *Research in Developmental Disabilities, 24,* 485–495.

Matson, J.L., & Minshawi, N.F. (2007). Functional assessment of challenging behavior: Toward a strategy for applied settings. *Research in Developmental Disabilities, 28,* 353–361.

Matson, J.L., & Neal, D. (2009). Psychotropic medication use for challenging behaviors in persons with intellectual disabilities: An overview. *Research in Developmental Disabilities, 30,* 572–586.

Matson, J.L., & Rivet, T.T. (2008). Characteristics of challenging behaviours in adults with autistic disorder, PDD-NOS, and intellectual disability. *Journal of Intellectual and Developmental Disability, 33,* 323–329.

Matson, J.L., Terlonge, C., & González, M.L., (2006). *Autism Spectrum Disorders-Comorbidity-Adult Version.* Baton Rouge, LA: Disability Consultants, LLC.

Matson, J.L., & Vollmer, T. (1995). *Questions About Behavioral Function (QABF).* Baton Rouge, LA: Disability Consultants, LLC.

Matson, J.L., Wilkins, J., & Macken, J. (2009). The relationship of challenging behaviors to severity and symptoms of autism spectrum disorders. *Journal of Mental Health Research in Intellectual Disabilities, 2,* 29–44.

Montes, G., & Halterman, J.S. (2007). Bullying among children with autism and the influence of comorbidity with ADHD: A population-based study. *Ambulatory Pediatrics, 7,* 253–257.

Mudford, O.C., Arnold-Saritepe, A.M., Phillips, K.J., Locke, J.M., Ho, I.C.S., & Taylor, S.A. (2008). Challenging behaviors. In J.L. Matson (Ed.), *Clinical assessment and intervention for autism spectrum disorders* (pp. 267–297). London: Elsevier Inc.

Newman, S.S., & Ghaziuddin, M. (2008). Violent crime in Asperger syndrome: The role of psychiatric comorbidity. *Journal of Autism and Developmental Disorders, 38,* 1848–1852.

Newton, J.T., & Sturmey, P. (1991). The Motivation Assessment Scale: Interrater reliability and internal consistency in a British sample. *Journal of Mental Deficiency Research, 35,* 472–474.

Nicholson, J., Konstantinidi, E., & Furniss, F. (2006). On some psychometric properties of the Questions About Behavioral Function (QABF) scale. *Research in Developmental Disabilities, 27,* 337–352.

O'Reilly, M.F. (1995). Functional analysis and treatment of escape-maintained aggression correlated with sleep deprivation. *Journal of Applied Behavior Analysis, 28,* 225–226.

O'Reilly, M., Rispoli, M., Davis, T., Machalicek, W., Lang, R., Sigafoos, J., et al. (2010). Functional analysis of challenging behavior in children with autism spectrum disorders: A summary of 10 cases. *Research in Autism Spectrum Disorders, 4,* 1–10.

Paclawskyj, T.R., Matson, J.L., Rush, K.S., Smalls, Y., & Vollmer, T.R. (2000). Questions About Behavioral Function (QABF): A behavioral checklist for functional assessment of aberrant behavior. *Research in Developmental Disabilities, 21,* 223–229.

Paclawskyj, T.R., Matson, J.L., Rush, K.S., Smalls, Y., & Vollmer, T.R. (2001). Assessment of the convergent validity of the Questions About Behavioral Function scale with analogue functional analysis and the Motivation Assessment Scale. *Journal of Intellectual Disability Research, 45,* 484–494.

Parrish, J.M., Cataldo, M.F., Kolko, D.J., Neef, N.A., & Egel, A.L. (1986). Experimental analysis of response covariations among compliant and inappropriate behaviors. *Journal of Applied Behavior Analysis, 19,* 241–254.

Petscher, E.S., Rey, C., & Bailey, J.S. (2009). A review of empirical support for differential reinforcement of alternative behavior. *Research in Developmental Disabilities, 30,* 409–425.

Piazza, C.C., Hanley, G.P., Fisher, W.W., Ruyter, J.M., & Gulotta, C.S. (1998). On the establishing and reinforcing effects of termination of demands for destructive behavior maintained by positive and negative reinforcement. *Research in Developmental Disabilities, 19,* 395–407.

Posey, D.J., Stigler, K.A., Erickson, C.A., & McDougle, C.J. (2008). Antipsychotics in the treatment of autism. *Journal of Clinical Investigation, 118,* 6–14.

Provenzano, G., & Mantia, G. (2008). Psychopharmacology in pre-school and school-age children. *Acta Medica Mediterranea, 24,* 109–112.

Reaven, J.A. (2009). Children with high-functioning autism spectrum disorders and co-occurring anxiety symptoms: Implications for assessment and treatment. *Journal for Specialists in Pediatric Nursing, 14,* 192–199.

Reynolds, C.R., & Kamphaus, R.W. (1992). *Behavior assessment system for children(ital) (2nd ed.).* Bloomington, MN: Pearson.

Ringdahl, J.E., Call, N.A., Mews, J.B., Boelter, E.W., & Christensen, T.J. (2008). Assessment and treatment of aggressive behavior without a clear social function. *Research in Developmental Disabilities, 29,* 351–362.

Rojahn, J., Schroeder, S.R., & Hoch, T.A. (2008). *Self-injurious behavior in intellectual disabilities.* Amsterdam: Elsevier.

Romano, J.P., & Roll, D. (2000). Expanding the utility of behavioral momentum for youth with developmental disabilities. *Behavioral Interventions, 15,* 99–111.

Shogren, K.A., & Rojahn, J. (2003). Convergent reliability and validity of the Questions About Behavioral Function and the Motivation Assessment Scale: A replication study. *Journal of Developmental and Physical Disabilities, 15,* 367–375.

Sigafoos, J., Kerr, M., & Roberts, D. (1994). Interrater reliability of the motivation assessment scale: Failure to replicate with aggressive behavior. *Research in Developmental Disabilities, 15,* 333–342.

Singh, A.N., Matson, J.L., Mouttapa, M., Pella, R.D., Hill, B.D., & Thorson, R. (2009). A critical item analysis of the QABF: Development of a short form assessment instrument. *Research in Developmental Disabilities, 30,* 782–792.

Sturmey, P., Seiverling, L., & Ward-Horner, J. (2008). Assessment of challenging behaviors in people with autism spectrum disorders. In J.L. Matson (Ed.), *Clinical assessment and intervention for autism spectrum disorders* (pp. 131–163). London: Elsevier, Inc.

Swaggart, B.L., & Gagnon, E. (1995). Using social stories to teach social and behavioral skills to children with autism. *Focus on Autistic Behavior, 10,* 1–16.

Tarbox, J., Wilke, A.E., Najdowski, A.C., Findel-Pyles, R.S., Balasanyan, S., Caveney, A.C., et al. (2009). Comparing indirect, descriptive, and experimental functional assessments of challenging behavior in children with autism. *Journal of Developmental and Physical Disabilities, 21,* 493–514.

Tenneij, N.H., & Koot, H.M. (2008). Incidence, types and characteristics of aggressive behaviour in treatment facilities for adults with mild intellectual disability and severe challenging behaviour. *Journal of Intellectual Disability Research, 52,* 114–124.

Thompson, R.H., Fisher, W.W., Piazza, C.C., & Kuhn, D.E. (1998). The evaluation and treatment of aggression maintained by attention and automatic reinforcement. *Journal of Applied Behavior Analysis, 31,* 103–116.

Thompson, R.H., & Iwata, B.A. (2001). A descriptive analysis of social consequences following problem behavior. *Journal of Applied Behavior Analysis, 34,* 169–178.

Toogood, S., & Timlin, K. (1996). The functional assessment of challenging behaviour: A comparison of informant-based, experimental and descriptive methods. *Journal of Applied Research in Intellectual Disabilities, 9,* 206–222.

Touchette, P.E., MacDonald, R.F., & Langer, S.N. (1985). A scatter plot for identifying stimulus control of problem behavior. *Journal of Applied Behavior Analysis, 18,* 343–351.

Tyrer, F., McGrother, C.W., Thorp, C.F., Donaldson, M., Bhaumik, S., Watson, J.M., et al. (2006). Physical aggression towards others in adults with learning disabilities: Prevalence and associated factors. *Journal of Intellectual Disability Research, 50*, 295–304.

Tyrer, P., Oliver-Africano, P.C., Ahmed, Z., Bouras, N., Cooray, S., Deb, S., et al. (2008). Risperidone, haloperidol, and placebo in the treatment of aggressive challenging behaviour in patients with intellectual disability: A randomised controlled trial. *Lancet, 371*, 57–63.

Van Camp, C.M., Lerman, D.C., Kelley, M.E., Contrucci, S.A., & Vorndran, C.M. (2000). Variable-time reinforcement schedules in the treatment of socially maintained problem behavior. *Journal of Applied Behavior Analysis, 33*, 545–557.

Vollmer, T.R., Borrero, J.C., Wright, C.S., Van Camp, C., & Lalli, J.S. (2001). Identifying possible contingencies during descriptive analyses of severe behavior disorders. *Journal of Applied Behavior Analysis, 34*, 269–287.

Vollmer, T.R., Iwata, B.A., Smith, R.G., & Rodgers, T.A. (1992). Reduction of multiple aberrant behaviors and concurrent development of self-care skills with differential reinforcement. *Research in Developmental Disabilities, 13*, 287–299.

Vollmer, T.R., Marcus, B.A., Ringdahl, J.E., & Roane, H.S. (1995). Progressing from brief assessments to extended experimental analyses in the evaluation of aberrant behavior. *Journal of Applied Behavior Analysis, 28*, 561–576.

Zarcone, J.R., Rodgers, T.A., Iwata, B.A., Rourke, D.A., & Dorsey, M.F. (1991). Reliability analysis of the Motivation Assessment Scale: A failure to replicate. *Research in Developmental Disabilities, 12*, 349–360.

# Biopsychosocial Features Influencing Aggression

CHAPTER

## A Multimodal Assessment and Therapy Approach

*William I. Gardner,*
*Dorothy M. Griffiths, and Jeffery P. Hamelin*

• • • • • • • • • • • • • • • • • • • • • • • • • • • • • • • • • • • • • • • • • • • • • • • • •

Tomas Cordosa, a 16-year-old youth with mild cognitive disabilities, resides in a group home for juvenile male offenders with recurring behavior difficulties. A recent episode involving one of his peers during a social skills training table game illustrates Tomas's inclination to impulsive aggression under conditions of provocation. Jay, one of four peers involved in the activity, called Tomas a "retard" when he was unable to complete a segment of the table game. Tomas immediately retorted with "I'll bust your mouth" as he jumped across the table and punched the peer in the face. Staff terminated the training session and escorted the peer to the staff office to tend to his injury. Tomas continued to yell repeatedly "I'm no retard" as staff redirected him into another area in the day room.

This chapter describes a triadic mental health therapy approach (TMHTA) to address recurring problems of aggression similar to those presented by Tomas. Specific therapy targets consist of interrelated triads of "*emotional/motivational → cognitive → behavioral*" components selected following comprehensive assessment of the biopsychosocial influences presumed to control a person's aggressive responding. Therapy approaches are selected to reduce or eliminate the problem triads and to replace these with competency alternatives.

## RATIONALE FOR A MULTIMODAL CASE FORMULATION

As background for description of the TMHTA, we present the rationale and features of a multimodal contextual case formulation from which the triads of therapy targets and related therapy procedures are derived. It is well documented that recurring difficulties involving aggressive and related agitated/disruptive behaviors presented by people with intellectual and developmental disabilities (IDD) may reflect the current influence of a range of *psychiatric* (Hemmings, 2007; Tuinier & Verhoeven, 1993), *neurological* (Barnhill, 1999; Sovner, Foxx, Lowry, & Lowry, 1993), *genetic* (Taylor & Oliver, 2008; Woodcock, Oliver, & Humphreys, 2009*), physical illness and chronic disease* (Carr & Owen-DeSchryer, 2007; Gardner & Whalen, 1996; Oeseburg, Jasen, Groothoff, Dijkstra, & Reijneveld, 2009), *psychological* (Carr, Levin, McConnachie, Carlson, Kemp, & Smith, 1994; Chiang, 2008; Gardner, 2002a), and *environmental* (Embregts, Didden, Huitink, & Schreuder, 2009; Tsiouris, 2001) conditions.

Seldom if ever does any single one of these conditions controlling aggressive responding occur in isolation from other conditions. Instead, these conditions most frequently occur in clusters and thus represent individually unique influences that, in interactive combination, control acts of aggression (Feldman, Condillac, Tough, Hunt, & Griffiths, 2002). When present, these conditions may serve to initiate (Embregts et al., 2009), may contribute to increase severity level (Gardner, 2002a), and, when aspects of these are changed following acts of aggression, may contribute to the likelihood of recurrence (Matson, Bamburg, Cherry, & Paclawskyj, 1999). These transactional relationships require that clinical practices involving assessment, and related interpretations of assessment results, be guided by an integrative bio-psychosocial case formulation to insure adequate attention to these possible multiple sources of influence.

## EFFECTS OF CASE FORMULATION ON CLINICAL PRACTICE

Review of the clinical and research literatures reveals reports of various case formulations and resulting treatment modalities for serious behavioral difficulties in people with IDD. These include case formulations associated with medical, psychiatric, genetic, psychological, developmental, behavior analytic, and various combinations. On examination of these, Gardner and Griffiths (2004) noted that the suppositions held by a clinician relative to the specific types of conditions that control occurrence of aggressive responding not only influence selection of a specific case formulation model but also determine the 1) assessment targets, 2) procedures used to gather assessment information as well as the 3) particular interpretations given assessment results. The assessment results obtained and the subsequent interpretation of these in turn influence both the specific *treatment objectives* and the *treatment and management procedures* selected to address the conditions identified as controlling various features of a person's aggressive acts.

It is unusual, as suggested previously, that recurring problems of aggression reflect a direct relationship to the presence, or absence, of a single set of conditions such as a psychiatric condition (e.g., mood disorder), a social condition (e.g., provocative peer), or a psychological condition (e.g., cognitive distortion). The nature and degree of influence of each may be modified significantly by the presence of other conditions that interact with these.

To illustrate these additive and interactive effects, psychiatric conditions such as schizophrenia or bipolar disorder may result in changes in cognitive functions, mood and affective states, emotional regulation, and psychomotor behaviors. These changing psychological and physical characteristics may influence occurrence of new behavioral or emotional difficulties or may contribute to occurrence or increased severity of problems that predated a current psychiatric episode (Lowry & Sovner, 1992). These symptoms in turn create more than usual changes in the manner in which the social environment responds to and interacts with the person and the problems that may occur (Dosen, Gardner, Griffiths, King, & Lapointe, 2007). These experiences with the social environment may, in a reciprocal manner, strengthen the problem behaviors or intensify the emotional arousal and the person's perceptions of the social feedback. An effective therapy program must be responsive to these complex interrelationships and provide attention to each set of influences (Gardner, Dosen, Griffiths, & King, 2006).

As a second example of the interactive effect, a person with a functional behavioral repertoire that includes a number of competency alternatives to aggressive acts may indeed decrease aggression by substituting functionally alternative acts under therapy conditions of contingent withdrawal of maintaining reinforcing events following aggressive acts. However, a person with a paucity of alternative coping behaviors in his or her skill repertoire, while perhaps demonstrating reduction in aggressive responding under similar changing reinforcement conditions, may be left without a coping functional alternative when confronted with similar distress-producing events in the future (Gardner, 2002b).

A diagnostic and related treatment case formulation approach thus often is desired that reflects the complex of antecedent instigating conditions, the individually specific manner in which these are mediated and potentially influenced by personal biomedical and psychological characteristics, and the possible interactions among these. To elaborate, this diagnostic case formulation should consider 1) the *salient environmental, psychological, and biomedical stimulus conditions* (i.e., conditions that create various levels of personal distress) that precede and serve to initiate and maintain the chain of events ending in specific episodes of behavioral acts, 2) the person's current biomedical and psychological *central processing* features that mediate and thus may serve either as risk/vulnerabilities or as immunities for engaging in these behavioral acts when confronted with an antecedent activating stimulus complex, as well as 3) proximate *consequences* that follow occurrences of behavioral challenges and, in combination with a current person's motivational conditions, determine the functionality and future strength of the resulting behaviors.

As noted, the antecedent stimulus complex may include the arousing and activating features of a range of external physical and social environmental as well as internal psychological and biomedical conditions. Embregts et al. (2009) provide a lengthy laundry listing of events that serve as precursors to aggressive activity. Gardner and colleagues (Gardner, Cole, Davidson, & Karan, 1986; Gardner, Karan, & Cole, 1984) demonstrated the individual nature of these antecedents and how specific events when combined with other environmental and biopsychological events significantly increased, or decreased, the conditional probability of aggressive responding. Thus these antecedent stimulus conditions are processed centrally, both neurochemically and psychologically, and subsequently transported into the motor tract as behavioral expressions that in most instances serve as coping actions (Bradley, 2000; Gardner, Watson, & Nania, 2004; Ratey, 2001).

## MULTIMODAL CONTEXTUAL CASE FORMULATION

Gardner and colleagues describe one such case formulation approach that reflects the complex of interactive influences (Gardner, 1996, 2002a; Gardner et al., 2006; Gardner & Sovner, 1994). This multimodal (*bio-*, *psycho-*, and *socioenvironmental* modalities of influences), contextual (*instigating, central processing*, and *maintaining* conditions that may involve multiple modalities of influence), case formulation approach directs the clinician to evaluate both psychosocial and biomedical conditions as possible contributors to occurrence, severity, variability, and habitual recurrence of aggressive acts. This model also provides a means of combining various medical and psychiatric diagnostic insights and related diagnostically based interventions with those that involve psychological and environmental influences.

### Context 1: Instigating Influences

Instigating influences consist of current external (e.g., instructional demands, conflict with peers, blocking by staff of ritualistic or compulsive routines, staff corrective feedback, invasion of personal space) and internal (e.g., high arousal level, anger, pain-related distress, deprivation states, dysphoric mood) stimulus conditions that contribute to the occurrence, severity levels, and variability of specific aggressive and related disruptive episodes (Benson & Fuchs, 1999; Carr & Durand, 1985; Lowry & Sovner, 1992; Tsiouris, 2001). These instigating stimulus conditions are relatively varied and highly specific to each person and, when present, represent risk factors to that person for initiating occurrence and related features (e.g., severity, variability) of incidents of aggressive responding (McComas, Hoch, Paone, & El-Roy, 2000). Similar stimulus conditions may not represent risk factors for aggressive responding in other people. As noted, it is not unusual for these controlling antecedent conditions to consist of combinations of psychosocial and biomedical influences that vary significantly among individuals.

### Context 2: Central Processing Influences

Central processing influences refer to personal features of a biomedical and psychological nature that place a person at increased risk for aggressive behaviors (Gardner 2002a, Dosen et al., 2007). These mediating features determine the influence on occurrence, severity, and variability of aggression of specific antecedent conditions such as a hostile postural manner of a peer (Gardner et al., 1984), unwanted staff directives (Tsiouris, 2001), an environment that provides insufficient social attention or opportunities for social interactions (Embregts et al., 2009), presence of a female (Lindsay, Marshall, Neilson, Quinn, & Smith, 1998), or a demanding work supervisor (Cole, Gardner, & Karan, 1985). Examination of central processing influences may suggest why one person is at increased risk for behavioral challenges involving aggression when another person is at minimal or no risk when both are exposed to these or similar antecedent conditions (e.g., Baker & Bramston, 1997; Fuchs & Benson, 1995).

### Classes of Personal Risk Conditions

Two major categories of central processing features that place a person at increased risk for behavioral challenges are of particular significance. A person's level of risk for aggressive responding when exposed to individually specific conditions of instigation is related to the type, number, and strength of these central processing vulnerability features (Gardner, 2002a).

***Psychobiological***   The initial major category consists of *psychobiological* features involving 1) neurological and related neurochemical abnormalities (Dosen et al., 2007; Barnhill, 1999), 2) psychiatric disorders and symptoms (Sovner & Lowry, 2001; Tuinier & Verhoeven, 1993), 3) other medical abnormalities (Gedye, 1997; Kastner, Walsh, & Fraser, 2001), and 4) genetic syndromes (Dykens, Hodapp, & Finucane, 2000; Woodcock et al., 2009) that influence the manner in which antecedent activating events are mediated by an individual and the transactions that may occur between these classes of events (Gardner 2002a).

More specifically, features such as an inclination for generalized affective arousal (hyperexcitability, hyperirritability) even to seemingly minor conditions of social or physical threat or provocation, impairments in the processes of modulating states of overarousal with the result that the person remains in an overaroused state for extended periods, and impairments in skills of inhibiting exaggerated impulsive aggressive reactions are present with increased frequency and severity among people with more severe cognitive and adaptive behavior limitations (Sovner & Fogelman, 1996). Similar personal features also are reported in people with intellectual disabilities who present with various psychiatric and personality disorders (Bradley, 2000; Mavromatis, 2000; Reiss, 1994).

People with psychiatric disorders also present with other more discrete features that may serve as mediating risk influences on aggressive responding. Various mood/affective (e.g., irritability, dysphoria, anxiety, emotional agitation), cognitive (e.g., delusional thought processes, flights of ideas), perceptual (e.g., auditory and visual hallucinations), and related symptoms associated with major mental disorders and various personality disorders and traits may influence the meaning or function of instigating stimulus events. To illustrate, a person may have a tendency to view the actions of others in a paranoid or hostile manner. Others and their actions or intent are viewed with suspicion and mistrust. These and similar paranoid traits are reported to occur with some frequency in people with intellectual disabilities who engage in disruptive behaviors (Bouras & Drummond, 1992; Reiss, 1990). This cognitive view of the actions of others will influence the information-processing activities involved in encoding and interpreting social events. This impaired cognitive-perceptual set interferes with the selection and evaluation of alternative means of coping with the perceived sources of threat. These, in combination with a strong habit of aggressive responding, are likely to be processed into an impulsive aggressive act in a coping attempt to reduce or remove the presumed source of threat (Benson, 2002; Taylor, 2002). This scenario emphasizes the dynamic transactions between instigating and central processing features.

***Psychological: Presence or Excessive Nature***    The second major category of central processing risk conditions consists of two groups of *psychological* features. The initial group, consisting of personal features of a cognitive, emotional/motivational, and behavioral nature, represents vulnerabilities for occurrence of aberrant responding due to their *presence or excessive* nature. This initial group is illustrated by such personal features as 1) presence of a strong habit of responding in an aggressive manner to distress-producing conditions, 2) cognitive abnormalities such as a cognitive hostile attributional bias (Baker & Bramston, 1997) or the presence of cognitive distortions (Lindsay et al., 1998), and 3) motivational aberrations such as a motivational inclination to enjoy sexual contact with children (Griffiths, 2002).

A person's *habit strength* of acts of aggression and related disruptive responding illustrates the role that psychological characteristics assume both in determining the effects of specific antecedent events as well as the manner in which assessment information about these personal characteristics influences clinical decisions concerning treatment selection. The effectiveness of interventions, whether a specific procedure such as extinction or a treatment package with multiple components, is determined both by the habit strength of aggressive responding as well as the presence and relative strength of functional alternatives to aggressive responding currently in the person's repertoire.

Specific interventions may be quite effective when used with an individual with low habit strength of aggressive responding and who also has behavioral alternatives to address the instigating motivational condition. The same intervention procedures or packages of procedures may be relatively ineffective when used with a person whose habit strength is quite high and who has minimal functional prosocial coping alternatives available for use. Bradley (2000) suggested that, following repeated acts as aggression, neural circuits are changed and thus are more resistant to treatment effects. Vlitiello, Behar, Hunt, Stoff, and Ricciuti (1990) offered similar observations in their supposition that impulsive aggression associated with emotional states of fear or anger toward conditions of provocation may be more neurologically "hardwired" and become more automatic and habitually used. As a result, more powerful interventions provided over repeated therapy experiences would be required for significant and enduring reduction in habit strength and successful replacement of the behavioral challenges with functionally appropriate behaviors.

In sum, consideration of habit strength, the presence and strength of functional alternatives, related motivational features, and similar current psychological features require a case formulation approach that considers these in selection of interventions and in speculation both about the potential effectiveness of specific interventions as well as the relative number and duration of therapy experiences required prior to expecting durable treatment effects.

***Psychological: Functional Absence or Low Strength*** A second grouping of psychological central processing features places the person at risk for occurrence of aggressive responding as a result of the *functional absence or low strength* of these. These features include such areas as 1) anger management skill deficits (Benson, Rice, & Miranti, 1986; Cole, Gardner et al., 1985), 2) relaxation skill deficits (To & Chan, 2000), 3) communication skill deficits (Bird, Dores, Moniz, & Robinson, 1989; Carr et al., 1994), 4) problem solving skill deficits (Benson, 2002), 5) deficits in prosocial skill alternatives to aberrant responding (Fredericks & Nishioka-Evans, 1999), 6) deficits in skills of self-regulating personal emotional and behavioral features (Cole, Gardner et al., 1985; Gardner, 1998, 2005; Gardner & Cole, 1989), and 7) deficits in significant components of a person's socialized motivational system (Gardner, 2002a).

These personal features increase the risk of aggressive responding when a person with an inclination to use aggression as coping responses is exposed to conditions of provocation that require the deficit psychological features for alternative socially appropriate action. To illustrate, a person with a communication skill deficit who is inclined to use aggression to cope with distress-producing conditions is at increased risk for these behaviors when exposed to situations that require some form of expressive communication. Under these conditions, acts of aggression may serve a communicative function in producing valued consequences (Carr & Durand, 1985; Carr et al., 1994; Schroeder, Reese, Hellings, Loupe, & Tessel, 1999).

Other people with a strong inclination to engage in aggressive acts under specific instigating conditions may have no functionally adequate prosocial coping alternative to aggressive responding. Under these circumstances, a number of writers have reported significant reduction of aggression following teaching of a range of coping alternatives. Singh, Wahler, Adkins, Myers, and the Mindfulness Research Group (2003) report reduction of aggression after teaching a mediating cognitive sequence that effectively interrupted the cognitive focus that resulted in anger, a precursor to aggression. In the initial demonstration, a self-controlling strategy was taught to an adult with IDD and mental illness whose aggressive behaviors had precluded successful community placement. Treatment consisted of teaching a simple mediation technique that required the adult to shift his attention and awareness from an anger-producing situation to the soles of his feet. After learning this technique, the adult was guided to use it in situations that normally resulted in heightened anger arousal and aggressive acts. This self-controlling technique resulted in 6 months of aggression-free behavior at which time the man was transitioned to the community. No acts of aggression were reported during a 1-year follow-up.

This mindfulness procedure with modifications was repeated with three adults with moderate IDD and significant problems of aggression. Following intervention, problem behaviors decreased and were maintained over a 2-year period (Singh et al., 2007).

It is not unusual for a combination of different central processing features to contribute to a person's aggressive responding. As illustration, when an intrusive peer violates his personal space, an adult with severe cognitive impairments may respond immediately with a sudden surge in emotional and motor agitation followed by impulsive acts of face slapping and physical aggression. Under these conditions of instigation, the adult has a number of personal characteristics that place him at high risk for disruptive responding. These include such features as an inclination to become hyperaroused under minor conditions of instigation, limited effective socially appropriate communicative means of expressing his distress, an impaired emotional modulation system, a strong habit of disruptive responding under conditions of distress, and limited cognitive and affective skills to inhibit these destructive acts (Gardner, 2002b).

A number of writers have report treatment success with addressing at least two interrelated components of the cognitive-emotional-behavior triad (Benson, 1992, 2002; Benson et al., 1986; Chapman, Shedlack, & France, 2006; Lindsay et al., 2004; Taylor, 2002, 2009; Thorne, 2005). In illustration, Chapman et al. (2006) used a self-control technique with three adults who presented with psychiatric illness and a range of aggressive and related disruptive behaviors. Each person was taught a Stop–Think–Relax cognitive sequence when experiencing anger or increased anxiety that typically led to impulsive disruptive acts. After acquiring these self-controlling skills, each person demonstrated a reduced likelihood of engaging in impulsive acts when confronted with previous conditions that produced heightened anger or anxiety. Benson and colleagues (1992, 2002), describe an anger management program (AMP) in reducing aggressive responding with people with mild to moderate intellectual disabilities. The AMP recognizes the interactive effects of feeling-thinking-doing (Benson, 2002), and addresses each in treatment components devoted to identifying emotions, relaxation training, self-instructional training, and problem solving skills involving competency alternatives to aggression. Benson et al. (1986) report success with the AMP in use with groups of adults with mental retardation and difficulties of conduct.

Cole et al. (1985) and Cole, Pflugard, Gardner, and Karan (1985) describe a comprehensive self-management training program that addresses individualized interrelated emotional/motivational, cognitive, and behavioral components involved in chronic aggressive behaviors in a group of adults with intellectual disabilities and coexisting psychiatric issues. These and related studies (Gardner, Clees, & Cole, 1983; Gardner, Cole, Berry, & Nowinski, 1983; Gardner et al., 1986) provided the conceptual and empirical background for evolution of the TMHTA. Each of these studies involved people with mild to moderate intellectual disabilities that presented chronic problems of impulsive aggression and related conduct difficulties. The problem cognitive-emotional/motivational-behavioral triads were used to construct alternative triads of competencies that served as functional replacements. To ensure generalization of gains made in individual therapy sessions, each study also provided and gradually faded therapeutic supports in situ sessions.

In the initial study (Gardner, Cole et al., 1983), a self-management therapy package was used with two adults who displayed high-rate verbal (teasing, taunting, swearing, name calling, threatening, yelling) and physical aggression during attendance at a vocational training program. Following baseline conditions in which the two adults received social praise and monetary reinforcement for displaying positive affect, ignoring provocative behaviors of peers, working quietly, being on task, and following staff directives, each adult was provided self-management training, initially in a training room and later, to ensure generalization of newly acquired skills, in the work setting. In therapy, each adult was taught to discriminate between occurrence of the previously demonstrated inappropriate actions and suitable replacement prosocial actions. Trainer modeling and role-play procedures were used in this discrimination training. The adult was next taught to self-evaluate his own actions as "adult behavior" or "not adult behavior." Behaviors relevant to each person's history of inappropriate actions were modeled and followed by prompting the adult to role-play appropriate and inappropriate responses to each and to self-evaluate his actions. To assist with this training, a card was used with a colored photograph of the person smiling pasted on one side (labeled "Adult Behavior"). The flip side of the card contained a photograph of the person with an angry frown (labeled "Not Adult Behavior"). Additional modeling and role-playing experiences were provided as the adult used the card to distinguish appropriate versus inappropriate ways to respond to sources of provocation. Specific training was provided in self-instructional training to ensure that each adult self-initiated occurrence of prosocial alternatives. Finally, each adult was taught to "self-consequate" his or her own behavior via learning to deliver monetary rewards following a period of appropriate adult behavior.

After acquiring self-management skills and practicing these in situ, each adult was provided a timer and taught to set the timer for a designated period of time. The adult was provided a choice of engaging in "Adult Behavior" as a means of earning money. On occurrence of inappropriate behaviors, the adult was prompted to stop the timer and flip the picture card to the "Not Adult Behavior" photo. During this work delay, no money was earned. The trainer prompted rehearsal of alternative ways of responding to the source of provocation and informed the adult that whenever he was ready to resume work, the card could be flipped to the "Adult Behavior" photo, timer reset, and work resumed. Trainer prompts were gradually faded. Training replacement competency triads via the self-management therapy package involving self-monitoring, self-evaluation, self-consequation, and self-instruction of appropriate competency alternatives resulted in an immediate and significant reduction in the disruptive behaviors. Therapy gains were maintained during a fading period and at 6-months follow-up.

A second study by Gardner, Clees et al. (1983) evaluated a similar self-management treatment package with a focus on changing disruptive behaviors and replacing these with triads of prosocial alternatives. High-rate disruptive vocalizations of a man with moderate intellectual disabilities while attending a vocational training program represented the target of concern. The content, frequency, and volume of these disruptive verbal behaviors produced agitated/disruptive reactions from peers requiring staff intervention. Following intervention, disruptive verbalizations reduced to near-zero level and were maintained through fading of the treatment package and at 6- and 12-month follow-up. In a third study (Cole, Gardner et al., 1985), the treatment package was successful in treatment of six adults with mild to moderate intellectual disabilities who displayed chronic and severe behavioral/emotional difficulties. Triads selected for intervention were individualized. In addition to the therapy program described previously, more detailed self-instructional and emotional desensitization therapies were provided via use of video and audio presentations of provocative situations. Staff modeling and client rehearsal of inappropriate and alternative cognitive-emotional-behavioral triads were included. During rehearsal, duration and intensity of the simulated provocation were increased gradually with client encouraged to use subvocal self-instruction of alternative ways of thinking-feeling-behaving. Following the individualized therapy sessions, each person was provided in situ training with frequent encouragement to self-instruct and rehearse desired coping alternatives under conditions of provocation. Following therapy, immediate and clinically significant reductions in severe conduct difficulties were obtained in all six people. Nine-month follow-up under different work conditions revealed continued maintenance of treatment gains.

## Context 3: Maintaining Conditions

As noted, aggressive acts in most instances become functional for a person based on the type of feedback effects of these behaviors. Aggressive acts may result in the removal (termination), reduction, or avoidance of internal or external stimulus conditions that are experienced by the person as distressful, unpleasant, or aversive (e.g., anxiety level, taunts from peers, attempts by others to block occurrence of compulsive or ritualistic behavior, parent criticism, unwanted teacher directives) or may reduce states of deprivation through producing, maintaining, or magnifying internal or external conditions experienced as pleasant or emotionally desirable (e.g., gaining social attention; gaining access to physical, cognitive, or sensory stimulating activities; being included in a valued peer group; creating distress in others) (Carr et al., 1994; Thompson & Symonds, 1999).

A specific contingent consequence serves to strengthen acts of aggression to the extent that the behavioral consequence addresses either the specific motivation state giving impetus to the behavior or an equally or more powerful unmet motivational state. A motivational analysis thus represents a process of identifying individually salient motivational states → consequences dyads. Gardner (1971, 1977, 2002a, 2007) and Reiss and Havercamp (1997, 1998) describe a number of aberrant motivational features of people with IDD that may require attention in this analysis, especially in people with significant mental health concerns. These become relevant to a specific behavioral consequence in relation to a specific emotional/motivational state or states that activate acts of aggression (Gardner, 2002a). A diagnostic hypothesis that these acts of aggression serve an "escape" function or a "social attention" function is incomplete until the specific motivational states related to the "escape" or "attention" are described (Carr, Langdon, & Yarborough, 1999). With this complete diagnostic information, an individualized intervention program may be designed to reduce the emotional/motivational state or states or to support acquisition and/or use of alternative prosocial means of coping with the motivational conditions.

## TRIADIC MENTAL HEALTH TREATMENT

As a potentially useful alternative to a primary treatment focus on removing or reducing pathological cognitions (e.g., hostile intent, faulty beliefs) *or* emotions (e.g., excessive anger, anxiety) *or* behaviors (e.g., aggression), the major focus of the TMHTA becomes one of replacing these controlling cognitions, and/or emotions/motivations, and the resulting aggressive behaviors, with interrelated cognitive $\rightarrow$ emotional/motivational $\rightarrow$ behavioral triads that serve as competency alternatives. These replacement triads may include self-initiated coping strategies of anger reduction (cognitive $\rightarrow$ emotional/motivational) when confronted with conditions of provocation as described previously by Chapman et al. (2006), and self-directed prosocial coping functional alternatives (cognitive $\rightarrow$ behavior) as illustrated by Benson (1992). The reader should note that these therapy targets address person-specific central processing vulnerabilities (e.g., inclination to excessive anger, hostile cognitive set, high strength of aggressive responding) identified during the multi-modal assessment process as representing critical contributors to a person's aggressive responding. As these alternative triads are developed and strengthened, the critical controlling pathological features are either reduced in influence or eliminated (Cole, Gardner, et al., 1985).

To accomplish these treatment goals, the specific therapy procedures deemed most likely to accomplish the therapeutic objectives of addressing these triads are selected for use. This selection, offered direction by empirical literatures that support efficacy with people with intellectual disabilities, may involve a range of social learning, relationship development, emotional enhancement, cognitive, cognitive-behavioral, and reinforcement strategies, including anger management and related emotional retraining, self-control training, impulse control training, social skills training, assertiveness training, interpersonal conflict resolution skills training, empathy training, social problem-solving strategies, emotional desensitization, relaxation training, cognitive retraining, and a range of contingency management procedures.

## CASE ILLUSTRATIONS OF TRIADIC MENTAL HEALTH THERAPY

The reader will recall the initial example of Tomas Cordosa (a fictitious name). Multimodal assessment implicated the following triad that needed replacement: Peers calling Tomas "retard" resulted immediately in heightened anger arousal $\rightarrow$ cognitions with a hostile intent $\rightarrow$ aggressive act. Assessment revealed that Tomas frequently used aggressive acts as means of coping with a range of social provocations, especially involving criticism of his cognitive abilities. When he was criticized or felt threatened, he quickly became angry. Having limited skills in modulating his anger and limited alternative problem solving or related skills of coping, his typical reaction was one of impulsive aggression. At the same time, Tomas was highly motivated to gain peer and staff acceptance and most typically following an aggressive episode would be apologetic to peers and staff about his aggressive behavior.

The therapy objective became one of replacing the problem triads with alternative prosocial ones that Tomas could use under similar situations in the future. Initially, through graduated exposure and coping skills training format, Tomas was taught alternative self-controlling statements that directed deep breathing and relaxation along with a neutral or positive cognitive statement. He then was taught a self-label of "Used My Head," or "I'm Smart" following each training trial following successful use of the alternative sequence. Following the emotional → cognitive → behavioral retraining, a series of alternative problem-solving behaviors were taught. Finally, he was prompted to self-instruct "Use my head" when confronted with provocations that required problem solving. These new replacement triads were practiced in increasingly realistic simulated situations that reflected the range of conditions in which Tomas previously had used aggression as his coping reaction to conditions of provocation. Staff prompting in situ was faded as Tomas demonstrated independent use of his newly acquired competency triads. Clinically significant reductions in impulsive anger arousal and aggressive responding were noted during and following therapy and at 6 months follow-up. In fact during the 3 weeks of observation at the 6-month period, no occurrences of aggression occurred even though he was confronted with multiple conditions of provocation that prior to therapy had resulted in impulsive aggressive episodes. Staff reported only infrequent occurrence of minor verbal threats. During these episodes, he was reported to point to his head and to verbalize "Be smart—use my head" as he coped successfully with the provocative conditions. He also was observed suggesting to disruptive peers that they "Be Smart. Use Your Head."

Experience with Carol Dunlap (a fictitious name), an adult with mild cognitive impairment and a lengthy history of verbal and physical aggression and related disruptive episodes, offers a second application of the TMHTA. Carol resides in a group home with staff trained to manage her aggressive episodes. History revealed a variety of unsuccessful pharmacological and behavioral attempts to manage her aggressive approach to coping with a range of interpersonal and program structure conditions that created emotional distress for her. On initiation of the triadic intervention, Carol's treatment program consisted of medications for an anxiety disorder and "her aggression and anxious/depressive mood" combined with behavioral approaches that involved: token reinforcement and praise every 4 hours for the absence of verbal or physical aggression paired with a redirection to a quiet area to calm following aggressive/disruptive episodes. Carol also had attended anger management and coping skills training group programs and, under conditions in which there was no in situ provocation, could verbalize socially appropriate ways of coping with aggravations. However, this cognitive knowledge had minimal influence over her emotional and behavioral reactions when confronted in situ with provocative conditions that she viewed as a threat to her.

Multimodal assessment revealed a number of central processing features that contributed to Carol's aggressive episodes. Carol was generally suspicious of the intent of others who attempted to interact with her and viewed a variety of actions of others as having hostile intent (e.g., corrective feedback, any intrusion into her ongoing behavior, teasing from peers, continued eye-contact, raised voice, peer or staff directives, and attempts by people unfamiliar to her to initiate interaction). These events produced increased anxiety/anger followed by a range of loud negative verbal reactions that quickly escalated into physical aggression until the situation was clarified or resolved (e.g., don't stare at me, don't tell me what to do, I didn't do anything, why are you mad at me, I don't know you, what do you want from me). In view of her large physical size and inclination to physical aggression, most of her peers soon learned to avoid contact with her.

The TMHTA program for Carol was designed to address the following: 1) strong inclination to attribute hostile intent to the actions of others, 2) strong inclination toward heightened anxiety/anger arousal when the actions of others were viewed as having hostile intent, 3) strong habit of impulsive verbal and physical aggression as means of coping with sources of perceived threat, 4) limited skills of anxiety or anger management, 5) limited repertoire of prosocial coping alternatives to aggressive responding, 6) limited problem solving or conflict resolution skills, and 7) limited skills of self-management.

Initiation of individual therapy sessions was preceded by rapport development with a behavior therapist via informal social contact (visits to coffee shops away from the group home, lunch in the community, a visit to the library, a visit to the shopping mall). To encourage Carol to develop a positive relationship with the new therapist, one or two group home staff members that currently had a positive relationship with Carol participated in these initial social outings. These staff members (one worked the morning shift and the other worked the evening shift in the group home) served as adjunct therapists. This was critical, as most adults in an authority position represented a threat to Carol. In addition, Carol was encouraged to select a peer on each occasion as her guest on these social outings. As Carol had few friends, this procedure was designed to increase the number of peers with whom she could share some positive experiences. This process of rapport building as an initial step is consistent with the conclusion of Buetler (2002) that therapeutic outcome is maximized when various "core conditions" are present, for example, "when the therapist is skillful and provides trust, acceptance, acknowledgment, collaboration and respect" (p. 1005).

After four outings over a 2-week period, a more formal therapy program was begun. Reinforcement procedures used with Carol involved a self-managed token program during which she was taught to self-monitor, self-evaluate, self-consequate, and self-instruct alternative prosocial coping behaviors. This self-managed procedure was used though out the formal therapy period. Exchange reinforcing events consisted of a range of community social activities selected by Carol. Each included one or more peers selected by Carol as her guests.

Carol was trained both by the behavior therapist and by either one of the two group home adjunct therapists. Initial content included anxiety and anger management skills followed by combining these with problem solving skills. In each of these therapy sessions, scenarios were created that represented problem areas (people, actions of others, situations) identified by Carol and staff that resulted in cognitive misinterpretations → anxiety/anger → verbal/physical aggression. These scenarios were gradually designed to be increasingly realistic and, with Carol's consent, involved those peers and staff involved in past negative experiences. Carol was guided to use her newly acquired prosocial coping strategies with each of the series of scenarios. She was prompted to self-monitor her responses to each and make the appropriate self-managed correction as needed. Following each session, Carol completed her token card. The adjunct therapists assisted in generalization of newly acquired triads of coping competencies by prompting use of these following formal therapy sessions as occasions arose in situ.

Carol's motivation for success was further enhanced by weekly telephone visits with her mother and older sister. She displayed considerable pride in informing her family about what she was learning, the social activities that she was earning, and her new friends. During monthly visits from her family, Carol also proudly shared her self-recorded graphic display of her progress during the month. In addition, to her family's considerable surprise, she insisted that one or two of her friends accompany them during the outings that she had with her family.

Formal therapy was gradually faded, with group home staff continuing to provide prompts and related supports as needed in situ to ensure maintenance. In addition, to ensure continuation of peer relationships, two social clubs (Coffee Club and Community Outing Club) with bimonthly meetings were organized. Each club was formalized with the election of officers, membership dues, dress codes, and activity committee. Carol was elected as the initial president of the Coffee Club.

During the 2-month baseline period prior to initiation of therapy, Carol had a weekly average of 6.5 incidents of verbal aggression and 2.0 incidents of physical aggression. Following initiation of the formal TMHTA program, staff reported a noticeable decrease in aggressive incidents. Carol was reported to value her self-managed token program and quickly learned to seek staff support when she felt threatened by others or situations. At 3-, 6-, and 9-month follow-ups following termination of her individual and group therapy sessions, only infrequent incidents of verbal threats occurred. Her medication was being tapered. Staff reported that, although Carol required occasional prompting, in most incidences of interpersonal conflict, she continued to successfully use her prosocial competency triads as coping alternative to previously demonstrated aggression.

## SUMMARY AND CONCLUSIONS

These examples illustrate that TMHTA procedures for each person are selected to target client-specific emotional → cognitive → behavioral triads with the objective of reducing or eliminating these problem triads by replacing these with cognitive → emotional → behavioral triads reflecting personal competencies. These newly acquired competencies serve as alternative means of coping with specific environmental, intrapersonal, and biological conditions that contribute to the problem behaviors.

Our extensive clinical experience combined with results of empirical studies with people who present with chronic and severe problems of aggression recommend use of a number of therapy strategies. To the extent possible, concrete rather than abstract cognitive representation of skill deficits are used to facilitate learning

(Chapman et al., 2006; Cole, Gardner, et al., 1985; Gardner, 2002a; Singh et al., 2007). Action based program components represent valued therapies. These include such procedures as participant modeling, role-playing and behavior rehearsal, graduated exposure to specific conditions of provocation, and eventual practice of newly acquired skills in situ (Benson, 2002; Chapman et al., 2006; Cole, Gardner, et al., 1985). Concrete means are used to represent contingent relationships between appropriate and inappropriate behaviors (pictorially, graphically, and/or physically depicted). Progress toward goal attainment is concretely represented and reviewed frequently via such procedures as self-monitoring of progress on a behavior checklist or recording on a graphic representation reflecting progress toward goal attainment (Gardner & Hunter, 2003). Situations in which problem triads occur are progressively reconstructed during therapy to insure the functional utility of the replacement competency triads for the person as these or similar stress-producing conditions are confronted in the future. Specific procedures are added to train for maintenance and generalization of new skills to future situations (Cole, Gardner. et al., 1985; Gardner, Watson, & Nania, 2004).

In conclusion, the overriding objective of the TMHTA is one of increasing the person's triads of cognitive-emotional/motivational-behavioral competencies. This initially is accomplished in individual and/or group therapies. To support the generalization of these newly acquired competencies, therapy is continued in situ and faded as the person is able to demonstrate independence in using these competencies in daily life. As noted, these competencies become functional replacements for the person's problem features identified during multimodal assessment as risk conditions for aggressive responding.

## RESEARCH NEEDS

In accepting responsibility for treatment of problems of aggression presented by people with IDD, the clinician initially defines the problem behaviors and then carefully describes the various environmental and personal (psychological and biomedical) contexts in which these occur. In this descriptive and analytic diagnostic process, the presumed controlling and contributing influences are identified. The next step becomes one of specifying which one or combination of the presumed controlling and contributing influences will become the target(s) of intervention efforts. Following selection of these events, the clinician carefully describes the outcome objectives associated with each. Finally, therapy approaches are selected that promise to be most effective and efficient in meeting the objectives. In this selection process, the clinician identifies those procedures that enjoy the best empirical support from studies with people with characteristics similar to the people being treated, and thoughtfully blends these with clinical experiences with clients who present with similar personal characteristics and circumstances.

A number of research questions arise at each step in this clinical process. As described earlier, the case formulation approach used (e.g., behavioral, mental illness, developmental, multimodal), and the theoretical and empirical literatures that support each, influence activities in each step in the clinical treatment process (diagnostics, selection of treatment targets, specification of treatment objectives, selection of interventions, measurement procedures used to evaluate attainment of treatment objectives). A major cluster of research questions relates to the efficacy and relative efficacy of the various case formulations selected to guide the clinical process. As illustration of one inquiry: "under what conditions, if ever, would a unimodal case formulation such as a mental illness or a physical illness or a behavioral, or a genetic case formulation be selected as the case formulation of choice in analysis and treatment of chronic problems of aggression?"

In reviewing decades of our clinical and research experiences, the authors found it difficult to recall an instance of chronically occurring aggression that was "just environmental," or "just medical," or "just psychiatric." If this observation holds true in general, what case formulation approach would best do justice to the potentially multiple and interactive influences that require identification and treatment? Even though our clinical experience supports use of an integrative multimodal case formulation, research support for our selection is absent from the IDD literature. Although there is considerable lip service recommending the use of an integrative multidisciplinary approach, there is little empirical evidence that the approach as typically practiced represents an integrative one. Our observations suggest that, most frequently in clinical practice, diagnoses and treatments are discipline specific, with no integrative paradigm to permit speculation about the specific and relative influence of the treated condition on aggressive responding. Would such an integrative paradigm add to the efficacy and efficiency of the treatment process?

More specific to the TMHTA approach and related multimodal contextual case formulation, a number of research questions arise. As noted earlier, relative efficacy and efficiency of the TMHTA in comparison to other case formulations and associated treatments are absent in the empirical literatures, leaving theoretical adherence and clinical experience rather than empirical support as guiding influences for selection of the specific case formulation used in addressing clients with IDD and significant issues of aggression. Although many of the individual treatment components used in the TMHTA enjoy research support, research data are lacking to support the supposition that best treatment results occur when these are used in a package to address interrelated problem triads of emotions-cognitions-behaviors and associated triads of competency replacements.

A final major research issue relates to the question of generalization and maintenance of treatment gains. In our clinical experience, every case referred for the TMHTA previously had been provided a variety of pharmacological, behavioral, and other psychological interventions that either were unsuccessful or else short-term gains were not maintained following termination of interventions. What therapy targets and procedures and what types of supports following termination of formal therapy are needed to enhance generalization and long-term maintenance? Does the the TMHTA approach that both emphasizes development and use of triads of competencies and trains transfer of these to in situ conditions facilitate long-term maintenance? In conclusion, a seemingly endless number of research questions in treatment of severe problems of aggression in people with IDD remain open to investigation.

## REFERENCES

Baker, W., & Bramston, P. (1997). Attributional and emotional determinents of aggression in people with mild intellectual disabilities. *Journal of Intellectual and Developmental Disabilities, 22,* 169–186.

Barnhill, J. (1999). The relationship between epilepsy and violent behavior in persons with mental retardation. *The NADD Bulletin, 2,* 43–46.

Benson, B.A. (1992). *Teaching anger management to persons with mental retardation.* Worthington, OH: IDS Publishing.

Benson, B.A. (2002). Feeling, thinking, doing: Reducing aggression through skill development. In W.I. Gardner, *Aggression and other disruptive behavioral challenges* (pp. 293–323). Kingston, NY: NADD Press.

Benson, B.A., & Fuchs, C. (1999). Anger-arousing situations and coping responses of aggressive adults with intellectual disabilities. *Journal of Intellectual and Developmental Disabilities, 24,* 207–215.

Benson, B.A., Rice, C.J., & Miranti, S.V. (1986). Effects of anger management training in mentally retarded adults in group treatment. *Journal of Consulting and Clinical Psychology, 54,* 728–729.

Bird, F., Dores, P.A., Moniz, D., & Robinson, J. (1989). Reducing severe aggression and self-injurious behaviors with functional communication training. *American Journal of Mental Retardation, 94,* 37–48.

Bouras, N., & Drummond, C. (1992). Behavior and psychiatric disorders of people with mental handicaps living in the community. *Journal of Intellectual Disability Research, 36,* 349–357.

Bradley, S.J. (2000). *Affect regulation and the development of psychopathology.* New York: The Guilford Press.

Buetler, L.E. (2002). David and Goliath. When empirical and clinical standards of practice meet. *American Psychologist, 55,* 997–1007.

Carr, E.G., & Durand, V.M. (1985). Reducing behavior problems through functional communication training. *Journal of Applied Behavior Analysis, 18,* 111–126.

Carr, E.G., Langdon, N.A., & Yarbourgh, S.C. (1999). Hypothesis-based interventions for severe problem behavior, In A.C. Repp & R.H. Horner (Eds.), *Functional analysis of problem behavior* (pp. 9–31). Belmont, CA: Wadsworth Publishing.

Carr, E.G., Levin, L., McConnachie, G., Carlson, J., Kemp, D.C., & Smith, C.E. (1994). *Communication-based intervention for problem behavior.* Baltimore: Paul H. Paul H. Brookes Publishing Co.

Carr, E.G., & Owen-DeSchryer, J.S. (2007). Physical illness, pain, and problem behavior in minimally verbal people with developmental disabilities. *Journal of Autism and Developmental Disorders, 37,* 413–424.

Chapman, R.A., Shedlack, K.J., & France, J. (2006). Stop-Think-Relax: An adapted self-control training strategy for individuals with mental retardation and coexisting psychiatric illness. *Cognitive and Behavioral Practice, 13,* 205–214.

Chiang, H. (2008). Expressive communication of children with autism: the use of challenging behaviour. *Journal of Intellectual Disability Research, 52,* 966–972.

Cole, C.L., Gardner, W.I., & Karan, O.C. (1985). Self-management training of mentally retarded adults presenting severe conduct difficulties. *Applied Research in Mental Retardation, 6,* 21–26.

Cole, C.L., Pflugard, D., Gardner, W.I., & Karan, O.C. (1985). *The self-management training program: Teaching developmentally disabled individuals to manage their disruptive behavior.* Champaign, IL: Research Press.

Dosen, A., Gardner, W.I., Griffiths, D.M., King, R., & Lapointe, A. (2007). *Practice guidelines and principles: Assessment, diagnosis, treatment, and related support services for persons with intellectual disabilities and problem behaviour—European Edition.* Gouda, The Netherlands: Centre of Consultation and Expertise.

Dykens, E.M., Hodapp, R.M., & Finucane, B.M. (2000). *Genetics and mental retardation syndromes: A new look at behavior and interventions* Baltimore: Paul H. Brookes Publishing Co.

Embregts, P.J. C.M., Didden, R., Huitink, C., & Schreuder, N. (2009). Contextual variables affecting aggressive behaviour in individuals with mild to borderline intellectual disabilities who live in residential facility. *Journal of Intellectual Disability Research, 53,* 255–264.

Feldman, M.A., Condillac, R.A., Tough, S., Hunt, S., & Griffiths, D. (2002). Effectiveness of community positive behavioral intervention for persons with developmental disabilities and severe behavioral challenges. *Behavior Therapy, 33,* 377–398.

Fredericks, B., & Nishioka,-Evans, V. (1999). Functional assessment for a sex offender population. In A.C. Repp, & R.H. Horner (Eds.), *Functional analysis of problem behaviors* (pp. 279–303). Belmont, CA: Wadsworth.

Fuchs, C., & Benson, B.A. (1995). Social information processing by aggressive and nonaggressive men with mental retardation. *American Journal of Mental Retardation, 100,* 244–252.

Gardner, W.I. (1971). *Behavior modification in mental retardation.* London: University of London Press.

Gardner, W.I. (1977). *Learning and behavior characteristics of exceptional children and youth.* Boston: Allyn & Bacon.

Gardner, W.I. (1996). A contextual view of nonspecific behavioral symptoms in persons with a dual diagnosis: A psychological model for selecting and monitoring drug interventions. *Psychology in Mental Retardation, 21*(3), 6–11.

Gardner, W.I. (1998). Teaching skills of self-management. In D.M. Griffiths, W.I. Gardner, & J. Nugent (Eds.), *Behavioral supports: Individual centered interventions* (pp. 259–274). Kingston, NY: NADD Press.

Gardner, W.I. (2002a). *Aggression and other disruptive behavioral challenges: Biomedical and psychosocial assessment and treatment.* Kingston, NY: NADD Press.

Gardner, W.I. (2002b). Psychological treatment of persons with mental retardation who present emotional and behavioral challenges. In R.F.B. Gues & D.A. Flikweert (Eds.), *Behandeling van psychische en gedragsproblemen* (pp.13–20). Utrecht, The Netherlands: NGBZ/NIZW.

Gardner, W.I. (2005). Impulse control difficulties in persons with an intellectual disability: Role in behavioral and psychiatric disorders. In *NADD Bulletin, 8*(3), 47–56.

Gardner, W.I. (2007). Aggression in persons with intellectual disabilities and mental disorders. In J. Jacobson, J. Mulick, & J. Rohjan (Eds.), *Handbook of intellectual and developmental disabilities* (pp. 541–562). New York: Springer.

Gardner, W.I., Clees, T.J., & Cole, C.L. (1983). Self management of disruptive verbal ruminations by a mentally retarded adult. *Applied Research in Mental Retardation, 4,* 41–58.

Gardner, W.I., & Cole, C.L. (1989). Self-management approaches. In E. Cipani (Ed.), *The treatment of severe behavior disorders: Behavior analysis approach* (pp. 19–36). Washington, DC: American Association on Mental Retardation.

Gardner, W.I., Cole, C.L., Berry, D.L., & Nowinski, J.M. (1983). Reduction of disruptive behaviors in mentally retarded adults: A self-management approach. *Behavior Modification, 7,* 76–96.

Gardner, W.I., Cole, C.L., Davidson, D.P., & Karan, O.C. (1986). Reducing aggression in individuals with developmental disabilities: An expanded stimulus control, assessment and intervention model. *Education and Training of the Mentally Retarded, 21,* 3–12.

Gardner, W.I., Dosen, A., Griffiths, D.M., & King, R., (2006). *Practice guidelines for diagnostic, treatment, and related support services for persons with developmental disabilities and serious behavior problems.* Kingston, NY: NADD Press.

Gardner, W.I., & Griffiths, D.M. (2004). Treatment of aggression and related disruptive behaviors in persons with intellectual disabilities and mental health issues. In J.L. Matson, R.B. Laud, & M. Matson (Eds.), *Behavior modification for persons with developmental disabilities: Treatments and supports.* (Vol. 1) (pp. 279–309). Kingston, NY: NADD Press.

Gardner, W.I., & Hunter, R.H. (2003). Psychosocial diagnosis and treatment services in inpatient psychiatric facilities for persons with mental retardation: Practice guides. *Mental Health Aspects of Developmental Disabilities, 6,* 1–13.

Gardner, W.I., Karan, O.C., & Cole, C.L. (1984). Assessment of setting events influencing functional capacities of mentally retarded adults with behavior difficulties. In A.S. Halpern & M.J. Fuhrer (Eds.), *Functional assessment in rehabilitation* (pp. 171–185). Baltimore: Paul H. Brookes Publishing Co.

Gardner, W.I., & Sovner, R. (1994). *Self-injurious behavior: A multimodal approach to diagnosis and treatment.* Willow Street, PA: Vida Publishing.

Gardner, W.I., Watson, E., & Nania, K. (2004). Persons with mental retardation who present significant behavioral and emotional challenges: A habilitative mental health therapy approach to treatment. In F. Chan, N.L. Berven, & K.R. Thomas (Eds.), *Counseling theories and techniques for rehabilitation health professionals* (pp. 459–487). New York: Springer.

Gardner, W.I., & Whalen, J.T. (1996). A multimodal behavior analytic model for evaluating the effects of medical problems on nonspecific behavioral symptoms in persons with developmental disabilities. *Behavioral Interventions: Theory and Practice in Residential and Community-Based Clinical Programs, 11,* 147–161.

Gedye, A. (1997). *Behavioral diagnostic guide for developmental disabilities.* Vancouver, BC, Canada: Diagnostic Books.

Griffiths, D.M. (2002). Sexual aggression. In W.I. Gardner, *Aggression and other disruptive behavioral challenges* (pp. 325–397). Kingston, NY: NADD Press.

Hemmings, C. (2007). The relationship between challenging behaviour and psychiatric disorders in people with severe intellectual disabilities. In N. Bouras & G. Holt (Eds.), *Psychiatric and behavioural disorders in intellectual and developmental disabilities* (pp. 62–75). Cambridge: Cambridge University Press.

Kastner, T., Walsh, K.K., & Fraser, M. (2001). Undiagnosed medical conditions and medication side effects presenting as behavioral/psychiatric problems in people with mental retardation. *Mental Health Aspects of Developmental Disabilities, 4,* 101–107.

Lindsay, W.R., Allan, R., Parry, C., Macleod, F., Cottrel, J., Overend, H., Smith, A.H.W. (2004). Anger and aggression in people with intellectual disabilities: Treatment and follow-up of consecutive referrals and a waiting list comparison. *Clinical Psychology and Psychotherapy, 11,* 255–264.

Lindsay, W.R., Marshall, I., Neilson, C., Quinn, K., Smith, A.H.W. (1998). The treatment of a man with a learning disability convicted of exhibitionism. *Research in Developmental Disabilities, 19,* 295–316.

Lowry, M.A.., & Sovner, R. (1992). Severe behavior problems associated with rapid cycling bipolar disorder in two adults with profound mental retardation. *Journal of Intellectual Disability Research, 36,* 269–281.

Matson, J.L., Bamburg, J.W., Cherry, K, E., & Paclawskyj, T. (1999). A validity study of the Questions about Behavioral Function (QABF) Scale: Predicting treatment outcome success for self-injury, aggression, and sterotypies. *Research in Developmental Disabilities, 20,* 163–175.

Mavromatis, M. (2000). The diagnosis and treatment of borderline personality disorders in persons with developmental disabilities: Three case studies. *Mental Health Aspects of Developmental Disabilities, 3,* 89–97.

McComas, J., Hoch, H., Paone, D., & El-Roy, D. (2000). Escape behavior during academic tasks: A preliminary analysis of idiosyncratic establishing operations. *Journal of Applied behavior Analysis, 33,* 479–493.

Oeseburg, B., Jasen, D.E.M.C., Groothoff, J.W., Dijkstra, G.J., & Reijneveld, S.A. (2009). Emotional and behavioural problems in adolescents with intellectual disability with and without chronic diseases. *Journal of Intellectual Disability Research, 54,* 81–89.

Ratey, J.J. (2001). *A user's guide to the brain.* New York: Pantheon Books.

Reiss, S. (1990). Prevalence of dual diagnosis in community based day programs in the Chicago metropolitan area. *American Journal of Mental Retardation, 94,* 578–585.

Reiss, S. (1994). *Handbook of challenging behavior: Mental health aspects of mental retardation.* Worthington, OH: IDS Publications.

Reiss, S., & Havercamp, S.M. (1997). Sensitivity theory and mental retardation: Why functional analysis is not enough. *American Journal of Mental Retardation, 101,* 553–566.

Reiss, S., & Havercamp, S.M. (1998). Toward a comprehensive assessment of fundamental motivation: Factor structure of the Reiss Profiles. *Psychological Assessment, 10,* 97–106.

Schroeder, S.R., Reese, R.M., Hellings, J., Loupe, J., & Tessel, R.E. (1999). The causes of self-injurious behavior and their implications. In N.A. Wieseler & R. Hanson (Eds.), *Challenging behavior in persons with mental health disorders and severe developmental disabilities* (pp. 65–87). Washington, DC: AAMR Monograph Series.

Singh, N.N., Lancioni, G.E., Winton, A.S.W., Adkins, A.D., Singh, J., & Singh, A.N. (2007). Mindfulness training assists individuals with moderate mental retardation to maintain their community placement. *Behavior Modification, 31,* 800–814.

Singh, N.N., Wahler, R.G., Adkins, A.D., Myers, R.E., & the Mindfulness Research Group. (2003). Soles of the feet: A mindfulness-based self-control intervention for aggression by an individual with mild mental retardation and mental illness. *Research in Developmental Disabilities, 24,* 158–169.

Sovner, R., & Fogelman, S. (1996). Irritability and mental retardation. *Seminars in Clinical Neuropsychiatry, 1,* 105–114.

Sovner, R., Foxx, C.J., Lowry, M.J., & Lowry, M.A. (1993). Floretine treatment of depression and associated self-injury in two adults with mental retardation. *Journal of Intellectual Disability Research, 37,* 301–311.

Sovner, R. & Lowry, M. (2001). Mood and affect as determinants of psychotropic drug therapy: Response in mentally retarded persons with organic mental syndromes. In A. Dosen & K. Day (Eds.), *Treating metal illness and behaviour disorders in children and adults with mental retardation* (pp. 265–282). Washington, DC: American Psychiatric Press.

Taylor, J. (2002). A review of the assessment and treatment of anger and aggression in offenders with intellectual disabilities. *Journal of Intellectual Disability Research, 46,* 57–73.

Taylor, J.L. (2009). Treatment of anger and aggression in offenders with intellectual disabilities in secure settings. In R. Didden & X. Moonen (Eds.), *Met het oog op behandeling 2,* pp. 9–14. Amersfoort, The Netherlands: Bergdrukkerij.

Taylor, L., & Oliver, C. (2008). The behavioural phenotype of Smith-Magenis syndrome: Evidence for a gene-environment interaction. *Journal of Intellectual Disability Research, 52,* 830–841.

Thompson, T., & Symonds, F.J. (1999). Neurobehavioral mechanisms in drug action. In N.A. Wieseler & R.H. Hanson (Eds.), *Challenging behaviors of persons with mental health disorders and severe developmental disabilities* (pp. 125–150). Washington, DC: American Association on Mental Retardation.

Thorne, I. (2005). Individual cognitive-behavioural anger treatment for people with mild-borderline intellectual disabilities and histories of aggression: A controlled trial. *British Journal of Clinical Psychology, 44,* 367–382.

To, M.Y.F., & Chan, S. (2000). Evaluating the effectiveness of progressive muscle relaxation in reducing the aggressive behaviors of mentally handicapped patients. *Archives of Psychiatric Nursing, 14,* 39–46.

Tsiouris, J.A. (2001). Diagnosis of depression in people with severe/profound mental retardation. *Journal of Intellectual Disability Research, 45,* 115–120.

Tuinier, S.A., & Verhoeven, W.M.A. (1993). Psychiatry and mental retardation: Toward a behavioral pharmacological concept. *Journal of Intellectual Disability Research, 37,* 16–24.

Vlitiello, B., Behar, D., Hunt, J., Stoff, D., & Ricciuti, A. (1990). Subtyping aggression in children and adolescents. *Journal of Neuropsychiatry, 2,* 189–192.

Woodcock, K.A., Oliver, C., & Humphreys, G.W. (2009). A specific pathway can be identified between genetic characteristics and behaviour profiles in Prader-Willi syndrome via cognitive, environmental and physiological mechanisms. *Journal of Intellectual Disability Research, 53,* 493–500.

# III

SECTION

# Sexual Offending Behavior

# Risk Assessment for Sexual Offending

## William R. Lindsay

**CHAPTER 6**

The recent development of risk assessment instruments has produced a significant impact on risk prediction and management of offenders in forensic and clinical services. Several instruments were produced based on research correlating developmental, offense-related, adult adjustment, and psychiatric/psychological assessment variables with offending. Even in their early use, these variables produced better predictions about who would and who would not commit a general criminal offense when compared to clinical judgment. Several authors went on to continue the research toward constructing risk assessments for the prediction of aggressive and violent offenses.

This chapter reviews the topic of risk assessment for sexual offending among people who have intellectual and developmental disability (IDD). I describe standardized assessment instruments as well as structured clinical judgment and dynamic risk evaluation with sex offenders. Although the focus of the chapter is on offenders with IDD, individuals who do not have IDD also are considered because much of the research with this population is relevant to people with disabilities.

## RISK ASSESSMENT

### Standardized Instruments

Prior to constructing the Violence Risk Appraisal Guide (VRAG), Quinsey, Harris, Rice, and Cormier (1998, 2005) conducted a wide ranging investigation on 191 recidivists and 427 nonrecidivists who had previously offended and been admitted for psychiatric assessment and treatment (Harris, Rice, & Quinsey 1993). They grouped variables into four categories: 1) developmental variables from childhood, 2) adult adjustment variables, 3) variables related to the index offense, and 4) assessment variables from psychological and psychiatric investigations. Quinsey et al. (1998, 2005) included a total of 42 promising candidate variables that had emerged from previous research as possible predictors for future violent and sexual offenses. Eleven of these variables contributed to a regression model that was significantly successful in predicting who would and who would not commit a further violent offense. Quinsey et al. (1998, 2005) also developed a sister risk assessment for sexual offenses, the Sex Offender Risk Appraisal Guide (SORAG), and these two assessments have become standard comparators against which other risk assessments have been gauged for predictive accuracy. The VRAG has been cross validated on a variety of forensic psychiatric populations and prisoner samples and in their original evaluation Quinsey et al. (1998) found that it was as accurate with offenders who had IDD (IQ less than 80) as with offenders who did not. However, because their study was not confined to offenders with IDD, the sample sizes for those with lower intellectual functioning were very small.

The VRAG is a static risk assessment, relying on actuarial variables that cannot change. For example, if the individual has had behavioral problems at school, this will contribute to their risk score and can never be taken from the person's history. For the most part, static risk can only increase. If individuals have committed violent offenses, the offenses can never be taken from their histories, and it will always contribute to their risk assessments. However, by committing another violent offense, static risk will increase. This effect is true for every variable on the VRAG except for age, which varies inversely with risk.

Hanson (1997) developed the Rapid Risk Assessment for Sexual Offence Recidivism (RRASOR), and shortly thereafter, the Static-99 assessment (Hanson & Thornton, 1999), both of which were specifically designed to assess risk of future sexual offenses. The principle of these two instruments is the Static-99 which has 10 items: 1) number of prior charges or convictions for sexual offenses, 2) current age, 3) any male victims, 4) any unrelated victims, 5) number of prior sentencing dates, 6) any convictions for noncontact sexual offenses, 7) nonsexual violence dealt with at the time of sentencing for the index offense, 8) prior nonsexual violence, and 9) any stranger victims and cohabitation status (living with a partner for at least 2 years). It can be seen immediately that the Static-99 includes variables related to the sexual offense but also variables related to general antisociality (e.g., prior nonsexual violent offenses) and a general attachment variable (ever lived with a partner for at least 2 years). The VRAG and Static-99 have become standards for violent and sexual recidivism, respectively.

As research on risk assessment developed over the subsequent 10 years, several groups of researchers compared the predictive accuracy of different risk assessment instruments on a range of databases. Barbaree, Seto, Langton, and Peacock (2001) compared the VRAG, SORAG, RRASOR, Static-99, and the Minnesota Sex Offender Screening Tool–Revised (MnSOST-R: Epperson, Kaul, Huot, Hesselton, Alexander, & Goldman, 1998). Barbaree et al. (2001) used a Canadian database of 215 sex offenders who had out of prison for an average of 4.5 years and found that all of the instruments except the MnSOST-R successfully predicted general recidivism and sexual recidivism. Following from this research, Langton, Barbaree, Seto, Peacock, Harkins, and Hansen (2007) extended the study with 468 main-stream sex offenders followed up for an average of 5.9 years. Langton et al. used the same assessments as previously with the addition of the updated Static-2002 (Hanson & Thornton, 2003). With the addition of these extra 253 participants, the VRAG and SORAG now showed the largest effect sizes for any offending, and those two assessments plus the Static-2002 showed the largest effect sizes for serious offending.

Other authors have compared the predictive accuracy of various instruments across a range of clients and cultures. Bartosh, Garby, Lewis, and Gray (2003) compared the Static-99, RRASOR, MnSOST-R, and SORAG in predictions for recidivism in 251 sexual offenders. They categorized their participants in terms of index offense type and found that none of the four tests had consistent predictive validity across categories. The Static-99 and the SORAG emerged as the instruments with greatest consistency in terms of predictive accuracy for future sexual offenses. In a further follow-up to their original series of studies, Harris, Rice, Quinsey, Lalumiere, Boer, and Lang (2003) compared the VRAG, SORAG, RRASOR, and Static-99 in predicting recidivism for 396 sexual offenders in Canada. All four instruments predicted recidivism with significantly greater accuracy than chance. Predictions of violent recidivism were consistently higher for the VRAG and SORAG with the effect sizes large for violent recidivism and moderate for sexual recidivism.

Given these and other studies, there is little doubt that prediction of future sexual and violent offending based on actuarial and historical variables can be conducted with a reasonable degree of accuracy.

## Structured Clinical Judgment

Contiguous with the development of actuarial risk assessments, risk assessments based on structured clinical judgment were also being developed. The first and most widely used was the Historical Clinical Risk–20 Items (HCR-20) developed by Webster, Eaves, Douglas, and Wintrup (1995). This is a risk assessment for future violence that has been adopted extensively for a range of offenders, including those with mental illness and IDD.

The HCR-20 is organized into historical (10 items), clinical (5 items), and risk (5 items) sections, with each item rated on a three-point scale from 0 (no evidence of the variable), 1 (some evidence of the variable), and 2 (clear evidence of the variable). The total score is the sum of the items, although the authors do not recommend making decisions on the basis of the total scores. Instead, they recommend that the items are structured in order to establish a comprehensive range of variables for arriving at a final judgment. This way, historical variables are combined with an assessment of current clinical status and a consideration of future risk variables.

The HCR-20 has been researched in many settings for mainstream offenders within correctional and mental health facilities. Because this instrument has a range of clinical variables, much of the research has been carried out in forensic psychiatric settings or with mentally disordered offenders. A few examples of the extensive research illustrate its use. Kroner and Mills (2001) compared the predictive accuracy of a range of instruments including the HCR-20 with 97 mainstream offenders in Canada. The VRAG had the highest predictive correlations with minor and major incidents, although there were no statistically significant differences between any of the risk assessments.

Generally, studies have used receiver operator characteristics to evaluate the significance of the risk predictions. This statistic is calculated by setting a cutoff on a set of individual risk assessments for predicting a violent or sexual incident. The cutoff is then gauged against whether an incident does or does not happen, and this gives an effect size for the predictive value of the risk assessment. The effect size is termed *area under the curve* (AUC), and an AUC of .5 is no better than chance, .7 indicates a significant prediction with a medium effect, and 1.0 would indicate perfect prediction. Grann, Belfrage, and Tengstrom (2000) followed up for a period of 2 years 404 forensic patients who had committed violent offenses. They found that the H Scale predicted significantly for both offenders with a diagnosis of schizophrenia (AUC = .71) and offenders with personality disorder (AUC = .71). In a 2-year follow-up of 70 psychiatric patients who had committed violent acts, Dolan and Khawaja (2004) reported that the HCR-20 total score significantly predicted self- or collateral reports of violence (AUC = .76) and documented incidents of reoffending (AUC = .71). Several studies have compared the predicted value of the HCR-20 with other commonly used risk assessments such as the Violence Risk Appraisal Guide (VRAG: Quinsey et al., 1998).

With offenders who have mental illness, work on the HCR-20 has developed to investigate a range of other variables. Douglas and Ogloff (2003) examined the effect of rater confidence on the accuracy of the prediction of risk. They followed up on 100 forensic psychiatric patients, 79% of whom had a violent index offense. In addition to completing HCR-20 judgments, raters were also asked to indicate their confidence in the judgment on a 10-point scale. The AUC value for the high confidence group was 0.84 for any violence and for the low confidence group, the AUC value was .52 for any violence. Therefore, when clinicians have greater confidence in their HCR-20 ratings, the accuracy of prediction was markedly greater.

In a comparison of male ($n = 85$) and female ($n = 63$) forensic patients, Strand and Belfrage (2001) found no differences in scale or total scores between the two groups. The only significant gender differences were on individual items, with males scoring higher on previous violence, violence at a young age, substance use, and negative attitudes. Females scored higher on personality disorder, impulsivity, and stress. However, de Vogel and de Ruiter (2005) in a comparison of 42 women and 42 men in a forensic psychiatric service found that the HCR-20 was a better violence predictor for men (AUCs for total and scale scores ranged between .75 and .88) than women (AUCs ranged from .52 to .63). In a further development, Grevatt, Thomas-Peter, and Hughes (2004) investigated the extent to which the HCR-20 could predict short-term violence within 6 months of admission to a forensic unit. Although the H Scale and total score were not predictive, the C Scale significantly predicted any incidents (AUC =.72) and verbal abuse (AUC =.81). Belfrage and Douglas (2002) also found that the C Scale and the R Scale reduced significantly in response to treatment in hospital.

A significant amount of research has now been carried out using the HCR-20 with offenders with IDD in clinical practice and in forensic settings. Gray, Fitzgerald, Taylor, MacCulloch, and Snowden (2007) assessed the predictive accuracy of the HCR-20 in relation to the VRAG and Psychopathy Checklist-Screening Version (PCL-SV; Hart, Cox, & Hare, 1995). Gray et al. employed

118 men and 27 women with IDD who had all been discharged from hospital following admission for conviction of a criminal offense or exhibiting behavior that might have led to a conviction in different circumstances. This IDD group was compared with a similar control group of 843 men and 153 women who were mainstream, mentally ill offenders without IDD. Following up these individuals for a period of 5 years, Gray et al. (2007) found that all these instruments predicted violence recidivism with large effect sizes. For violent offending, the HCR historical items predicted recidivism with an AUC of .81, the clinical items with an AUC of .71, and the risk management items with an AUC of .64. These predictive values were considerably better than those found with the non-IDD group, which were .69, .55, and .63 respectively.

Lindsay et al. (2008) conducted a study on 212 offenders with IDD drawn from a range of community, low secure, medium secure, and maximum secure settings. They compared the predictive validity of a number of risk assessments including the HCR-20 and found that the VRAG and HCR-20 had similar predictive values with AUCs of .71 and .72, respectively. Taylor et al. (2010) conducted a more extensive analysis on the HCR-20 data reported in summary fashion by Lindsay et al. (2008). Taylor et al. (2010) found that on the H Scale, community offenders with IDD had significantly lower scores than those in low secure, medium secure, or maximum secure settings. This orderly result was not mirrored with the Risk and Clinical items that are more dynamic in nature (see discussion later on dynamic risk). On the Clinical scale, there were no significant differences between the groups and on the Risk management scale, the medium secure–low secure participants had significantly lower scores than either the community of maximum secure group. One might expect individuals in medium secure and high secure services to have higher risk management scores than those in the community. However, it should be remembered that any community forensic service caters to individuals who live at home with their families, in supported accommodation, and in group homes. In the Taylor et al. (2010) study most individuals had constant unsupervised access to the community, so they would present a constant risk as judged by the services. Therefore, it is perhaps less surprising that they were judged as having higher risk scores. In comparisons between individuals who did and did not perpetrate violent incidents in the follow-up period, there were significant differences between the groups on all three scales with those who committed further incidents having higher scores. When Taylor et al. (2010) calculated the predictive accuracy of the HCR-20 for those who did and did not perpetrate a further incident, they found an AUC = .68 for the H scale, AUC = .67 for the C scale, AUC = .62 for the R scale, and AUC = .72 for the total scale. It seems, then, that the HCR-20 has reasonable predictive accuracy across this range of settings.

In relation to risk for future sexual incidents, Boer, Hart, Kropp, and Webster (1997) created the Sexual Violence Risk-20 Items (SVR-20). This instrument was produced to complement the HCR-20 but has generated far less research than its violence assessment counterpart. Sjostedt and Langstrom (2002) compared the accuracy of several assessments including the VRAG, RRASOR, Hare Psychopathy Checklist–Revised (PCL-R; Hare, 1991), and SVR-20. They followed up 51 mainstream offenders convicted of rape in Sweden for an average of 92 months. Only the RRASOR showed predictive accuracy for sexual recidivism, whereas the other instruments, including the SVR-20, showed some predictive accuracy with violent nonsexual recidivism.

The SVR-20 is organized into three sections: psychosocial adjustments (11 items), sexual offenses (7 items), and future plans (2 items). As with the HCR-20, each of the SVR-20 items can be rated on a three-point scale (0, 1, and 2) from no evidence to clear evidence of the variable. Again, it is recommended that the items are structured to consider a range of variables when formulating a risk management plan. To date, there are no research reports about using the SVR-20 with sex offenders with IDD; however, Boer, Frize, Pappas, Morrissey, and Lindsay (2010) have published guidelines for implementing the SVR-20 with this clinical population. The general principles for the guidelines were that first, consideration should be given to the extent to which any sexual behavior is primarily challenging behavior rather than a paraphilia that is driven by some deviant sexual preference. In this way, these authors were making a distinction that Hingsburger, Griffiths, and Quinsey (1990) distinguished between men with IDD who commit sexual offenses because of some form of deviancy from those men who exhibit similar behavior through naivety, lack of experience, lack of appropriate opportunities, or lack of understanding of the law (a so-called "counterfeit deviance"). This distinction is an important consideration in any risk assessment for sex offenders with IDD.

The psychosocial adjustment items in the SVR-20 include sexual deviation, being a victim of child abuse, psychopathy as measured by the PCL-R, major mental illness, substance use problems, suicidal/homicidal ideation, relationship problems, employment problems, past nonsexual violent offenses, past nonviolent offenses, and past supervision failures. Clearly, these items are a mixture of those relating to sexual issues and those related to antisociality. For example, it has been found that sex offenders with IDD have a higher rate of sexual abuse in childhood than nonsexual offenders. Lindsay, Law, Quinn, Smart, and Smith (2001) found that 38% of sex offenders with IDD in their sample had experienced sexual abuse as children, whereas 13% of the nonsexual offenders had similar abuse experiences. On the other hand, 33% of the nonsexual (violent) offenders with IDD had experienced physical abuse as children in contrast to 13% of the sexual offenders. Therefore, it seemed that the experience of sexual abuse may influence the development of deviance in sexual preferences in clients with IDD. Lindsay (2009) has pointed out that in this study, 62% of the sexual offenders had not been sexually abused in childhood, whereas 13% of the violent offenders, who had not committed a sexual offense, had also been sexually abused in childhood. So, although there is a relationship with sexual abuse in childhood, it is by no means the complete explanation for offending in adulthood. Nevertheless, past sexual abuse seems to contribute toward risk.

The sexual offending items in the SVR-20 include high-density sex offenses, multiple sex offense types (e.g., adults and children, males and females, contact, and no contact), physical harm to the victim during the sex offense, using weapons or threats of death in sex offenses, escalation in frequency or severity of the sex offenses, extreme minimization or denial of sex offenses, and attitudes that support or condone the sexual offenses. With reference to the latter two items, Kolton, Boer, and Boer (2001) found that sex offenders with IDD had higher rates of cognitive distortions on the Abel Screening assessment (Abel, Gore, Holland, Camp, Becker, & Rathner, 1989) than control participants. Lindsay, Whitefield, and Carson (2007) also found that sex offenders with IDD endorsed higher rates of cognitive distortions related to a range of sexual offending situations when compared to nonsexual offenders and nonoffenders, all with IDD. Therefore, cognitive schema that support denial of offenses or distorted attitudes that might support or condone offenses are a risk factor in sex offenders with IDD.

The final section of the SVR-20 concerned with future plans includes whether or not the offender lacks realistic plans and has negative attitudes toward intervention. Lindsay, Elliot, and Astell (2004) found that negative response to treatment among 52 sexual offenders was significantly related to reoffending and made a unique contribution to the regression model predicting those who would and those who would not sexually offend. Accordingly, there exists detailed guidelines for Structured Clinical Judgment assessment of risk in relation to sexual offenders and many of these items have received empirical support.

## Dynamic Risk in Sex Offenders with Intellectual Disability

Although actuarial risk assessments rely on static, historical factors that cannot be changed, dynamic risk assessment incorporates variables that are more proximal to the sex offenses. The variables can be conceptualized as factors involved in the cycle leading to the index incident or the reoffense. Hanson and Harris (2000) proposed a dichotomy in dynamic risk variables of "stable" dynamic and "acute" dynamic. Stable dynamic factors are propensities that individuals may have to put themselves in a state of dynamic risk such as a tendency to abuse alcohol. Acute dynamic factors are situations where the environment or the individual themselves sharply increases the risk through a stress on the stable dynamic state as when a man goes into a bar or starts drinking alcohol. Therefore, dynamic risk factors incorporate contextual, proximal, and temporal variables as antecedents to index incidents. Correspondingly, treatment, intervention, or self-regulation can impinge on these factors providing protective circumstances against committing crime. Consideration of dynamic factors certainly takes account of the offense process and it is on these factors that the clinician would begin assessment and consider treatment.

Hanson and Harris (2000) studied the predictive effects of dynamic risk variables on 208 sex offense recidivists and 201 nonrecidivist offenders who had completed probation. Significant variables were poor social support, attitudes tolerant of sexual assault, antisocial lifestyle, poor self-management strategies, poor cooperation with supervision/treatment, and increased anger and subjective stress just before reoffending. They constructed a regression model that significantly predicted reoffending and, importantly, they also ascertained that these dynamic variables provided additional predictive value when static risk assessment was statistically covaried (i.e., taken into account).

Thornton (2002) developed a framework for the assessment of dynamic risk factors in sex offenders. He set out four domains, the first of which was socioaffective functioning or the way an individual relates to other people when angry, anxious, depressed, or experiencing low self-esteem. In relation to sexual incidents, low self-esteem and loneliness can be antecedents to inappropriate or violent sexual behavior (Beech, Friendship, Erikson, & Hanson, 2002). The second domain relates to distorted attitudes and beliefs where there has been a considerable interest in relation to cognitive distortions for sex offenders (e.g., Ward, Hudson, & Keenan, 1998; Ward & Hudson, 2000). The third domain, self- management, refers to the individual's current ability to engage in appropriate problem solving, impulse control, and ability to regulate personal behavior. Clearly these are offense related issues and deficits in such self-regulation would be relevant for the assessment of increased immediate risk. Self-regulation has also been employed as a fundamental principle guiding recent developments in the assessment and treatment of sex offenders (Ward & Hudson, 2000) and has been even more heavily indicated for sex offenders with IDD (Lindsay, 2009). The fourth domain mentioned in the Thornton (2002) framework was offense related sexual preference, which was split into sexual drive and deviant sexual preference.

For sex offenders with IDD socioaffective functioning is extremely important. Antisocial and hostile attitude emerged most frequently from studies reviewing dynamic risk factors in offenders. Indeed, in the field of IDD, hostility and anger have attracted most of the research when compared with other dynamic risk factors. Taylor (2002) found that aggressive behavior presents a serious risk for staff in IDD services and is the primary reason why people with IDD are admitted or readmitted to institutions. However, although hostile attitude and anger emerged persistently from studies assessing risk for future violent incidents, it has to be acknowledged that sex offenders with IDD tend to show lower levels of anger than other offenders with IDD. Lindsay, Michie et al. (2006), Lindsay, Steele et al., (2006) and Lindsay, Steptoe, Haut, and Brewster (2011), in evaluations of a forensic IDD service on 247 and 309 offenders, respectively, found that sex offenders show significantly lower levels of anger and aggression and lower levels of other emotional difficulties than other male offenders or female offenders.

In consideration of the second group of factors, distortions in attitudes, cognitions, and beliefs, a considerable amount of work has been completed with sex offenders with IDD. The most widely reported assessment of attitudes and beliefs associated with sexual offending that has been developed for men with IDD is the Questionnaire on Attitudes Consistent with Sexual Offending (QACSO: Lindsay et al., 2007). The QACSO consists of seven scales assessing attitudes that could be considered permissive of or consistent with seven different types of sexual offenses. The types of attitudes assessed are those which minimize harm to victim, which mitigate the offender's responsibility, which moves some of the responsibility for the offense onto the victim, and other attitudes that might excuse the actions of the offender for various reasons. The seven sections include rape and attitudes to women, voyeurism, exhibitionism, dating abuse, stalking, homosexual assault (offenses against men), and offenses against children. Lindsay et al. (2007) compared

41 sex offenders with IDD, 34 other types of male offenders with IDD (generally violent or alcohol-related offenses), 30 nonoffenders with IDD, and 31 mainstream nonoffending males. The QACSO had good reliability and internal consistency and differentiated between the four groups with sex offenders endorsing a significantly greater number of cognitive distortions in all other groups. The effect sizes for these differences were large. Langdon and Talbot (2006) also used the QACSO to assess levels of cognitive distortion in sex offenders and found that sex offenders with IDD had significantly higher scores on the QACSO than nonoffenders.

Lindsay, Michie et al., (2006) *applies to both study sites* tested attitudinal differences between offenders against women, offenders against children, and exhibitionists. In two separate studies, on two separate sites, offenders against women had higher scores than the other cohorts on the rape and attitudes to women scale, whereas the offenders against children had higher scores on the child scale than the other cohorts. Therefore, there was some indication of specificity in cognitive distortions between offenders against women and offenders against children.

Lindsay and Beail (2004) conducted a study that examined the predictive value of a large number of known risk assessment variables. They employed a sample of 52 sex offenders with IDD, 18 of whom went on to commit a further sexual offense following treatment. They found that antisocial attitude, low self-esteem, attitudes tolerant of sexual crimes, low treatment motivation, deteriorating treatment compliance, and staff complacency all contributed to the predictive regression model. Dynamic predictors were most significant: 1) antisocial attitude, 2) denial of crime, 3) allowances made by staff, and 4) deteriorating compliance. It was interesting that of the 50 variables used, the most significant contribution with the strongest predictive power came from three variables—allowances made by staff, antisocial attitude, and poor relationship with mother. It can be seen that two of these are dynamic, and more dynamic variables generally contributed to the regression model than did static variables in this study.

Boer, Tough, and Haaven (2004) outlined several variables that they considered to be important in the structured assessment of future recidivism by sex offenders with IDD. These variables comprised four categories: 1) stable dynamic (staff and environment), 2) acute dynamic (staff and environment), 3) stable dynamic (offenders), and 4) acute dynamic (offenders). In total, Boer et al. (2004) reviewed 30 dynamic variables including such items as communication amongst supervisory staff, client-specific knowledge of staff, new staff entering the clinical team, monitoring of the offender by staff, attitudes toward compliance of the offender, mental health problems, relationship skills, impulsiveness, changes in social support, changes in dynamic abuse, and coping strategies of the offender. This research did not provide empirical support for the model, and it is likely that with 30 dynamic variables there would be significant colinearity among the variables with some redundancy. However, as a theoretical framework, the model considers important aspects for current management of sexual offenders with IDD. Of note, Blacker, Beech, Wilcox, and Boer (2011) studied 44 sex offenders with special needs, many of whom had IDD, and found that the assessment developed by Boer et al. (2004) was a reasonable predictor of sexual recidivism.

## CLINICAL AND TREATMENT IMPLICATIONS OF RISK FRAMEWORK

As indicated in the preceding review, risk assessment has made a significant contribution to good clinical practice by placing historical information within a coherent structure and providing a broad template for the clinician. Although most clinicians would always have had a purpose when gathering information on attachments, schooling, relationships through childhood and adolescence, history of alcohol and substance abuse, and so on, all of this information can now be placed within a broad framework for risk assessment. Studies have previously shown that clinical judgment, unsupported by research information on risk assessment, has provided very poor risk predictions (Litwack, 2001; Quinsey et al., 1998). Risk assessment also allows the clinician to give appropriate weighting and importance to various pieces of information taken during a history. In some ways, actuarial risk assessment may seem like common sense. For example, it may appear that conduct disorder and attachment difficulties as a child would likely contribute to risk as an adult. However, the fact that clinical risk assessment has been so poor as a predictor suggests that what we now consider common sense has changed. In this way, I believe that common sense has caught up with available research conducted through the 1980s and 1990s. Indeed, in relation to IDD, McMillan, Hastings, and Coldwell (2004) found that a combined clinical judgment on behalf of the clinical team, including psychologists, psychiatrists, and nurses, was as good a predictor as an actuarial assessment incorporating previous violence.

Completing a historical risk assessment places an individual within a band of risk for future incidents. The band is likely to be low risk, medium risk, high risk, very high risk, or some such graduation. For example, while the Static-99 has such a series of risk gradings, (low risk to very high risk), the VRAG has nine risk bands. The author uses actuarial risk assessment as a background against which to place further information about the individual and prefers a simple three- or four-category evaluation from low risk to very high risk.

Once this background has been set, information on dynamic variables can be considered more meaningfully, as depicted in the following case illustrations:

### Case of John

John is an individual with mild IDD who had several sexual incidents with other males. These incidents were noncontact or minimal contact convictions. He has been convicted of indecent exposure on two occasions in parks with other adult men and has also been charged and convicted with touching other men on the buttocks or legs on top of their clothing. He has never been convicted of violent offenses and has no history of violence.

John was brought up by both his parents and still visits them regularly while living in supported accommodation. He is quite effeminate in his interpersonal style and said that he had had a few short, same-sex encounters as a teenager and as a young adult. He enjoyed school and had no history of truancy or disruption. Although he admitted a few occasions of being intoxicated, he did not have a history of alcohol abuse and alcohol was never involved in any of his offenses. When assessed, he had a low risk for violent offending but a very high risk for sexual offenses. He was not of an antagonistic or violent nature, currently did not abuse alcohol or drugs, had no history of confrontation or antagonism toward authority or any occupational regime, and was generally cooperative with his daily routines. These various risk assessments were helpful when discussing his management with authorities. The police, having conducted a risk assessment for sexual violence, had concluded, rightly, that he was a high risk. They therefore thought that he should be either escorted 24 hours a day or managed in a secure setting. However, when the other risk assessments were discussed with the various individuals involved, it became clear that a long-term treatment program would be sufficient to address his needs and the needs of the local community.

In fact, the treatment program was highly successful and John was able to live a normal life free from escort and secure environments as long as he maintained his treatment sessions. In this way, risk assessment (including various psychological assessments to review cognition and emotion) was a powerful clinical too to develop appropriate treatment and management programs and to make the argument that undue restriction for John was unnecessary while an appropriate treatment program was important. "High risk" was placed in context so that various officers involved could understand its meaning and subtlety.

## Case of Ian

Ian was a man with mild learning disabilities who had been convicted of violent offenses. His father had abused alcohol and maltreated the family throughout his childhood and his parents had separated when he was 8 years old. Ian had a history of school disruption and had been excluded and eventually expelled when he was 14 years old because of violence toward other pupils and staff. He then attended a residential school for boys with disruptive behavior and IDD. He began drinking alcohol at an early age and continued alcohol abuse throughout his teenage years and early adulthood. His first conviction was at 16 years of age for stealing alcohol from a local shop. When confronted by the shopkeeper, he was violent toward him. This pattern continued with incidents of theft and occasional incidents of violence until his referral for treatment.

In Ian's case, he was assessed as having a high risk for future violence and also had a number of dynamic risk features in his current case profile. He continued to be antagonistic, abused alcohol, was noncompliant with various regimes, and had contravened the conditions of his probation on two previous occasions. Psychological assessment revealed cognitions consistent with violence. For example, Ian believed that you had to be aggressive with people or they would take advantage of you. He also thought that if other people were irritating him he should become aggressive toward them. These factors, suggesting a high level of dynamic risk, were placed in the context of an individual who is a high actuarial risk for future violence. One positive feature in Ian's case was that he had never been physically aggressive toward others—accordingly, community placements were still willing to accept him as long as there was some assurance that treatment services would be provided. With colleagues, the author was able to offer high intensity treatment services involving day attendance for anger management, social problem-solving groups, alcohol education and treatment, and help with daily living skills. We also offered 2 days in occupational placement activity and attendance at a drop-in day center. With such frequent attendance at services, housing associations were willing to offer him supported accommodation so that at other times during the week we could coordinate someone going into his house and supporting him with daily living skills and community shopping activities. This level of support was success-ful with a few setbacks. He was occasionally confrontational with others at the occupational placement. When he was aggressive with other service users or staff, all of the information could be used during treatment sessions so that the various services were coordinated.

When one works in forensic IDD services, it is apparent that representatives of community services such as the police and housing associations are more tolerant of high-risk aggressive offenses than high-risk sexual offenses, even when the latter are relatively low level. Had Ian been assessed as having a high actuarial risk of sexual incidents (rather than violent incidents) and had a high dynamic risk of confrontation and violence, the community agencies would have been much less willing to accept him as a client. In the author's experience, the police would also have had much greater involvement, placing pressure to have Ian under constant or frequent escort. Had he continued to have occasional sexual offenses or inappropriate sexual behavior, it is suggested that others' tolerance would not have lasted. However, the risk assessments led to decisions being made about his placement and concomitant high-intensity treatment over a long period of time. Although he continued to have occasional aggressive outbursts, treatment and placement over subsequent years proved extremely successful. His aggression was reduced, he stopped stealing, and his alcohol intake was reduced (although he continued to have occasional binge-drinking episodes).

## SUMMARY AND CONCLUSIONS

The evaluation of risk for sexual offenders and general offenders with IDD has significantly advanced in the last few years. Studies that have been conducted on offenders with IDD suggest that the results of risk assessment, based on actuarial variables, allow prediction of violent and sexual incidents as well as they do in mainstream offender groups. In one study (Gray et al., 2007) it was found that the historical items in the HCR-20 showed superior predictive accuracy on offenders with IDD when compared to mainstream offenders. One further study (Lindsay et al., 2004) found that many of the risk variables for future sexual offenses emerged from a regression analysis in a manner similar to that found in mainstream offenders. However, these authors also noted that dynamic risk variables appeared to emerge with greater potency than static risk variables, suggesting that assessment of dynamic risk variables or more important for offenders with IDD than for mainstream offenders.

Dynamic variables are important considerations for this population both from the point of determining proximal risk and from the point of view of developing a treatment program. In summary, dynamic risk variables are those that are of interest to professionals who may be assessing with a view to implementing a treatment program. The case illustrations have shown the way in which such risk assessment can flow into considerations for treatment and management of sex offenders. Therefore, although research and risk assessment for sex offenders with IDD is at a relatively early stage, it already seems clear that such assessment is of crucial value both in helping to organize an approach to a clinical case and in establishing programs of treatment and management.

## REFERENCES

Abel, G.G., Gore, D. K., Holland, C.L., Camp, N., Becker, J.V., & Rathner, J. (1989). The measurement of the cognitive distortions of child molesters. *Annals of Sex Research, 3,* 135–153.

Barbaree, H.E., Seto, M.C., Langton, C.M., & Peacock, E.J. (2001). Evaluating the predictive accuracy of six risk assessment instruments for adult sex offenders. *Criminal Justice & Behaviour, 28,* 490–521.

Bartosh, D.L., Garby, T., Lewis, D., & Gray, S. (2003). Differences in the predictive validity of actuarial risk assessments in relation to sex offender type. *International Journal of Offender Therapy & Comparative Criminology, 47,* 422–438.

Beech, A., Friendship, C., Erikson, M., & Hanson, R.K. (2002). The relationship between static and dynamic risk factors and reconviction in a sample of UK child abusers. *Sexual Abuse: A Journal of Research & Treatment, 14,* 155–167.

Belfrage, H. & Dougals, K.S. (2002). Treatment effects on forensic psychiatric patients measures with the HCR-20 violence risk assessment scheme. *International Journal of Forensic Mental Health, 1,* 25–36.

Blacker, J., Beech, A.J., Wilcox D.T., & Boer, D.P. (2011). The Assessment of Dynamic Risk and Recidivism in a Sample of Special Needs Sexual Offenders. *Psychology Crime and Law, 17,* 75–92.

Boer, D.P., Frize, M., Pappas, R., Morrissey, C, & Lindsay, W. (2010) Adaptations to the SVR-20 for Offenders with Intellectual Disabilities. In L. Craig, W.R. Lindsay and K. Browne (Eds.) *Assessment and Treatment of Sexual Offenders with Intellectual Disability: A Handbook.* Chichester, UK: Wiley Blackwell.

Boer, D.P., Hart, S.D., Kropp, P.R., & Webster, C.D. (1997). Manual for the sexual violence risk-20: Professional guidelines for assessing risk of sexual violence. Vancouver, BC: British Columbia Institute on Family Violence & Mental Health, Law & Policy Institute, Simon Fraser University.

Boer, D.P., Tough, S., & Haaven, J. (2004). Assessment of risk manageability of developmentally disabled sex offenders. *Journal of Applied Research in Intellectual Disabilities, 17,* 275–284.

de Vogel, V., & de Ruiter, C. (2005). The HCR-20 in personality disordered female offenders: A comparison with a matched sample of males. *Clinical Psychology and Psychotherapy, 12,* 226–240.

Dolan, M., & Khawaja, A. (2004). The HCR-20 and post discharge outcome in male patients discharged from medium security in the UK. *Aggressive Behaviour, 30,* 469–483.

Douglas, K.S. and Ogloff, J.R. (2003). The impact of confidence on the accuracy of structured professional and actuarial violence risk judgements in a sample of forensic psychiatric patients. *Law and Human Behaviour, 27,* 573–87.

Epperson, D.L., Kaul, J .D., Huot, S.J., Hesselton, D., & Alexander, W. (1998). *Minnesota Sex Offender Screening Tool—Revised (MnSOST-R).* St. Paul, MN: Minnesota Department of Corrections.

Grann, M., Belfrage, H., & Tengstrom, A. (2000). Actuarial assessment of risk for violence: predictive validity of the VRAG and the historical part of the HCR-20. *Criminal Justice and Behaviour, 27,* 97–114.

Gray, N.S., Fitzgerald, S., Taylor, J., MacCulloch, M & Snowden, R. (2007) Predicting Future Reconviction in Offenders with Intellectual Disabilities: The Predictive Efficacy of the VRAG, PCL-SV and the HCR-20. *Psychological Assessment, 19,* 474–79.

Grevatt, M., Thomas-Peter, B., & Hughes, G. (2004). Violence, mental disorder and risk assessment; can structured clinical assessments predict the short-term risk of inpatient violence? *Journal of Forensic Psychiatry and Psychology, 15,* 278–292.

Hanson, R.K. (1997). *The development of a brief actuarial risk scale for sexual offence recidivism* (user report 1997–2004). Ottawa: Department of the Solicitor General of Canada.

Hanson, R.K., & Harris, A.J.R. (2000). Where should we intervene? Dynamic predictors of sexual offence recidivism. *Criminal Justice & Behaviour, 27,* 6–35.

Hanson, R.K., & Thornton, D. (1999). *Static-99: Improving actuarial risk assessments for sex offenders* (user report 1999-02). Ottawa: Department of the Solicitor General of Canada.

Hanson, R.K., & Thornton, D. (2003). *Notes on the development of Static-2002* (user report 2003-01). Ottawa, Ontario: Department of the Solicitor General of Canada.

Hare, R.D. (1991). *The Hare Psychopathy Checklist–Revised*. North Tonawanda, NY: Multi-Health Systems.

Harris, G.T., Rice, M.E., & Quinsey, V.L. (1993). Violent recidivism of mentally disordered offenders: the development of a statistical prediction instrument. *Criminal Justice and Behaviour, 20,* 315–335.

Harris, G.T., Rice, M.E., Quinsey, V.L., Lalumiere, M.L., Boer, D., & Lang, C. (2003). A multi-site comparison of actuarial risk instruments for sex offenders. *Psychological Assessment, 15,* 413–425.

Hart, S.D., Cox, D.N., & Hare, R.D. (1995). *The Hare PCL:SV.* Toronto, Ontaria: Multi-health Systems.

Hingsburger, D., Griffiths, D. & Quinsey, V. (1991) Detecting counterfeit deviance: differentiating sexual deviance from sexual inappropriateness. *Habilitation Mental Health Care Newsletter, 10,* 51–54

Kolton, D.J.C., Boer, A., & Boer, D.P. (2001). A revision of the Abel and Becker Cognition Scale for intellectually disabled sexual offenders. *Sexual Abuse: A Journal of Research & Treatment, 13,* 217–219.

Kroner, D.G.& Mills, J.F. (2001). The accuracy of five risk appraisal instruments in predicting institutional misconduct and in knew convictions. *Criminal Justice and Behaviour, 28,* 471–489.

Langdon, P.E., & Talbot, T.J. (2006). Locus of control and sex offenders with an intellectual disability. *International Journal of Offender Therapy & Comparative Criminology, 50,* 391–401.

Langton, C.M., Barbaree, H.E., Seto, M.C., Peacock, E.J., Harkins, L., & Hansen, K.T. (2007). Actuarial assessment of risk for re-offence amongst adult sex offenders: Evaluating the predictive accuracy of the Static-2002 and five other instruments. *Criminal Justice & Behaviour, 24,* 37–59.

Lindsay, W.R. (2009) *The treatment of sex offenders with developmental disabilities: A practice workbook.* Chichester, UK: Wiley Blackwell.

Lindsay, W.R., & Beail, N. (2004). Risk assessment: actuarial prediction and clinical judgment of offending incidents and behaviour for intellectual disability services. *Journal of Applied Research in Intellectual Disabilities, 17,* 229–234.

Lindsay, W.R., Elliot, S., & Astell, A. (2004). Predictors of sexual offence recidivism in offenders with intellectual disability. *Journal of Applied Research in Intellectual Disabilities, 17,* 267–274.

Lindsay, W.R., Hogue, T., Taylor, J.L., Steptoe, L., Mooney, P., Johnston., S., et al. (2008). Risk assessment in offenders with intellectual disabilities: A comparison across three levels of security. *International Journal of Offender Therapy & Comparative Criminology, 52,* 90–111.

Lindsay, W.R., Law, J., Quinn, K., Smart, N., & Smith, A.H.W. (2001). A comparison of physical and sexual abuse histories: Sexual and nonsexual offenders with intellectual disability. *Child Abuse & Neglect, 25,* 989–995.

Lindsay, W.R., Michie, A.M., Whitefield, E., Martin, V., Grieve, A., & Carson, D. (2006). Response patterns on the Questionnaire on Attitudes Consistent with Sexual Offending in groups of sex offenders with intellectual disability. *Journal of Applied Research in Intellectual Disabilities, 19,* 47–54.

Lindsay, W.R., Steele, L., Smith, A.H.W., Quinn, K. & Allan, R. (2006). A community forensic intellectual disability service: 12 year follow-up of referrals, analysis of referral patters and assessment of harm reduction. *Legal and Criminological Psychology, 11,* 113–130.

Lindsay, W.R., Steptoe L., Haut, F., & Brewster, C. (2011) An evaluation and 20 year follow up of a community forensic intellectual disability service. Manuscript submitted for publication.

Lindsay, W.R., Whitefield, E., & Carson, D. (2007). An assessment for attitudes consistent with sexual offending for use with offenders with intellectual disability. *Legal & Criminological Psychology, 12,* 55–68.

Litwack, T.R. (2001). Actuarial versus clinical assessments of dangerousness. *Psychology, Public Policy & Law, 7,* 409–443.

MacMillan, D., Hastings, R. & Coldwell, J. (2004). Clinical and actuarial prediction of physical violence in a forensic intellectual disability hospital: a longitudinal study. *Journal of Applied Research in Intellectual Disabilities, 17,* 255–266.

Quinsey, V.L., Harris, G.T., Rice, M.E. & Cormier, C.A. (1998). *Violent offenders: Appraising and managing risk.* Washington DC: Americal Psychological Association.

Quinsey, V.L., Harris, G.T., Rice, M.E., & Cormier, C.A. (2005). *Violent offenders, appraisal and managing risk.* 2nd Ed. Washington DC: American Psychological Association.

Sjostedt, G., & Langstrom, N. (2002). Assessment of risk for criminal recidivism among rapists: A comparison of four different measures. *Psychology, Crime & Law, 8,* 25–40.

Strand, S., & Belfrage, H. (2001). Comparison of HCR-20 scores in violent mentally disordered men and women. Gender differences and similarities. *Psychology, Crime & Law, 7,* 71–79.

Taylor, J.L. (2002). A review of the assessment and treatment of anger and aggression in offenders with intellectual disability. *Journal of Intellectual Disability Research, 46*(Suppl. 1), 57–73.

Taylor, J.L., Lindsay, W.R., Hogue, T.E., Mooney, P., Steptoe, L., Johnston, S., et al. (2010). Use of the HCR-20 in offenders with intellectual disability. Paper presented to British Psychological Society Forensic Division Conference, Edinburgh.

Thornton, D. (2002). Constructing and testing a framework for dynamic risk assessment. *Sexual Abuse: A Journal of Research & Treatment, 14,* 139–153.

Ward, T., & Hudson, S.M. (2000). A self-regulation model of the relapse prevention process. In D.R. Laws, S.M. Hudson, & T. Ward (Eds.), *Remaking relapse prevention with sex offenders: A source book* (pp. 79–101). Thousand Oaks, CA: Sage.

Ward, T., Hudson, S.M., & Keenan, T. (1998). A self-regulation model of the sexual offence process. *Sexual Abuse: A Journal of Research & Treatment, 10,* 141–157.

Webster, C.D., Eaves, D., Douglas, K.S., & Wintrup, A. (1995). *The HCR-20: The Assessment of Dangerousness and Risk.* Vancouver, Canada: Simon Fraser University and British Columbia Forensic Psychiatric Services Commission.

CHAPTER 7

# Behavioral Assessment and Intervention for Sex Offenders with Intellectual and Developmental Disabilities

*Timothy R. Vollmer,*

*Jorge R. Reyes, and Stephen F. Walker*

The focus of the chapter is behavioral assessment and intervention for sex offenders with intellectual/developmental disabilities (IDD). Sex offending of any kind is a critical problem, but in the chapter we focus on sex offenses committed by individuals with IDD directed at children. In addition, we concentrate on male sex offenders because female sex offenders are relatively rare (Laws & O'Donohue, 1997), and have not been a focus of our clinical work. We discuss the reasons why sex offenses by individuals with IDD create a unique set of clinical challenges. The chapter also reviews the historical context of behavioral approaches and then discusses and proposes modern applied behavior analytic methods. In the past 8 years or so, we have been developing an applied behavior analysis model for sex offenders with IDD. Accordingly, we present data from our work in clinical applications and research that has been either published, is in press, is under review for publication, or soon to be reviewed for publication. Furthermore, we suggest areas for future research and propose a clinical model ranging from assessment to generalization and maintenance.

## SEX OFFENDING BY INDIVIDUALS WITH INTELLECTUAL AND DEVELOPMENT DISABILITIES

Sexual abuse is one of the most disturbing forms of child maltreatment. Almost daily a story is publicized about child abduction, child molestation, child pornography, or rape of a child. It is less known by the culture at large that in many residential and treatment facilities, including group homes in neighborhoods around the United States and other countries, reside individuals with IDD who have committed a sex crime or crimes toward children but were adjudicated incompetent to stand trial or were otherwise placed in residential neighborhoods. As a culture, how are we addressing this issue? On one hand, we must first and foremost protect children and other members of our society such as vulnerable housemates. On the other hand, we must recognize that individuals adjudicated incompetent have not been convicted of a crime and therefore, by law, will be served under the same rules and regulations as many other individuals with IDD. Unfortunately, there is no foolproof method of addressing this challenge or for striking a good balance. However, we contend that an approach based on applied behavior analysis is the most likely to be effective and acceptable, due to its rigor in assessment, its reliance on repeated measurement, its focus on individual data, its emphasis on generalization and maintenance, and its emphasis on social validity. That said, sex offending by individuals with IDD presents several unique challenges to behavior analysts (Luiselli, 2000).

One reason that sex offending by individuals with IDD is a unique clinical challenge for applied behavior analysts is that sex offending of any kind (let alone by individuals with IDD) has characteristics that do not easily conform to behavior analytic methodology. For example, in most cases, the behavior occurs when no one (other than the offender and the offended) is watching. This is a difficult challenge for a field that relies largely on direct behavioral observation (as opposed to verbal or anecdotal report). Also, the very nature of the behavior disorder is such that we can never allow it to happen because it is far too dangerous. This is a difficult challenge for a field that relies on functional analysis as a principal form of behavioral assessment (in a functional analysis, the behavior must occur in order to test possible antecedent and consequent events responsible for maintenance of behavior). Thus, whether the individual is IDD or non-IDD, the behavior associated with sexual offending is not easily translated to common behavior analytic methodology.

A second reason for the unique challenge is that the individuals have IDD. This is a complication because the typically expected cultural practice of sentencing an individual to prison or jail usually does not happen. Because the offender is adjudicated incompetent to stand trial, he or she has the same rights to effective and active treatment as many other IDD individuals. In other words, the offender usually must have opportunities to learn skills, receive behavioral supports and services, and has a right to the least restrictive placement. It is incumbent on any interdisciplinary team to ensure that the individual is placed in as safe an environment as possible. It is also incumbent on the interdisciplinary team to ensure that any risk of reoffense, no matter what the placement, is minimized (to the greatest extent possible). Thus, when a non-IDD offender is released to the community, it is the duty of law enforcement to protect the community. When an IDD offender resides in the community or even visits the community, it is not only the duty of law enforcement to protect others, but also the duty of professional staff including behavior analysts to protect the individual and others as best as possible via intervention and treatment. A serious concern is that direct care staff are frequently not aware of court orders in place and staff monitoring is not consistent or safe enough.

The next three reasons for the unique challenge relate to social validity. Wolf (1978) proposed that relative to intervention efforts, social validity refers to the social significance of the goals, the social appropriateness of the procedures, and the social importance of the effects. On one level, few would argue the significance of the goal of eliminating reoffense. However, what about the goal of least-restrictive placement? To date, we have found no studies evaluating whether a majority of individuals favor placement of offenders in unlocked facilities even if they are deemed by a team of professionals as safe to do so. Thus, we can rely only on the fact that our legal system represents to a degree the value system of our culture. To that end, the goal of least-restrictive placement must be viewed as acceptable until otherwise challenged. If our culture ultimately decides that all sex offenders should remain indefinitely in locked facilities, much of our discussion that follows is moot. We are not taking a position one way or another; instead, we aim to address the problem given the current cultural practices.

What about the procedures? As shown later in the chapter, many of the assessment and intervention components may be unacceptable to either the offenders themselves or to others. One example of a procedure that may be unacceptable to offenders (clients) is if they are watched via hidden camera without their knowledge. On the other hand, members of our culture may recognize covert assessment as a necessary test of the offender's behavior during unsupervised activity. An example of a procedure that may be acceptable to the offender but unacceptable to others is if offenders visits community settings, such as a shopping mall or public park, in order to evaluate their level of arousal in the presence of children and other adults (Rea, DeBriere, Butler, & Saunders, 1998). From a standpoint of assessment and treatment, it is critical to know how the offender will respond, but from a standpoint of the community, such activity might be fear inducing (unacceptable) even if the activity is highly supervised by professionally trained staff.

What about the effects? With many behavioral problems commonly addressed by behavior analysts, a goal of, say, 80%–90% reduction is acceptable. For example, if self-injurious behavior is greatly reduced, an occasional episode does not necessarily damage the acceptability of the treatment outcome. Conversely, with a child sex offense, there is necessarily zero tolerance for a single episode of reoffense. Thus, can any amount of data ever produce a level of comfort for our consumers (in this case, consumers would be the community members we aim to protect)? The fact is that our legal system is arranged such that offenders with IDD sometimes end up living in neighborhoods. Lawyers have at least in some cases successfully argued that the individual has not been convicted of a crime and, therefore, requires the least-restrictive placement. Given this, a more meaningful way of framing the social validity question is as follows: Would our culture be more accepting of a neighbor who has offended toward children but has received no assessment or intervention, or would they prefer a neighbor of the same sort who has received as thorough an assessment and ongoing intervention and follow-through as possible? The answer seems obvious. Hence, we move forward on the assertion there is a role for applied behavior analysis.

## HISTORICAL BEHAVIORAL APPROACHES

Behavioral approaches were predominant in the early days of systematic assessment and treatment of sex offenders. Over time, a reliance on assessing and changing the arousal response (a common target in behavioral applications) was viewed as limited. Cognitive behavioral approaches became favored because they were more comprehensive and focused on other facets of sex offending, such as problems with stimulus control, empathy, social skills, and so on. Thus, there were advantages to the cognitive behavioral approach. However, in that approach, there is often a reliance on verbal understanding of the expected behavior change and less emphasis on measuring actual behavior change. Thus, we contend that an applied behavior analysis approach will combine the virtues of a rigorous behavioral model and a comprehensive (so-called) cognitive behavioral model. To better clarify some historical factors leading to this assertion. We discuss some of the early behavioral approaches as follows.

Before attempting any form of treatment for problem behavior, it is critical to have effective and reliable assessment methods capable of producing clear and informative outcomes. Without the information from a complete and accurate assessment, the effectiveness and durability of a treatment could be compromised. Whenever possible, assessments in behavior analysis involve systematic manipulations of conditions to identify the function of behavior, or, in other words, to identify the specific variables responsible for the occurrence and non-occurrence of behavior (e.g., Iwata, Dorsey, Slifer, Bauman, & Richman, 1982/1994). Thus, assessments for IDD sex offenders should be designed in order to identify the conditions under which an offense is most likely to occur.

A complete assessment of sexual offending would need to include aspects related to both the operant and respondent features (i.e., arousal) of sexual offending. Early examples of behavioral assessments for sex offenders tended to focus primarily on the respondent features of the sexual offenses by attempting to identify individuals' sexual preferences via detection of the arousal response (Simon & Schouten, 1991). Focusing on sexual preferences generally assumes that offenses are sexually motivated to a large degree, and research has validated that point showing that sexual preferences for children is an important factor in committing a sexual offense against a child; however, other factors, such as social support (which might be interpreted as supervision), emotional state, and substance abuse, are also considered important (Marshall & Fernandez, 2003a)

Historically, various assessment methods have been used in order to identify sexual preferences. Some of these methods have been more successful than others, and some are still in use today. Many of the earlier types of assessments involved gathering information through indirect methods, whereby individuals would be asked to report on their sexual preferences (Murphy & Barbaree, 1994). Self-reporting in general is a notoriously unreliable source of information (Miltenberger, 2008); self-reporting of sexual preferences, however, can be especially problematic because the reporter is likely motivated to provide false information. The problems inherent to self-report are not unique to the IDD population, but it becomes an even more complicated issue when taking into consideration the intellectual and verbal functioning of the individual. For example, taking self-report measures may be impossible in cases where an individual does not have the requisite skills to respond to questions about sexual preference or activity.

## Plethysmography

Although indirect methods may have value under certain conditions or when combined with other sources of information, it is not appropriate to rely on them solely. Direct assessment methods are more commonly favored in behavior analysis and their outcomes are considered to have greater utility (Miltenberger, 2008). Direct measurement of an individual's sexual arousal level is called *phallometry* or *penile plethysmography*. Phallometric assessments typically involve measuring an individual's arousal in response to some visual or auditory stimulation. The most commonly used measurement device consists of a mercury-in-rubber strain gauge worn around the shaft of the penis, which measures circumferential changes of the erectile response (Bancroft, Jones, & Pullan, 1966). The data produced from the gauges are measured through the use of a computerized interface and the combination of the strain gauge and measurement apparatus is commonly referred to as a penile plethysmograph (Laws & Marshall, 2003). This type of assessment methodology has been one of the most widely researched and yet controversial topics in the area of sexual offending assessment, and continues to be a source of debate in terms of its overall utility (Launay, 1999). For the most part, phallometry research has primarily focused on sex offenders without IDD with only a few published data sets using penile plethysmography with IDD offenders (Murphy, Coleman, & Haynes, 1983; Rea et al., 1998; Reyes et al., 2006; Rosenthal, 1973). According to Murphy, Coleman, & Haynes (1983), some literature has suggested possible problems in using phallometric assessments with individuals with IDD, but the cited references are anecdotal reports and no clear data support those claims.

There has generally been a great deal of variation in stimulus types used in arousal assessments and very little consistency exists across institutions that conduct these types of assessments (Howes, 1995). Although such variation exists, some authors have reported general strategies that address common assessment goals. For example, Lalumière and Harris (1998) reported that assessments of age and gender preferences are best accomplished by using stimuli depicting males and females at different developmental stages. Overall, however, the stimuli used in an arousal assessment can vary across a number of dimensions including the content in terms of the degree of sexually explicit content depicted (Marshall & Fernandez, 2003a), whether the stimuli are presented via videos, pictures or slides, audiotape descriptions with and without accompanying video or pictures, written text, or fantasy (Howes, 1995; Kalmus & Beech, 2005; Marshall & Fernandez, 2003a; Murphy & Barbaree, 1994), and the overall number of stimuli used in an assessment as well as the duration of each stimulus presentation (Lalumière & Harris,1998; Murphy & Barbaree,1994). It is important to note that state and federal laws often prohibit the use of sexually explicit material (Marshall & Ferndandez, 2003a). Thus, most United States–based groups use non-explicit materials, such as video clips of individuals wearing bathing suits.

Data from plethysmography are generally analyzed in terms of their raw scores (e.g., millimeter change), converting the data to percentage of full erection, and expressing the data using statistics such as z-scores (Howes, 1995; Lalumière &

Harris, 1998; Marshall, 2006a; Murphy & Barbaree, 1994). In our work, we have focused on raw measures of penile circumference, as that approach requires no modification of existing data (Reyes et al., 2006). That approach is consistent with other behavior analytic methods but represents a departure from most sex offender plethysmograph applications.

Despite the potential variability across different aspects of the assessment methodology, phallometric assessments can provide useful information in the overall assessment and treatment of sexual offenders. For example, phallometric assessments are often evaluated in terms of their predictive utility (i.e., how assessment outcomes relate to the future probability of an individual committing another offense). A consistent finding has been that showing arousal to child stimuli is one of the best predictors of reoffense (e.g., Barbaree & Marshall, 1988; Hanson & Bussiére, 1998; Hanson & Morton-Bourgon, 2004; Quinsey, Chaplin, & Carrigan, 1980). Although no studies have explicitly reported on reoffense by individuals with IDD, it makes sense to use it as a predictor given the outcomes for other sex offender populations. Furthermore, the predictive use of plethysmograph assessments appears to be even more powerful when combined with other sources of information, such as previous offenses (Quinsey, Rice, & Harris, 1995).

## Historical Behavioral Treatment Approaches

Treatment for sexual offending is a complicated concept in that it is difficult to evaluate success. In general, treatment efficacy is primarily evaluated in terms of future rates of reoffending; however, there are numerous potential problems with obtaining such information (Barbaree & Marshall, 1998). For example, studies have shown that actual reoffense rates may be underestimated or reflect behavior other than what was targeted in treatment, such as learning to avoid being caught (see Barbaree & Marshall, 1998; Hanson & Morton-Bourgon, 2004). On a more practical level, other issues stem from the problems inherent in attempting to conduct or interpret studies on treatment efficacy. For example, it is often impossible to compare outcomes across studies given that there are methodological differences and different subject populations (e.g., Hanson et al., 2002). Nonetheless, future rates of reoffending remain the standard and arguably most logical measure of treatment success. On a more molecular level, however, treatments are often first evaluated in terms of changes in deviant arousal following treatment or changes in other more subjective variables such as self-reports.

In general, early approaches to the treatment of sexual offenders were based on the assumption that deviant sexual preferences were the result of conditioning processes that had occurred at some point throughout an individual's developmental history (Laws & Marshall, 1990). As a result, the majority of early treatments tended to focus on behavioral techniques to reduce or eliminate deviant sexual preferences (for discussion, see Laws & Marshall, 2003; Quinsey & Marshall, 1983). Furthermore, given more recent research demonstrating the relationship of deviant sexual arousal to reoffending (e.g., Hanson & Bussiére, 1998; Hanson & Morton-Bourgon, 2004), the modification of deviant sexual preferences was a logical approach and it seems reasonable to assume that it would still be an important component of current treatment approaches.

Historically, the most common behavioral treatments were based on classical conditioning models including aversion therapy, covert sensitization, satiation therapy, and orgasmic reconditioning. The basic procedures involved in aversion therapies involve pairing an aversive event with an inappropriate stimulus or delivering the aversive event contingent on arousal to the inappropriate stimulus (Callahan & Leitenberg, 1973; Quinsey & Earls, 1990). The most commonly used aversive events that have been evaluated include electric shock and foul odors (Maletzky & McGovern, 1991); some studies have also investigated the use of nausea-inducing substances (Quinsey & Marshall, 1983). Overall, aversion procedures consisting of both electric shock and olfactory aversion have yet to be fully explored with IDD sex offenders and would likely be met with justified ethical concerns. Only one published study (i.e., Rosenthal, 1973) has evaluated the use of electric shock with this population, and in that study the lack of any direct measures of arousal does not allow for proper evaluation of the outcomes. Some researchers have discussed the use of aversion therapies with IDD sex offenders (Murphy, Coleman, & Haynes, 1983; Plaud, Plaud, Kolstoe, & Orvedal, 2000); however, no conclusive evidence of their effectiveness has been provided. Although there may be ethical issues with the use of aversion therapies with IDD individuals, these therapies should not be entirely discounted, especially when considered in relation to the severity of committing a sexual offense.

The procedures involved in covert sensitization are similar to those used in aversion therapies, but there is no direct contact with an aversive event. In general, deviant sexual situations or acts are described to a participant followed by a description of aversive scenes or consequences (Barbaree & Seto, 1997). The descriptions of aversive consequences can be individually tailored but can involve socially based consequences such as being discovered, going to jail (Maletzky, 1974; Murphy, Coleman, & Abel, 1983), or physically aversive consequences such as thoughts about vomiting, etc (Levin, Barry, Gambaro, Wolfinsohn, & Smith, 1977). As with aversion therapies, there does not appear to be any studies investigating the effectiveness of covert sensitization with adult male sex offenders with IDD. Some researchers have discussed using these procedures with the IDD population, but there have not been any published outcomes (e.g., Haaven, Little, & Petre-Miller, 1990; Murphy, Coleman, & Haynes, 1983). Even though covert sensitization is less intrusive than procedures involving actual contact with an aversive event (e.g., olfactory aversion), its effectiveness would have to be repeatedly demonstrated before being incorporated as an evidence-based treatment component for IDD sex offenders.

Satiation therapy involves having an individual masturbate for extended periods of time while fantasizing about deviant sexual interests (Murphy, Coleman, & Haynes, 1983). The basic idea is to have the individual continue to masturbate past ejaculation so that arousal levels are minimized while the deviant sexual fantasies are still occurring. A related form of satiation therapy, referred to as verbal satiation, consists of having an individual continually engage in deviant sexual fantasies without masturbating (Laws, 1995). Overall, the evidence supporting satiation therapy is limited within the non–IDD sex offender population, and there have not been any published accounts of satiation therapy or verbal satiation therapy with sex offenders with IDD. It is possible that the use of satiation therapy may be applicable with the IDD population, but factors stemming from an individual's level of functioning could potentially make the procedure difficult to implement. At this point, however, no definitive conclusions can be made regarding the effectiveness of using satiation therapy to reduce deviant arousal in either IDD or non–IDD sex offenders.

As a complement to decreasing deviant arousal, some treatments have been designed to increase arousal to appropriate stimuli (e.g., Earls & Castonguay, 1989; Laws, Meyer, & Holmen, 1978). As with the previously mentioned approaches, procedures to increase appropriate arousal are generally based on the theory that conditioning processes are responsible for sexual preferences and, therefore, the goal of these procedures is generally to pair masturbation and ejaculation with appropriate stimuli. Similar to the approaches attempting to decrease inappropriate arousal, orgasmic reconditioning has not been attempted with sex offenders with IDD and its usefulness with the non–IDD sex offender population is questionable as well.

Perhaps due to the overall limited information about the effectiveness of behavioral treatments, and due to the focus on arousal (reflexive behavior) rather than operant features of offending, behaviorally based sex offender treatment declined beginning in the 1980s in favor of treatments that incorporated cognitive processes. Even when decreased arousal was obtained in clinical laboratory contexts, there was no evidence that the effects spread (generalized) to other environments. According to Marshall and Laws (2003), professionals in the field believed that approaches to sex offender treatment needed to include procedures that addressed other aspects of offending such as social skills, sex education, assertiveness, empathy training, and cognitive distortions. Some researchers in the field have even proposed that the direct modification of deviant arousal is unnecessary for successful treatment. For example, Marshall and Fernandez (2003b) argued that deviant sexual preferences could be modified by focusing more on cognitive aspects such as empathy and assertiveness training. Although the basic components that make up cognitive behavioral therapy vary widely, it appears that this therapeutic approach is generally accepted as an effective treatment for sexual offenders. Cognitive behavioral treatments have become prevalent with the IDD offender population and currently appear to be the most commonly used treatment (Wilcox, 2004). *It is important, however, that to date there is little empirical justification for the use of cognitive behavioral treatment packages for sex offenders with IDD.*

In a sense, then, because historical behavioral approaches were limited, cognitive behavioral treatments began with the purpose of addressing both arousal and cognitive processes. Interestingly, current researchers in the sex offender treatment field have highlighted a drift away from the inclusion of behavioral procedures and have called for their return (Fernandez, Shingler, & Marshall, 2006). In our view, the features of offending that are deemed "cognitive" are, in fact, operant in nature and should be in the purview of behavior analytic approaches. Although it is true that procedures targeting deviant arousal only address one of the components of sexual offending, it is not clear whether the inclusion of cognitive approaches was the correct course of action to broaden the field of sex offender treatment. Early behavioral approaches were, in fact, limited, and it appears that the focus on deviant arousal of early behavioral approaches was partially responsible for a decrease in popularity. An alternative to the inclusion of cognitive treatment components, however, would be to include assessment and treatment procedures to address operant features of sexual offending in addition to the arousal-based features of offending. The goals of these procedures would be to teach, via operant conditioning, skills that may compete with or possibly even replace sexual offending. Some of these skills might include avoidance of risk situations, developing stimulus control to discriminate appropriate versus inappropriate occasions for social interaction, learning appropriate social skills, job skills, and so on. A difference between a behavioral model and a cognitive model is that the former places an emphasis on demonstration of competency and the latter places an emphasis on verbal recognition of social rules and expectations. Therefore, a modern behavioral approach would involve a combination of assessment and treatment components related to both the respondent and operant features of sexual offending, using direct behavioral measures as evidence of improvement. By "modern" behavior analytic approaches, we mean applied behavior analysis.

## APPLIED BEHAVIOR ANALYSIS AND SEX OFFENDING BY INDIVIDUALS WITH INTELLECTUAL AND DEVELOPMENTAL DISABILITIES

### Assessment

The overarching goal of a behavioral assessment of sex offending is to identify any context that could represent a high risk for reoffense. Thus, information must be obtained about the state of the individual during offenses (e.g., substance abuse), the characteristics of victims, and hypothesized sources of reinforcement (e.g., sexual reinforcement vs. other reactions for the victim or social environment). Such information can be obtained via three features of a behavioral assessment, including indirect methods (e.g., interviews and record reviews to identify the age, gender, and characteristics of victims as well as the stimulus context of the offense), preference assessments, and phallometric assessments.

We have recently explored stimulus preference assessments using a paired choice approach similar to Fisher et al. (1992). Using a computer program, the client is given a choice between two pictures of the individuals from the phallometric assessment stimuli. The frames chosen from each video were selected from a similar part in each video in order to make the pictures as similar as possible. Every attempt was made to select pictures only showing the individual's face, but some pictures also included parts of an individual's upper body as well. A picture was selected by using the computer mouse to click on the picture. Once a picture was selected, the other picture disappeared and the selected picture was enlarged to approximately 3 inches by 3 inches and appeared in the middle of the screen for 5 seconds. After 5 seconds, the picture disappeared and the computer screen remained blank for a period of 5 seconds, after which two new pictures appeared. The computer program cycled through each of the pictures until each picture was presented with every other picture and counterbalanced for a total of 18 presentations per picture. If a participant failed to select a picture within 30 seconds of the start of a trial, a prerecorded vocal prompt to select one of the pictures was presented automatically. Figure 7.1 shows the outcomes of a preference assessment (Reyes, 2009). Interestingly, the most preferred age category is consistent with the highest level of arousal by age category for this individual during a plethysmograph assessment.

One concern with prior research on phallometric assessments is that characteristically very few measures of arousal are obtained. In some cases, the individuals are exposed to multiple stimuli within a particular age category but are only exposed to each stimulus on one occasion and the average level of responding to that category is measured (e.g., Lalumière & Harris, 1998; Laws & Osborn, 1983). On the rare occasions when multiple exposures to the stimuli are presented, it is done in the context of either a pre- or posttreatment evaluation or in order to assess test-retest reliability. There are many potential limitations involved with evaluating outcomes based on few exposures to assessment stimuli. For example, there could be a number of different variables that affect how an individual will respond during an arousal assessment, such as illness, lack of sleep, and time since masturbation. Using a repeated-measures approach to arousal assessments would not control for the influence of extraneous variables, but it would allow for a more complete picture of an individual's level of arousal across time; any outlying data points would be more clearly visible, and the strategy would therefore allow for more careful evaluation of arousal patterns. Figure 7.2 is from Reyes et al. (2006) showing differentiated deviant arousal in the presence of female stimuli (these stimuli are from commercially available video clips of males and females wearing bathing suits) in the age groups of kindergarten, 6–7 years, 8–9 years, teenage, and adult.

In addition to assessing an individual's level of arousal under laboratory conditions, it is also important to assess how an individual may respond under naturalistic conditions. The ability to conduct arousal assessments in naturalistic environments using a portable plethysmograph would help to provide a potentially more accurate assessment of an individual's deviant interests given that some community settings would better approximate the conditions under which offenses were or could be committed. Aside from its use as an assessment tool, naturalistic assessments aid in evaluating generalization and maintenance of treatments that can be initiated in the clinical setting. Any interventions that are found to decrease deviant arousal in a laboratory setting would need to be evaluated outside of a laboratory setting in order for the intervention to have any practical utility. Rea et al. (1998) presented a promising approach using a portable plethysmograph, through which an offender's arousal could be tracked in community settings. We too have incorporated portable plethysmograph methodology into our clinical regimen. One example of an outcome is seen below in Figure 7.3, taken from an individual's routine visit to a community setting (Reyes, 2009). Of course, all safety precautions such as careful staff monitoring were used. Noteworthy is the increase in arousal in the presence of females ranging in age from 6–7 and 8–9 years.

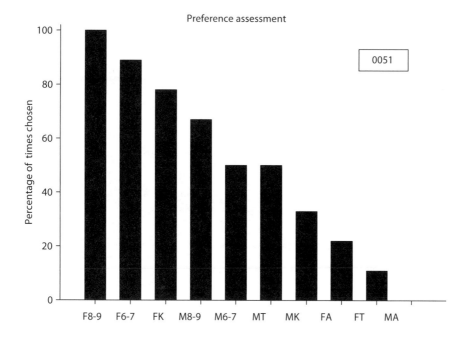

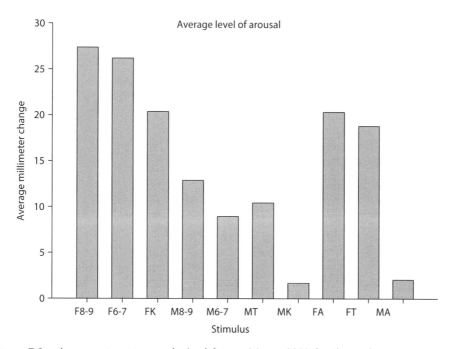

**Figure 7.1.** Assessment outcomes obtained for participant 0051 for the preference assessment (upper panel) and arousal assessments (lower panel). F and M refer to gender and numbers and descriptors refer to general age groups (K means "kindergarten" as it is presented as such in the commercially available stimulus set). (*Source:* Reyes, 2009.)

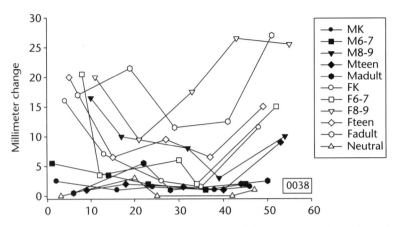

**Figure 7.2.** Assessment results for participant 0038. F and M refer to gender and numbers and descriptors refer to general age groups (K means "kindergarten" as it is presented as such in the commercially available stimulus set). (From Reyes, J.R., Vollmer, T.R., Sloman, K.N., Hall, A., Reed, R., & Jansen, G.M. [2006]. Assessment of deviant arousal in adult male sex offenders with developmental disabilities. *Journal of Applied Behavior Analysis, 39*[2], 173–188.)

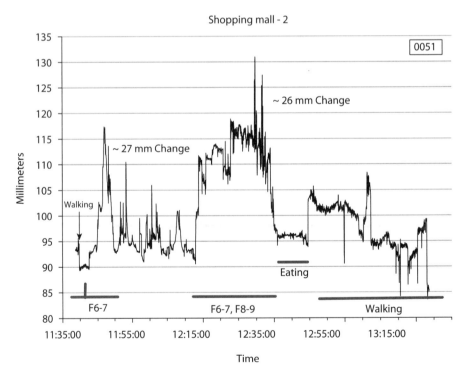

**Figure 7.3.** Arousal assessment outcomes obtained for participant 0051 during the second session at a shopping mall. Duration of relevant stimuli and events are denoted by the horizontal lines. (*Key:* F, female; numbers following F refer to the age group.) (*Source:* Reyes, 2009.)

Given that the direct observation of a sexual offense is very unlikely, it may be possible to measure other responses related to sexual offending without endangering anyone in the community. The assessment process should involve evaluating how individuals respond while in situations considered to be high risk (e.g., when the individual believes he is alone). Some offense-related behavior may include watching children, approaching areas where children are present, and frequenting locations where children could be nearby. Under ordinary circumstances, because the individuals are being closely supervised, they learn to avoid such approach responses. A critical test is how they behave when they believe they are alone.

Thus, ideally, assessments of high-risk situations would take place under conditions where individuals were led to believe that they were not being observed, but also without placing anyone in danger. These types of covert assessments have been used previously in behavioral research. For example, Himle, Miltenberger, Flessner, and Gatheridge (2004) observed children to see if they would touch or play with (unloaded artificial) handguns. Similarly, Poche, Brouwer, and Swearingen (1981) observed children to see if they would leave with a confederate "stranger" posing as a child abductor. These prior studies offer a useful methodology that could be applied in the assessment of sex offenders with IDD. For example, a situation could be arranged wherein an individual would be brought to a location for some false purpose and left alone in the context of a waiting room. Various cues could be left to signal that children may be present in an adjacent room such as the presence of toys, or even a tape-recorded voice of a child and data would be collected on how the individual responded through the use of a hidden video camera or live video feed. Information would be obtained on whether the individual attempted to move toward and enter the room, or if the individual left the area and notified someone that he was in a potentially dangerous situation.

We recently conducted several individualized assessments to see if sex offenders with IDD would attempt to look at child-related stimuli (e.g., clothing magazines with pictures of children) under conditions where they believed they were alone in a waiting room. The situation was arranged such that the waiting room had both appropriate materials (e.g., non-child–related sports or automotive magazines) and inappropriate materials (e.g., child-related clothing and toy magazines) available for browsing. Data were collected via hidden cameras (their use had been court approved and approved by a human rights committee). The primary data of interest involved which magazines the participant viewed and whether or not he tried to tear out pages of children. In one case, we found that an individual who was ordinarily a "model citizen" when supervised, repeatedly viewed and even tore out and hid photos of young children, indicating he was still a community risk despite mounds of data to the contrary in other contexts where he had been closely supervised. Similar data have been obtained in our work with offenders who steal, have a history with substance abuse (which, incidentally, can be a common antecedent for sex offending), or have a history of poor interpersonal social skills (i.e., they are observed interacting with a confederate "stranger.")

**Treatment**

One criticism of prior behavioral treatments, such as aversion therapy, is that the treatment may (or may not) be effective in a clinical context and determining whether generalization to other environments will occur needs to be explored more comprehensively (e.g., Laws, 2001). One tenet of the applied behavior analysis approach is that treatments identified in one context should be generalized to a target environment. Thus, a goal of sex offender treatment is to test and ensure efficacy in settings other than the clinical laboratory. Treatments can fall into two broad categories: those that address arousal and those that address operant features of offending.

One potential treatment component related to arousal involves masturbation but used in a different manner than treatments such as satiation therapy. The basic idea is to take advantage of the refractory period following ejaculation, during which arousal levels are generally lower. We have recently evaluated this procedure in the clinical laboratory and found that an individual who was previously aroused in the presence of child video stimuli (children wearing bathing suits), was not aroused after the opportunity to masturbate. These effects have not yet been tested in community settings, nor have the parameters of the refractory period been assessed on an individual basis. However, the early results suggest a promising line for future application, as follows:

If the evaluation showed (as it did) that arousal levels during the masturbation phases were consistently lower than in the other phases, then these procedures could be used as a possible treatment component. For example, individuals could masturbate before going into community settings where they might encounter children. The masturbation could potentially give them a window of time during which they might be less likely to become aroused and pose less of a risk to the children in the community. However, there are some potential limitations to consider. First, it is likely that different individuals have different refractory periods, so the arousal–arousal interval would vary. Each individual would have to undergo a parametric analysis whereby the time between ejaculation and assessment was varied to find the critical period of time before arousal levels return to previous strength. Second, it is not known whether refractory periods in a lab would predict refractory periods outside a lab. Thus, it would be critical to evaluate the effects of this procedure outside of the laboratory via portable plethysmograph (discussed previously). To be clear, this procedure is being proposed for use as only one component of an overall much larger treatment package.

Another potential arousal-related treatment would be designed to take advantage of the well-documented potential for individuals to suppress arousal (e.g., Laws & Rubin, 1969). The fact that individuals are capable of suppressing arousal is generally considered to be a serious limitation of arousal assessments involving the penile plethysmograph (Laws & Rubin, 1969). Instead of viewing it as a limitation, however, suppression potentially could be used as a treatment component. For example, an individual could be taught to bring his erectile responses under instructional control and to teach himself to suppress under conditions that may be high-risk for reoffending. We recently evaluated this type of intervention for two individuals in the clinical laboratory. Using a single-subject reversal design, the individuals were instructed to suppress arousal during certain phases of the plethysmograph evaluation and arousal levels would be compared to those phases where the individual was not instructed to suppress. Results for one of the individuals are presented in Figure 7.4.

A potential limitation of this suppressive approach is that once an individual had been taught to suppress his arousal, he may continue to suppress even in the conditions in which he was not instructed to do so. In short, teaching this strategy may confound plethysmograph assessments. A second potential limitation is that suppression in the laboratory may not predict suppression outside the laboratory. As with the masturbation manipulation described previously, evaluating the suppression procedures outside of a laboratory setting would be critical to determine their potential usefulness. Despite potential drawbacks, the suppression procedure would be fairly unobtrusive. Again, this is proposed as only one component of a larger intervention strategy.

Both of the foregoing procedures (the masturbation manipulation and the use of suppression) could be criticized in terms of the focus on reducing deviant arousal. As discussed previously, there does not appear to be enough evidence to show that reductions in deviant arousal alone translate into reduced levels of reoffense. However, a critical difference between these procedures and those used previously involves the embedded evaluation outside of laboratory settings. It is possible that showing decreases in arousal outside of laboratory settings does in fact more readily translate into a reduced likelihood of reoffense. That empirical question remains to be addressed.

In the currently proposed approach, addressing deviant sexual arousal is considered critical, but the treatments would also involve interventions for the operant features of sexual offending. For example, data from the covert observations would be used to determine what skills a particular individual would need to be taught in order to respond appropriately under potentially problematic situations or how to avoid those situations altogether if possible. The following is a brief passage taken from a covert observation of a sex offender and a young adult female confederate (who was actually a highly trained behavior analyst also posing as a waiting room guest). This excerpt demonstrates clearly that a target for skills training for this individual would be interpersonal interactions:

| | |
|---|---|
| Participant: | Oh, you don't have none (money), see what I'm saying, I'm your friend, I help you out, alright? |
| Confederate: | Thanks. |
| Participant: | *In a louder tone:* I'm talking, I get no answer, you like "thanks." |
| Confederate: | I've got money for food. |
| Participant: | *Still louder tone:* I know, you see what I'm saying, if you don't, if you don't have none! |
| Confederate: | Okay. |
| Participant: | *Even louder tone:* (laughs) You gotta listen to me some time. |

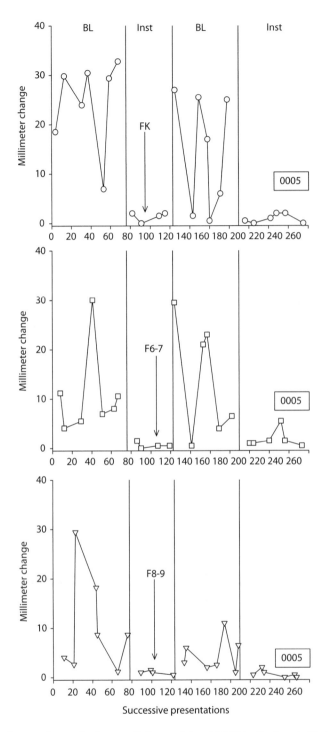

**Figure 7.4.** Suppression evaluation results for participant 0005 to the female kindergarten stimulus (upper panel), the female 6-7 stimulus (middle panel), and the female 8-9 stimulus (lower panel). (*Key:* BL, baseline; Inst, instruction.) (From Reyes, J.R., Vollmer, T.R., & Hall, A. [2011]. The influence of presession factors in the assessment of deviant arousal. *Journal of Applied Behavior Analysis, 44,* 707–717.)

| Confederate: | Mhm. |
| Participant: | *Loudest tone:* You gotta, you see, you gotta start listening to me, you be looking at the books and things. |
| Confederate: | Okay. |
| Participant: | *Walks over to confederate and yells:* You know, look look look, you lookin' that book, you don't pay no attention to me. |
| Participant: | *Stands directly in front of confederate, grabs her hand, leans down and looks into her face.* What I am saying, see what I am saying, I be telling you, if you don't have none, you don't have the money, I will help you out as a friend. |
| Confederate: | Thank you. |

At this point the therapist came back into the room and the client ran back to his chair.

Among the skills that are frequently focused on for sex offenders include social skills training and sex education (Murphy, Coleman, & Haynes, 1983). Deficits in any of these areas could be important factors related to the likelihood of reoffending, and the teaching of these skills could be accomplished via behavioral skills training. Although teaching these skills is not a novel idea in the treatment of sexual offenders (e.g., Barbaree & Marshall, 1998), cognitive–behavioral practices involve focus on changing a client's verbal behavior without necessarily changing their nonverbal behavior. Even current practitioners who follow a cognitive behavioral model have recently called for the inclusion of behavioral procedures such as modeling and role-playing for training purposes, and becoming fluent in the application of behavioral principles such as reinforcement and extinction (Fernandez et al., 2006). An applied behavior analysis model would require a demonstration of competency on the part of the participant. Behavioral skills training usually involves some combination of the following components: 1) verbal instructions, 2) modeling, 3) role playing, 4) immediate feedback, 5) delayed feedback, and 6) unobtrusive follow up observations to test competency (Miltenberger, 2008).

The covert probes described previously also could be used as a baseline for evaluating the efficacy of behavior reduction procedures including intermittent supervision, fixed-time reinforcement schedules, and differential reinforcement of other/alternative behavior. For example, we recently explored a test situation to evaluate whether we could suppress viewing child magazines and/or stealing pictures from the magazines in a waiting room. A therapist intermittently reentered the room for various reasons (e.g., "forgot my keys," "you doing okay?" etc.). We were able to suppress inappropriate behavior in this context. Such intermittent supervision is not a treatment per se, but it provides an evaluation of the level of supervision that is likely necessary in a less restrictive environment.

## ROLE AND POTENTIAL ROLE OF MODERN TECHNOLOGY

Modern technology (i.e., virtual reality (VR), video games, global positioning system (GPS) tracking) has many implications for the assessment, treatment, and placement of sex offenders, including those diagnosed with IDD. However, research demonstrating the clinical usefulness of these technologies is lacking. Additionally, the little research that has been done has focused on non-IDD offenders. This section describes current research, potential contributions, and how modern technology might be integrated with the assessment and treatment of sex offenders with IDD.

## Virtual Reality

The application of VR technology to the assessment of sexual offenders is the biggest advancement in the field since the development of the penile plethysmograph by Freund in 1963. The use of VR has allowed the field to address some of the primary criticisms of the plethysmograph: 1) the use of pictures and videos of real children and 2) the possibility of participants avoiding (i.e., not looking at) potentially arousing stimuli. As Laws (2009) stated,

> I believe… that the future belongs to virtual reality. This is a giant step forward in that it permits us to tailor entire stimulus environments to a particular individual and promises technological evaluation of a host of behaviors, internal as well as external. For many years, these have been the stuff of dreams. Now, at last, they are at hand. (p. 26)

Renaud and colleagues have led the field in the area of integrating existing assessment techniques, such as phallometric assessment, and VR technology. A study presented by Renaud, Rouleau, Granger, Barsetti, and Brouchard (2002) was the first to use a stimulus set consisting entirely of computer-generated images (avatars). A study presented by Renaud et al. (2005) was the first to simultaneously record participant's erectile response and eye movements using VR (guaranteeing that participants were attending to the stimuli). Most recently, the study presented by Renaud et al. (2009) was the first to empirically evaluate the usefulness of avatars as an assessment tool with sex offenders.

The use of avatars, although it addresses the ethical issue of using real children's pictures, provides the field with additional opportunities that until now have been impossible. First, one of biggest assumptions in the field is that increases in erectile response, once observed, are due to the age and gender of the presented stimulus (Laws, 2009). The pictures and videos that are often used as stimuli are highly complex; they often vary across a number of features (e.g., hair color, eye color, torso length) leaving open the possibility that one of the other stimulus features, besides age and gender, are controlling the erectile response. Avatars permit the modification of specific stimulus features allowing the effects of other stimulus features to be empirically evaluated. Second, the fact that avatars are modifiable leaves open the possibility of the offender being able to construct their own stimulus set. The utility of stimuli constructed by the sexual offender himself has yet to be empirically evaluated and requires further research. Finally, the use of avatars allows researchers to control the virtual environment in which the stimulus is presented. Often stimuli are either presented in a fixed environment (e.g., poolside) or in a barren environment (e.g., black background) making it impossible to evaluate the effects of different environmental settings (e.g., poolside vs. playground). It is possible that the environment in which the stimulus is presented could serve as a primary determinant of erectile response; however, this has yet to be empirically demonstrated.

Another application of VR technology that has yet to be applied to the assessment and treatment of sexual offenders is the use of video games, and virtual environments, to assess typical patterns of offense-related behavior prior to treatment, and as a means of assessing treatment effectiveness. Laws and Gress (2004) describe the general approach:

> A typical option would be to examine approach and avoidance behaviours. Let us imagine that the participant enters a VE that is more or less generic to his known or presumed sexual preferences, e.g. paedophilia. The VE would be filled with choice points, some leading toward deviant behaviour and some leading away. The VE would also be heavily laden with numerous high-risk factors of differing intensity (schoolyards, playgrounds, swimming pools, etc.). The subject would encounter models appropriate to his presumed deviant interest who, depending on what he did or said to them, would reply in kind (i.e. deviant or non-deviant). This type of VE could be used in at least two ways. First, it could be used to initially assess how an offender typically deals with risky situations in his environment. Later, as a product of treatment, his ability to use relapse prevention skills to deal with risky situations could be evaluated. (p. 193)

Along with being a useful assessment tool, video games and virtual environments could be used as a component of treatment. All that it required to transform video games into a possible treatment is the addition of a few straightforward contingencies (i.e., reinforce appropriate avoidance behavior, and provide corrective feedback for inappropriate approach behavior) to the already arranged choice points. This method of treatment has several potential benefits: 1) it would require little staff effort, 2) it would allow for training across wide numbers environmental situations, and 3) the reinforcement of appropriate behavior and corrective feedback for inappropriate behavior would be provided immediately after the target behavior. Empirical support for these assertions is needed.

## Global Positioning Systems

The use of GPS tracking devices has been the topic of much discussion in the sex offender literature and poses two primary questions: 1) is it ethical to track someone continuously every moment of their lives (Nellis, 2010), and 2) how effective is the technology at decreasing the likelihood of recidivism (Renzema & Mayo-Wilson, 2005)? The answer to the first question is difficult. As discussed previously, the IDD–offender population brings with it a unique set of legal issues that are not applicable to non-IDD offenders (e.g., offenders with IDD have been adjudicated incompetent to stand trial; therefore, they are entitled to the least-restrictive placement deemed safe for themselves and community at large). The answer to the second question is a matter of conducting more precise evaluations of the technology.

Before discussing these issues in depth, some understanding of the technical details of GPS technology is needed. With GPS tracking, it is possible to program specific "exclusion zones" for individuals. For instance, it would be possible to designate certain high-risk areas (e.g., playgrounds) as exclusions zones for an individual who has offended against children. It is then possible to set up a variety alerts (e.g., phone calls to staff, loud alarms that are worn by the individual) that would activate contingent on an individual entering or approaching a high-risk area (Nellis, 2010).

There are three different methods by which the individual can be tracked (Nellis, 2010). The GPS can be set in active mode, during which the individual's location is continuously reported, via cellular upload, to the tracking agency. Although this method is the most costly of the three, it is the most immediate and does not require the GPS data to be downloaded and analyzed at a later time. One significant benefit of this method of GPS tracking is that it allows for the individual and staff to be notified as soon as the individual approaches an exclusion area.

Second alternative, the GPS can be set to passive mode (Nellis, 2010). While the GPS is in passive mode, the individual is continuously tracked, but the data are not transmitted in real time. This method requires that the individual or his staff download the tracking data once the individual has returned home. A major limitation to this method of tracking is that if the individual approaches or enters an exclusion zone, staff is not notified until the next day.

The third alternative is the hybrid mode that blends active and passive options. As long as the individual does not approach or enter an exclusion zone, the GPS functions as it would in passive mode. However, once the individual approaches an exclusion zone the GPS switches over to active mode, alerting the individual and staff that an exclusion zone is being approached (Nellis, 2010). This third mode seems to be the best of both worlds, it is less costly than the active mode, but still provides immediate feedback to the individual and staff if an exclusion zone is approached.

At face value, the benefit of GPS tracking is obvious for the treatment and placement of offenders with IDD. When the alternatives (e.g., institutional placement, intensive supervision) are considered, GPS tracking is a less restrictive alternative. GPS tracking allows for the individual to reside in a less restrictive placement without the need of intensive staff supervision. However, researchers still question how effective GPS technology is at decreasing the likelihood of recidivism. The results of the most recent meta-analysis indicate that GPS technology is not effective in reducing the likelihood of recidivism (Renzema & Mayo-Wilson, 2005). However, it should be noted that the only two studies that showed beneficial effects of GPS tracking reported ongoing treatment during the evaluation. Given that the effects of GPS tracking have never been evaluated with offenders with IDD, and that the existing research leaves much to be desired (i.e., more controlled research is needed), the effectiveness of GPS tracking warrants empirical investigation.

One promising area for behavior analytic research using the GPS is contingency management, similar to the procedures used effectively in substance abuse treatment programs (e.g., Silverman, Chutuape, Bigelow, & Stitzer, 1999). Just like substance abuse clinicians essentially "track" substance abuse via webcam drug testing (e.g., Dallery, Glenn, & Raiff, 2007), sex offender clinicians could track violations of exclusion zones. For intervals during which violations do not occur, individuals could earn reinforcers such as store and restaurant vouchers in a differential reinforcement arrangement. It would be somewhat controversial to "pay" offenders for behaving appropriately, but every mechanism should be explored to compete against the dangerous target behavior of reoffense.

## SOME REMAINING QUESTIONS

Avoidance of child-related material (e.g., TV shows or magazines containing children) is a widely accepted component of treatment for child sexual offenders, including those diagnosed with IDD. At first glance, the avoidance of child-related material appears to be a sensible treatment recommendation. Why would you want child sex offenders to have access to pictures of children? However, there has been no empirical research demonstrating that avoidance of child-related material actually decreases the likelihood deviant arousal and offense-related behavior. In fact, depending on the underlying behavioral mechanisms, it is possible that denying child sex offender's access to child-related material could actually increase the likelihood of deviant arousal and other offense related behavior. It is likely that the origin of this often-recommended treatment component evolved from the relapse prevention (cognitive behavioral) literature (discussed previously). Like the other components of the relapse prevention model, the avoidance of child-related material warrants further investigation. It is likely that the effects of deprivation from child-related material will be idiosyncratic, which suggests a need for individualized assessment. Three potential patterns of arousal during plethysmographic assessments are hypothesized. First, some individuals might show greater levels of deviant arousal when they are not allowed to view child related material outside of sessions. Second, some individuals might show greater levels of deviant arousal when allowed to view child related material outside of sessions. Finally, some individuals might show the same levels of deviant arousal across conditions. Only in the second case would the avoidance of child-related material be a potentially useful treatment component. Three similar patterns could occur if, rather than plethysmograph assessments were used, covert observations were conducted to evaluate approach responses to child-related material or child areas when the individual is observed unobtrusively.

A related question centers on allowing child sex offenders to masturbate to pictures and videos of children. At first glance many readers will dismiss the usefulness of allowing child sex offenders to masturbate to pictures/videos of children (or, perhaps better, virtual children) as a component of treatment. However, just like avoidance of child-related material, this is a component of treatment that warrants further investigation. Specifically, does allowing child sex offenders the opportunity to masturbate to pictures/videos of children decrease or increase the likelihood of deviant arousal and other offense-related behavior? Again, it is likely that the effects of the masturbation manipulation will be idiosyncratic. Nevertheless, the results of these evaluations will provide valuable information that can be incorporated into an individualized treatment plan.

## CONCLUSION

The assessment and treatment of sex offenders with IDD is a challenging task for applied behavior analysts. We recommend a model of assessment that involves 1) reviewing documents and records relating to the offense, 2) interviewing the offender and those knowledgeable about the events surrounding the case, 3) conducting clinic-based plethysmography, 4) conducting community-based plethysmography, 5) conducting preference assessments, and 6) conducting covert probes of risk-related behavior. We recommend a model for treatment that involves arousal reduction methods and operant conditioning via behavioral skills training to teach appropriate replacement behavior during role play, virtual reality, and in situ. Making sure that all staff is aware of the person's high risks, past offenses, and current intervention strategies is also extremely important in a community group home.

However, these suggestions only scratch the surface of a very complex cultural issue. Any treatments developed will only be successful if clear efforts are made to transfer intervention procedures to less restrictive environments, such as group or family homes. Intensive staff training and the use of technology, such as GPS, will likely be required. A promising approach might be contingency management where the individual's location is tracked via GPS and reinforced in a manner similar to those found to be successful with substance abusers. That said, there is no room for error.

## REFERENCES

Bancroft, J.H., Jones, H.G., & Pullan, B.R. (1966). A simple transducer for measuring penile erection, with comments on its use in the treatment of sexual disorders. *Behaviour Research and Therapy, 4*(3), 239–241.

Barbaree, H.E., & Marshall, W.L. (1988). Deviant sexual arousal, offense history, and demographic variables as predictors of reoffense among child molesters. *Behavioral Sciences & the Law, 6*(2), 267–280.

Barbaree, H.E., & Marshall, W.L. (1998). Treatment of the sexual offender. In R.M. Wettstein (Ed.), *Treatment of offenders with mental disorders* (pp. 265–328). New York, NY: Guilford Press.

Barbaree, H.E., & Seto, M.C. (1997). Pedophilia: Assessment and treatment. In D.R. Laws & W.T. O'Donohue (Eds.), *Sexual deviance: Theory, assessment, and treatment.* (pp. 175–193). New York, NY: Guilford Press.

Callahan, E.J., & Leitenberg, H. (1973). Aversion therapy for sexual deviation: Contingent shock and covert sensitization. *Journal of Abnormal Psychology, 81*(1), 60–73.

Dallery, J., Glenn, I.M., & Raiff, B.R. (2007). An Internet-based abstinence reinforcement treatment for cigarette smoking. *Drug and Alcohol Dependence, 86*(2–3), 230–238.

Earls, C.M., & Castonguay, L.G. (1989). The evaluation of olfactory aversion for a bisexual pedophile with a single-case multiple baseline design. *Behavior Therapy, 20*(1), 137–146.

Fernandez, Y.M., Shingler, J., & Marshall, W.L. (2006). Putting "behavior" back into the cognitive-behavioral treatment of sexual offenders. In W.L. Marshall, Y.M. Fernandez, L.E. Marshall, & G.A. Serran (Eds.), *Sexual offender treatment: Controversial issues* (pp. 211–224). New York, NY: John Wiley & Sons Ltd.

Fisher, W., Piazza, C.C., Bowman, L.G., Hagopian, L.P., Owens, J.C., & Slevin, I. (1992). A comparison of two approaches for identifying reinforcers for persons with severe and profound disabilities. *Journal of Applied Behavior Analysis, 25,* 491–498.

Freund, K. (1963). A laboratory method for diagnosing predominance of homo- or hetero-erotic interest in the male. *Behaviour Research and Therapy, 1*(1), 85–93.

Haaven, J., Little, R., & Petre-Miller, D. (1990). *Treating intellectually disabled sex offenders.* Orwell, VT: The Safer Society Press.

Hanson, R.K., & Bussiére, M.T. (1998). Predicting relapse: A meta-analysis of sexual offender recidivism studies. *Journal of Consulting and Clinical Psychology, 66*(2), 348–362.

Hanson, R.K., Gordon, A., Harris, A.J.R., Marques, J.K., Murphy, W., Quinsey, V.L., & Seto, M.C. (2002). First report of the Collaborative Outcome Data Project on the effectiveness of psychological treatment for sex offenders. *Sexual Abuse: Journal of Research and Treatment, 14,* 169–194.

Hanson, R.K., & Morton-Bourgon, K. (2004). *Predictors of sexual recidivism: An updated meta-analysis.* (cat. no.: PS3-1/2004-2E-PDF). Public Works and Government Services Canada (ISBN: 0-662-36397-3).

Himle, M.B., Miltenberger, R.G., Flessner, C., & Gatheridge, B. (2004). Teaching safety skills to children to prevent gun play. *Journal of Applied Behavior Analysis, 37*(1), 1–9.

Howes, R.J. (1995). A survey of plethysmographic assessment in North America. *Sexual Abuse: Journal of Research and Treatment, 7*(1), 9–24.

Iwata, B.A., Dorsey, M.F., Slifer, K.J., Bauman, K.E., & Richman, G.S. (1982/1994). Toward a functional analysis of self-injury. *Journal of Applied Behavior Analysis, 27*(2), 197–209.

Kalmus, E., & Beech, A.R. (2005). Forensic assessment of sexual interest: A review. *Aggression and Violent Behavior, 10(2),* 193–217.

Lalumière, M.L., & Harris, G.T. (1998). Common questions regarding the use of phallometric testing with sexual offenders. *Sexual Abuse: Journal of Research and Treatment, 10*(3), 227–237.

Launay, G. (1999). The phallometric measurement of offenders: An update. *Criminal Behaviour and Mental Health, 9*(3), 254–274

Laws, D.R. (1995). Verbal satiation: Notes on procedure, with speculations on its mechanism of effect. *Sexual Abuse: Journal of Research and Treatment, 7*(2), 155–166.

Laws, D.R. (2001). Olfactory aversion: Notes on procedure, with speculations on its mechanism of effect. *Sexual Abuse: Journal of Research and Treatment, 13*(4), 275–287.

Laws, D.R. (2009). Penile plethysmography: Strengths, limitations, innovations. In D. Thornton & D.R. Laws (Eds.), *Cognitive approaches to the assessment of sexual interest in sexual offenders* (pp. 7–29). New York, NY: John Wiley and Sons Ltd.

Laws, D.R., Gress, C.L.Z. (2004). Seeing things differently: The viewing time alternative to penile plethysmography. *Legal and Criminological Psychology, 9,* 183–196.

Laws, D.R., & Marshall, W.L. (1990). A conditioning theory of the etiology and maintenance of deviant sexual preference and behavior. In W.L. Marshall, D.R. Laws, & H.E. Barbaree (Eds.), *Applied clinical psychology* (pp. 209–229). New York, NY: Plenum Press.

Laws, D.R., & Marshall, W.L. (2003). A brief history of behavioral and cognitive behavioral approaches to sexual offenders: Part 1. Early developments. *Sexual Abuse: Journal of Research and Treatment, 15*(2), 75–92.

Laws, D.R., Meyer, J., & Holmen, M.L. (1978). Reduction of sadistic sexual arousal by olfactory aversion: A case study. *Behaviour Research and Therapy, 16*(4), 281–285.

Laws, D.R., & O'Donohue, W. (1997). Fundamental issues in sexual deviance. In D.R. Laws & W. O'Donohue (Eds.), Sexual deviance: Theory, assessment, and treatment (pp. 1–21) New York, NY: Guilford Press.

Laws, D.R., & Osborn, C.A. (1983). How to build and operate a behavioral laboratory to evaluate and treat sexual deviance. In J.G. Greer, & I.R. Stuart (Eds.), *The sexual aggressor: Current perspectives on treatment* (pp. 293 R. 335). New York, NY: Van Nostrand Reinhold.

Laws, D.R., & Rubin, H.B. (1969). Instructional control of an autonomic sexual response. *Journal of Applied Behavior Analysis, 2*(2), 93–99.

Levin, S.M., Barry, S.M., Gambaro, S., Wolfinsohn, L., & Smith, A. (1977). Variations of covert sensitization in the treatment of pedophilic behavior: A case study. *Journal of Consulting and Clinical Psychology, 45*(5), 896–907.

Luiselli, J.K. (2000). Presentation of paraphilias and paraphilia-related disorders in young adults with mental retardation: Two case profiles. *Mental Health Aspects of Developmental Disabilities, 3,* 42–46.

Maletzky, B.M. (1974). "Assisted" covert sensitization in the treatment of exhibitionism. *Journal of Consulting and Clinical Psychology, 42*(1), 34–40.

Maletzky, B.M., & McGovern, K.B. (1991). *Treating the sexual offender.* Thousand Oaks, CA: Sage Publications Inc.

Marshall, W.L. (2006). Clinical and research limitations in the use of phallometric testing with sexual offenders. *Sexual Offender Treatment, 1*(1), 1–18.

Marshall, W.L., & Fernandez, Y.M. (2003a). *Phallometric testing with sexual offenders: Theory, research, and practice.* Brandon, VT: Safer Society Press.

Marshall, W.L., & Fernandez, Y.M. (2003b). Sexual preferences: Are they useful in the assessment and treatment of sexual offenders? *Aggression and Violent Behavior, 8*(2), 131–143.

Marshall, W.L., & Laws, D.R. (2003). A brief history of behavioral and cognitive behavioral approaches to sexual offender treatment: Part 2. The modern era. *Sexual Abuse: Journal of Research and Treatment, 15*(2), 93–120.

Miltenberger, R.G. (2008). *Behavior modification: Principles and procedures* (4th ed.). Belmont, CA: Wadsworth.

Murphy, W.D., & Barbaree, H.E. (1994). *Assessments of sex offenders by measures of erectile response: Psychometric properties and decision making.* Brandon, VT: The Safer Society Press.

Murphy, W.D., Coleman, E.M., & Abel, G.G. (1983). Human sexuality in the mentally retarded. In J.L. Matson & F. Andrasik (Eds.), *Treatment issues and innovations in mental retardation.* New York, NY: Plenum Press.

Murphy, W.D., Coleman, E.M., & Haynes, M.R. (1983). Treatment and evaluation issues with the mentally retarded sex offender. In J.G. Greer & I.R. Stuart (Eds.), *The sexual aggressor: Current perspectives on treatment* (pp. 22–41). New York, NY: Van Nostrand Reinhold.

Nellis, M. (2010). Eternal Vigilance Inc.: The satellite tracking of offenders in "real time." *Journal of Technology in Human Services, 28*(1–2), 23–43.

Plaud, J.J., Plaud, D.M., Kolstoe, P.D., & Orvedal, L. (2000). Behavioral treatment of sexually offending behavior. *Mental Health Aspects of Developmental Disabilities, 3,* 54–61.

Poche, C., Brouwer, R., & Swearingen, M. (1981). Teaching self-protection to young children. *Journal of Applied Behavior Analysis, 14*(2), 169–176.

Quinsey, V.L., Chaplin, T.C., & Carrigan, W.F. (1980). Biofeedback and signaled punishment in the modification of inappropriate sexual age preferences. *Behavior Therapy, 11*(4), 567–576.

Quinsey, V.L., & Earls, C.M. (1990). The modification of sexual preferences. In W.L. Marshall, D.R. Laws, & H.E. Barbaree (Eds.), *Applied clinical psychology* (pp. 279–295). New York, NY: Plenum Press.

Quinsey, V.L., & Marshall, W.L. (1983). Procedures for reducing inappropriate sexual arousal: An evaluation review. In J.G. Greer, & I.R. Stuart, (Eds.), *The sexual aggressor: Current perspectives on treatment.* (pp. 267–289). New York: Van Nostrand Reinhold.

Quinsey, V.L., Rice, M.E., & Harris, G.T. (1995). Actuarial prediction of sexual recidivism. *Journal of Interpersonal Violence, 10*(1), 85–105.

Rea, J.A., DeBriere, T., Butler, K., & Saunders, K.J. (1998). An analysis of four sexual offenders' arousal in the natural environment through the use of a portable penile plethysmograph. *Sexual Abuse: Journal of Research and Treatment, 10*(3), 239–255.

Renaud, P., Chartier, S., Rouleau, J.L., Proulx, J., Decarie, J., Trottier, D., et al. (2009). Gaze behavior nonlinear dynamics assessed in virtual immersion as a diagnostic index of sexual deviancy: preliminary results. *Journal of Virtual Reality and Broadcasting, 6,* 1–11.

Renaud, P., Proulx, P., Rouleau, J.L., Bouchard, S., Madrigrano, G., Bradford, J., (2005). The recording of observational behaviors in virtual immersion: A new research and clinical tool to address the problem of sexual preferences with paraphiliacs. *Annual Review of Cyber Therapy and Telemedicine, 3,* 85–92.

Renaud, P., Rouleau, J.L., Granger, L., Barsetti, D.P., & Bouchard, S. (2002). Measuring sexual preferences in virtual reality: A pilot study. *Cyberpsychology and Behavior, 5,* 1–9.

Renzema, M., & Mayo-Wilson, E. (2005). Can electronic monitoring reduce crime for moderate to high-risk offenders? *Journal of Experimental Criminology, 1*(2), 215–237.

Reyes, J.R. (2009). Assessment of sex offenders with developmental disabilities. *Dissertation Abstracts International, 69*(10). (UMI No. 3334500)

Reyes, J.R., Vollmer, T.R., & Hall, A. (2011). The influence of presession factors in the assessment of deviant arousal. *Journal of Applied Behavior Analysis, 44,* 707–717.

Reyes, J.R., Vollmer, T.R., Sloman, K.N., Hall, A., Reed, R. Jansen, G., M. (2006). Assessment of deviant arousal in adult male sex offenders with developmental disabilities. *Journal of Applied Behavior Analysis, 39*(2), 173–188.

Rosenthal, T.L. (1973). Response-contingent versus fixed punishment in aversion conditioning of pedophilia: A case study. *Journal of Nervous and Mental Disease, 156*(6), 440–443.

Silverman, K., Chutuape, M.A., Bigelow, G.E., & Stitzer, M.L. (1999). Voucher-based reinforcement of cocaine abstinence in treatment-resistant methadone patients: Effects of reinforcement. *Psychopharmacology 146,* 128–138.

Simon, W.T., & Schouten P.G.W. (1991). Plethsmography in the assessment and treatment of sexual deviance: An overview. *Archives of Sexual Behavior, 20*(1), 75–91.

Wilcox, D.T. (2004). Treatment of intellectually disabled individuals who have committed sexual offences: A review of the literature. *Journal of Sexual Aggression, 10*(1), 85–100.

Wolf, M.M. (1978). Social validity: The case for subjective measurement or how applied behavior analysis is finding its heart. *Journal of Applied Behavior Analysis, 11*(2), 203–214.

# Problem-Solving Treatment for Sexual Offending

**CHAPTER**

*Christine Maguth Nezu,*
*Travis A. Cos, and Arthur M. Nezu*

Problem-solving therapy (PST) is a cognitive–behavioral intervention that focuses on training individuals in the effective application of adaptive problem-solving attitudes and skills (A.M. Nezu, 2004). Originally developed for individuals with average intellectual functioning (D'Zurilla & Goldfried, 1971; D'Zurilla & Nezu, 2001, 2007), PST has been also adapted for people with intellectual and developmental disabilities (IDD) and found to be effective in improving their psychological and adaptive functioning and decreasing certain challenging social behaviors (e.g., Loumidis & Hill, 1997; C.M. Nezu, A.M. Nezu, & Arean, 1991). More recently, it has been applied as a treatment for sexual offending in general (e.g., C.M. Nezu, D'Zurilla, & Nezu, 2005), and to individuals with IDD as well (e.g., C.M. Nezu, Fiore, & Nezu, 2006). We begin this chapter with a description of sexual offending among individuals with IDD, followed by an overview of PST and its underlying conceptual framework. In addition, we provide treatment guidelines and end with a series of recommendations for future research and service delivery.

## SEXUAL OFFENDERS

Sexual offenders are individuals who have committed a sex offense or engaged in sex offending behavior (C.M. Nezu, Nezu, Klein, & Clair, 2007). The term "sex offending" is a psycholegal one that encompasses a broad set of behaviors such as nonconsensual sexual conduct with an adult or sexual behavior with a minor (Lanyon, 2001). Many individuals identified as sex offenders are also characterized as having deviant sexual interests or diagnosed with specific paraphilias, such as pedophilia or voyeurism. However, having these interests is different from committing a sex offense; some individuals with paraphilias and other deviant sexual interests may never actually engage in sex offending behavior. Similarly, it is possible for individuals to commit a sex offense in the absence of deviant sexual interests or a diagnosed paraphilia. In general, there is a significant degree of heterogeneity among individuals who commit sex offenses (C.M. Nezu et al., 2007). Individuals who commit such offenses vary across age, race, gender, socioeconomic status, offending history, and many other variables.

## Sex Offenders with Intellectual or Developmental Disabilities

Although numerous studies have attempted to identify the actual percentage of individuals with IDD who commit sex offenses, as well as the percentage of sexual offenders who have IDD, methodologies of studies investigating such incidence rates are so variable that conclusions are difficult to draw (Lindsay, 2002a). Lindsay (2002b), for example, notes that variability in estimates are often a function of specific inclusion criteria (e.g., what type of sexual offenses are included as inclusion criteria), how IDD is actually diagnosed (e.g., IQ criteria), and the source of a particular sample (e.g., prison vs. hospital).

## Vulnerability Factors for Sex Offending

It is generally accepted that sex offending behavior among the general population does not have a single cause, but is the result of a combination of factors (Marshall, Anderson, & Fernandez, 1999). Various behavioral and cognitive pathways comprising these risk factors interact to affect an individual's unique vulnerability for engaging in sex offending behavior. Marshall et al. (1999) describe vulnerability as an individual's attitudes, beliefs, cognitions, behavior patterns and emotions, and emphasize the importance of the role of learning in the development and maintenance of these factors. Deficits or deviance in any one or combination of these areas can increase one's vulnerability, and thus one's risk, for committing a sex offense (C.M. Nezu et al., 2007).

The empirical literature has identified several factors as possible determinants of vulnerability in the general sex offending population. Some are *static* factors, such as individual characteristics, living alone (Marques, Day, Nelson, & West, 1994), abusive early environments (Seghorn, Prentky, & Boucher, 1987), and past behavioral patterns of sex offending with a range of victims (Prentky, Knight, & Lee, 1997). Other risk factors consist of *dynamic* or changeable characteristics, such as deviant sexual preferences (Hanson & Bussiere, 1998), social incompetence (Marshall, Earls, Segal, & Drake, 1983), poor stress management (Marques et al., 1994), cognitive distortions (Ward, Hudson, & Marshall, 1995), avoidance (Prentky & Knight, 1991), psychopathy (Rice, Chaplin, Harris, & Couts, 1994), non-adherence to treatment (Marshall et al., 1999), and ineffective social problem-solving ability (C.M. Nezu, Nezu, Dudek, Peacock, & Stoll, 2005).

## Vulnerabilities in Sexual Offenders with Intellectual and Developmental Disabilities

Although the empirical literature that provides evidence for the presence of vulnerability factors in offenders with IDD is much less than for sexual offenders in general, many researchers and clinicians have suggested that similar vulnerability factors exist for sex offenders with such disabilities (C.M. Nezu et al., 2007). In general, these vulnerabilities can be categorized into two types: deviance and deficits. *Deviance* theories suggest that sexual offending behavior is a result of deviant sexual desires learned through conditioning (Marshall et al., 1999). Deviant cognitions have also been linked with risk for sex offending and have been observed in both with and without disabilities sex offenders (C.M. Nezu et al., 1998). For example, many offenders tend to distort and minimize their own behavior, as well as the intentions and consequences on their victims.

Vulnerability factors categorized as *deficits* represent variables related to poor or deficient life skills or abilities. These include poor interpersonal skills, poor coping skills, social incompetence, and poor problem solving. These deficits appear to be quite similar in both IDD and non-IDD sex offender populations (C.M. Nezu et al., 2007).

Sex offenders with IDD also face additional problems and unique vulnerabilities. These individuals may have a significant history of developmental factors that contribute to their risk for sex offending. In some cases, factors that contribute to the disability itself (e.g., abuse or neglect) may also serve as risk factors for sex offending behaviors. For example, IDD sex offenders often misinterpret sociosexual cues in their environment, have deficits in their ability to identify and interpret negative affect or distress, and have difficulties in their ability to effectively and appropriately express emotions (C.M. Nezu et al., 2007). In addition, sex offenders with IDD tend to have less access to resources and services needed to address and remediate such problems.

Moreover, the lives of individuals with IDD, including their sexual expression, often are influenced by societal factors. For example, such individuals are stereotyped either as being "innocent, naive individuals with no sexual desires" (Szollos & McCabe, 1995, p. 205), or as "promiscuous, criminal individuals with uncontrollable sexual desires" (Lumley & Scotti, 2001, p. 110). Social stigmas, fears, and inaccurate perceptions or negative attitudes toward sexuality in this population have led society to often isolate individuals with IDD, restrict their sexual behavior, and avoid providing them with reasonable educational experiences regarding sexuality and intimacy. These factors, in turn, can potentially lead to deficits in sexual knowledge, decreased access to sexual expression, and negative emotions regarding issues of sexuality, such as anger, frustration, confusion, sadness, and loneliness. Furthermore, individuals with IDD may have an increased vulnerability to sexual offending due to a history of institutionalization that serves to increase the likelihood of experiencing sexual victimization themselves (C.M. Nezu et al., 1998). Collectively, such problems in living require effective, but often complex, solutions. One means to reduce these unique vulnerabilities may be to specifically direct treatment at increasing these individuals' ability to cope more effectively with such stressful difficulties—hence, the rationale for teaching problem-solving skills to sexual offenders with IDD.

## SOCIAL PROBLEM SOLVING

Social problem solving (i.e., the type of problem solving that occurs in an interpersonal or social environment) is the cognitive-behavioral process by which individuals attempt to identify, create, or discover effective or adaptive solutions to specific problems encountered in their everyday lives (D'Zurilla & Nezu, 2007;

A.M. Nezu, 2004). This process incorporates overt, purposeful, and conscious efforts to change one's reactions to a problem, to change the problem itself, or both, depending on the nature of the situation. We define a *problem* as a task or event that necessitates an effective or adaptive response but for which there is no such response immediately available or apparent due to existing obstacles or barriers (A.M. Nezu, 2004). The origin of the demands of a particular problem may lie in the environment (e.g., external barriers to a goal, such as limited access to appropriate sexual partners), within the individual being confronted with the problem (e.g., inability to reach a personal goal, such as difficulties with emotional regulation regarding sexual arousal), or between individuals (e.g., conflicting goals, such as disagreements between two individuals as to what constitutes appropriate sex). The obstacles to an effective or adaptive response, and thus goal attainment, can include uncertainty, ambiguity, lack of resources, novelty, conflicting demands, or skill deficits.

With regard to a pathway leading to sexual offending, problems may be "causally" linked to internal origins (e.g., deviant thoughts, emotional arousal, learned reactions), or external stressors (e.g., interpersonal problems, lack of training opportunities, life changes), or a combination of both. Moreover, a problem can be a single event (e.g., getting fired from work), a series of related events (e.g., repeated social rejections), or a chronic situation (e.g., social stigmatization, loneliness). The demand in the problem may originate in the environment (e.g., restrictions at a group residence, arguments with supervisors, access to potential victims) or within the person him- or herself (e.g., viewing a child as seductive, deviant arousal, lack of personal control).

Within this framework, we define a *solution* as any coping response designed to alter the nature of the situation so that it is no longer problematic, one's maladaptive negative reaction to it, or both (A.M. Nezu, 2004). However, not all solutions are "effective." According to this definition, many destructive or harmful behaviors are viewed as ill-fated solutions, such as substance abuse, extensive avoidance, or coercive acts toward others. An *effective* solution, on the other hand, is one that not only achieves a positive or prosocial goal, but also leads to positive consequences and minimal negative consequences. Within a problem-solving conceptualization, sexual offending deviance and behavior reflect *a limited and destructive solution to the perpetrator's problems*. As such, sex offending may provide some relief to an immediate problem (e.g., psychological distress, threats to self-esteem, sexual tension, desire for sexual or physical intimacy) but also often leads to significant negative consequences for both the victim and offender.

## Multidimensional Model of Problem Solving

Based on decades of research, problem-solving outcomes are viewed as being largely determined by two general, but partially independent, dimensions: 1) problem orientation, and 2) problem-solving style (D'Zurilla & Nezu, 2007; A.M. Nezu, 2004). *Problem orientation* is the set of relatively stable cognitive-affective schemas that represent a person's generalized beliefs, attitudes, and emotional reactions about problems in living and one's ability to successfully cope with such problems. One's "general" problem orientation can be either positive or negative. A *positive problem orientation* involves a tendency to 1) appraise problems as challenges, 2) be optimistic in believing that problems are solvable, 3) perceive one's own ability to solve problems as strong, 4) believe that successful problem solving involves time and effort, and 5) accept that negative emotions are a normal part of life. When individuals characterized by a strong positive orientation experience an immediate negative emotional reaction (e.g., sadness or fear) to a stressful event, they use such experiences as important sources of personal information to denote that a problem exists and as a means to inform themselves regarding how to go about coping with the stressor. Conversely, a *negative problem orientation* is one that involves the tendency to 1) view problems as threats, 2) expect problems to be unsolvable, 3) doubt one's own ability to solve problems successfully, and 4) become especially frustrated and upset when faced with problems or confronted with negative emotions. Although intuitively viewed initially as two ends of the same continuum, positive and negative orientations have been repeatedly found to be independent and largely orthogonal constructs (D'Zurilla & Nezu, 2007). Moreover, some people may have a positive orientation for some types of problems they experience (e.g., careers, jobs), but a negative orientation with regard to other problem areas (e.g., relationships). As can be assumed from its description, one's problem orientation serves a motivational function (D'Zurilla & Nezu, 2001). For example, a positive orientation can lead to positive affect and approach motivation, which in turn can foster effective problem-solving efforts (e.g., willingness to attend to difficult situations rather than avoid them). Conversely, a negative orientation can engender negative affect, such as depressive symptoms and avoidance motivation, which can serve later to inhibit or disrupt subsequent problem-solving attempts.

The second major dimension, *problem-solving style*, refers to the core cognitive-behavioral activities that people engage in when attempting to cope with problems in living (D'Zurilla & Nezu, 2007). There are three differing styles that have been empirically identified—one of which is adaptive, whereas the remaining two reflect maladaptive ways of coping. *Rational problem solving* is the constructive problem-solving style that involves the systematic and planful application of certain skills, each of which makes a distinct contribution toward the discovery of an adaptive solution or coping response. This style encompasses four specific rational problem-solving skills: problem definition and formulation, generation of alternatives (GOA), decision making, and solution implementation and verification. The goal of *problem definition and formulation* is to accurately delineate the factors that describe why a given situation is a problem for a particular individual (e.g., the presence of obstacles), as well as to specify a set of realistic goals and objectives to help guide further problem-solving efforts. The purpose of the GOA task is to create, using various brainstorming principles, a large pool of possible solutions in order to increase the likelihood that the most effective ideas will be ultimately identified. The goal of *decision making* is to conduct a systematic cost–benefit analysis of these alternatives by identifying and then weighing their potential positive and negative consequences if carried out, and then, based on this evaluation, to develop an overall solution plan. Finally, the purpose of *solution implementation and verification* is to carry out the solution plan, monitor and evaluate its effectiveness, and troubleshoot if the outcome is unsatisfactory.

Two additional problem-solving styles have been identified, both of which are dysfunctional or maladaptive in nature (D'Zurilla & Nezu, 2007). An *impulsive/careless style* involves the generalized response pattern characterized by impulsive, hurried, and careless attempts at problem resolution. Although the individual characterized by this style actively attempts to apply various strategies to address problems, such attempts are narrow, hurried, and incomplete. For example, a person with this style is likely to consider only a few solution alternatives, often impulsively implementing the first idea that comes to mind. In addition, the narrow range of options and their consequences are scanned quickly, carelessly, and unsystematically. For example, people with a problem-solving style marked by impulsivity/carelessness may engage in an aggressive or provocative behavioral pattern because they report *"I can't help it, I was upset and felt like I had to do something."* This represents an impulsive action pattern following autonomic or limbic arousal, whereby problem-solving training is geared to teach individuals how to dampen their arousal, reduce the urge to respond immediately, and instead, orient oneself to engage in adaptive problem-solving coping activities.

*Avoidance style* is the second maladaptive problem-solving pattern, this one characterized by procrastination, passivity, and overdependence on others to provide solutions (D'Zurilla & Nezu, 2007). This type of problem solver generally avoids problems rather than confronting them "head on," puts off addressing problems for as long as possible, waits for problems to resolve themselves, and attempts to shift the responsibility for solving one's problems to other people. In general, both styles can lead to ineffective or unsuccessful problem resolution. In fact, they are likely to worsen existing problems or even create new ones. For example, use of drugs and alcohol may provide some relief or numbing of negative thoughts or feelings that an individual seeks to avoid, but can create a more maladaptive or destructive situation.

PST treatment objectives, then include 1) fostering a positive orientation, 2) decreasing a negative orientation, 3) enhancing rational problem solving, 4) minimizing impulsivity and carelessness, and 5) decreasing avoidance.

## Relevance of Problem-Solving Therapy for Sex Offenders

The potential efficacy of PST for the treatment of sex offenders is based in part on both clinical observations and empirical data that links deficits in social problem solving to aggression (e.g., Basquill, Nezu, Nezu, & Klein, 2004), as well as sex offending behavior (C.M. Nezu et al., 2005). More specifically, deficient problem-solving skills are viewed as one important dynamic factor that is related to sexual aggression and deviance (C.M. Nezu et al., 1998). As such, PST is hypothesized to help sex offenders better identify those stressful problems and situations that serve either distally or proximally as triggers for sex offending behaviors, including aggression towards others (C.M. Nezu et al., 2005). In addition, it is also geared to help teach such individuals to engage in alternative ways of coping with these stressful situations that are more adaptive and result in less negative consequences. Identifying trigger situations, according to the PST approach, also entails overcoming various cognitive distortions, such as *justification* (e.g., "she wanted to have sex with me—she was wearing sexy lipstick") and *minimization* (e.g., "I was the only one who cared about loving that child"), as well as *denial* (e.g., "I didn't do anything"). Such deviant thought patterns are often well learned and serve as major obstacles for the offenders themselves to validly understand the chain of events that ultimately led them to engage in sex offenses. Although it was once thought that such cognitive distortions were not relevant to understanding psychopathology among individuals with IDD (i.e., intellectual limitations equals lack of cognitive phenomena operative among the general population), research conducted during the past few decades have proved this assumption to be false (e.g., Kalal, Nezu, Nezu, & McGuffin, 1999; C.M. Nezu, Nezu, Rothenberg, DelliCarpini, & Groag, 1995).

Consider the following clinical example as an illustration of how problem solving can be related to sexual offending. Freddie is a 25-year-old man with a diagnosis of mild intellectual disability. Historically, he has a history of being stigmatized and bullied as a result of his intellectual limitations, is generally impulsive in nature, and has had no age-appropriate sexual relationships. Freddie has sexual interests in 9- to 11-year-old females, especially as he has found them to be particularly approachable. He frequently engages in sexual fantasies regarding such girls that culminate in masturbation. One day, while Freddie is experiencing a heightened level of sexual desire, he sees a 10-year-old girl from his neighborhood who says "hello" on recognizing him while at a local convenience store. He begins to think about having sex with her and what it would be like. The more he fantasizes about it, the more aroused he becomes. According to our model, the "problem" that Freddie is experiencing involves strong sexual feelings toward this 10-year old girl. Unfortunately, the "solution" to this problem would be to engage in behavior that on one hand could provide immediate sexual satisfaction but obviously carries myriad negative consequences for him, the girl, and potentially others (e.g., both sets of families). Given that the strong sexual arousal exists, a more "effective" solution would be to leave the situation and seek more socially and age-appropriate ways of either obtaining sexual gratification (e.g., masturbation) or tension alleviation (e.g., deep breathing). Barriers that exist for Freddie to be able to engage in the more socially appropriate solution may include a negative problem orientation (e.g., inability to tolerate negative emotional arousal) and/or poor problem-solving skills (e.g., poor impulse control, inability to identify alternative ways of handling sexual arousal). PST, then, would be geared to help Freddie to develop a more positive problem orientation (e.g., motivation to handle negative arousal more appropriately) and to use a rational problem-solving style as a means of developing socially appropriate options to deal with high-risk situations (e.g., being around young girls).

## PROBLEM-SOLVING THERAPY: IMPLICATIONS AND RECOMMENDATIONS

Following are basic guidelines for implementing PST for sexual offenders with IDD. Readers interested in a more detailed description of PST for general populations are referred to the treatment manuals contained in D'Zurilla and Nezu (2007) and A.M. Nezu, Nezu, & D'Zurilla (2007). One important consideration when adapting PST as an intervention for individuals with developmental disabilities is to optimally tailor the intervention to the intellectual level of the patients receiving treatment (C.M. Nezu, Nezu, & Arean, 1991). A full description of such guidelines for adapting psychosocial intervention strategies such as PST can be found in C.M. Nezu, Nezu, and Gill-Weiss (1992), including incorporating strategies to maintain attention, having individuals with IDD serve as teaching models, repeating training exercises, using concrete examples, and including specific reinforcers for newly learned skills. In addition, we strongly suggest the use of 1) handouts that incorporate pictures and icons to help explain concepts, 2) concrete language, and 3) videotaped role plays as teaching tools.

### Training in Problem Orientation

An important goal of training in problem orientation (PO) is to overcome possible cognitive distortions that serve to justify sexual offending behavior as appropriate (e.g., "I was only teaching her about sex"). One PST strategy to help achieve this treatment objective is the "reversed advocacy role play" technique. Here, the therapist first proposes a clearly false belief but one that is benign in nature and unrelated to the sexual misconception (i.e., "if I make a mistake, that means I am a complete failure"). The task presented to the offender is to provide reasons why such a belief or attitude is "wrong, irrational, illogical, incorrect, or maladaptive." The therapist's job is to become more extreme in his or her examples and counterarguments in order to make it easier for the offender to identify reasons to dispute the proposed belief. This is to foster the ability to develop alternative ways of thinking and understanding. Finally, examples become more and more challenging, and more related to the problem at hand, moving, for example, into direct opposition with a particular core belief of the offender (e.g., "It's okay to have sex with a 10-year-old girl"), requiring the offender to develop alternative and more adaptive arguments.

We also recommend engaging in the exercise called the "A–B–C Way of Healthy Thinking" in order to help the offender better understand the link among specific antecedent events, corresponding beliefs, and subsequent feelings and actions. Offender-relevant examples are used to demonstrate how certain *activating events* (e.g., a member of the opposite sex does not smile in response to the offender's greeting) often elicit the offender's *belief* (e.g., "She's a b****! Why doesn't she smile at me!? I should hurt her for being nasty!"), which can then lead to inappropriate *emotional* (e.g., anger, disappointment, sadness) and *behavioral* (e.g., verbal aggression toward girl) reactions. Over time, this provides an opportunity to provide instruction in developing more adaptive thinking (e.g., "It's okay if she doesn't smile at me—not everyone has to like me—I don't like everyone in the world myself") to help better self-regulate negative emotions and behavior.

This exercise is a prelude to teaching offenders to "STOP and THINK" as a means of engaging in better self-control and problem solving. Specifically, participants are taught to 1) label emotions (e.g., feelings of anger, deviant sexual arousal) as a "signal" to the presence of a problem (e.g., "when I feel angry I should try to see a 'red flag, stop sign, or flashing traffic light' that tells me that a problem exists, and if I don't deal with it okay, I might get into trouble or hurt someone"), 2) inhibit the tendency to respond automatically (e.g., "the red light means that I should stop myself from hurting someone"), and 3) try to think of alternative ways of dealing with the problem (e.g., "I should just walk away," "maybe I can talk to a friend," "another way to deal with this is to try to relax").

The process of "STOP and THINK" is repeatedly practiced, including using a picture of a red stop sign to remind the individual to initiate the various rational problem-solving activities when experiencing negative physical or emotional reactions. Self-talk, deep breathing, visualizing success in problem solving, and talking to others are also introduced to help the offenders better manage negative mood and foster developing a more positive orientation.

## Training in Problem Definition and Formulation

This skill emphasizes developing a concrete, specific, and accurate definition of a problem following the premise that "a problem well-defined is half solved." Training in problem definition and formulation (PDF) involves teaching individuals to effectively gather information about a problem, separate facts from assumptions, develop realistic goals, and identify obstacles or barriers that exist to achieving the goal (C.M. Nezu et al., 2006). We have found that a useful way to develop the ability to separate facts from assumptions involves having the person look at a picture in a magazine and to answer the basic question "what is going on in this picture?" Inevitably, a good part of the overall answer will involve assumptions. Using such a response as a springboard, the PST therapist can provide feedback and point out why some "facts" really are assumptions, and why some facts are indeed facts.

Crucial in this training is the ability to delineate realistic, as well as appropriate, goals. Here, particularly for a sex offender population, conducting a cost–benefit analysis becomes crucial with regard to the actual choices of goals (e.g., having sex with a 10-year-old girl versus having consensual sex with someone who is closer to the offender's age). Often values clarification training needs to occur.

Identifying barriers that exist for a given individual limiting his ability to achieve such goals is also a crucial part of PST. During this process, the therapist can also better assess various skill deficits characteristic of a given offender (i.e., lack of personal resources necessary to achieve a goal), such as poor communication skills, ineffective interpersonal skills, deficient assertive skills, and so forth. As such, the therapist can deviate slightly from PST in order to attempt to provide additional skills training in other deficient areas.

## Training in Generation of Alternatives

The rational problem-solving task of GOA involves creatively thinking of a variety of possible solution ideas geared to reach one's goal using three basic brainstorming principles (C.M. Nezu et al., 2006: 1) *the quantity principle* (e.g., the more solution ideas that are produced, the more likely an effective solution will eventually be identified); 2) *deferment-of-judgment principle* (e.g., it is important to withhold one's evaluation of a given alternative until after brainstorming is complete); and 3) *strategies–tactics principle* (e.g., ideas can be subdivided into strategies or general ways to approach a solution, as well as specific tactics or different ways of carrying out a given strategy). We suggest that a useful teaching tool to foster skill acquisition of GOA involves initially practicing with nonemotional goals. For example, we often ask individuals to "think of as many ways you can use a single brick as possible" as a means of demonstrating how to use the brainstorming principles. Moreover, additional tips are provided regarding how to overcome "feeling stuck" (e.g., combine two different ideas to make a third, think of how different people might use a brick, such as a favorite relative, movie star, musician, sports figure, politician, or neighbor). Once the individual has developed this skill, more personally relevant problems are addressed, including how to deal with deviant sexual urges.

## Training in Decision Making

This component emphasizes learning how to effectively conduct another cost–benefit analysis, this time in order to select the most appropriate solution(s) for a given problem. Therapists also seek to remind offenders of the problem, the obstacles to solving the problem, and the goals before this step is practiced in session. Training involves teaching offenders how to identify and determine the "pros and cons" of each alternative idea, as well as fostering the ability to consider a wide range of differing types of consequences (e.g., the effects on oneself versus the effects on others) (C.M. Nezu et al., 2005). Consideration of the effects on others becomes especially important to emphasize with this population. Decision-making skills are practiced by starting with less difficult problems, such as determining a "better way to get to work" (e.g., driving, walking, taking a bus, hitchhiking). As individuals become more proficient, more directly relevant problems are tackled (e.g., considering the differing consequences of asking a much younger girl for a date). If the individual has difficulty identifying the various consequences for a given alternative, he is encouraged to use the brainstorming principles as an aid. Based on a cost–benefit analysis of the various alternatives previously generated for a given problem, individuals are guided to select those ideas that are associated with the most positive consequences and the least negative outcomes in order to develop an overall solution plan.

## Training in Solution Implementation and Verification

This final rational problem-solving task involves carrying out the chosen solution plan and evaluating its relative success in reaching one's problem-solving goals

(C.M. Nezu et al., 2005). If the individual is initially hesitant to carry out the plan, obstacles that led to this avoidance are identified (e.g., anxiety, passivity, or a changed problem situation), and the overall rational problem-solving approach is applied to help overcome these performance obstacles. When a solution plan is carried out, individuals are taught to match the expected outcome with what actually occurred. If the match is satisfactory, then the individual is directed to engage in self-reinforcement. If not, the offender is taught to go through each of the rational problem-solving tasks (i.e., PDF, GOA, decision making, solution implementation and verification) to determine "where one went wrong" (e.g., "Was the problem not well defined? Was enough alternatives generated? Was a good decision made? Was the solution plan not carried out well?"). This process is repeated until the problem is solved satisfactorily.

## Guided Practice

A significant amount of treatment efforts should be devoted to helping the individual apply the various problem-solving skills to a variety of relevant problems. Beyond actually solving problems, continuous in-session practice serves three additional purposes: 1) the individual can receive "professional" feedback from the therapist, 2) increased facility with the overall PST model can decrease the amount of time and effort necessary to apply the entire model with each new problem, and 3) practice fosters maintenance and generalization of the skills. In addition to focusing on resolving and coping with current problems, practice sessions should also allow for "future forecasting" whereby the individual is encouraged to look to the future and anticipate where potential problems might arise in order to apply such skills in a preventive manner (e.g., moving to a better neighborhood, but actually closer to a schoolyard).

## Empirical Support for Problem-Solving Therapy for Sexual Offenders with Intellectual and Developmental Disabilities

Although no controlled studies have been conducted to date directly evaluating the efficacy of PST for sex offenders with IDD, significant evidence does exist supporting the efficacy of PST in general for a variety of health and mental health problems, including populations of adults with IDD (D'Zurilla & Nezu, 2007; Malouff, Thorsteinsson, & Schutte, 2007). In addition, clinical case reports by C.M. Nezu, Greenberg, and Nezu (2006) document its relevance and potential efficacy regarding sex offenders with IDD. For example, of the first 25 men who underwent treatment in Project STOP, an outpatient program developed to treat adult sex offenders with IDD that included PST as a pivotal treatment ingredient, a 12-year recidivism rate of 4% was identified (i.e., only one patient committed another sexual offense)(C.M. Nezu, Greenberg, et al., 2006). Although such program evaluation data needs to be viewed with caution, it does underscore the potential efficacy of this approach. Moreover, preliminary results from a randomized controlled trial that identified significant reductions in sexual deviance related to a

PST intervention (as compared to a waiting list control) for adult sex offenders with average intellectual functioning provides further support for its potential efficacy for such individuals with IDD (C.M. Nezu, 2003).

## FUTURE RESEARCH AND SERVICE DELIVERY

Due to the dearth of research that exists regarding both the assessment and treatment of sex offenders with IDD (Lindsay, 2002; C.M. Nezu et al., 2007), the obvious recommendation for the future is to conduct additional studies. Unfortunately, due to a variety of legal and social liability issues, conducting well-controlled treatment studies with this population is particularly difficult, especially when focusing on individuals already convicted of a sex crime. As such, researchers need to be creative in developing methodologies that can yield empirically sound results. One possibility is for researchers to pool their resources and conduct multisite studies in order to develop large enough pools of research participants to have sufficient statistical power.

Another area of research that needs to be continued is the relevance of various dynamic psychosocial factors that are etiologically related to sex offending behavior in this population, including deficient social problem-solving ability. Although some research suggests that poor problem solving regarding real-life stressors is characteristic of offenders without IDD in general (McMurran, Egan, Richardson, & Ahmadi, 1999), as well as with specific regard to non-IDD sex offenders (C.M. Nezu et al., 2005), efforts should be extended to determine whether this variable is predictive of sex offending behavior among adults with IDD.

Related to this issue is the need to have psychometrically sound measures of those constructs relevant to this overall area. For example, a popular and psychometrically sound measure of social problem solving among the general population, the Social Problem-Solving Inventory–Revised (SPSI-R; D'Zurilla, Nezu, & Maydeu-Olivares, 2002), has recently been found to have sound reliability and validity properties when testing a large sample ($N = 499$) of male adult sex offenders (Wakeling, 2007). However, in part because the SPSI-R is a self-reporting measure, it remains an empirical question whether it can be useful with a sample of adults with intellectual and/or reading limitations.

In addition to well-controlled studies of PST to evaluate its efficacy for the treatment of sex offenders, what is needed further is to determine whether improvements in problem solving actually mediate changes in relevant outcome (e.g., sexual deviance, reoffense rates). For example, Kirsch and Becker (2006) argue that a major problem within the sex offending literature in general is the overall lack of convincing evidence linking a particular etiological theory of sex offending with recidivism outcomes. In addition, they suggest that problems exist with regard to how a given treatment is actually implemented (i.e., treatment delivery). This suggests that researchers especially need to consider issues of treatment dissemination, treatment fidelity, and therapist training when developing and conducting empirical investigations (A.M. Nezu & Nezu, 2008).

## REFERENCES

Basquill, M., Nezu, C.M., Nezu, A.M., & Klein, T.L. (2004). Aggression-related hostility bias and social problem-solving deficits in adult males with mental retardation. *American Journal on Mental Retardation, 109,* 255–263.

D'Zurilla, T.J., & Goldfried, M.R. (1971). Problem solving and behavior modification. *Journal of Abnormal Psychology, 78,* 107–126.

D'Zurilla, T.J., & Nezu, A.M. (2001). Problem-solving therapies. In K.S. Dobson (Ed.), *The handbook of cognitive-behavioral therapies* (2nd ed., pp. 211–245). New York, NY: Guilford.

D'Zurilla, T.J., & Nezu, A.M. (2007). *Problem-solving therapy: A positive approach to clinical intervention* (3rd ed.). New York, NY: Springer.

D'Zurilla, T.J., Nezu, A.M., & Maydeu-Olivares, A. (2002). *Manual for the social problem-solving inventory-revised.* North Tonawanda, NY: Multi-Health Systems.

Hanson, R. K., & Bussiere, M. T. (1998). Predicting relapse: A meta-analysis of sexual offender recidivism studies. *Journal of Consulting and Clinical Psychology, 66,* 348–362.

Kalal, D.M., Nezu, C.M., Nezu, A.M., & McGuffin, P.W. (1999). Cognitive distortions in sex offenders with intellectual deficits. In B. Schwartz (Ed.), *The sex offender: Theoretical advances, treating special populations and legal developments* (Vol. 3, pp. 31.1–31.15). Kingston, NJ: Civic Research Institute.

Kirsch, L.G., & Becker, J.V. (2006). Sexual offending: Theory of problem, theory of change, and implications for treatment effectiveness. *Aggression and Violent Behavior, 11,* 208–224.

Lanyon, R.I. (2001). Psychological assessment procedures in sex offending. *Professional Psychology: Research and Practice, 32,* 253–260.

Lindsay, W.R. (2002a). Integration of recent reviews on offenders with intellectual disabilities. *Journal of Applied Research in Intellectual Disabilities, 15,* 111–119.

Lindsay, W. R. (2002b). Research and literature on sex offenders with intellectual and developmental disabilities. *Journal of Intellectual Disability Research, 46*(Suppl. 1), 74–85.

Loumidis, K.S., & Hill, A. (1997). Training social problem-solving skill to reduce maladaptive behaviours in intellectual disability groups: The influence of individual difference factors. *Journal of Applied Research in Intellectual Disabilities, 10,* 217–237.

Lumley, V.A., & Scotti, J.R. (2001). Supporting the sexuality of adults with mental retardation: Current status and future directions. *Journal of Positive Behavior Interventions, 3,* 109–119.

Malouff, J.M., Thorsteinsson, E.B., & Schutte, N.S. (2007). The efficacy of problem-solving therapy in reducing mental and physical health problems: A meta-analysis. *Clinical Psychology Review, 27,* 46–57.

Marques, J.D., Day, D.M., Nelson, C., & West, M.A. (1994). Effects of cognitive-behavioral treatment on sex offender recidivism: Preliminary results of a longitudinal study. *Criminal Justice and Behavior, 21,* 28–54.

Marshall, W.L., Anderson, D., & Fernandez, Y. (1999). *Cognitive behavioural treatment of sexual offenders.* West Sussex, UK: John Wiley & Sons.

McMurran, M., Egan, V., Richardson, C., & Ahmadi, S. (1999). Social problem-solving in mentally disordered offenders: A brief report. *Criminal Behaviour and Mental Health, 9,* 315–322.

Murphy, W.D., Coleman, E.M., & Haynes, M.A. (1983). Treatment evaluation issues with the mentally retarded sex offender. In J.G..Greer & I.R. Stuart (Eds.), *The sexual aggressor: Current perspectives on treatment* (pp. 22–41). New York, NY: Van Nostrand Reinhold.

Nezu, A.M. (2004). Problem solving and behavior therapy revisited. *Behavior Therapy, 35,* 1–33.

Nezu, A.M., & Nezu, C.M. (Eds.). (2008). *Evidence-based outcome research: A practical guide to conducting randomized clinical trials for psychosocial interventions.* New York, NY: Oxford University Press.

Nezu, A.M., Nezu, C.M., & D'Zurilla, T.J. (2007). *Solving life's problems: A 5-step guide to enhanced well-being.* New York, NY: Springer Publishing.

Nezu, C.M. (2003). Cognitive-behavioral treatment for sex offenders: Current status. *Japanese Journal of Behavior Therapy, 29,* 15–24.

Nezu, C.M., D'Zurilla, T.J., & Nezu, A.M. (2005). Problem-solving therapy: Theory, practice, and application to sex offenders. In M. McMurran & J. McGuire (Eds.), *Social problem solving and offenders: Evidence, evaluation and evolution* (pp. 102–123). Chichester, UK: John Wiley & Sons.

Nezu, C.M., Fiore, A.A., & Nezu, A.M. (2006). Problem-solving treatment for intellectually disabled sex offenders. *International Journal of Behavioral Consultation and Therapy, 2,* 266–276.

Nezu, C.M., Greenberg, J., & Nezu, A.M. (2006). Project STOP: Cognitive behavioral treatment for intellectually disabled sex offenders. *Journal of Forensic Psychology Practice, 6,* 87–103.

Nezu, C.M., Nezu, A.M., & Arean, P.A. (1991). Assertiveness and problem-solving therapy for persons with mental retardation and dual diagnosis. *Research in Developmental Disabilities, 12,* 371–386.

Nezu, C.M., Nezu, A.M., & Dudek, J.A. (1998). A cognitive behavioral model of assessment and treatment for intellectually disabled sexual offenders. *Cognitive and Behavioral Practice, 5,* 25–64.

Nezu, C.M., Nezu, A.M., Dudek, J.A., Peacock, M., & Stoll, J. (2005). Problem-solving correlates of sexual deviancy among child molesters, *Journal of Sexual Aggression, 11,* 27–35.

Nezu, C.M., Nezu, A.M., & Gill-Weiss, M.J. (1992). *Psychopathology of persons with mental retardation: Clinical guidelines for assessment and treatment.* Champaign, IL: Research Press.

Nezu, C.M., Nezu, A.M., Klein, T., & Clair, M. (2007). Sex offending behavior. In J.A. Mulick & J.W. Jacobson (Eds.), *Handbook of mental retardation and developmental disabilities* (pp. 635–655). New York, NY: Kluwer.

Nezu, C.M., Nezu, A.M., Rothenberg, J. L., DelliCarpini, L., & Groag, I. (1995). Depression in adults with mild mental retardation: Are cognitive variables involved? *Cognitive Therapy and Research, 19,* 227–239.

Prentky, R.A., & Knight, R.A. (1991). Identifying critical dimensions for discriminating among rapists. *Journal of Consulting and Clinical Psychology, 59,* 643–661.

Prentky, R.A., Knight, R.A., & Lee, A.F.S. (1997). Risk factors associated with recidivism among extrafamilial child molesters. *Journal of Consulting and Clinical Psychology, 65,* 141–149.

Rice, M.E., Chaplin, T.C., Harris, G.T., & Couts, J. (1994). Empathy for the victim and sexual arousal among rapists and nonrapists. *Journal of Interpersonal Violence, 9,* 435–449.

Seghorn, T.K., Prentky, R.A., & Boucher, R.J. (1987). Childhood sexual abuse in the lives of sexually aggressive offenders. *Journal of the American Academy of Child and Adolescent Psychiatry, 26,* 262–267.

Szollos, A.A., & McCabe, M.P. (1995). The sexuality of person with mild intellectual disability: Perceptions of clients and caregivers. *Australia and New Zealand Journal of Developmental Disabilities, 20,* 205–222.

Wakeling, H.C. (2007). The psychometric validation of the social problem-solving inventory-revised with UK incarcerated sexual offenders. *Sexual Abuse: A Journal of Research and Treatment, 19,* 217–236.

Ward, T., Hudson, S.M., & Marshall, W.L. (1995). Cognitive distortions and affective deficits in sexual offenders: A cognitive deconstructionist interpretation. *Sexual Abuse: Journal of Research & Treatment, 7,* 67–83.

# Health-Threatening Eating Disorders

SECTION IV

# Behavioral Assessment and Treatment of Pica

*Louis P. Hagopian,*
*Natalie U. Rolider, and Griffin W. Rooker*

CHAPTER

Pica is defined diagnostically as 1) consumption of nonnutritive items for more than a month, 2) consumption of nonnutritive items inappropriate to developmental age, 3) eating that is not part of culturally sanctioned activity, and 4) a behavior severe enough to require independent clinical attention when other clinical services are being provided for another mental disorder (American Psychological Association, 2000). Several severe health risks are associated with pica (Decker, 1993), including lead poisoning, intestinal perforation and obstruction (sometimes necessitating surgical removal of the item), and death (Chisholm & Kaplan, 1968; Greenberg, Jacobziner, McLaughlin, Fuerst, & Pellitteri, 1958). The research literature describes three populations of individuals that engage in pica, including typically developing individuals with a nutritional disorder, typically developing individuals who engage in obsessive-compulsive disorder (OCD), and individuals diagnosed with intellectual and developmental disability (IDD).

For individuals with a nutritional disorder, research on pica has been related to the prevention of lead poisoning (Chisolm & Kaplan, 1968) and pica is the manifestation of poor diet, specifically anemia (Gutelius, Millican, Layman, Cohen, & Dublin, 1962; Lanzkowsky, 1959). Pica is directly related to an imbalance in the diet and thus can be treated by correcting the deficiency; however, no connection has been made about the types of items consumed and their relation to specific dietary deficiencies. For individuals with OCD or impulse control disorder (Luiselli, 1996), pica is related to the ritualistic nature of the disorder. Therefore, medications such as a serotonin reuptake inhibitor (SRI) have been an important part of treatment (Stein, Bouwer, & van Heerden, 1996). For individuals with IDD, which is the focus of the current chapter, pica can involve ingestion of inedible items (e.g., dirt; Bucher, Reykdal, & Albin, 1976), edible but insufficiently prepared food (e.g., raw potatoes; Lacey, 1990), and food that is contaminated (see Table 9.1).

The prevalence of pica in people with IDD has been reported to be between 5.7% and 25.8% (Ashworth, Hirdes, & Martin, 2009). In the largest study, Danford & Huber (1982) reviewed the records of 991 institutionalized individuals and found that pica occurred in 25.8% of the sample. The authors also evaluated the frequency of different forms of pica based on the type of items ingested (e.g., inappropriate food vs. nonfood items) and concluded that nonfood pica was the most prevalent (16.7%), followed by food pica (5.4%), and finally combinations of food and nonfood pica (3.7%). In addition, research suggests that pica is more prevalent among lower functioning individuals (Ali, 2001). Kinnell (1985) conducted a case-review of 140 individuals who attended an in- or outpatient hospital, 70 diagnosed with autism and 70 with Down syndrome, and found that 60% of those with autism and 4% of those with Down syndrome engaged in pica, respectively. However, it is possible that the difference between the groups was so great because of the inclusion criteria. That is, because individuals with autism selected for the Kinnell review were also diagnosed with profound intellectual disability, these participants were already more likely to engage in pica. Table 9.1 shows the participant characteristics of 25 studies that assessed and treated pica through behavior analytic procedures.

## BEHAVIORAL ASSESSMENT OF PICA

### Functional Behavioral Assessment

To assess the operant contingencies maintaining pica, a functional behavioral assessment (FBA) is recommended (Iwata, Dorsey, Slifer, Bauman, & Richman, 1994). A variety of FBA procedures have been described, and can be categorized as involving indirect or direct methods. Indirect methods include interviews and questionnaires aimed at identifying controlling variables based on the report of others. Direct methods involve observation of the behavior of interest and can be further categorized as correlational or experimental. Correlational methods include observation of environmental antecedents and consequences and require the clinician to make inferences about functional relations between those environmental variables and the behavior of interest. Experimental methods (i.e., functional analysis, FA) are the most rigorous and involve directly manipulating relevant antecedent and consequent variables and then observing their effects on behavior. In light of the level of rigor and control inherent in experimental FA, this approach has become the clinical standard for identifying the variables that maintain problem behavior such as aggression and self-injury (Iwata & Worsdell, 2005).

Although FBA using indirect methods have not proven to be sufficiently valid to endorse their use for assessment of severe aggression and self injury (Camp, Iwata, Hammond, & Bloom, 2009; Lerman & Iwata, 1993), there is some evidence that indirect methods may be valid for assessment of pica. Wasano, Borrero, and Kohn (2009) assessed the pica of three individuals using indirect and direct methods (FA) and found that in all three cases the results of the indirect assessment matched the results of the FA. Wasano et al. also showed that indirect assessments required less time to complete than the FA. These findings suggest that indirect assessments may be more accurate for pica than for other behaviors because pica is usually maintained by nonsocial reinforcers. Nevertheless, we recommend conducting an experimental FA particularly if earlier interventions based on indirect assessments are not effective, and if the individual can be kept safe in the interim.

### Use of Safe and Simulated Pica Items

Because an FA requires repeated observation of the target behavior, caution should be taken to ensure the individual's safety during an FA of pica. Many studies

**Table 9.1.** Published pica treatment studies

| Authors | Participants | Items reportedly consumed | Assessment procedures, and results | Safe or simulated pica items | Treatments used and successful |
|---|---|---|---|---|---|
| Foxx and Martin (1975) | 30 y.o. F, pID<br>31 y.o. F, pID<br>20 y.o., pID<br>33 y.o., pID | Trash, feces, any small items, cigarette butts | No formal assessment of function of pica | None used | Punishment* |
| Bucher, Reykdal, and Albin (1976) | 6 y.o. M, pID<br>6 y.o. F, pID | Grass, stones, dirt, food off floor, tiny objects, feces | No formal assessment of function of pica | Corn flakes and Melba toast (simulated); during treatment only | Punishment* |
| Mulick, Barbour, Schroeder, and Rojahn (1980) | 28 y.o. M, pID<br>23 y.o. F, pID | Wire, paper clips, straight pins, rocks, hand towel, tacks, coins, screws, safety pins; string bits of clothing, small nonnutritive objects | No formal assessment of function of pica | Bits of cloth, paper, string, placebo capsules (safe); during treatment only | Punishment* |
| Favell, McGimsey, and Schell (1982) | 19 y.o. F, pID<br>13 y.o. F, pID<br>16 y.o. M, pID | Clothing, bed linen, paper, pieces of toys | No formal assessment of function of pica | None used | Noncontingent Reinforcement (NCR)<br>NCR + DRA (1 of 3 cases)* |
| Finney, Russo, and Cataldo (1982) | 3.5 y.o. M<br>3.75 y.o. M<br>5.67 y.o. F<br>2.25 y.o. F<br>Class IIIV lead poisoning | Paint chips, ashtray, spatula, plastic lid, body parts | No formal assessment of function of pica | Edible items resembling paint chips made from flour and water (simulated); during treatment only | DRO (2 of 4 cases)*<br>DRO + Punishment (2 of 4 cases)* |
| Singh and Winton (1984) | 24 y.o. F, pID | Cigarette butts, string, buttons, leaves | No formal assessment of function of pica | None used | DRO + Punishment* |
| Mace and Knight (1986) | 19 y.o. M, pID | Shredded clothing or other material | No formal assessment of function of pica | None used | Punishment* |

(Continued)

**Table 9.1.** Published pica treatment studies *(continued)*

| Authors | Participants | Items reportedly consumed | Assessment procedures, and results | Safe or simulated pica items | Treatments used and successful |
|---|---|---|---|---|---|
| Rojahn, McGonigle, Curcio, and Dixon (1987) | 16 y.o. F, ASD sID | Tacks, staples, crayons, strings, woven material, paper, cigarette butts | No formal assessment of function of pica | Strings, small pieces of paper, and pieces of cigarettes (safe); during treatment only | Punishment* |
| Donnely and Olczak (1990) | 38 y.o. M, ID<br>44 y.o. M, ID<br>26 y.o. F, ID | Cigarettes | No formal assessment of function of pica | None used | DRI* |
| Fisher, Piazza, Bowman, Kurtz, Sherer, and Lachman (1994) | 3 y.o. F, sID<br>5 y.o. M, pID<br>3 y.o. M, sID | Feces, pet hair, insects, cigarette butts, grass, string, glass, tile adhesive, rocks, wood chips | No formal assessment of function of pica | Edible items resembling nonfood items (e.g., "paint chips" made from flour and water — i.e., (simulated); during treatment only | NCR<br>NCR + DRA + Punishment* |
| Bogart, Piersel, and Gross (1995) | 21 y.o. F, pID | Plastics, foam rubber, strings, paper, assorted training material | No formal assessment of function of pica | None used | Punishment<br>DRI + Punishment* |
| Piazza, Hanley, and Fisher (1996) | 17 y.o. M, sID | Cigarette butts | Functional analysis<br>Results: Automatic | Clean cigarette butts (safe) | NCR<br>NCR + Punishment* |
| Piazza, Fisher, Hanley, LeBlanc, Worsdell, Lindauer, and Keeney (1998) | 4 y.o. F, pID<br>17 y.o. F, sID<br>5 y.o. M, ASD | Furniture, clothing, oxygen tube, string, hair, keys, rocks, plastic game pieces, crayons, coins, cloth, paper, twigs | Functional analysis<br>Results: Automatic, automatic, attention | Velcro strips, tape, paper, a chair cushion, plastic toy, birthday candles, uncooked beans and pasta, stuffed bear, cloth towel (safe) | NCR (2/3)*<br>NCR + RB/RI<br>(1 of 3 cases)* |

| Authors | Participants | Items reportedly consumed | Assessment procedures, and results | Safe or simulated pica items | Treatments used and successful |
|---|---|---|---|---|---|
| Goh, Iwata, and Kahng (1999) | 40 y.o. M, pID<br>49 y.o. F, sID<br>44 y.o. M, pID<br>46 y.o. M, pID | Cigarettes | No formal assessment of function of pica | None used | NCR (dense)*<br>DRA + RB/RI (3 of 4 cases)*<br>DRA + RB/RI + punishment |
| Piazza, Hanley, Blakeley-Smith, and Kinsman (2000) | 9 y.o. M, pID | Floors, walls, body parts, clothes | Functional analysis conducted on SIB not pica, but pica frequency was measured (likely automatic) | None used | Increased response effort* |
| Hagopian and Adelinis (2001) | 26 y.o. M, mID | Paper, pencils, paint chips, human feces | Functional analysis<br>Results: automatic | Paper (safe) | RB<br>RB + redirection* |
| Rapp, Dozier, and Carr (2001) | 6 y.o. F, ASD | Rocks, dirt, grass, balloons | Functional analysis with simulated pica items<br>Results: automatic | Broken pieces of animal crackers (simulated) | NCR (dense)*<br>RB/RI<br>Punishment<br>NCR + punishment* |
| Piazza, Roane, Kenney, Boney, and Abt (2002) | 19 y.o. F, sID<br>14 y.o. F, sID<br>15 y.o. F, sID | Car keys, rocks, sticks, dirt, rubber gloves, alkaline batteries, plastic, feces, soap, cloth | Functional analysis with simulated pica items<br>Results: automatic | Uncooked edible items (pasta, turnip, and beans), paper, onion skins, and collard greens, plastic blocks, candles, PlayDoh, crayons (simulated) | Increased response effort* |
| Ricciardi, Luiselli, Terrill, and Reardon (2003) | 7 y.o. M, ASD | Wood chips, dirt, stones, paper, plastic, tar | Indirect and descriptive FBA<br>Results: automatic | None used | RB/RI<br>RB/RI + punishment* |

*(continued)*

**Table 9.1.**  Published pica treatment studies (continued)

| Authors | Participants | Items reportedly consumed | Assessment procedures, and results | Safe or simulated pica items | Treatments used and successful |
|---|---|---|---|---|---|
| McCord, Grosser, Iwata, and Powers (2005) | 48 y.o. M, pID<br>40 y.o. M, pID<br>44 y.o. M, pID | Straw, grass, plants, coins, plastic, Styrofoam, cleaning fluid, paint chips, dirt | Sole condition of functional analysis Only<br><br>Results: automatic | Paper towel, styrofoam, and leaves (safe) | RB/RI* |
| Ferreri, Tamm, and Wier (2006) | 4 y.o. M, ASD | Ends of plastic toys | No formal assessment of function of pica | None used | Punishment* |
| Kern, Starosta, and Adelman (2006) | 8 y.o. M, sID<br>18 y.o. M, ASD, sID | Fabric, metal, plastic, foam padding from chairs, human hair, string, dust, paper, Velcro | Functional analysis<br>Results: automatic | Paper (safe) | RB/RI + DRI* |
| Falcomata, Roane, and Pabico (2007) | 12 y.o. M, ASD | Rocks, small pieces of plastic or metal | Functional analysis with simulated pica items<br>Results: automatic | Dried grits, uncooked beans (simulated) | NCR<br>NCR + punishment* |
| Wasano, Borrero, and Kohn (2009) | 9 y.o. M, ID<br>5 y.o. F, ID<br>14 y.o. F, ID | Leaves, grass, tree bark, feces, furniture, spiderwebs, rocks, hair, paper, magazines | Functional analysis with simulated pica items<br>Results: automatic<br>Indirect assessments: QABF and MAS | Cotton candy, little chocolates, licorice jelly beans, beef jerky, spring mix lettuce, crumbled pieces of cookies, brownies (simulated) | N/A |
| Gonzalez and Hagopian (2009) | 13 y.o. F, sID | Motor oil, Miracle Grow, detergent | Functional analysis with simulated pica items<br>Results: automatic | Rice cakes, Play Doh®, crayons, seaweed, and two types of rice paper (simulated) | NCR + RB +<br>Redirection + DRI* |

*Key:* pID, profound intellectual disability; sID, severe intellectual disability; mID, moderate intellectual disability; y.o., years old; M, male; F, female; ASD, autism spectrum disorder; DRA, differential reinforcement of alternative behavior; DRI, differential reinforcement of incompatible behavior; RB, response blocking; RI, response interruption; NCR, noncontingent reinforcement; FBA, functional behavioral assessment; QABF, Questions about Behavioral Function; MAS, Motivation Assessment Scale; *Effective treatment.

describing FAs of pica have involved "baiting" the environment with safe pica items (i.e., items that are safe to ingest) or with simulated pica items that are similar to items the individual has historically ingested but are safe to consume in controlled amounts. Eight of the studies listed in Table 9.1 have used simulated pica items, and eight have used safe pica items. Safe pica items have included paper, small pieces of string, and pieces of cigarettes. Simulated pica items have included imitation paint chips (flour and water), metal pieces (cake toppings), cleaning fluid (water with food coloring), ceiling tiles (animal crackers), lint (cotton candy), small twigs (beef jerky), rocks (licorice jelly beans), leaves and plants (salad greens), and dirt (ground-up cookies), as well as several items that are generally not considered edible but were not specified to directly mimic another item (e.g., uncooked pasta, uncooked beans, onion skins, rice cakes, seaweed, rice paper, nontoxic molding clay). Use of safe or simulated pica items for assessment permits pica to occur while ensuring a person's safety. Whether using simulated or safe pica items, we advise having medical staff knowledgeable about the individual review the items and define how much can be ingested safely.

## Functional Analysis of Pica

The most commonly used FA procedures involve four conditions (alone, attention, play, and demand) that are alternated in a multielement design (Iwata et al., 1994). In the "alone" condition, the individual is in a room alone and there are no programmed consequences for pica. This condition tests whether pica occurs in the absence of social consequences. If so, the conclusion is that pica is maintained by sensory reinforcement. In the "attention condition," the individual and a therapist are in the room and the therapist does not attend to the individual unless pica occurs, at which time a comment is made (e.g., "No, don't put that in your mouth!"). This condition tests whether pica is sensitive to access to positive reinforcement in the form of attention. In the "demand" condition, the individual and the therapist are in the room with various task materials. The therapist instructs the individual to complete tasks and removes them briefly when pica is displayed. This condition tests whether problem behavior is maintained by negative reinforcement in the form of escape from demands. In the "play" condition, the individual and therapist are present in the room with various toys and no demands are presented. If pica occurs, the therapist does not attend to the individual. This condition serves as the control condition against which other conditions are compared.

Early studies often did not conduct an FA of pica and it was often assumed that pica was maintained by sensory consequences. This assumption has generally been borne out in most studies employing FA but is not always the case (see Table 9.1). Piazza et al. (1998) showed that pica was maintained by attention for one of three individuals for whom an FA was conducted. In total, 11 studies have conducted a FBA (indirect or direct methods) to determine the maintaining variables of pica. These studies reported on a total of 20 individuals, 19 of which (95%) had pica that was maintained by sensory reinforcement. Despite these findings, conducting some type of FBA of pica is recommended to ensure that the relevant controlling variables are identified prior to developing treatment. We reiterate that conducting an experimental FA with baited safe or simulated pica items is recommended for cases with frequent and high-risk pica.

## BEHAVIORAL TREATMENT OF PICA

Although the type of population being considered may play an important factor in developing a treatment for pica, two broad classes of intervention have been shown to be successful: medical and behavioral interventions. Within the context of medical interventions, correcting identified nutritional deficits has shown the most promise. When medical interventions are unsuccessful, or there is no reason to believe that a nutritional deficit exists, behavior analytic interventions have been shown to be extremely effective at reducing pica. Treatments often involve multiple components, and can be divided into three classes of behavioral interventions: *antecedent interventions* (including noncontingent reinforcement and effort manipulations), *consequent interventions* (including reinforcement, response blocking, punishment, and reinforcement interventions), and *combined antecedent and consequent interventions* (including noncontingent reinforcement in combination with consequent interventions).

## Antecedent Interventions

### Noncontingent Reinforcement

Noncontingent reinforcement (NCR) involves delivering a reinforcer on a timed schedule (usually variable or fixed time) independent of the individual's behavior. Two possible mechanisms may account for NCR's effectiveness: extinction (EXT) or satiation (Hagopian, Crockett, van Stone, DeLeon, & Bowman, 2000). First, NCR may be effective because it contains an EXT component. That is, the response–reinforcer relation is broken because the consequences for problem behavior are provided independently of problem behavior. Second, NCR may be effective because free access to reinforcement decreases the motivation to perform the behavior.

These procedures have sufficient evidence supporting their effectiveness for aggression and self-injury to be characterized as "empirically supported treatments" (Carr, Severtson, & Lepper, 2009). NCR is the most commonly reported intervention for pica (see Table 9.1; Falcomata, Roane, & Pabico, 2007; Favell, McGimsey, & Schell, 1982; Fisher et al., 1994; Goh, Iwata, & Kahng, 1999; Gonzalez & Hagopian, 2009; Piazza, Hanley, & Fisher, 1996; Piazza et al., 1998; Rapp, Dozier, & Carr, 2001). As a treatment for pica, NCR involves providing noncontingent access to reinforcing stimuli. For example, Favell et al. (1982) provided non-contingent access to edible and leisure items to three individuals with IDD that engaged in pica. Goh et al. (1999) found that a dense schedule of NCR (edibles delivered every 10 seconds for 5 minutes) successfully reduced pica for one individual with IDD. However, Hagopian and Adelinis (2001) found that NCR alone was not sufficient to reduce pica—blocking plus redirection (a consequent intervention) had to be implemented as additional procedures.

Noncontingent reinforcement is relatively easy to implement, as it requires simply providing the individual access to edible or leisure items. The challenge is identifying the stimuli that compete with reinforcement maintaining problem behavior. A competing stimulus assessment (CSA) has become the preferred approach for identifying stimuli that are associated with reduced pica (Goh et al., 1999). The assessment involves systematically exposing individuals to stimuli (one at a time) and observing how access to them affects rate of pica relative to a no-stimulus control. The CSA should be conducted in an environment baited with simulated pica materials that are safe to ingest (e.g., Goh et al., 1999; Piazza et al., 1996; Piazza et al., 1998).

### Response Effort Manipulations

Response effort manipulations have been used to treat self-injury and pica maintained by sensory reinforcement. The goal is to increase the effort required to engage in the response beyond the level supported by obtained reinforcement. To illustrate, Piazza, Roane, Kenney, Boney, and Abt (2002) reduced pica of three individuals by increasing the relative effort required to perform the inappropriate behavior. The authors found that when items associated with pica and appropriate alternative food items were available, individuals were more likely to consume the alternative item. When the response effort to obtain an item (pica-associated item or appropriate alternative) was increased, the participants consumed whatever item could be obtained with the least effort. In addition, Piazza, Hanley, Blakeley-Smith, and Kinsman (2000) reduced pica and increased appropriate toy play by attaching toys to a string for one individual who was blind and found that when it was less effortful to locate toys, the individual played with toys rather than engaging in pica. Therefore, this intervention combined both NCR (free access to toys) and effort manipulation (reducing effort to obtain toys). Although research findings are sparse, results to date suggest that manipulations of response effort may be a highly effective procedure for behavior that is automatically reinforced. Additional research is needed to examine whether response effort manipulations must be maintained over time to remain effective, or whether exposure over extended periods of time may establish alternative repertoires.

## Consequent Interventions

### Reinforcement-Based Procedures

Reinforcement is defined as both an operation and a process. Reinforcement is an operation (or procedure) involving the contingent addition (positive) or removal (negative) of a stimulus that increases the future probability of a response (process). Differential reinforcement procedures have been effective with different problem behaviors, including pica, in a number of populations (see Cooper, Heron, & Heward, 2007). Specifically, differential reinforcement of alternative (DRA) or incompatible behavior (DRI) involve providing a reinforcer contingent on a specific response that is an alternative to pica or topographically incompatible with it respectively. Studies using differential reinforcement to treat pica have targeted eating nonpica items, playing with alternative items, or discarding/exchanging potential pica items. For example, Fisher et al. (1994) provided 30 seconds of reinforcement for appropriate eating, as well as punishment for inappropriate eating, to decrease pica in three individuals. However, appropriate eating did not increase significantly. Donnelly and Olczak (1990) provided participants with chewing gum and delivered praise and an edible item for every 5 seconds in which participants were chewing the gum. This procedure decreased the latency to pica for all three participants. Kern, Starosta, and Adelman (2006) trained two participants to hand pica items to therapists in exchange for preferred edibles. In addition, if the participants did not exchange the item, the therapist prompted them accordingly. This procedure was effective for both participants. Finally, Gonzalez and Hagopian (2009) provided reinforcement for throwing away pica items combined with response blocking.

Differential reinforcement of other behavior (DRO) involves providing a reinforcer for not engaging in pica (rather than specifying a particular alternative or incompatible response). As the sole treatment for pica DRO has been described in only one study (Finney, Russo, & Cataldo, 1982). In that study, DRO alone was effective in two of four cases. DRO was combined with punishment in the form of overcorrection for the other two cases for which DRO alone was not effective.

### Response Blocking/Response Interruption

Response blocking or response interruption (RB/RI) involves preventing a behavior from occurring and has been shown to be effective in reducing problem behavior maintained by sensory reinforcement (see Cooper et al., 2007). RB/RI to treat automatically maintained problem behavior may be effective because it prevents the individual from obtaining reinforcement. However, RB/RI is an atypical EXT procedure, in that most EXT procedures allow the response to occur and then withhold reinforcement. In RB/RI both the response itself, as well as the reinforcer, are restricted. Alternatively, there is some evidence that RB/RI may function as punishment (Lerman and Iwata, 1996). Concerning pica, McCord, Grosser, Iwata, and Powers (2005) successfully treated three individuals by blocking them from touching pica items. However, pica was not entirely suppressed in all cases. In another study, Ricciardi, Luiselli, Terrill, and Reardon (2003) interrupted one individual from displaying pica by redirecting him back to tasks in a classroom setting, eventually adding a positive practice procedure to eliminate the behavior.

### Punishment-Based Procedures

Similar to reinforcement, punishment is both an operation and process. Punishment is defined as the contingent addition (positive) or removal (negative) of a stimulus that decreases the frequency or probability of that behavior as the result of a stimulus (Cooper et al., 2007). An example of positive punishment would be the pica-contingent oral hygiene routine described by Mulick, Barbour, Schroeder, and Rojahn (1980). An example of negative punishment would be withholding attention following pica (Mace & Knight, 1986).

The use of punishment procedures for pica is proportionally more prominent than for other types of behaviors, perhaps because pica can be life threatening. And yet, only a few studies have evaluated punishment procedures alone (see Table 9.1; Buchar et al., 1976; Ferreri, Tamm, & Wier, 2006; Foxx & Martin, 1975; Mulick et al., 1980; Rojahn, McGonigle, Curcio, & Dixon, 1987; Singh & Winton, 1984). One of the earliest studies that used punishment to treat pica was conducted by Foxx and Martin (1975). In this study, positive punishment (overcorrection) decreased pica over 90% for all four participants. Similarly, Buchar et al. (1976) assessed the effectiveness of positive punishment (brief contingent restraint) on the pica behavior of two individuals. The authors found that pica was reduced to zero when both a reprimand and brief contingent restraint were used in conjunction for touching a pica item.

### *Multicomponent Consequent Interventions*

Punishment and RB procedures are usually used in conjunction with reinforcement procedures. Typically, punishment or RB/RI is added to the treatment when reinforcement procedures alone are insufficient to decrease problem behavior. Of note, Lerman and Vorndran (2002) suggested that punishment may be necessary when the reinforcer for problem behavior cannot be controlled or behavior is so severe that significant injury is possible. Both of these conditions are satisfied in some cases of pica, so it is not surprising that punishment is often used concurrently with reinforcement-based procedures. For example, Goh et al. (1999), mentioned previously, assessed the same reinforcement component with two different additions (DRA and RB as well as DRA and punishment) and found that DRA plus RB increased the latency to pica for three participants but that little difference was seen between DRA plus RB and DRA plus punishment.

### **Antecedent and Consequent Interventions**

Noncontingent reinforcement has been used in conjunction with reinforcement-based, punishment-based, and reinforcement and punishment-based treatments (see Table 9.1; Donnelly & Olczak, 1990; Falcomata et al., 2007; Favell et al., 1982; Fisher et al., 1994; Goh et al., 1999; Gonzalez & Hagopian, 2009; Piazza et al., 1998; Piazza et al., 1996; Piazza et al., 2002; Rapp et al., 2001). As mentioned previously, NCR may be a necessary component for the differential reinforcement treatments because of the nature of the response. For example, Donnelly and Olczak (1990) provided three participants with chewing gum and then delivered coffee and praise for every 5 seconds the participants were chewing gum and not engaging in pica. The authors found that the latency to pica increased over the course of 15-minute sessions. Similarly, Kern et al. (2006) trained two individuals to trade pica items for preferred edibles. Here, the turning over of pica items is incompatible with eating pica items, and the exchange behavior is maintained by access to highly preferred items. This procedure was effective for reducing pica for both individuals. Favell et al. (1982) found that adding DRA to NCR had idiosyncratic effects for each of three participants. Pica was further reduced for one participant; no difference in pica was observed for another participant, and pica disrupted the effects of NCR for the third participant. These results suggest that the use of DRA plus NCR may be effective in some cases; however, counter therapeutic effects are possible. For an example of how NCR can interact with DRA, see also Goh et al. (2000).

The use of NCR and punishment has also been investigated. Piazza et al. (1996) first examined noncontingent access to edible items as a treatment for pica, found it ineffective, and added a verbal reprimand effectively for one individual. Conversely, Rapp et al. (2001) evaluated several antecedent and consequent procedures for decreasing pica, and found that NCR plus punishment was not effective.

A unique set of studies have examined NCR plus DRA and punishment or RB. For example, Fisher et al. (1994) evaluated noncontingent access to edible items, differential reinforcement for eating food items, and a facial screen for pica among three individuals. The procedures decreased pica and slightly increased appropriate eating for all of the participants. Similarly, Gonzalez and Hagopian (2009) studied the effects of noncontingent access to leisure items, RB, and DRA for edible items. During the DRA, the participants identified and discarded inedible items to earn edible ones. The combination of these procedures was effective at decreasing pica for two individuals.

## CONCLUSIONS AND RECOMMENDATIONS

As noted by Mace (1994), the widespread use of functional analysis ushered in a shift toward the development of interventions based on an understanding of the determinants of behavior in lieu of using default procedures to override existing (and often unknown) contingencies. Technological and conceptual advances in the assessment and treatment of problem behavior (aggression, self-injury) described in recent decades have been extended to the assessment and treatment of pica. The increased proportion of reinforcement-based procedures relative to punishment procedures for problem behavior and self-injury associated with these advancements (Kahng, Iwata, & Lewin, 2002; Luiselli, 2004; Pelios, Morren, Tesch, & Axelrod, 1999) is also evident in the literature on the treatment of pica (Table 9.1).

Although some behavior analytic treatments such as punishment have been used consistently to treat pica, two general trends in pica research have been observed in the last 40 years: 1) the proportion of studies that have incorporated reinforcement-based procedures has increased, and 2) more treatment components have been employed concurrently as part of treatment packages for pica. With the introduction of analog FA as described by Iwata and colleagues (beginning in 1984), the number of studies that incorporated reinforcement procedures increased. For example, between 1970 and 1995, six studies used punishment alone as a treatment procedure, whereas only three studies used differential reinforcement alone as treatment. However, between 1995 and 2010, an equal number of studies examined punishment and differential reinforcement procedures—and punishment was generally not the sole treatment component.

Research on the treatment of self-injury maintained by sensory reinforcement in particular has informed and has been informed by developments in the treatment of pica. The application of NCR as a treatment component for pica also has increased with the more common use of FBA of pica. This increase in the number of studies that use NCR and competing stimuli is not surprising given that pica is typically found to be maintained by sensory reinforcement. The parallel development of treatments for self-injury maintained by sensory reinforcement and for pica is perhaps most evident if one examines the procedures used to identify stimuli intended to produce competing sources of reinforcement. Although early studies selected stimuli to compete with problem behavior and pica (Favell et al., 1982) using informal methods, current studies use competing stimulus assessments to systematically select stimuli based on the extent to which they decrease the response, presumably via reinforcer competition (e.g., Piazza et al., 1996).

The inherent risks associated with pica pose a significant barrier to safe and thorough behavioral assessment and treatment evaluation. Baiting the environments with simulated pica items or safe pica items during assessment and treatment is a significant development that allows pica to occur without threat to the individual. Simulated pica items are needed in cases where none of the items the individual has consumed are safe to ingest, even in small quantities. However, to increase the generality of treatment, some training should be conducted where the actual pica materials are present, noting that precautions must always be taken to ensure safety. In cases where the threat of harm is particularly severe (e.g., eating feces) some form of response blocking could be used to ensure safety. Using a progression of simulated pica items to actual pica items will validate that the treatment effects are not related to the particular items used in treatment and will remain effective outside of the current treatment conditions.

Interventions developed in clinic settings have value only if their effects generalize to the natural environments of the individual. Successful generalization is more likely to be achieved by explicitly programming for generalization. Thus, treatment of a child's pica at school would have to be extended to the home if it occurs in that setting. Similarly, effective intervention for one form of pica, say, cigarettes, does not guarantee a similar outcome for other pica objects. Accordingly, programmed generalization for pica treatment should entail cross-setting implementation by all care-providers and for a broad class of pica behaviors.

The goal of treatment of pica should be to establish edible and inedible items as separate and distinct stimulus classes that occasion different responses. To reiterate, items may be inedible because of their location (on the ground, in the garbage) or type (nails, bleach). Therefore, individuals who engage in pica should be trained to respond differentially to stimuli that are of the edible and inedible class. This type of stimulus control training has been demonstrated in several studies (e.g., Bogart, Piersel, & Gross, 1995; Finney et al., 1982; Gonzalez & Hagopian, 2009; Piazza et al., 1996). Establishing these stimulus classes can be accomplished through the use of differential consequences for consumption of the different items paired with schedule-correlated stimuli. Supplemental stimuli can be used in the early stages of treatment, but the ideal intervention would be designed to establish naturally occurring stimuli as discriminative for what items can and cannot be ingested.

Like generalization, intervention effects for pica are more likely to be maintained over time if addressed through formal programming. For example, if a four-component treatment package successfully eliminated pica, it would be prudent to systematically remove single components of the package while maintaining previous treatment gains. Ultimately, it is advantageous to withdraw the full strength of intervention so that low- to no-frequency pica can be supported with natural contingencies. Of course, it may not be possible to remove treatment completely but instead, make it more practical.

Intervention integrity (Hagermoser-Sanetti & Kratochwill, 2008) is critical given the seriousness of pica and the requirement, at least initially, for intensive treatment. Treating professionals must carefully monitor care providers to verify that they apply procedures accurately. Intervention integrity assessment is conducted through direct observation that documents adherence to the procedures that comprise a treatment plan. Feedback in the form of positive reinforcement and correction is given to care providers based on their intervening at or below criterion, respectively. A nontreatment effect with good intervention integrity would indicate that the treatment plan should be revised. As important, a nontreatment effect with poor intervention integrity would signal further training and supervision of care providers. Because behavior analytic treatment plans for pica typically have more than one procedure and must be implemented by multiple care providers, intervention integrity assessment is integral to success.

Finally, practitioners should work with care providers to create a safe environment where opportunities for pica are decreased. This includes providing a sufficient level of supervision, and keeping the environment clean to minimize access to potential pica items. As noted previously, more recent interventions have sought to involve the individual in this process, by teaching him or her to clean the environment and appropriately discard potential pica materials (e.g., Gonzalez & Hagopian, 2009; Kern et al., 2006). Any safety precautions, however, should be as least restrictive as needed to ensure that the individual continues to have opportunities to engage in a normalized routine, access preferred activities, and live in a stimulating environment.

## REFERENCES

Ali, Z. (2001). Pica in people with intellectual disability: A literature review of aetiology, epidemiology and complications. *Journal of Intellectual & Developmental Disability, 26,* 205–215.

American Psychiatric Association. (2000). *Diagnostic and statistical manual of mental disorders* (4th ed., rev.). Washington, DC: Author.

Ashworth, M., Hirdes, J.P., & Martin, L. (2009). The social and recreational characteristics of adults with intellectual disability and pica living in institutions. *Research in Developmental Disabilities, 30,* 512–520.

Bogart, L.C., Piersel, W.C., & Gross, E.J. (1995). The long-term treatment of life-threatening pica: A case study of a woman with profound mental retardation living in an applied setting. *Journal of Developmental and Physical Disabilities, 7,* 39–50.

Bucher, B., Reykdal, B., & Albin, J. (1976). Brief physical restraint to control pica in retarded children. *Journal of Behavior Therapy & Experimental Psychiatry, 7,* 137–140.

Camp, E.M., Iwata, B.A., Hammond, J.L., & Bloom, S.E. (2009). Antecedent versus consequent events as predictors of problem behavior. *Journal of Applied Behavior Analysis, 42,* 469–483.

Carr, J.E., Severtson, J.M., & Lepper, T.L. (2009). Noncontingent reinforcement is an empirically supported treatment for problem behavior exhibited by individuals with developmental disabilities. *Research in Developmental Disabilities, 30,* 44–57.

Chisholm, J.J. & Kaplan, E. (1968). Lead poisoning in childhood-comprehensive management and prevention. *Journal of Pediatrics, 73,* 942–950.

Cooper, J.O., Heron, T.H., and Heward, W.L. (2007). *Applied Behavior Analysis.* (2nd ed.). Columbus, OH: Prentice Hall.

Danford, D.E., & Huber, A.M (1982) Pica among mentally retarded adults. *American Journal of Mental Deficits, 87,* 141–146.

Decker, C.J. (1993). Pica in the mentally handicapped: A 15-year surgical perspective. *Canadian Journal of Surgery, 36,* 551–554.

Donnelly, D.R., & Olczak, P.V. (1990). The effect of differential reinforcement of incompatible behaviors (DRI) on pica for cigarettes in persons with intellectual disabilities. *Behavior Modification, 14,* 81–96.

Falcomata, T.S., Roane, H.S., & Pabico, R.R. (2007). Unintentional stimulus control during the treatment of pica displayed by a young man with autism. *Research in Autism Spectrum Disorders, 1,* 350–359.

Favell, J.E., McGimsey, J.F., & Schell, R.M. (1982). Treatment of self-injury by providing alternate sensory activities. *Analysis and Intervention in Developmental Disabilities, 2,* 83–104.

Ferreri, S.J., Tamm, L., & Wier, K.G. (2006). Using food aversion to decrease severe pica by a child with autism. *Behavior Modification, 30,* 456–471.

Finney, J.W., Russo, D.C., & Cataldo, M.F. (1982). Reduction of pica in young children with lead poisoning. *Journal of Pediatric Psychology, 7,* 197–207.

Fisher, W.W., Piazza, C.C., Bowman, L.G., Kurtz, P.F., Sherer, M.R., & Lachman, S.R. (1994). A preliminary evaluation of empirically derived consequences for the treatment of pica. *Journal of Applied Behavior Analysis, 27,* 447–457.

Foxx, R.M., & Martin, E.D. (1975). Treatment of scavenging behavior (coprophagy and pica) by overcorrection. *Behavior Research & Therapy, 13,* 153–162.

Goh, H., Iwata, B.A., & DeLeon, I.G. (2000). Competition between noncontingent and contingent reinforcement schedules during response acquisition. *Journal of Applied Behavior Analysis, 33,* 195–205.

Goh, H., Iwata, B.A., & Kahng, S. (1999). Multicomponent assessment and treatment of cigarette pica. *Journal of Applied Behavior Analysis, 32,* 297–316.

Gonzalez, M.L., & Hagopian, L.P (2009). The treatment of pica through response chain alternations. In L.P. Hagopian (Chair), *Assessment and treatment of behavior maintained by automatic reinforcement.* Symposium conducted at the Annual Convention of the Association for Behavior Analysis International, Phoenix, AZ.

Greenberg, M., Jacobziner, H., McLaughlin M.C., Fuerst, H.T., & Pellitteri, O. (1958). A study of pica in relation to lead poisoning. *Pediatrics, 22,* 756–760.

Gutelius, M.F., Millican, F.K., Layman, E.M., Cohen, G.J., & Dublin, C.C. (1962). Nutritional studies of children with pica. *Pediatrics, 29,* 1012–1023.

Hagermoser-Sanetti, L.M., & Kratochwill, T.R. (2008). Treatment integrity in behavioral consultation: Measurement, promotion, and outcomes. *International Journal of Behavioral Consultation and Therapy, 4,* 95–114.

Hagopian, L.P., & Adelinis, J.D. (2001). Response blocking with and without redirection for the treatment of pica. *Journal of Applied Behavior Analysis, 34,* 527–530.

Hagopian, L.P., Crockett, J.L., van Stone, M., DeLeon, I.G., & Bowman, L.G. (2000). Effects of noncontingent reinforcement on problem behavior and stimulus engagement: The role of satiation, extinction, and alternative reinforcement. *Journal of Applied Behavior Analysis, 33,* 433–449.

Iwata, B.A., Dorsey, M.F., Slifer, K.J., Bauman, K.E., & Richman, G.S. (1994). Toward a functional analysis of self-injury. *Journal of Applied Behavior Analysis, 27,* 197–209. (Reprinted from *Analysis and Intervention in Developmental Disabilities, 2,* 3–20, 1982).

Iwata, B.A., & Worsdell, A.S. (2005). Implications of functional analysis methodology for the design of intervention programs. *Exceptionality, 13,* 25–34.

Kahng, S., Iwata, B.A., & Lewin, A.B. (2002). Behavioral treatment of self-injury, 1964 to 2000. *American Journal on Mental Retardation, 107,* 212–221.

Kern, L., Starosta, K., & Adelman, B.E. (2006). Reducing pica by teaching children to exchange inedible items for edibles. *Behavior Modification, 30,* 135–158.

Kinnell, H.G. (1985). Pica as a feature of autism. *British Journal of Psychiatry, 147,* 80–82.

Lacey, E.P. (1990). Broadening the perspective of pica: Literature review. *Public Health Reports, 105,* 29–35.

Lanzkowsky, P. (1959). Investigation into the aetiology and treatment of pica. *Archives of Disease in Childhood, 34,* 140–148.

Lerman, D.C., & Iwata, B.A. (1993). Descriptive and experimental analysis of variables maintaining self-injurious behavior. *Journal of Applied Behavior Analysis, 26,* 293–319.

Lerman, D.C., & Iwata, B.A. (1996). A methodology for distinguishing between extinction and punishment effects associated with response blocking. *Journal of Applied Behavior Analysis, 29,* 231–234.

Lerman, D.C., Vorndran, C.M. (2002). On the status of knowledge for using punishment implications for treating behavior disorders. *Journal of Applied Behavior Analysis, 35*(4), 431–464.

Luiselli, J.K. (1996). Pica as obsessive compulsive behavior. *Journal of Behavior Therapy & Experimental Psychiatry, 27,* 96–97.

Luiselli, J.K. (2004). Current issues in behavior support for persons with developmental disabilities. In J.L. Matson, R.B. Laud, & M.L. Matson (Eds.), *Behavior modification for persons with developmental disabilities: Treatments and Supports.* New York, NY: NADD Press.

Mace, F.C. (1994). The significance and future of functional analysis methodologies. *Journal of Applied Behavior Analysis, 27,* 385–392.

Mace, F.C., & Knight, D. (1986). Functional analysis and treatment of severe pica. *Journal of Applied Behavior Analysis, 19,* 411–416.

McCord, B.E., Grosser, J.W., Iwata, B.A., Powers, L.A. (2005). An analysis of response-blocking parameters in the prevention of pica. *Journal of Applied Behavior Analysis, 38,* 391–394.

Mulick, J.A., Barbour, R., Schroeder, S.R., & Rojahn, J. (1980). Overcorrection of pica in two profoundly retarded adults: Analysis of setting effects, stimulus, and response generalization. *Applied Research in Mental Retardation, 1,* 241–252.

Pelios, L., Morren, J., Tesch, D., & Axelrod, S. (1999). The impact of functional analysis methodology on treatment choice for self-injurious and aggressive behavior. *Journal of Applied Behavior Analysis, 32,* 185–195.

Piazza, C.C., Fisher, W.W., Hanley, G.P., LeBlanc, L.A., Worsdell, A.S., Lindauer, S.E., & Keeney, K.M. (1998). Treatment of pica through multiple analyses of its reinforcing functions. *Journal of Applied Behavior Analysis, 31,* 165–189.

Piazza, C.C., Hanley, G.P., Blakeley-Smith, A.B., & Kinsman, A.M. (2000). Effects of search skills training on the pica of a blind boy. *Journal of Developmental and Physical Disabilities, 12,* 35–41.

Piazza, C.C., Hanley, G.P., & Fisher W.W. (1996). Functional analysis and treatment of cigarette pica. *Journal of Applied Behavior Analysis, 29,* 437–450.

Piazza, C.C., Roane, H.S., Keeney, K.M., Boney, B.R., Abt, K.A. (2002). Varying response effort in the treatment of pica maintained by automatic reinforcement. *Journal of Applied Behavior Analysis, 35,* 233–246.

Rapp, J.T., Dozier, C.L., & Carr, J.E. (2001). Functional assessment and treatment of pica: A single-case experiment. *Behavioral Interventions, 16,* 111–125.

Ricciardi, J.N., Luiselli, J.K., Terrill, S., & Reardon, K. (2003). Alternative response training with contingent practice as intervention for pica in a school setting. *Behavioral Interventions, 18,* 219–226.

Rojahn, J., McGonigle, J.J., Curcio, C., & Dixon, M.J. (1987). Suppression of pica by water mist and aromatic ammonia. *Behavior Modification, 11,* 65–74.

Singh, N.N., & Winton, A.S.W. (1984). Effects of a screening procedure on pica and collateral behaviors. *Journal of Behavior Therapy & Experimental Psychiatry, 15,* 59–65.

Stein, D.J., Bouwer, C., & van Heerden, B. (1996). Pica and the obsessive-compulsive spectrum disorders. *South African Medical Journal, 86,* 1591–1592.

Wasano, L.C., Borrero, J.C., & Kohn, C.S. (2009). Brief report: A comparison of indirect versus experimental strategies for the assessment of pica. *Journal of Autism and Developmental Disorders, 39,* 1582–1586.

# Ruminative Vomiting

### Jonathan Tarbox,
### Amy L. Kenzer, and Michele R. Bishop

CHAPTER

Rumination involves repeated regurgitation, chewing, and reswallowing of previously ingested food. Rumination is a high-risk behavior because it can result in negative outcomes such as weight loss, malnutrition, tooth decay, halitosis, and electrolyte imbalances (Chial, Camilleri, Williams, Litzinger, & Perrault, 2003). Chronic rumination may have the less tangible, but perhaps equally important, negative social effect of driving peers and others away due to the smell and sight of regurgitated food in one's mouth. Despite being an unusual behavior, rumination is more common than might be expected, with a prevalence rate of up to 5%–10% in individuals with intellectual disabilities (Gravestock, 2000). The form and frequency of rumination varies considerably across individuals, some rejecting regurgitated food (i.e., vomiting), and others rechewing and reswallowing it (Rogers, Stratton, Victor, Kennedy, & Andres, 1992). Most rumination appears to occur during or soon after mealtimes and these time periods are also when the behavior has typically been studied in treatment research.

Rumination may appear to be a medical problem because most occurrences of regurgitation outside of rumination can be attributed to medical causes (with the obvious exception of bulimia nervosa). However, according to the *Diagnostic and Statistical Manual of Mental Disorders* (4th ed., revised), rumination disorder cannot be attributed purely to a medical cause (*DSM-IV-TR;* American Psychiatric Association, 2000). Many or most cases of rumination disorder likely involve medical variables as contributing factors to some degree, but the environment virtually always plays a role as well. It appears as though the behavior of ruminating produces stimulation that is reinforcing, thereby resulting in automatic reinforcement for the behavior (see discussion of functional assessment of rumination following). The specific sources of stimulation that serve as reinforcement are unknown, but researchers have hypothesized that oral stimulation and esophageal stimulation are at least two possibilities (Rast, Johnston, Allen, & Drum, 1985). In any case, it appears likely that many cases of rumination may originate from a medical condition (e.g., gastroesophageal reflux or vomiting due to illness), in which regurgitation occurred involuntarily, and then due to behavior-contingent consequences, may have come under operant control via automatic reinforcement (Kedesdy & Budd, 1998; Rogers et al., 1992). The behavior may then be maintained over long periods of time, often in the absence of any clear medical contributing factors. Thus, as we discuss as follows, the majority of empirically validated treatments for rumination include environmental manipulation. However, it must be noted that rumination is a disorder with obvious multidisciplinary factors involved, and it is therefore always prudent to convene a multidisciplinary team for assessment and treatment.

In this chapter, we review research on the various empirically validated treatments for rumination, provide recommendations for how clinicians can implement treatment in the context of a multidisciplinary team, and conclude with a discussion for potential directions for future research.

## REVIEW OF RESEARCH

A review of research on the behavioral treatment of rumination is presented below (also see Davis & Cuvo, 1980; Fredericks, Carr, & Williams, 1998; McAdam & Cole, 2007; Singh, 1981; and Starin & Fuqua, 1987, for additional reviews). We focus on treatments that have repeated replications of effectiveness, published by two or more different research groups. Nonintrusive treatments are also emphasized, as well as research on the functional assessment of rumination.

### Punishment

Some of the earliest research demonstrating the effective treatment of rumination used punishment procedures consisting of aversive consequences applied contingent on each occurrence of rumination. Most of these procedures consisted of applying a substance with an aversive taste to the mouth, sometimes referred to as "response–contingent taste aversion." An early study used contingent lemon juice to punish rumination in a 6-month-old infant (Sajwaj, Libet, & Agras, 1974). A similar lemon juice procedure was demonstrated to be effective in a 16-year-old boy with profound intellectual disability (Marholin, Luiselli, Robinson, & Lott, 1980). In an additional participant, an 11-year-old boy with tuberous sclerosis, profound intellectual disability, and a seizure disorder, Marholin et al. found lemon juice to be ineffective but found contingent application of Tabasco sauce to produce robust decreases in rumination. More recently, a mildly aversive "tart" lemonade was included as part of a treatment package to treat rumination (Sanders-Dewey & Larson, 2006). Singh, Manning, and Angell (1982) used an "oral hygiene" procedure to decrease the rumination of a pair of 17-year-old monozygotic twins with profound intellectual disabilities. The oral hygiene procedure had the participants brush their teeth for 2 minutes, using a toothbrush soaked in oral antiseptic (Listerine), and then wipe their lips with a cloth soaked in oral antiseptic.

Other punishment procedures have included verbal reprimands (Marholin et al., 1980; Simpson & Sasso, 1978), shock (Luckey, Watson, & Musick, 1968; White & Taylor, 1967), and time-out (Kedesdy & Budd, 1998; Smeets, 1970). Research on punishment of rumination has consistently demonstrated robust treatment effects but punishment-based interventions should only be considered following failure of less intrusive treatments and for more severe cases. In the vast majority of cases, empirically supported nonintrusive treatments are likely to be effective.

## Differential Reinforcement

A variety of differential reinforcement procedures for the treatment of rumination have been investigated, including differential reinforcement of other behavior (DRO), differential reinforcement of incompatible behavior (DRI), and differential reinforcement of alternative behavior (DRA). Many of these interventions involve delivery of appetitive or gustatory reinforcers (Conrin, Pennypacker, Johnston, & Rast, 1982; McKeegan, Estill, & Campbell, 1987; O'Neil, White, King, & Carek, 1979; Sanders-Dewey & Larson, 2006). However, contingent delivery of vibratory stimulation (Barmann, 1980), and physical touch accompanying social praise (Mulick et al., 1980) have also been used. Differential reinforcement procedures are also often combined with other treatments including punishment (Sanders-Dewey & Larson, 2006), manipulation of food quantity (O'Neil et al., 1979), and paced meals (McKeegan et al., 1987).

O'Neil et al. (1979) demonstrated the effective treatment of rumination with a DRO procedure in which honey water was delivered contingent on the absence of rumination. The DRO procedure was implemented with and without punishment procedures (time-out and contingent lemon juice) and resulted in reduced levels of rumination with each implementation. A DRO scheduled based on the mean interresponse time resulted in rapid reductions in rumination with near-zero levels at shorter interval durations (Conrin et al., 1982). In another study, DRI was combined with a taste aversion procedure to produce rapid decreases in rumination (Sanders-Dewey & Larson, 2006). In this study, both preferred liquid and verbal praise were initially provided, with the subsequent removal of the preferred liquid, then aversive stimulus and eventually, only verbal praise remained with further decrements in rumination observed across each phase of the intervention, as well as maintenance of treatment effects at follow-up. In a related study, Barmann (1980) successfully eliminated ruminative vomiting with a DRO procedure for hand mouthing, a behavior that consistently preceded vomiting. Similarly, a DRO procedure further reduced ruminative responding when combined with pacing the meal (McKeegan et al., 1987). A comparison of DRO, DRI, and DRA revealed similar reductions in responding across each procedure with DRI proving slightly more effective (Mulick et al., 1980).

These data suggest that differential reinforcement can be an effective method for reducing rumination. However, the resulting reduction in rumination is variable and does not always produce total cessation (Mulick et al., 1980). Additionally, the combination or sequencing of differential reinforcement procedures with other empirically validated interventions limits our understanding of the independent effects of differential reinforcement, particularly with respect to edible reinforcers.

## Food Quantity

Several empirically validated treatment procedures for rumination involve increasing the amount of food consumed during, following, or between meals. Increased food quantity has been provided in the form of larger meals, supplemental feedings, and satiation procedures. Research on the relation between food quantity and rumination has revealed an inverse relationship between the amount of rumination that occurs and the amount of food which has been consumed (Rast, Johnston, & Drum, 1984). One exception to this general relationship is found when only slight increases in food quantity are provided, often resulting in increases in rumination (Johnston & Greene, 1992; Kenzer & Wallace, 2007). A substantial increase in the amount of food provided for consumption is often necessary for treatment effects to be observed, with "all-you-can-eat" satiation procedures proving most effective, as described below (Rast, Johnston, Drum, & Conrin, 1981; Rast et al., 1984; Rast & Johnston, 1986).

## Satiation

Satiation procedures involve providing the individual with an additional, unlimited amount of food following completion of the regular meal, often while providing prompts to continue eating until the individual will no longer consume the food (Johnston & Greene, 1992). Satiation procedures are among the earliest and most researched treatment procedures for rumination, with the first published account provided by Jackson, Johnson, Ackron, and Crowley (1975). Satiation procedures typically include the provision of starchy foods (e.g., potatoes, Cream of Wheat, white bread, peanut butter, and rice cakes; Dudley, Johnson, & Barnes, 2002; Rast et al., 1981, Rast et al., 1984; Rast et al., 1985, Rast & Johnston, 1986, Rast, Johnston, Lubin, & Ellinger-Allen, 1988; Yang, 1988). The frequent use of starchy foods in satiation procedures has led to the common use of the term "starch satiation" to refer to it. Fruits and vegetables have also been used successfully, although a greater volume of food is typically consumed under these conditions and fruits and vegetables have rarely been evaluated alone (Dunn, Lockwood, Williams, & Peacock, 1997; Rast et al., 1985). Lobato, Carlson, and Barrera (1986) also observed a reduction in rumination following satiation with a variety of low calorie foods such as pudding, toast, and diluted juice. Finally, Saloviita (1999) provided additional portions of the regular meal along with spoonfuls of honey to decrease rumination.

Satiation procedures are easy to implement and often produce immediate and substantial decreases in ruminating. Satiation effects have been observed to carry over to subsequent postmeal observation periods with the amount of food consumed having a cumulative effect across the day (Johnston & Greene, 1992). In a parametric evaluation of food quantity and rumination, both ascending and descending amounts of food were provided systematically across sessions with the amounts staggered across breakfast and lunch meals (Rast et al., 1984). Results demonstrated that less rumination was observed following lunch when more food was consumed during breakfast, even when the amount of food provided during lunch was reduced.

Satiation-based interventions frequently result in collateral weight gain; a significant advantage considering many individuals who engage in chronic rumination are also malnourished and underweight (Yang, 1988). For example, Rast et al. (1981) reported that a starch satiation procedure resulted in substantial weight gain for three participants whose baseline weight was 10 to 30 pounds below their ideal weight range.

Conversely, the characteristic weight gain resulting from satiation procedures can be a significant disadvantage for some. Collateral weight gain is inappropriate if it continues beyond the ideal range for that individual or if the client begins intervention at his or her ideal weight (Johnston & Greene, 1992). Weight gain can be minimized by fading out the satiation treatment after treatment effects are stable or by transitioning from starchy foods to low calorie foods such as fruits and vegetables. Several investigations have successfully faded satiation interventions while maintaining reductions in rumination (Thibadeau, Blew, Reedy, & Luiselli, 1999; Yang, 1988). Yang systematically decreased the number of bread slices each week until no additional food was provided with zero to near-zero levels of rumination maintained through a 12-week follow-up. In contrast, Rast et al. (1984) observed an increase in rumination for the participant exposed to descending amounts of food suggesting fading procedures may not always be successful. Dunn et al. (1997) demonstrated the effectiveness of a fruits and vegetables satiation procedure following an initial decrease in rumination under starch-satiation conditions. Treatment effects were maintained following the switch to fruits and vegetables and a stabilization of weight observed. In addition, the amount of fruits and vegetables was successfully reduced by 50% to further minimize weight gain.

## Supplemental Feedings

Supplemental feedings have also been found to reduce ruminative vomiting (Barton & Barton, 1985; Greene et al., 1991; Kenzer & Wallace, 2007; Lyons, Rue, Luiselli, & DiGennaro, 2007). Supplemental feedings involve the delivery of pre-specified amounts of food during the meal, following completion of the meal, or between meals without an attempt to achieve satiation. Barton and Barton (1985) provided supplemental feedings of peanut butter to treat rumination in four children with mental retardation. The children were fed 2–4 tablespoons of peanut butter every 2–3 hours during the school day and mealtime liquids were reduced. The supplemental peanut butter effectively eliminated ruminating for all participants. The supplemental food was gradually faded and rumination remained at zero levels at a 30-day follow-up. Saloviita (1999) found similar results with one participant who was fed supplemental peanut butter and honey immediately following the meal. The thick, sticky consistency of the peanut butter and honey were hypothesized to make rumination more effortful and therefore less likely to occur. Greene et al. (1991) evaluated the effect of food consistency on rumination by comparing supplemental feedings of peanut butter to a peanut butter "shake" and found that although both foods reduced rumination, a greater reduction was observed with the regular peanut butter.

Supplemental feedings have also been provided in small amounts, spaced over time following the meal. Spaced supplemental feeding involves the delivery of a single bite of food on a fixed-time schedule for 15–30 minutes following completion of the regular meal (Kenzer & Wallace, 2007; Lyons et al., 2007; Masalsky & Luiselli, 1998). Masalsky and Luiselli (1998) provided bites of white bread every 30 seconds for 30 minutes following the meal. A decrease in rumination was observed and maintained as the duration of the supplemental feeding was reduced to 15 minutes. A decrease in rumination was also observed when a variety of different foods were provided across sessions for 30 minutes postmeal (Kenzer & Wallace). However, rumination increased when the supplemental feeding was reduced to 15 minutes. The evaluation of spaced supplemental feedings requires that rumination is measured during and following the supplemental feeding to ensure that the supplemental feeding does not simply delay rumination.

The delivery of supplemental food can circumvent unwanted weight gain because the amount of additional food provided is typically less than that consumed during satiation-based treatments. However, supplementing feeding procedures often produce reductions in rumination that are less dramatic and immediate than those produced by satiation. Additionally, lengthy supplemental feedings that span several minutes postmeal or occur across the entire day can be more effortful and time intensive to implement.

## Portion Manipulation

Perhaps the simplest means of increasing food quantity is to increase the meal size. One of the earliest investigations of food quantity and rumination included a large portions condition in which the regular meal portions were increased by a factor of 1.5 at lunch and doubled at breakfast (Rast et al., 1981). Instead of a therapeutic effect, larger meal portions resulted in an increase in rumination. Similarly, an increase in rumination was observed when an additional 10 ounces of food was provided following the regular meal (Rast et al., 1984). Kenzer and Wallace (2007) also found a slight increase in rumination with larger portions. Despite the ease of implementation, portion manipulation has not proven an effective intervention.

## Mechanisms of Change

Although the effectiveness of increased food quantity for the treatment of rumination has been repeatedly demonstrated, only a handful of investigations have sought to identify the necessary and sufficient variables responsible for its effectiveness. Increasing the amount of food consumed simultaneously increases the number of calories consumed, produces greater oral and pharyngeal stimulation, and increases stomach distention and gastric load (Rast et al., 1985). Any one or combination of these components may contribute to the decrease in rumination observed.

If an individual ruminates because he or she is hungry, the increased caloric intake and sense of "fullness" produced by greater stomach distension would likely produce therapeutic effects. This may be the case when food is restricted and the regular baseline meals are associated with weight loss (Rast et al., 1981). In a study by Rast et al. (1985), the caloric density of food was increased while keeping the volume, weight, and chewing requirements of the meal constant. Caloric intake was manipulated by substituting low calorie foods with high-calorie foods (e.g., whole milk substituted for skim milk), adding butter and oil, and increasing the amount of starchy vegetables. A moderate to large, but variable, decrease in rumination was observed with the increase in calories. Greene et al. (1991) found similar results when they compared supplemental feedings of high-calorie peanut butter to low-calorie peanut butter. High-calorie peanut butter produced greater reductions in rumination than the low-calorie peanut butter. This difference was not evident, however, when the consistency of the peanut butter was also manipulated by providing the peanut butter in a "shake" form. The high- and low-calorie peanut butter shakes were equally effective in producing a slight decrease in rumination.

Only a single study evaluated the role of stomach volume in satiation procedures by providing participants with supplemental feedings of wheat bran to produce greater stomach distention while keeping caloric intake and oral stimulation constant (Rast et al., 1985). A slight, but consistent, decrease in rumination was observed under these conditions.

The influence of oropharyngeal stimulation in the reduction of rumination has also been evaluated. If rumination is automatically maintained by the oral or esophageal stimulation produced by regurgitation and rechewing of food, it stands to reason that an increase in similar stimulation produced by consumption of large quantities of food would function to decrease the reinforcing properties of stimulation produced by rumination (Jackson et al., 1975) by decreasing the individual's level of deprivation from that sort of stimulation. Rast et al. (1985) increased both food volume and weight in an attempt to approximate the amount of chewing and thus oropharyngeal stimulation produced during satiation procedures while minimizing any concurrent increase in calories. The result was a slight decrease in rumination.

Oropharyngeal stimulation has also been evaluated by manipulating food consistency as well as amount of premeal chewing. Food consistency may influence the amount of stimulation produced during food consumption with pureed food requiring less chewing and therefore producing less stimulation. In a comparison of regular versus pureed food, the regular food was effective in reducing rumination, whereas an increase in rumination occurred following pureed meals (Johnston & Greene, 1990). Inconsistent effects of food consistency on rumination were observed in another study comparing regular peanut butter with peanut butter in a shake form with two participants displaying less rumination under regular peanut butter conditions and two participants displaying less rumination following consumption of the peanut butter shake (Greene et al., 1991).

Finally, the role of oropharyngeal stimulation on rumination was examined by matching the amount of premeal gum chewing to the amount of chewing observed during meal consumption and ruminative episodes (Rast et al, 1988). The premeal gum chewing resulted in slight decrease in rumination following completion of a regular meal. Taken together, the results of these studies suggest that each of these variables—caloric intake, stomach distension, and oropharyngeal stimulation—each contribute to the decrease in rumination produced by satiation and supplemental feeding procedures.

## Liquid Rescheduling

Several studies have found that rescheduling the opportunity to consume liquids, typically by withholding liquids until after meals have been consumed, can help decrease rumination. Luiselli, Haley, and Smith (1993) evaluated liquid rescheduling, in the context of a multicomponent treatment for rumination, with a 16-year-old boy with severe multiple disabilities. The liquid rescheduling component of the intervention consisted of scheduling an interval of at least one hour between consumption of food and liquids. Similarly, Heering, Wilder, and Ladd (2003) successfully treated the rumination of a 19-year-old man with autism by withholding all liquids during meals and presenting liquids a minimum of 1.5 hours after meal completion. It is not known why liquid rescheduling decreases rumination, but it is possible that withholding liquids during mealtimes makes regurgitation of the consumed food more difficult.

## Other Procedures

A small number of other procedures, which are not easily classified into the categories already addressed above, have been shown to be effective for treating rumination. For example, Watson and Scott (1994) used a treatment package, combining time-out from food and attention with DRO, to decrease the rumination of a 52-year-old man with severe intellectual disabilities and esophagitis. It is not known which intervention components produced the decrease in rumination, but it is worth noting that the use of time-out from attention and food is significantly less intrusive than the response-contingent taste aversion procedures used in other studies on the punishment of rumination.

In a recent case study, our group evaluated the effects of continuously available chewing gum on the rumination of a child with autism (Rhine & Tarbox, 2009) for whom starch satiation had previously been found to be ineffective. Continuous access to chewing gum produced robust decreases in rumination and did not interfere with ongoing educational tasks. In another study, more conservative effects were found when gum chewing was limited to the premeal time period (Rast et al., 1988).

Another intervention that has shown some promise is slowing the pace of the meal. In a study on ruminative vomiting, a participant was taught to eat his meal more slowly, only taking bites after the previous bite had been chewed and swallowed (Azrin, Jamner, & Besalel, 1986). Pacing the meal effectively reduced vomiting but did not have an effect on subsequent rumination (reconsumption) of the vomitus. The pace of food consumption was also examined by Rast et al. (1981) with their spaced baseline condition in which the regular meal was presented in small pieces, one at a time. The pacing of the regular meal did not influence the rate of rumination observed. Pacing of supplemental food following completion of the regular meal has been shown to produce more consistent decreases in rumination.

Reductions in rumination have been demonstrated when supplemental feedings were slowly paced over 15–30 minutes following the meal (Kenzer & Wallace, 2007; Lyons et al., 2007; Masalsky & Luiselli, 1998). However, the food quantity, slower pace, or combination of variables may have contributed to the effectiveness of the intervention. In an effort to separate the effects of food quantity and pacing, Kenzer and Wallace compared supplemental food provided as part of the meal to supplemental feedings paced over 30 minutes following meal completion. A decrease in rumination was observed when the supplementary food was slowly paced, but an increase in rumination was observed when the additional food was provided as part of the meal even though the amount of additional food consumed was comparable under both conditions.

## Comparison Studies

Few empirical studies have compared the relative effectiveness of different treatments for rumination (Borreson & Anderson, 1982; Kenzer & Wallace, 2007; Wilder, Draper, Williams, & Higbee, 1997). Borreson and Anderson (1982) compared a satiation procedure to satiation plus time-out from music, and satiation plus time-out from music and time-out from tactile stimulation. Rumination was eliminated during the satiation plus time-out from music and time-out from tactile stimulation condition. Results also indicated that lower levels of rumination were observed when the consequence was delivered contingent upon antecedents to rumination instead of after ruminative behavior was observed.

Wilder et al. (1997) compared showers after meals (selected because singing frequently occurred in the shower and singing is incompatible with rumination), noncontingent supplemental feedings every 20 seconds for 30 minutes after a meal, and liquid rescheduling (i.e., no liquids were provided for 30 minutes before a meal, during the meal, or for 1.5 hours after a meal). Results indicated that the supplemental feeding intervention was the most effective relative to the other treatments implemented, but it did not completely eliminate rumination.

Kenzer and Wallace (2007) compared noncontingent supplemental feedings every minute for 30 minutes after a meal, noncontingent supplemental feedings every minute for 15 minutes after a meal, and a large meal equivalent to a typical meal plus the amount of food consumed during a 30-minute supplemental feeding. The lowest levels of rumination were observed during the 30-minute supplemental feeding condition. These preliminary data suggest that a critical variable may be the length of time during which food is consumed given that the amount of food in the 30-minute supplemental feeding and large-meal interventions was comparable.

## CLINICAL IMPLICATIONS

In what follows, we provide a research-based practically oriented set of recommendations for the treatment of rumination including pretreatment assessments, intervention selection, implementation of satiation procedures, and observation, measurement, and data-collection techniques.

### Pretreatment Assessment

Rumination may be a result of a medical condition, environmental contingencies, or a combination of both; therefore, it is essential to formulate treatment protocols on data from thorough medical and functional assessments. An inadequate assessment of the cause of rumination may result in the implementation of an ineffective treatment and the worsening of a serious behavior.

## Medical Assessment

Researchers have reported an association between gastroesophageal abnormalities and rumination (Kuruvilla & Trewby, 1989; Rogers et al., 1992). For instance, Rogers et al. performed medical assessments on 23 adults with developmental disabilities and rumination and found significant gastroesophageal abnormalities in 22 of 23 (91%) participants. In addition, some medications commonly prescribed to individuals with developmental disabilities (e.g., benzodiazepines and neuroleptics) may effect swallowing and gastroesophageal function (Rogers et al., 1992). Given these findings, it is recommended that a comprehensive evaluation be made by a gastroenterologist, who will conduct medical assessments, such as a barium swallow, esophagram, evaluations for gastroesophageal reflux, and gastric emptying, in order to rule out any physiological conditions that may be contributing to rumination (Fredericks et al., 1998; Gravestock, 2000; Kerwin & Berkowitz, 1996; Starin & Fuqua, 1987).

## Functional Assessment

Traditional efforts at determining the cause of rumination have focused on the differentiation between rumination as a physiological response (e.g., regurgitation caused by certain types of food such as tomatoes and fats), adjunctive behavior, and operant responding (Rast et al., 1984). Rumination is often considered an operant behavior maintained by automatic reinforcement. That is, the behavior itself produces the reinforcing consequences maintaining it. The topography of rumination may contribute to this perspective. The repeated pattern of regurgitation, rechewing, and reswallowing, is somewhat stereotypical and suggestive of automatic reinforcement. Furthermore, the most effective interventions for rumination have involved punishment and satiation procedures; neither of which have required the identification of the function to ensure efficacy of the intervention.

Some have suggested that a functional difference between rumination and vomiting may exist due to their differing topographies and resulting probability of social consequences for each (Johnston & Greene, 1990). Vomiting involves expelling previously ingested food from the mouth, it is more likely to be observed by others and result in a variety of social interactions (e.g., cleaning body, clothing, and/or furniture). In contrast, rumination may go relatively unnoticed, with little or no vomit leaving the mouth and is therefore less likely to result in obvious social interactions. Furthermore, rumination sometimes results in a decrease in social interactions due to the offensive smell produced.

Very few published studies on rumination have included a functional assessment but results of existing studies consistently demonstrate automatic reinforcement. Dudley et al. (2002) noted that indirect and direct assessments of the rumination of a 9-year-old girl diagnosed with autism revealed no sensitivity to social contingencies. Similarly, indirect assessments of self-injurious behavior, including rumination, revealed that most topographies were maintained in the absence of socially mediated reinforcers (Applegate, Matson, & Cherry, 1999; Matson et al., 2005). A brief functional analysis of rumination with two children diagnosed with autism and global developmental delays revealed undifferentiated patterns of responding, suggesting automatic reinforcement (Lyons et al., 2007). Finally, a multielement functional analysis on the rumination of a man with profound intellectual disability revealed undifferentiated patterns of responding, also suggesting automatic reinforcement (Kenzer & Wallace, 2007). In the same study, extended sessions of a no-interaction condition revealed consistently high levels of rumination, thereby further supporting the hypothesis that rumination was maintained by automatic reinforcement.

When medical assessments reveal a physiological condition that contributes to rumination it is important to pursue a medical intervention for this underlying cause. An important second step, regardless of the results of the medical assessments, is to conduct a functional assessment to determine any potential environmental contingencies maintaining rumination (McAdam & Cole, 2007). Previous research has consistently found that rumination is maintained by automatic reinforcement (McAdam & Cole); however, it is still advisable to confirm this hypothesis with a functional assessment. Research has demonstrated that function-based interventions can be more effective than non–function-based interventions (Ingram, Lewis-Palmer, & Sugai, 2005). If indeed some other form of consequence (e.g., attention, escape from work, etc.) contributes to maintaining rumination and this variable is not identified before implementing an intervention, it is possible that caretakers may inadvertently continue to deliver that consequence following rumination, thereby decreasing the effectiveness of the treatment.

We recommend conducting both an indirect and descriptive functional assessment, given that these two forms of assessment tend to be inexpensive, easy to implement, and do not generally require extensive specialized training. When conducting a descriptive functional assessment of rumination, it is important to schedule observations during the times when rumination is most likely to occur. Research suggests that ruminative behavior tends to occur following meals (Barton & Barton, 1985; Greene et al., 1991; Mulick et al., 1980; Rast et al., 1988), and it is recommended that observations occur 20 to 60 minutes postmeal.

## Selecting an Intervention

It is generally considered the most ethical option to begin with the least restrictive intervention possible and move to more intrusive options only when others have been shown to be ineffective (Cooper, Heron, & Heward, 2007; McAdam & Cole, 2007). Therefore, despite research on the effectiveness of punishment procedures (e.g., contingent taste aversion) used to treat rumination, we recommended that less intrusive environmental manipulations (e.g., starch-satiation procedures, liquid rescheduling) or reinforcement-based procedure (e.g., differential reinforcement) be implemented first. It may be reasonable to consider a more intrusive punishment procedure (Fredericks et al., 1998), particularly in severe cases where all less intrusive interventions have been implemented with high fidelity and have failed and where there is a present or highly likely medical emergency caused by rumination (e.g., aspiration pneumonia, electrolyte imbalance, tooth decay, severe weight loss, erosion of the esophagus). In such cases, a full review by a competent interdisciplinary treatment team, including obtaining human rights approval, should be conducted before implementing contingent taste aversion. It should also be noted that punishment procedures may produce unwanted side effects, such as emotional and aggressive behavior (Cooper et al., 2007). In addition, Fredericks et al. (1998) noted that punishment interventions are difficult to fade. In contrast, there are published data suggesting that nonaversive treatments for rumination have been successfully faded (Dunn et al., 1997; Thibadeau et al., 1999; Yang, 1988).

## Implementing Satiation Interventions

Given the relative ease of implementation and consistent effectiveness, satiation interventions are recommended as the treatment of choice. Although caution must be taken when implementing a satiation-based treatment for individuals who are not underweight, fading procedures and altering the types of food provided can minimize potential risks associated with unnecessary weight gain. In a summary of their 10-year research program on the relation between ruminating and quantity of food consumed, Johnston and Greene (1992) outline the satiation procedure including food type, delivery, and criteria for terminating the meal.

The supplementary food can be of any type, though starchy vegetables are the most commonly used food. Ideally, the additional food should vary within and across meals to prevent habituation to a particular flavor (Johnston & Greene, 1992). The foods should be tolerable otherwise the individual may stop eating prematurely before satiation has occurred. Low-calorie foods may be substituted for higher-calorie foods when weight gain is a concern.

Supplementary foods may be provided as part of the regular meal or following completion of the regular meal. In either case, an unlimited amount of the additional food is presented until satiation occurs. The delivery of supplemental foods involves the following components: 1) double the normal portion sizes of the meal, 2) present the larger portions on a full plate or tray, 3) refill the plate or tray as the food is consumed, and 4) prevent the tray from ever becoming empty. Supplemental food is continually provided and staff should "gently but persistently" prompt the individual to continue consuming food until he or she is no longer willing to eat. The termination criteria outlined by Johnston and Greene (1992) involves prompting the individual to eat if he or she pushes the food away, attempts to leave the table, or slows their eating pace. If three successive prompts are delivered and the individual fails to eat, the meal is terminated.

## Observation, Measurement, and Data Collection

Rumination can be a difficult behavior to measure. Some individuals engage in a visible "retching" motion of the neck when actively regurgitating, whereas others can regurgitate without displaying any overt signs that regurgitation is occurring. Staff often report that such individuals "suddenly appear to be chewing on something." Therefore, if it is desired to track the number of occurrences of regurgitation, it may be difficult to do so with some individuals. The behavior of rechewing regurgitated food can also be difficult to track because it does not necessarily have a clear beginning and end. Also, if clients have their mouths closed, it may be impossible to see inside their mouths to determine whether regurgitated food is present. For this reason, clinicians often resort to asking clients to open their mouths at regular intervals (or contingent on the appearance that they might be ruminating), in order to check for regurgitated food. In cases such as these, the presence of regurgitated food in the mouth may need to be measured instead of occurrence of the behavior of regurgitating or the act of rechewing regurgitated food per se.

In cases where the behavior of regurgitating itself is clearly visible, it would be advisable to collect frequency data if staff is available to do so. Tracking the ongoing frequency per unit time (i.e., rate) in such cases is likely to give the most accurate measurement possible. Additionally, duration measures contribute information about another important dimension of the behavior. Although frequency and duration may vary at the same time, the correspondence may not always be perfect and an examination of both frequency and duration measures contributes to an analysis of the overall level of behavior.

If regurgitating cannot be easily observed, data will need to be collected either on the sight of regurgitated food in the client's mouth or the behavior of chewing. For example, rumination can be defined as chewing when it is known that the client should have nothing to chew on. Because chewing is a behavior of varying duration, without a clearly marked beginning and end, it may be more practical to collect partial interval or momentary time-sampling data in these cases. As in any other interval data collection system, some compromise must be sought between long intervals (which provide a gross estimate of behavior but which are less labor intensive) and short intervals (which provide a more accurate estimate of behavior but which may be too labor intensive).

A final variable to consider when planning how to measure rumination is the time of the day during which observations will be made. Ideally, direct observation data would be collected on rumination during all waking hours, either by a parent or by a staff member. However, this is frequently impossible, so a smaller portion of the day may need to be chosen to provide an estimate of the overall occurrence of rumination. Rumination often occurs during or immediately after meals and research suggests that rumination is unlikely to occur if it is not observed within 20 minutes of meal completion (Greene et al., 1991). Under these circumstances, data collection may be shortened (Barton & Barton, 1985). However, when rumination does occur, it may continue several hours after the end of a meal. In order to avoid missing occurrences of rumination, it is recommended that data be collected on rumination for at least 1 hour following each meal. Furthermore, if a supplemental feeding procedure is used, in which food is made available for longer periods of time after a meal, our recommendation is that data be collected continuously for at least 1 hour after the last portion of food is given. This provision will avoid the possibility that rumination is simply delayed, thereby hiding it from measurement and thus producing a false positive result in the treatment evaluation data.

## FUTURE RESEARCH

More research on effective treatments for rumination is needed. Very few comparison studies have been conducted with a limited number of participants and functional assessments have not been systematically incorporated into these investigations. Specifically, more direct comparisons of the various empirically validated treatments would provide a better understanding of the conditions under which each is most effective. The evaluation of generalization and maintenance is also limited. In addition, much of the research reviewed in this chapter implemented package treatments, so further studies using component analyses to identify the active treatment components would be helpful. Additional research evaluating the separate and combined effects of medical versus behavioral interventions for rumination would also be beneficial.

More comparison studies are needed on the effects of supplemental feedings, satiation procedures, and differential reinforcement interventions using edible reinforcers. Each of these interventions involves increased food consumption, although to different levels. Although satiation procedures generally produce greater reductions in rumination than supplemental feedings or differential reinforcement procedures, a large amount of variability exists. That is, complete elimination of rumination has been produced in some studies, whereas more modest reductions have been observed in others. Therefore, further investigation of the relative effectiveness of each intervention is needed.

An interesting potential question for future research is whether a relationship exists between weight, treatment effectiveness, and maintenance. Several studies have included body weight as a secondary dependent measure (Dunn et al., 1997; Rast et al., 1981; Yang, 1988). Dunn et al. (1997) were able to successfully fade a satiation procedure by decreasing the amount of food provided by 50%. This reduction was implemented after the individual had gained nearly 40 pounds during the satiation procedure, and treatment effects were successfully maintained for 2 years until the participant experienced substantial weight loss and subsequently an increase in rumination was observed. The satiation procedure was again implemented, weight increased, and rumination ceased. In another study, weight loss and increased rumination were observed during a reversal to baseline meals (Rast et al., 1981). These data suggest that although satiation procedures concurrently produce weight gain and rumination reduction, standard meal portions may produce weight loss and increased rumination with some participants. These data also suggest that maintenance of treatment effects may be influenced by fluctuations in weight. Although some attempts to fade satiation interventions have been successful, other studies have failed to demonstrate maintenance as conditions are reversed or the food quantity is systematically reduced (Rast et al., 1984). It is possible that attempts to fade the intervention are more successful after an individual's weight has increased to a particular level—perhaps a proportion of their recommended weight. Interestingly, the nature of the satiation procedure allows the client to control the amount of food consumed. As a result, "self-fading" has been reported in which a participant consumes less food over time while maintaining low levels of rumination (Dunn et al., 1997; Yang, 1988). During "self-fading," consumption and weight stabilizes at levels greater than baseline but lower than that observed during the initial satiation conditions (Dunn et al., 1997; Yang, 1988). In short, future research should attempt to parse out the contribution of body weight (if any) from that of satiation procedures.

Another area of future research is the role of habituation in satiation interventions. Food satiation procedures are so named because their effectiveness is assumed to be a result of decreased reinforcer efficacy due to increased exposure to the maintaining reinforcer, food (e.g., Jackson et al., 1975). A problem arises, however, with the term "satiation" in relation to edible stimuli. Historically, and in other fields such as physiology, satiation is used to refer to the physiological effects produced by appetitive stimuli such as stomach distention, gastric load, and nutritional state (McSweeney, Hinson, & Cannon, 1996). Thus, using the term "satiation" can imply that physiological changes resulting from increased food consumption are the primary mechanism of behavior change. However, research suggests that oropharyngeal stimulation along with caloric density and gastric load contribute to the effectiveness of satiation procedures (Rast et al., 1985). As such, both satiety and habituation effects may combine to produce a maximally effective intervention (McSweeney, 2004).

Habituation is defined as a decrease in responding following repeated or prolonged exposure to a stimulus (Hinde, 1970). Relatively recent investigations within operant conditioning have revealed that habituation may also occur with reinforced responses (McSweeney et al., 1996; Murphy, McSweeney, Smith, & McComas, 2003). Within a habituation paradigm, motivated responding for food has been demonstrated to decrease over repeated presentations and consumption of food with typically developing children and adults (Epstein et al., 2003; Ernst & Epstein, 2002). Therefore, habituation may allow for a more parsimonious account of how increased oropharyngeal stimulation contributes to satiation procedures and that decreases in responding are not due solely to satiation (McSweeney, 2004; McSweeney & Murphy, 2000). Future research is needed to determine if and how habituation to the sensory properties of food contribute to the effectiveness of satiation interventions.

## REFERENCES

American Psychiatric Association. (2000). *Diagnostic and Statistical Manual of Mental Disorders*, (4th ed., revised). Washington, DC: Author.

Applegate, H., Matson, J.L., & Cherry, K.E. (1999). An evaluation of functional variables affecting severe problem behaviors in adults with mental retardation by using the Questions About Behavioral Function scale (QABF). *Research in Developmental Disabilities, 20,* 229–237.

Azrin, N.H., Jamner, J.P., & Besalel, V.A. (1986). Vomiting reduction by slower food intake. *Applied Research in Mental Retardation, 7,* 409–413.

Barmann, B.C. (1980). Use of contingent vibration in the treatment of self-stimulatory hand-mouthing and ruminative vomiting behavior. *Journal of Behavioral Therapy and Experimental Psychiatry, 11,* 307–311.

Barton, L.E., & Barton, C.L. (1985). An effective and benign treatment of rumination. *Journal of the Association of Persons with Severe Handicaps, 10,* 168–171.

Borreson, P.M., & Anderson, J.L. (1982). The elimination of chronic rumination through a combination of procedures. *Mental Retardation, 20,* 34–38.

Chial, H.J., Camilleri, M., Williams, D.E., Litzinger, K., & Perrault, J. (2003). Rumination syndrome in children and adolescents: Diagnosis, treatment, and prognosis. *Pediatrics, 111,* 158–162.

Conrin, J., Pennypacker, H.S., Johnston, J., & Rast, J. (1982). Differential reinforcement of other behaviors to treat chronic rumination of mental retardates. *Journal of Behavioral Therapy and Experimental Psychiatry, 13,* 325–329.

Cooper, J.O., Heron, T.E., & Heward, W.L. (2007). *Applied behavior analysis* (2nd ed.). Upper Saddle River, NJ: Pearson Merrill Prentice Hall.

Davis, P.K., & Cuvo, A.J. (1980). Chronic vomiting and rumination in intellectually normal and retarded individuals: Review and evaluation of behavioral research. *Behavior Research of Severe Developmental Disabilities, 1,* 31–59.

Dudley, L.L., Johnson, C., & Barnes, R.S. (2002). Decreasing rumination using a starchy food satiation procedure. *Behavioral Interventions, 17,* 21–29.

Dunn, J., Lockwood, K., Williams, D.E., & Peacock, S. (1997). A seven year follow-up of treating rumination with dietary satiation. *Behavioral Interventions, 12,* 163–172.

Epstein, L.H., Saad, F.G., Handley, E.A., Roemmich, J.N., Hawk, L.W., & McSweeney, F.K. (2003). Habituation of salivation and motivated responding for food in children. *Appetite, 41,* 283–289.

Ernst, M.M., & Epstein, L.H. (2002). Habituation of operant responding for food in humans. *Appetite, 38,* 224–234.

Fredericks, D.W., Carr, J.E., & Williams, W.L. (1998). Overview of the treatment of rumination disorder for adults in a residential setting. *Journal of Behavior Therapy and Experimental Psychiatry, 29,* 31–40.

Gravestock, S. (2000). Eating disorders in adults with intellectual disability. *Journal of Intellectual Disability Research, 44,* 625–637.

Greene, K.S., Johnston, J.M., Rossi, M., Rawal, A., Winston, M., & Barron, S. (1991). Effects of peanut butter on ruminating. *American Journal on Mental Retardation, 95,* 631–645.

Heering, P.W., Wilder, D.A., & Ladd, C. (2003). Liquid rescheduling for the treatment of rumination. *Behavioral Interventions, 18,* 199–207.

Hinde, R.A. (1970). Behavioral habituation. In G. Horn & R.A. Hinde (Eds.), *Short-term changes in neural activity and behavior* (pp. 3–40). London & New York: Cambridge University Press.

Ingram, K., Lewis-Palmer, T., & Sugai, G. (2005). Function-based intervention planning: Comparing the effectiveness of FBA function-based and non-function-based intervention plans. *Journal of Positive Behavior Support, 7,* 224–236.

Jackson, G.M., Johnson, C.R., Ackron, G.S., & Crowley, R. (1975). Food satiation as a procedure to decelerate vomiting. *American Journal of Mental Deficiency, 80,* 223–227.

Johnston, J.M., & Greene, K.S. (1990). Effects of food constincy on ruminating. *Psychological Record, 40,* 609–618.

Johnston, J.M., & Greene, K.S. (1992). Relation between ruminating and quantity of food consumed. *Mental Retardation, 30,* 7–11.

Kedesdy, J.H., & Budd, K.S. (1998). *Childhood feeding procedures: Biobehavioral assessment and intervention.* Baltimore, MD: Paul H. Brookes Publishing Co.

Kenzer, A.L., & Wallace, M.D. (2007). Treatment of rumination maintained by automatic reinforcement: A comparison of extra portions during a meal and supplemental postmeal feedings. *Behavioral Interventions, 22,* 297–304.

Kerwin, M.E., & Berkowitz, R.I. (1996). Feeding and eating disorders: Ingestive problems of infancy, childhood, and adolescence. *School Psychology Review, 25,* 316–328.

Kuruvilla, J., & Trewby, P.N. (1989). Gastro-oesophageal disorders in adults with severe mental impairment. *British Medial Journal, 299,* 95–96.

Lobato, E., Carlson, E.I., & Barrera, R.D. (1986). Modified satiation reducing ruminative vomiting without excessive weight gain. *Applied Research in Mental Retardation, 7,* 337–347.

Luckey, R.E., Watson, C.M., & Musick, J.K. (1968). Aversive conditioning as a means of inhibiting vomiting and rumination. *American Journal of Mental Deficiency, 73,* 139–142.

Luiselli, J.K., Haley, S., & Smith, A. (1993). Evaluation of a behavioral medicine consultative treatment for chronic, ruminative vomiting. *Journal of Behavior Therapy and Experimental Psychiatry, 24,* 27–35.

Lyons, E.A., Rue, H.C., Luiselli, J.K., & DiGennaro, F.D. (2007). Brief functional analysis and supplemental feeding for postmeal rumination in children with developmental disabilities. *Journal of Applied Behavior Analysis, 40,* 743–747.

Marholin, D., Luiselli, J.K., Robinson, M., & Lott, I.T. (1980). Response-contingent taste-aversion in treating chronic ruminative vomiting of institutionalised profoundly retarded children. *Journal of Mental Deficiency Research, 24,* 47–56.

Masalsky, C.J., & Luiselli, J.K. (1998). Brief report: Effects of supplemental feedings of white bread on chronic rumination. *Behavioral Interventions, 13,* 227–233.

Matson, J.L., Mayville, S.B., Kuhn, D.E., Sturmey, P., Laud, R., & Cooper, C. (2005). The behavioral function of feeding problems as assessed by the questions about behavioral function (QABF). *Research in Developmental Disabilities, 26,* 399–408.

McAdam, D.B., & Cole, L. (2007). A review of behavioral interventions to reduce the rumination of persons with developmental disabilities. In J.S. Jerome (Ed.), *Eating disorders and weight loss research* (pp. 77–104). New York: Nova Science Publishers.

McKeegan, G.F., Estill, K., & Campbell, B. (1987). Elimination of rumination by controlled eating and differential reinforcement. *Journal of Behavioral Therapy and Experimental Psychiatry, 18,* 143–148.

McSweeney, F.K. (2004). Dynamic changes in reinforcer effectiveness: Satiation and habituation have different implications for theory and practice. *Behavior Analyst, 27,* 177–188.

McSweeney, F.K., Hinson, J.M., & Cannon, C.B. (1996). Sensitization-habituation may occur during operant conditioning. *Psychological Bulletin, 120,* 256–271.

McSweeney, F.K., & Murphy, E.S. (2000). Criticisms of the satiety hypothesis as an explanation for within-session decreases in responding. *Journal of the Experimental Analysis of Behavior, 74,* 347–361.

Mulick, J.A., Schroeder, S.R., & Rojahn, J. (1980). Chronic ruminative vomiting: A comparison of four treatment procedures. *Journal of Autism and Developmental Disorders, 10,* 203–213.

Murphy, E.S., McSweeney, F.K., Smith, R.G., & McComas, J.J. (2003). Dynamic changes in reinforcer effectiveness: theoretical, methodological, and practical implications for applied research. *Journal of Applied Behavior Analysis, 36,* 421–438.

O'Neil, P.M., White, J.L., King, Jr., C.R., & Carek, D.J. (1979). Controlling childhood rumination through differential reinforcement of other behavior. *Behavior Modification, 3,* 355–372.

Rast, J., & Johnston, J.M. (1986). Social versus dietary control of ruminating by mentally retarded persons. *American Journal of Mental Deficiency, 90,* 464–467.

Rast, J., Johnston, J.M., Allen, J.E., & Drum, C. (1985). Effects of nutritional and mechanical property of food on ruminative behavior. *Journal of the Experimental Analysis of Behavior, 44,* 195–206.

Rast, J., Johnston, J.M., & Drum, C. (1984). A parametric analysis of the relationship between food quantity and rumination. *Journal of the Experimental Analysis of Behavior, 41,* 125–134.

Rast, J., Johnston, J.M., Drum, C., & Conrin, J. (1981). The relation of food quantity to rumination behavior. *Journal of Applied Behavior Analysis, 14,* 121–130.

Rast, J., Johnston, J.M., Lubin, D., & Ellinger-Allen, J. (1988). Effects of premeal chewing on ruminative behavior. *American Journal on Mental Retardation, 93,* 67–74.

Rhine, D., & Tarbox, J. (2009). Chewing gum as a treatment for rumination in a child with autism. *Journal of Applied Behavior Analysis, 42,* 381–385.

Rogers, B., Stratton, P., Victor, J., Kennedy, B., & Andres, M. (1992). Chronic regurgitation among persons with mental retardation: A need for combined medical and interdisciplinary strategies. *American Journal on Mental Retardation, 96,* 522–527.

Sajwaj, T., Libet, J., & Agras, S. (1974). Lemon-juice therapy: The control of life-threatening rumination in a six-month-old infant. *Journal of Applied Behavior Analysis, 7,* 557–563.

Saloviita, T.J. (1999). Dietary control of rumination: Two case studies. *Scandinavian Journal of Behaviour Therapy, 28,* 176–180.

Sanders-Dewey, N.E.J., & Larson, M.E. (2006). Chronic rumination reduction in a severely developmentally disabled adult following combined use of positive and negative contingencies. *Journal of Behavior Therapy and Experimental Psychiatry, 37,* 140–145.

Simpson, R.L., & Sasso, G.M. (1978). The modification of rumination in a severely emotionally disturbed child through an overcorrection procedure. *AAESPH Review, 3,* 145–150.

Singh, N.N. (1981). Rumination. In N.R. Ellis (Ed.), *International Review of Research in Mental Retardation, 10,* 139–182.

Singh, N.N., Manning, P.J., & Angell, M.J. (1982). Effects of an oral hygiene punishment procedure on chronic rumination and collateral behaviors in monozygous twins. *Journal of Applied Behavior Analysis, 15*, 309–314.

Smeets, P.M. (1970). Withdrawal of social reinforcers as a means of controlling rumination and regurgitation in a profoundly retarded person. *Training School Bulletin, 67*, 158–163.

Starin, S.P., & Fuqua, R.W. (1987). Rumination and vomiting in the developmentally disabled: A critical review of the behavioral, medical, and psychiatric treatment research. *Research in Developmental Disabilities, 8*, 575–605.

Thibadeau, S., Blew, P., Reedy, P., & Luiselli, J.K. (1999). Access to white bread as an intervention for chronic ruminative vomiting. *Journal of Behavior Therapy and Experimental Psychiatry, 30*, 137–144.

Watson, T.S., & Scott, J.B. (1994). Case study: Initiating and maintaining a nonruminative response in an adult male who is profoundly retarded. *Behavioral Interventions, 9*, 191–198.

White, D.A., & Taylor, D.J. (1967). Noxious conditioning as a treatment for rumination. *Mental Retardation, 5*, 30–33.

Wilder, D.A., Draper, R., Williams, W.L., & Higbee, T.S. (1997). A comparison of noncontingent reinforcement, other competing stimulation, and liquid rescheduling for the treatment of rumination. *Behavioral Interventions, 12*, 55–64.

Yang, L. (1988). Elimination of habitual rumination through the strategies of food satiation and fading: A case study. *Behavioral Residential Treatment, 3*, 223–234.

# Obesity and Weight Regulation

*Richard K. Fleming*

**CHAPTER 11**

Obesity represents a significant health problem among people with intellectual and developmental disabilities (IDD), affecting both children (Yamaki, Rimmer, Lowry, & Vogel, 2011) and adults (Melville et al., 2008; Rimmer & Yamaki, 2006). Overweight and obesity have been associated with chronic health conditions in the general population, including type 2 diabetes, asthma, cardiovascular disease, orthopedic problems, sleep apnea, and menstrual irregularities (Must & Strauss, 1999). Recent evidence suggests that many of these conditions also affect people with IDD and can become established by adolescence (Yamaki et al., 2011). Healthy People 2010 (Office of Disease Prevention and Health Promotion, 2000) and the Surgeon General's report, "Call to Action to Improve the Health and Wellness of Persons with Disabilities" (U.S. Department of Health and Human Services, 2005) are both examples of a national call to action to decrease obesity and its health correlates in the IDD population. As further testament to the need to better address the problem of obesity in children with IDD and associated health disparities, the National Institute of Child Health and Human Development (NICHD) convened a meeting in July 2010 to hear and discuss expert scientific commentary on obesity causes, prevention, and intervention in this population. There was broad consensus on the urgent need for more research in these areas, particularly toward developing interventions to prevent and treat childhood overweight and obesity. Several of the papers presented at the NICHD meeting are referenced in this chapter.

This chapter reviews the extant literature on overweight and obesity in people with IDD, including 1) its estimated prevalence among children and adults, 2) its secondary health risks, 3) an overview of the ecological model for studying its individual, interpersonal, organizational, community, and societal determinants, 4) interventions targeting weight loss and weight regulation in both the non–IDD and IDD populations, and 5) recommendations for future research and practice.

## PREVALENCE OF OVERWEIGHT AND OBESITY

Determination of overweight and obesity has used body mass index (BMI), which is weight in kilograms divided by height in meters squared ($kg/m^2$). In adults

The author's research described in this chapter was supported by grant R03DK070627-01A2 (Fleming, Principal Investigator) from the National Institute of Diabetes and Digestive and Kidney Diseases.

($\geq$ 20 years), overweight refers to a BMI of 25.0–29.9; obesity refers to a BMI of > 30. In children, because body composition varies with development and by sex, BMI is age and gender specific and is calculated using growth charts (e.g., the 2000 CDC Growth Chart for the United States) and expert committee. Overweight in children (aged 2–19 years) refers to a BMI at or above the 85th percentile but lower than the 95th percentile, whereas obesity refers to a BMI at or above the 95th percentile, for children of the same age and gender. Obesity in the general population has risen dramatically in the past 20 years, with current estimates at 32.2% among adult men and 35.5% among adult women (2007–2008 data from the National Health and Nutrition Examination Survey, or NHANES). When overweight and obesity are combined, prevalence rates increase to 68.0% and 72.2% in men and women, respectively (Flegal, Carroll, Ogden, & Curtin, 2010). Obesity among the general population of children has also increased, although the largest increase appears to have occurred from 1980 to 1998, with a plateau apparent from 1999 to 2006 (Ogden, Carroll, Curtin, Lamb, & Flegal, 2010). Ogden and colleagues (2010) recently extended this timeframe by analyzing BMI data from the 2007–2008 NHANES, which included a sample of 3281 children and adolescents ages 2–19 years. Weight status was reported at three BMI levels: BMI for age at or above the 97th percentile, which they called "high BMI," at or above the 95th percentile, and at or above the 85th percentile. Results indicate that 11.9% of the children were at or above the 97th percentile, 16.9% were at or above the 95th percentile, and 31.7% were at or above the 85th percentile. Although no statistically significant differences were found for gender at each BMI level, significant differences were found for age and race and ethnic groupings at each of the three BMI levels. Overall, the prevalence of childhood obesity was found to have remained stable through 2007–2008, except for an observed increase in boys ages 6–19 years at the heaviest BMI level ($\geq$ 97th percentile). The authors call for continued research "to identify the behavioral, biological and environmental factors sustaining these levels of high BMI in US children" (Ogden et al., 2010, p. 249).

Estimates of the prevalence of overweight and obesity in the population of people with IDD have varied widely (Humphries, Traci, & Seekins, 2009; Maiano, 2011), in part due to the different measures of overweight and obesity used, and in part because statistics have been derived largely from convenience samples, as opposed to larger, more comprehensive databases such as NHANES. Unfortunately the NHANES does not distinguish IDD in its categories of "developmental disorders." Bandini and colleagues analyzed NHANES data collected from 1999 to 2002 to determine the percentage of overweight among children with "developmental disorders" ages 6.0–17.9 years (Bandini, Curtin, Hamad, Tybor, & Must, 2005). Developmental disorders were categorized as children with physical limitations (4.1% of sample), attention deficit disorders (9.6%), learning disabilities (11.6%), and children receiving special education or early intervention services (10.7%). Using a slightly older BMI designation, the authors classified children as "at risk for overweight" if they had a BMI > 85th percentile (the current desig-nation for overweight), and "overweight" if they had a BMI > 95th percentile (the current designation for obese) based on age and gender. The prevalence of at risk for overweight was 50.9% for children with physical limitations, which was significantly greater than children without physical limitations; 33.4% for children receiving special education services; 29.5% for children with attention deficit disorder; and 35.4% for children with learning disabilities. The prevalence of overweight was 29.7% for children with physical limitations, 17.4% for children receiving special education services, 14.5% for children with attention deficit disorder, and 21.9% for children with learning disabilities, which was significantly greater than children without learning disabilities.

In a convenience sample of 461 adolescents (12–18 years) that included categories that better encompassed IDD (Rimmer, Yamaki, Lowry, Wang, & Vogel, 2010) the following rates of overweight and obesity were observed for five classes of disabilities: autism spectrum disorder (ASD) (42.5% overweight, 24.6% obese), Down syndrome (55.0% overweight, 31.2% obese), intellectual disability (27.2% overweight, 12.4% obese), cerebral palsy (14.8% overweight, 4.0% obese), and spina bifida (64.5% overweight, 18.6% obese). These percentages were compared by disability against a sample of youth without disability ($N$ = 12,973) whose overall percentage of overweight and obesity was 28.8% and 13.0%, respectively. The major findings were that youth with ASD, Down syndrome, and spina bifida were found to be significantly more overweight and obese than their non-IDD counterparts.

The prevalence of overweight and obesity in children with IDD has also been studied in a metropolitan area Australian sample (De, Small, & Baur, 2008). The authors conducted a chart review of 98 children and adolescents ages 2–18 years with intellectual disability (ID) or "global developmental delay" (GDD), a term generally used in Australia for younger children awaiting a more valid intelligence assessment when they are older. The study population was just over two thirds male and included 63 children ages 2–6 years (64% of sample), 25 children ages 7–12 years (26% of sample), and 10 adolescents ages 13–18 years (10% of sample). This ID/GDD group was compared for both overweight and obesity with an existing national school sample of typically developing children ($N$ = 5403) ages 5–16 years. Prevalence of overweight was 24% in the ID/GDD sample, compared with 17% in the typically developing sample, whereas prevalence of obesity was 15% in the ID/GDD sample versus 6% in the typically developing sample. The prevalence of children with ID/GDD who were overweight or obese (the two categories combined) was 40%, which was significantly higher than the prevalence of overweight and obese in the typically developing sample (23%). No significant differences were found in the ID/GDD group for age, gender, or severity of ID.

In sum, whereas studies to date have differed in measures used to define levels of overweight and obesity, and in population sampling methods, it appears that even young children and adolescents with IDD are in need of the development of effective obesity prevention and weight-loss/weight regulation interventions. Weight regulation in childhood, established through family-mediated diet and physical activity lifestyles and other school and community efforts, may prove critical in preventing obesity later, in young adulthood and adulthood (Rimmer, Rowland, & Yamaki, 2007).

The prevalence of obesity in adults with IDD has also been studied. Rimmer and Yamaki (2006) reviewed the prevalence data on obesity in the adult ID population and discussed environmental factors, such as greater availability of high-caloric-density foods and the lack of incentives to be physically active versus sedentary, both of which likely contribute directly to obesity. In one of the studies they reviewed, Yamaki (2005) examined U.S. population-level household survey data in the 16 years from 1985 to 2000. The sample included 3499 adults with IDD, with body weight status and obesity (BMI $\geq$ 30) determined using self-reported height and weight. This sample was compared with adults in the same survey population without IDD. Comparisons between these groups were presented across four 4-year observation intervals. Prevalence of obesity increased steadily for both groups over the 16-year period, with obesity among adults with IDD being significantly higher at each 4-year interval. Rates of obesity at each interval for people with IDD and without IDD, presented in that order, were 1) 1985–1988: 19.4%, 11.4%; 2) 1989–1992: 24.7%, 13.4%; 3) 27.4%, 16.0%; and 4) 34.6%, 20.6%.

In another study included in the Rimmer and Yamaki review (2006), Rimmer and Wang (2005) analyzed obesity (BMI $\geq$ 30) and extreme obesity (BMI $\geq$ 40) in a small nonrandomized convenience sample ($N = 306$) of adults with disabilities in the Chicago area. The sample included a subset of individuals with IDD. Although caution must be taken in generalizing from this sample, the finding that 70.7% of adults with Down syndrome and 60.6% of adults with IDD but not Down syndrome were obese is striking. In addition, extreme obesity was 19.0% in the Down syndrome sample and 12.1% in the IDD without Down syndrome sample.

Rimmer and Yamaki (2006) concluded their review with an analysis of the potential role of several environmental variables in determining adult obesity in IDD. Living arrangement appears to play an important role. Adults with IDD in the United States living in the least-restrictive less-supervised settings (at home with family, or independently), which accounts for as much as two thirds of this population, were found to have higher levels of obesity than those living in more supervised settings (community residential facilities). If these findings hold true, it suggests that intervention efforts must focus on the promotion of nutritional knowledge, choice-making strategies, self-motivation, and peer support in the IDD population. Low-income status, which is associated with limited food choices and resources for physical activity, also appears to be a barrier to weight regulation, but a supportive social network might facilitate better weight control. In short, in examining environmental correlates using the data available, Rimmer and Yamaki (2006) have identified high-potential targets for obesity prevention and treatment interventions.

Outside of the United States, in a Scottish sample of 945 adults with IDD, Melville and colleagues found 39.3% of women and 27.8% of men were obese (BMI $\geq$ 30), compared with 25.1% of women and 22.7% or men without IDD (Melville et al., 2008). Women with IDD were significantly more likely to be obese than men, and in an analysis of obesity rates associated with four levels of IDD (mild, moderate, severe, profound), obesity was observed to increase dramatically from profound to mild. For example, among participants with mild IDD, 52.2% of women and 41.0% or men were obese, compared with rates in the profound category of 13.9% or women and 12.0% or men. Finally, it should be noted that among adults with Down syndrome, 79.1% of women and 81.4% of men were obese, which further supports the need for weight loss and weight regulation research in this subpopulation of IDD.

In concluding this section on the prevalence of child/adolescent and adult overweight and obesity in IDD, it is clear that across the lifespan individuals with IDD are at similar or (more likely) greater risk of obesity than their counterparts without IDD. Differences within the IDD population appear to exist with age, gender, and type and degree of IDD, living arrangements, incomes status, and social network.

## HEALTH RISKS ASSOCIATED WITH OVERWEIGHT AND OBESITY

Health conditions associated with obesity in the general population include type 2 diabetes, asthma, cardiovascular disease, orthopedic problems, sleep apnea, and menstrual irregularities (Must & Strauss, 1999). Research on obesity-related chronic health conditions in people with IDD has been more limited. However, Yamaki and colleagues (Yamaki et al., 2011) conducted an investigation with a convenience sample of 643 families of adolescent children ages 12–18 years with IDD, 208 with a mobility limitation and 435 without. Parents or guardians were surveyed using the 32-item *Health and Lifestyles of Youth with Disabilities Survey* developed by the authors (unpublished). Fifteen chronic health conditions (and two cognitive/emotional correlates) common in the general population were evaluated, including "asthma, high blood pressure, high blood cholesterol, diabetes, depression, fatigue, gastrointestinal problems, joint or bone pain, sleep apnea, liver or gallbladder problems, low self-esteem, preoccupation with weight, Blount's disease, early maturation, and pressure ulcers" (Yamaki et al., 2011, p. 282).

Among adolescents with mobility limitations, 22.1% were overweight (24.8% of males, 19.0% of females), compared with adolescents without such limitations where 38.6% were overweight (39.2% of males, 38.2% of females). In both groups (with and without mobility limitations), adolescents who were overweight had a significantly higher number of chronic health conditions than those who were not overweight. In the mobility limitations group, overweight adolescents had an average of 2.74 health conditions versus 1.74 for those not overweight. In the nonmobility limitations group, overweight adolescents had 1.79 conditions on average, whereas their nonoverweight counterparts had 1.45 conditions.

The three health conditions most associated with overweight were asthma, high blood cholesterol, and diabetes. Overweight adolescents in both mobility groups had significantly higher blood cholesterol levels than their healthy weight peers. Asthma and early maturation increased with overweight in both mobility groups but were only statistically significant in the nonmobility limitations group. The prevalence rates of virtually all other health conditions were higher in overweight versus healthy weight individuals but did not reach levels of statistical significance. Limitations to this study include the high representation of white participants in the disabilities sample (81.1% of participants with mobility limitations, 84.7% of those without mobility limitations) and families with high incomes (45.7% of participants with mobility limitations, and 49.9% of participants without mobility limitations with parent incomes ≥ $75,000). Lower parent income of ≤ $34,999 was represented by only 15.8% of participants with mobility limitations and 16.1% with no mobility limitations.

In sum, recent survey research into the health conditions associated with overweight and obesity in children and adolescents with various forms of IDD clarifies the nature and degree of risk if overweight and obesity goes unchecked in this population. A better understanding of the etiology of obesity and development of prevention and weight loss interventions are needed.

## DETERMINANTS OF OVERWEIGHT AND OBESITY

Substantial research has been devoted to understanding the complex, interconnected, and often overlapping set of variables that have contributed to the current obesity epidemic in the United States. Many of the these variables have been applied to children with special health care needs, including children with IDD, and presented in the context of an ecological model (Minihan, Fitch, & Must, 2007). The model encompasses five primary domains that are described here and referenced throughout the remainder of the chapter as research and practice are discussed. The first domain concerns *individual* child or adult factors, which include energy balance between kilocalories consumed and kilocalories burned through physical activity, observed patterns of overeating and sedentary behavior, medication usage, physiological states, and more. *Interpersonal* factors, the second domain, relate broadly to interactions between family members and peers, the quality of which may be influenced by family stressors, resources, and perspectives on diet and physical activity. The third domain, *organizational* factors, addresses what occurs in schools and health care sites. In schools there exists a network of potent contingencies, such as the availability of health-promoting versus unhealthy foods, personnel attitudes, and many social influences. In health care organizations, variables such as pediatric screening of overweight, the availability of parent counseling on healthy eating, physical activity and limit setting with children, and the availability of informational materials can affect the course of weight regulation. *Community* factors, the fourth domain, consist of the physical makeup of the "built environments" that exist in different neighborhoods, and which affect opportunities for physical activity, social and cultural perspectives on diet, openness and tolerance of people with IDD, and more. Finally, *societal* factors, the fifth domain, include national policies, laws, and regulations that are seen to have a powerful effect on the quality, availability, cost, and marketing of the foods present in our everyday environments (Schwartz & Brownell, 2007). It is emphasized that the ecological model is gaining traction as a heuristic to better understand the network of interlocking contingencies that combine to affect obesity in both the general population and in IDD (Minihan et al., 2007; Humphries, 2010; Rimmer, 2010).

## RESEARCH ON WEIGHT LOSS
## AND WEIGHT REGULATION INTERVENTIONS

As noted, there is a dearth of research on obesity and its prevention and treatment in the existing IDD literature. Clearly, there is a challenge to researchers who have the opportunity to adapt and build on a much larger body of controlled research in weight loss and weight regulation in the general (non-IDD) pediatric and adult literature. In this section, we describe selected intervention research in people without IDD and then review existing obesity intervention research in children and adults with IDD. Weight loss interventions with people with Prader Willi syndrome are not included in this review because of the more extreme challenge of appetite control in this population and the highly specialized behavioral controls that are typically needed (e.g., locked food storage areas).

### Adapting Research in the General Population to People with Intellectual and Developmental Disabilities

Research on obesity interventions for people with IDD has been particularly limited, especially with children and adolescents. In addition, the existing research, although suggestive and helpful in beginning to address individual, interpersonal, and even community factors in weight regulation, has not been sufficiently controlled and experimental. That is, it has not included between-groups randomized controlled trials (RCTs) or within-subject, quasi-experimental designs to determine the efficacy of the interventions. Fortunately, an extensive body of controlled clinical research in the non-IDD population provides a model for future research while acknowledging that adaptations will need to be made to address the additional needs of people with IDD (Fleming, 2010; Fleming et al., 2008). Two particularly promising areas that address individual, interpersonal, and community domains in the ecological model are family-based behavioral weight loss interventions (Epstein, Paluch, Roemmich, & Beecher, 2007; Wilfley, Tibbs et al., 2007) and community-based interventions (Economos & Irish-Hauser, 2007).

Epstein and colleagues pioneered the development of family-supported behavioral interventions in the non-IDD child and adolescent population with 25 years of impressive short- and long-term results (Epstein et al., 2007; Epstein et al., 1990). In the adult population, Wing and colleagues have done extensive research on participant (self)-controlled behavioral interventions and further described lifestyle characteristics of individuals who have maintained weight loss of 15 kg or more (Wing, Tate, Gorin, Raynor, & Fava, 2006). These and other researchers have established a relatively standardized and replicable approach based in behavioral theory, defined broadly to include behavior analytic (operant), social-cognitive, cognitive-behavioral, and other related approaches (Baranowski, Cullen, Nicklas, Thompson, & Baranowski, 2003). Most weight-loss intervention packages have included the following set of core procedures: behavioral monitoring, stimulus control (environmental) arrangements, goal setting, feedback, and positive reinforcement (Epstein et al, 2007; Wadden, Butryn, & Byrne, 2004; Wilfley, Tibbs et al., 2007). These procedures are familiar to many parents of children with IDD, as well as teachers, paraprofessionals, and professional staff who work with this population. For this reason it is possible that family-based and school-based weight control interventions will be more acceptable for youth who have IDD.

Economos and colleagues (Economos, Hyatt et al., 2007) conducted a non-randomized controlled trial to test an 8-month community-based participatory research (CBPR) intervention designed to decrease BMI z score in a group of elementary school children ($N$ = 1178). The intervention was designed to increase the children's physical activity and expose them to more healthful foods every day, at home, in school, and in the community. The intervention was tested in a culturally diverse urban city in Massachusetts, with two similar cities in Massachusetts serving as controls. Prior to the intervention, more than one third of the children were at risk for overweight or were overweight. The intervention produced a modest but significant change in the children's BMI z score, which was viewed as encouraging given the otherwise "obesogenic" environment in which the study took place.

## Weight Regulation Research in People with Intellectual and Developmental Disabilities

Hamilton and colleagues reviewed case-control and cohort studies published from 1985 to 2006 that targeted weight loss, physical activity, and health promotion (Hamilton, Hankey, Miller, Boyle, and Melville, 2007). Among weight loss studies, behavioral interventions were shown to be somewhat effective (but less so than in the non-IDD population), with caretaker involvement especially critical for maintaining weight loss. The authors characterized the research to date in this area as having "design weaknesses, including small sample sizes and a lack of controlled studies" (Hamilton et al., 2007, p. 343), but they also pointed to the promising foundation set for the further development of interventions to promote behavior change and at least short-term weight loss.

Given that increasing their child's future independence is the goal of most parents of children and adolescents with Down syndrome, family-based interventions for weight loss and weight regulation appears warranted. Family-based behavioral interventions have been moderately to highly effective in growing body of efficacy research with children without IDD (Epstein et al., 2007; Wilfley, Tibbs et al., 2007), but to date, to our knowledge, no such controlled weight loss interventions with people with IDD have been published.

The author and his research group recently completed a small ($N$ = 21) RCT to test the efficacy of a 16-session, 6-month family-based weight loss intervention for overweight and obese adolescents and young adults, ages 14–26, with Down syndrome (submitted for publication). An earlier publication described the nutritional and physical activity curriculum, the behavioral procedures employed, and preliminary results (Fleming et al., 2008). Therefore, we describe the study briefly here, with limited reporting of results. The RCT compared a group that received nutrition and physical activity education (NAE) with a group that received NAE plus parent training in behavioral intervention (BI) for use at home

(NAE + BI). Measures included body weight, BMI, percent body fat (using bioelectrical impedance), self-reported dietary intake (3-day food records), and physical activity (7-day accelerometry) taken at four intervals: baseline (BL), 10 weeks, 6 months (end of program), and 12 months (follow-up). Adolescent and parent satisfaction were also assessed.

Results for weight loss indicate that adolescents in the NAE + BI group lost significantly more weight than did their counterparts in NAE, as determined by a linear mixed-effects regression analysis that compared between-group differences in weight change at each time interval: BL-10 weeks, BL-6 months, BL-12 months. Weight loss was moderate at 2–6 kg for the majority of adolescents in the NAE + BI group, with promising maintenance of weight loss at 12 months. However, one adolescent in NAE + BI lost approximately 12 kg by the end of the program (6 months) and had continued weight loss during the follow-up period (between months 6 and 12), ending at 18 kg lost. In addition, both NAE and NAE + BI were extremely well received by adolescents and parents alike. In short, this study reflects a systematic replication in IDD of the family-based behavioral intervention model found to have efficacy in the non-IDD population (Epstein et al., 2007; Wilfley, Tibbs et al., 2007).

Community-based interventions attempt to teach and support lifestyle behaviors in order to promote healthy weight and physical fitness by intervening on a large scale, and by involving community constituents in program design and implementation. CBPR is becoming established as a model for involving the community as part of the development, design, and implementation of research to address public health problems (Economos & Irish-Hauser, 2007; Israel, Schulz, Parker, Becker, Allen, & Guzman, 2003).

In one such CBPR study, a research team partnered with constituents in a large community to develop, implement, and evaluate a physical activity program— the Healthy Lifestyle Change Program (HLCP) (Bazzano et al., 2009)—designed to reduce existing high rates of obesity and sedentary behavior among the community's adults with developmental disabilities. The HLCP included peer mentoring, supervision for physical activity, personal health management education and advocacy, a supportive social environment, behavioral supports, and more. HLCP was associated with moderate weight loss, increased physical activity, and increased self-efficacy. However, the study was conducted as a single group, pre- and posttest comparison, with no control group or condition, so no causative statements can be made. Still, favorable participant response and promising results provide a foundation for conducting more controlled research at the community level using the CBPR model. This may be an avenue for intervening with and supporting community members with IDD who live independently, a living arrangement associated with increased risk of developing obesity (Rimmer & Yamaki, 2006).

## FUTURE DIRECTIONS FOR RESEARCH AND PRACTICE

In their review of obesity and its secondary conditions in adolescents with IDD, Rimmer et al. (2007) pointed squarely to the discrepancy between research on weight regulation interventions for typically developing youth and those with IDD. The authors concluded, "The lack of effective interventions for weight management in youth with disabilities substantially limits opportunities to improve their current health status and reduce future health risks associated with obesity" (p. 227). They also called for research to develop interventions for the IDD population that are "cost-effective and culturally and functionally relevant for this population" (2007, p. 227). Furthermore, interventions must address variables such as ability; motivation; physical, sensory and cognitive limitations; and a host of social and environmental barriers. A similar need exists for research on weight regulation among adults with IDD.

There is an urgent need for more research that builds upon the promising foundation of research on weight regulation in people without IDD, by adapting and extending it to people with IDD. The ecological model described earlier provides a framework for identifying research questions at different levels of analysis. For example, research at the individual level might further address differences in energy metabolism in people with certain types of developmental disabilities (Bandini, 2010), or the weight and health effects of restricted eating in people on the autism spectrum. At the interpersonal level, family-based behavioral interventions have worked well in children without disabilities and appear to hold promise in children with IDD (Fleming, 2010; Fleming et al., 2008), although larger efficacy studies are needed. Furthermore, research on the relationship between family stressors, which are known to adversely impact families of children with ASD, and weight gain is encouraging. At the community level, recent CBPR-based health-promotion interventions targeting diet and physical activity have had promising results. The Healthy Lifestyle Change Program developed by Bazzano and colleagues (2009), with ongoing participation from community members, is a good example of a large-scale weight-regulation intervention adapted for people with IDD, although the study was preliminary and lacked a control or comparison group.

Schools and health care settings represent another targeted area for weight regulation research with children and youth who have IDD, with opportunities to study peer modeling and support for making healthy food choices, or modification to physical education programs to promote increased physical activity. At the societal level, policy initiatives designed to alter what has been referred to as an "obesogenic" environment, with inexpensive, high-caloric density food available at seemingly every corner in our communities, may gradually lead to a everyday environments that are much more conducive to healthful lifestyles (Schwartz & Brownell, 2007).

Obesity research in the general population and the IDD population alike should also become more translational in nature, systematic in its scientific path toward demonstrating large-scale effectiveness, and valid with respect to measurement of cost effectiveness. Epstein and Wrotniak (2010) suggested these major new directions for research in pediatric obesity, including the need for 1) treatment development that incorporates more translational research from basic behavioral science to practice, 2) treatment evaluation, including movement from efficacy studies, with their high internal validity, to effectiveness studies, which address external validity in the form of generalizing from clinic-based to community interventions; and 3) cost effectiveness, incorporating various models to compare the short- and long-term benefits (including health cost savings) of different levels of weight loss against the intervention costs needed to achieve it.

Finally, although weight loss interventions in the adult non-IDD population have been reasonably effective in producing moderate weight loss, they have too often resulted in poor long-term maintenance in the form of weight regain, thus pointing to the need for more research on sustainable weight-regulating lifestyles (Lemmens, Oenema, Klepp, Henriksen, & Brug, 2008). In one of the 11 obesity prevention studies reviewed by Lemmens et al. (2008) an intervention group of premenopausal women ages 44–50 years received a 20-week 15-session behavioral dietary and physical activity program followed by a maintenance intervention characterized by "less frequent sessions…where participants were provided additional behavioural skills, support and motivation…" (Simkin-Silverman, Wing, Boraz, & Kuller, 2003, p. 452). At a postintervention 4.5-year follow-up, participants in the intervention group maintained their bodyweight while participants in an assessment-only control group gained 2.4 kg. A similar assessment has been made regarding the need for maintenance interventions in children without IDD (Wilfley, Stein et al., 2007). It is not yet known, but perhaps can be anticipated, that the barriers to weight maintenance found in the non-IDD population will also challenge people with IDD.

In conclusion, there is an urgent need for research on interventions designed to prevent and treat the conditions of overweight and obesity in children, adolescents, and adults with IDD. Left unchecked, obesity in this population will result in many secondary health conditions, including high blood cholesterol, diabetes, and asthma, among others. Although controlled research in the IDD population has been scant, this has not been the case in the non-IDD population. Clinical and community-based intervention studies, along with other areas of obesity research that may be more translational in nature, provide a model for replication with individuals with IDD.

## REFERENCES

Bandini, L.G. (2010, July). Energy balance in children with developmental disabilities. Eunice Kennedy Shriver National Institute of Child Health and Human Development (NICHD) Conference: Obesity in Children with Developmental and/or Physical Disabilities. Washington, DC.

Bandini, L.G., Curtin, C., Hamad, C., Tybor, D.J. & Must, A. (2005). Prevalence of overweight in children with developmental disorders in the continuous National Health and Nutrition Examination Survey (NHANES) 1999–2002. Journal of Pediatrics, 146(6), 738–743.

Baranowski, T., Cullen, K.W., Nicklas, T., Thompson, D., & Baranowski, J. (2003). Are current health behavioral change models helpful in guiding prevention of weight gain efforts? Obesity Research, 11, 23S–43S.

Bazzano, A.T., Zelden, A.S., Diab, I.R.S., Garro, N.M., Allevato, N.A., Lehrer, D., & the WRC Project Oversight Team. (2009). The Healthy Lifestyle Change Program: A pilot of a community-based health promotion intervention for adults with developmental disabilities. American Journal of Preventive Medicine, 37, S201–S208.

De, S., Small, J., & Baur, L.A. (2008). Overweight and obesity among children with developmental disabilities. Journal of Intellectual & Developmental Disability, 33(1), 43–47.

Economos, C., Hyatt R., Goldberg, J., Must, A., Naumova, E., Collins, J. & Nelson, M. (2007). A community-based environmental change intervention reduces BMI z-score in children: Shape Up Somerville first year results. *Obesity, 15,* 1325–1326.

Economos, C.E., & Irish-Hauser, S. (2007). Community interventions: A brief overview and their application to the obesity epidemic. *Journal of Law, Medicine and Ethics, 35,* 131–137.

Epstein, L.H., Paluch, R.A., Roemmich, J.N., & Beecher, M.D. (2007). Family-based obesity treatment, then and now: Twenty-five years of pediatric obesity treatment. *Health Psychology, 26*(4), 381–391.

Epstein, L.H., Valoski, A.M., Wing, R.R., & McCurley, M.A. (1990). Ten year follow-up of behavioral, family-based treatment for obese children. *Journal of the American Medical Association, 264*(19), 2519–2523.

Epstein, L.H., & Wrotniak, B H. (2010). Future directions for pediatric obesity treatment. *Obesity, 18*(1), S8–S12.

Flegal, K.M., Carroll, M.D., Ogden, C.L., & Curtin, L.R. (2010). Prevalence and trends in obesity among US adults, 1999–2008. *Journal of the American Medical Association, 303*(3), 235–241.

Fleming, R.K. (2010, July). *Translating general pediatric weight loss interventions for application with children with intellectual and developmental disabilities.* Eunice Kennedy Shriver National Institute of Child Health and Human Development (NICHD) Conference: Obesity in Children with Developmental and/or Physical Disabilities, Washington, DC.

Fleming, R.K., Stokes, E.A., Curtin, C., Bandini, L.G., Gleason, J., Scampini, R., ... Hamad, C. (2008). Behavioral health in developmental disabilities: A comprehensive program of nutrition, exercise and weight reduction. *International Journal of Behavioral Consulting and Therapy, 4*(3), 287–296.

Hamilton, S., Hankey, C.R., Miller, S., Boyle, S., & Melville, C.A. (2007). A review of weight loss interventions for adults with intellectual disabilities. *Obesity Reviews, 8,* 339–345.

Humphries, K. (2010, July). Understanding obesity as an ecological phenomenon. *Eunice Kennedy Shriver National Institute of Child Health and Human Development (NICHD) Conference: Obesity in Children with Developmental and/or Physical Disabilities.* Washington, DC.

Humphries, K., Traci. M.A., & Seekins, T. (2009). Nutrition and adults with intellectual or developmental disabilities: Systematic literature review results. *Intellectual and Developmental Disabilities, 47*(3), 163–185.

Israel, B.A., Schulz, A.J., Parker, E.A., Becker, A.B., Allen, A., & Guzman, J.R. (2003). Critical issues in developing and following community-based participatory research principles. In M. Minkler & N. Wallerstein (Eds.), *Community-based participatory research for health* (pp. 56–73). San Francisco, CA: Jossey-Bass.

Lemmens,V.E.P.P., Oenema,A., Klepp, K.I., Henriksen, H.B., & Brug, J. (2008). A systematic review of the evidence regarding efficacy of obesity prevention interventions among adults. *Obesity Reviews, 9,* 446–455.

Maiano, C. (2011). Prevalence and risk factors of overweight and obesity among children and adolescents with intellectual disabilities. *Obesity Reviews, 12*(3), 189–197.

Melville, C.A., Cooper, S.A., Morrison, J., Allan, L., Smiley, E., & Williamson, A. (2008). The prevalence and determinants of obesity in adults with intellectual disabilities. *Journal of Applied Research in Intellectual Disabilities, 21,* 425–437.

Minahan, P.M., Fitch, S.N. & Must, A. (2007). What does the epidemic of childhood obesity mean for children with special health care needs? *The Journal of Law, Medicine & Ethics, 35*(1), 61–77.

Must, A., & Strauss, R.S. (1999). Risks and consequences of childhood and adolescent obesity. *International Journal of Obesity, 23*(Suppl), S2–S11.

Office of Disease Prevention and Health Promotion (2000). *Healthy People 2010: Understanding and improving health* (2nd Ed.) Washington, D.C.: U.S. Department of Health and Human Services.

Ogden, C.L., Carroll, M.D., Curtin, L.R., Lamb, M.M., & Flegal, K.M. (2010). Prevalence of high body mass index in US children and adolescents, 2007–2008. *Journal of the American Medical Association, 303*(3), 242–249.

Rimmer, J.H. (2010, July). Current state of the science in obesity in youth with disabilities-what we know and where we need to go. *Eunice Kennedy Shriver National Institute of Child Health and Human Development (NICHD) Conference: Obesity in Children with Developmental and/or Physical Disabilities.* Washington, DC.

Rimmer, J.H., Rowland, J.L., & Yamaki, K. (2007). Obesity and secondary conditions in adolescents with disabilities: Addressing the needs of an underserved population. *Journal of Adolescent Health, 41*(3), 224–229.

Rimmer, J.H., & Wang, E. (2005). Obesity prevalence among a group of Chicago residents with disabilities. *Archives of Physical Medicine and Rehabilitation, 86*(7), 1461–1464.

Rimmer, J.H., & Yamaki, K. (2006). Obesity and intellectual disability. *Mental Retardation and Developmental Disabilities Research Reviews, 12,* 22–27.

Rimmer, J.H., Yamaki, K., Lowry, B.M.D., Wang, E., & Vogel, L.C. (2010). Obesity and obesity-related secondary conditions in adolescents with intellectual/developmental disabilities. *Journal of Intellectual Disability Research, 54*(9), 787–794.

Robinson, T.M. (1999). Behavioural treatment of childhood and adolescent obesity. *International Journal of Obesity, 28*(2), S52–S57.

Schwartz, M.B., & Brownell, K. (2007). Actions necessary to prevent childhood obesity: Creating the climate for change. *Journal of Law, Medicine and Ethics, 31*(5), 78–89.

Simkin-Silverman, L.R., Wing, R.R., Boraz, M.A,. & Kuller, L.H. (2003). Lifestyle intervention can prevent weight gain during menopause: Results from a 5-year randomized clinical trial. *Annals of Behavioral Medicine, 26*(3), 212–220.

U.S. Department of Health and Human Services. (2000). *Healthy people 2010: Understanding and improving health* (2nd ed.). Washington, DC: U.S. Government Printing Office.

U.S. Department of Health and Human Services. (2005). *The surgeon general's call to action to improve the health and wellness of persons with disabilities.* U.S. Washington, DC: Department of Health and Human Services, Office of the Surgeon General.

Wadden, T.A., Butryn, M.L., & Byrne, K.J. (2004). Efficacy of lifestyle modification for long-term weight control. *Obesity Research, 12*(Suppl), 151S–162S.

Wilfley, D.E., Stein, R.I., Saelens, B.E., Mockus, D.S., Matt, G.F., Hayden-Wade, H.A., et al. (2007). Efficacy of maintenance treatment approaches for childhood overweight: A randomized controlled trial. *Journal of the American Medical Association, 298*(14), 1661–1673.

Wilfley, D.E., Tibbs, T.L., Van Buren, D.J., Reach, K.P., Walker, M.S., & Epstein, L.H. (2007). Lifestyle interventions in the treatment of childhood overweight: A meta-analytic review of randomized controlled trials. *Health Psychology, 26*(5), 521–532.

Wing, R.R.. Tate, D.F., Gorin, A.A., Raynor, H.A., & Fava, J.L. (2006). A self-regulation program for maintenance of weight loss. *New England Journal of Medicine, 355*(15), 1563–1571.

Yamaki, K. (2005). Body weight status among adults with intellectual disability in the community. *Mental Retardation, 43,* 1–10.

Yamaki, K., Rimmer, J.H., Lowry, B.D., & Vogel, L.C. (2011). Prevalence of obesity-related chronic health conditions in overweight adolescents with disabilities. *Research in Developmental Disabilities, 32,* 280–288.

SECTION

# Criminal Behavior

**CHAPTER**

# People with Intellectual and Developmental Disabilities in the Criminal Justice System

*Susan Carol Hayes*

Research and clinical evidence paints a picture of offenders with intellectual disabilities (ID) or developmental disabilities (DD) as having multiple disadvantages. People with intellectual and/or developmental disabilities (IDD) who engage in offending behavior are likely to be isolated from their family and community, lonely, often homeless, and lacking any productive activity during the day (Simpson & Hogg, 2001; Vanny, Levy, Greenberg, & Hayes, 2009). These people may have substance abuse problems that affect their financial situation, resulting in offenses being committed in order to obtain food, alcohol, or drugs, or criminal behavior as a result of intoxication (Vanny, Levy, & Hayes, 2008; Vanny et al., 2009). Recidivism rates are high (Klimecki, Jenkinson, & Wilson, 1994; Lindsay & Holland, 2000). A further complicating factor is the evidence that compared with the general population, people with IDD have a markedly increased risk of developing mental health problems (Holland & Koot, 1998; Lunsky, 2004; Lunsky & Palucka, 2004).

Poverty is yet another determinant of social inequality that many offenders with IDD experience. People with IDDs and their families are overrepresented in the poorest strata of society (Emerson & Hatton, 2005). Furthermore, a higher prevalence of IDD and coexisting mental illness has been found in local courts located in low socioeconomic areas (Hayes, Levy, Vanny, & Greenberg, 2008), a finding that links financial disadvantage to both IDD and mental disorder as well as to offending behavior. This finding also helps to explain the differences in prevalence in different jurisdictions, prisons, and court systems because variations in prevalence may reflect the higher or lower socioeconomic indicators of the area in which research is conducted.

---

The term *offender* will primarily be used in this chapter for the sake of simplicity, although much of the research in this area has been conducted with samples where no formal determination of guilt has been made, or on pretrial populations who are remanded in custody or are on bail and have not been formally adjudicated, or with individuals with IDD who are diverted from the criminal justice system into community or forensic services.

Identifying an offender as having IDD, it has been argued, merely adds a label to that person and has little effect on the fairness of his or her treatment in the criminal justice system or outcome of the case. On the other hand, lack of identification may have serious implications for the individual's rights to receive a fair trial, including being able to participate in the defense, fitness to be tried, understanding the police caution or Miranda warning and the right to silence, fairness in admitting evidence including a confession, competence to give evidence, and appropriate sentencing or diversion from the criminal justice system. In addition, lack of identification may result in people with IDD missing out on appropriate diversions from the criminal justice system or participation in reha- bilitation programs. Holland (2004), while emphasizing the need for further research into prevalence, risk factors, and preventative interventions, raises the issue of the ethical and political complexities surrounding this and other vulnerable and minority groups in the criminal justice system; the potential for people with IDD, psychiatric patients; and ethnic minorities to become scapegoats; and the possible emergence of repressive policy developments. For example, diversion from the criminal justice system may appear to be a desirable option for people with IDD, but human rights issues need to be observed to ensure that diversion does not mean indefinite incarceration without review, by another name. A fine line exists between attempting to improve the situation of people with IDD in the criminal justice system and overprotection or inhibition of individual human rights.

## CASE STUDY

Joy, age 37 years, has an ID and her parents are her legal guardians. Joy has been diagnosed with a borderline personality disorder, very challenging and complex behaviors including violence and self-harming, and anxiety disorders that mani- fest themselves as obsessive and compulsive behaviors. Joy lived in a supported environment in a nongovernment residential group home in a country town, where she had full-time care, sharing the residential accommodation with nine other adults. Her life was simple, contented, and with few responsibilities. She attended supported employment full time. Joy then convinced herself that she was capable of living in the general community and she walked out of her group home to move into a two-bedroom apartment with a male friend, who quickly became her partner. Joy lived independently in the community in public housing for 5 years until she had an argument with her partner and threatened him with a kitchen knife. A Domestic Violence Order (DVO) was put in place preventing her from having contact with him. This DVO effectively ended her relationship with her partner. About a year after moving out of the group home, she had ceased working in the supported employment setting. She found the complexities and difficulties that a person with ID confronted living in the general community to be numerous and beyond her comprehension or ability to cope.

Joy was provided with 24.5 hours of support each week, which her parents considered to be insufficient for the complex needs of their daughter. After moving out of the supported environment, Joy's life lurched from disaster to disaster. She experienced frustration at being unable to manage her daily affairs (e.g., relationships, finances, shopping, cooking, paying bills, welfare payment) leading to serious violent attacks against her partner, or, when at home, against her mother. She also began to harm herself by cutting her forearms and hitting her arms and legs with her fists. Her parents were constantly reacting to crisis situations. Joy's ID made it difficult for her to learn consequences and accept responsibility for her behaviors and actions. She was before a local court on more than 10 occasions charged with stealing, shoplifting, and possession of stolen property. She was placed on probation, given community service, and fined heavily, but no consequence altered her behavior. The judge warned her on two occasions that the next time she appeared before the court there would be no alternative other than to give her a custodial sentence. A report was obtained from a forensic psychiatrist, stating that Joy is permanently unfit for trial. However, Joy has pleaded guilty to indictable matters on seven occasions. The duty lawyers were working within a system that did not allow them the time or resources to properly consider her ID. About 5 years after beginning her offending Joy began to receive legal services from a project delivering free specialized legal assistance to people with IDD and mental illness living in the local community.

Joy's parents believed that she needed close supervision and involvement in social, recreational, and work-related activities. She required close supervision with all activities in which she participates because of her dishonesty and unreliability. Her main social interaction was walking through shops daily for hours at a time. In a 4-month period, she received some extra supervision and support through a grant of crisis funding. Her case was referred to a behavior support team, where she could receive intervention for physical aggression, stealing, refusal to take medication, risk-taking behavior, and disruptive behavior in her neighborhood. A behavior intervention and management plan was developed by a team, headed by a psychologist, and agreed to by all parties who worked or associated with Joy. Her parents applied for her to enter an innovative housing project, but spaces were limited and she was not accepted. Her parents believed that in a secure, closely supervised environment, Joy could receive intensive behavior modification and intervention by skilled, experienced professionals, followed by close supervision and monitoring by skilled staff as she moved into more independent living arrangements. It is almost inevitable that Joy will commit further serious offenses if she is not admitted to supervised accommodation with a behavior management program.

The services that Joy has received have been fragmented and ad hoc, lacking continuity. The short-term nature of the support and intervention is such that no major changes in her behavior or living skills have been achieved. It is significant that each time a brief intervention ceases, she reoffends. Although her needs appear to be complex and multifaceted, they are, in fact, fairly simple—she needs ongoing long-term supervision and support with accommodation, social and recreational activities, vocational activities, programs to encourage development of skills of independent living including financial management, and intervention and therapy for challenging behavior.

## INVOLVEMENT IN THE CRIMINAL JUSTICE SYSTEM

### Prevalence

Owing to the significance of the threat of losing one's liberty, most research has been focused on people with IDD in custody, and a large portion of research has investigated the prevalence of IDD in prisons and jails. Difficulties arise when attempting to compare prevalence between nations and jurisdictions because of methodological, diagnostic, and sampling differences. Additional concerns are that many studies define IDD solely on the basis of IQ testing; some use nonrandom samples of convenience; cutoff scores for IDD vary; and "offending" behavior may include actions that are violent or aggressive, but that have not been formally adjudicated in a court (Holland, 2004; Jones, 2007; Lindsay, Hastings, Griffiths, & Hayes, 2007).

A review of studies that included 12,000 prisoners in Australia, Dubai, New Zealand, the United Kingdom, and the United States concluded that the prevalence of people with IDD ranged from 0 to 2.9% (Fazel, Xenitidis, & Powell, 2008), although the review omitted a number of studies that showed a higher prevalence (Crocker, Cote, Toupin, & St Onge, 2007; Hayes, 2000; Hayes, Shackell, Mottram, & Lancaster, 2007; Parton, Day, & White, 2004; Sondenaa, Rasmussen, Palmstierna, & Nottestad, 2008). The highest prevalence occurred in a study in Irish prisons, which sampled 10% of the prison population and found that 28% scored below 70 on an IQ test (Murphy, Harrold, Carey, & Mulrooney, 2000). Generally, research indicates that people with IDD are overrepresented in the offender population, although the extent of overrepresentation varies between jurisdictions and is a topic of controversy (Holland, 2004; Lindsay et al., 2007). If offenders with borderline intellectual ability (IQ = 70–79) are included, prevalence increases dramatically (Crocker et al., 2007).

In the United States, between 2% and 10% of the prison population has been estimated to have IDD (Anno, 1991; Dwyer & Frierson, 2006). The President's Committee on Mental Retardation estimated in 1991 that there were approximately 14,000 prisoners in state and federal prisons nationwide, an increase of 10% since 1988 (National Commission on Correctional Health Care, 1992). In the California corrections system, the estimated prevalence is 4% for prisoners and 2% for probationers. This group of offenders is more likely to be convicted, receive a prison sentence, and serve a greater portion of their prison term than their nondisabled peers (Petersilia, 1997a & 1997b).

A significant area of concern is the numbers of people with IDD who are on death row or who have been executed in the United States (Keyes, Edwards, & Perske, 2002). There is no definitive study of the prevalence of IDD amongst prisoners sentenced to death in the United States or elsewhere, although estimates range from 2% to 20% (Hall, 2002). The issue of whether or not a death row inmate has IDD is highly significant, given the decision by the U.S. Supreme Court in 2002 that the *"executions of mentally retarded criminals are 'cruel and unusual punishments'"* prohibited by the Eighth Amendment of the U.S. Constitution" (*Atkins v. Virginia*, 536 U.S. 304, 2002). Specifically, the Court expressed the opinion that:

> Because of their disabilities in areas of reasoning, judgment, and control of their impulses...they do not act with the level of moral culpability that characterizes the most serious adult criminal conduct. Moreover, their impairments can jeopardize the reliability and fairness of capital proceedings against mentally retarded defendants. (p. 1)

The few studies that have been conducted in courts rather than prisons indicated high prevalence, but also demonstrated significant variations in rates of IDD between courts within the same jurisdiction from a low of 1.7% to a high of 18.3% (Hayes, 1993, 1996; Hayes et al., 2008). These findings suggest that the controversy over prevalence of IDD in the criminal justice system will not be resolved in a clear and consistent manner because each jurisdiction is likely to have variations in prevalence within its own borders, as well as in comparison with other jurisdictions. Furthermore, prevalence may differ according to the stage of the criminal justice system that is under investigation. For example, there may be high prevalence of people with IDD presenting to some courts, who are then diverted out of the criminal justice system into community services or secure units or hospitals (Taylor et al., 1998).

Two large longitudinal birth cohort studies found that both men and women with ID were more likely than their peers in the general population to have been convicted of a criminal offense, with the relative risk being higher for violent offenses (Crocker & Hodgins, 1997; Hodgins, Mednick, Brennan, Shulsinger, & Engberg, 1996).

There may never be a clear determination of the debate about the extent to which people with IDD are overrepresented in the criminal justice system. Jurisdictions should be encouraged, however, to investigate this issue within their own systems in order to assist in facilitating planning of services both within the prison system as well as generalist and specialist services for people with IDD in the community. Systems of screening for IDD in police stations, courts, probation services, and prisons need to be introduced to allow interventions and supports to be established (Crocker et al., 2007; Hayes, 2000).

## PREDISPOSING FACTORS

Many offenders with IDD have not experienced stable, loving families, and in this characteristic they tend to differ from their nonoffending IDD counterparts while being similar to their peer group of offenders without disabilities who are also likely to have dysfunctional childhoods (Farrington, 2004). Two issues are significant, the first being that generally many families with IDD offspring are more likely than families with no offspring with disabilities to be in situations of disadvantage. Second, people with IDD who become offenders are even more likely to have abusive or neglecting family environments (Lindsay, Elliot, & Astell, 2004).

Relating to the first issue, families of children with IDD tend to experience difficulties such as low parental educational level, low socioeconomic status, psychopathology of the primary caregiver, single-parent situation, parental referral to mental health care, and family dysfunction (Dekker & Koot, 2003). Inadequate daily living skills, chronic physical conditions, social deficits, and negative life events predict a *DSM-IV* (*Diagnostic and Statistical Manual of Mental Disorders, Fourth Edition*; American Psychiatric Association, 2000) disorder in children with IDD. Disruptive behavior (as defined by the *Diagnostic Interview Schedule for Children–Parent Version: DISC-IV-PV*; Shaffer et al., 2000) is specifically predicted by inadequate daily living skills, family dysfunction, and low parental education. Mood disorder is uniquely predicted by negative life events, thus predisposing the children to challenging behavior (Dekker & Koot, 2003). Finally, being a witness to parental violence contributes to the development of anger and aggression in adulthood for people with IDD (Novaco & Taylor, 2008).

In relation to the second issue, the special disadvantage of offenders with IDD, Hayes (2004) reported in a study of sex offenders with ID that fewer than half the group had both parents present during their developmental years, prior to age 18; in half the cases, the mother was deceased, and in 43% of cases, their father was deceased. Fewer than 10% had supportive contact, or indeed any contact with their family currently, even though the whereabouts of parents, siblings, and sometimes grandparents were generally known to the participants. High rates of physical and sexual abuse were found among this group and the history of abuse was correlated with depression, suicidal ideation, and suicide attempts. Those sex offenders with IDD and depression were more likely to have used or threatened violence during the commission of the offense (Hayes, 2004). These results are consistent with other studies of physical and sexual abuse histories for offenders with ID, which conclude that sexual abuse in childhood may be a significant variable in the development of sexual offending in adulthood, whereas physical abuse in childhood was significantly more prevalent in nonsexual offenders (Lindsay, Law, Quinn, Smart, & Smith, 2001). The pattern for people with IDD entering forensic ID services includes economic and social deprivation in childhood, likelihood of a diagnosis of attention-deficit/hyperactivity disorder (ADHD), aggression, inappropriate sexual behavior, having been charged with an offense (Lindsay et al., 2010) and familial offending (Jones, 2007).

As mentioned earlier, psychiatric illness would logically seem to be a predisposing factor for people with IDD who offend. A comparison between offenders and nonoffenders both with IDD and psychiatric disorder found many similarities between the two groups, including a history of having been the victim of sexual abuse (Raina & Lunsky, 2010). However, the offender group was more likely to have higher cognitive functioning, diagnoses of psychotic disorder and/or impulse control/intermittent explosive disorder, and substance abuse history.

It has been suggested that two broad groups emerge from the prevalence studies: one group with mild levels of disability but with severely disadvantaged backgrounds, and a second group, known to IDD services, who may engage in rarer and potentially more dangerous behaviors (Holland, 2004). Holland comments upon the high levels of tolerance of possible offenses within IDD services, resulting in under-reporting of less serious offenses and possibly serious crimes such as rape, which may make it seem as though the group in contact with services is likely to engage in more dangerous and impulsive crimes.

In summary, offenders with IDD are likely to have suffered attachment disruption in early childhood, to have experienced childhood abuse, to be aggressive, to possess few conflict resolution skills, and to have developed psychiatric, behavioral, substance abuse, and emotional problems related to these negative early experiences.

## PEOPLE WITH INTELLECTUAL AND DEVELOPMENTAL DISABILITIES WHO COMMIT CRIMES

Most offenders with IDD function in the mild range of ID (Hayes, 2000; Jones, 2007). Of note, it can be difficult to differentiate this group from the mainstream prison population where the average IQ is in the low-average range of ability (Hayes et al., 2007). As emphasized in this chapter, the characteristics of offenders with IDD are not markedly different from their nondisabled counterparts (Salekin, Olley, & Hedge, 2010), many offenders with IDD are not known to specialist services (Hayes, 2000; Holland, Clare, & Mukhopadhyay, 2002), and they experience substance abuse problems, family dysfunction, accommodation instability, and unemployment (Hayes et al., 2008).

A recent study found that 12% of accused people appearing before local courts had IDD and 46% of this group had a coexisting mental health diagnosis (Vanny et al., 2009). Consistent with these high levels of coexisting psychiatric disorder, it has been demonstrated that 38% of a group of prisoners with IDD had received inpatient treatment in a psychiatric facility at some stage in their lives. Also, 29% had a recorded diagnosis of major psychiatric disorder, more than twice the rates found in another study of prisoners randomly selected from the same prison system (Glaser & Deane, 1999). Psychiatric disorder may be making a contribution, in its own right, to the behaviors and difficulties which lead to offending by people with IDD (Glaser & Florio, 2004). These authors commented,

> All the offenders in the study, already experiencing cognitive limitations, chaotic lifestyles and a lack of stable social networks, were repeatedly subjected to inconsistent (and often inaccurate) communications and interventions from multiple service providers in a situation where they had very little control over their destiny, limited opportunities to form permanent interpersonal relationships and very little sense of themselves as persons who could effectively understand and communicate their own concerns. (p. 600)

There is a grave risk of many offenders with dual diagnosis falling in between service and policy responsibilities (Myers, 2004). Compared with nonoffenders with IDD, those in the offending subgroup are more likely to be young and male (Holland et al., 2002), lacking specialist disability accommodation, not receiving services, unemployed (Simons, 2000), and in the borderline/mild range of intellectual functioning rather than the more serious categories of IDD (Cockram, 2005b).

## WOMEN OFFENDERS

Only a handful of research studies have been conducted with women who have IDD and offend (Hayes, 2007). One reason for this limited literature is the small proportion of women prisoners worldwide. In June 2008, 207,700 women were in U.S. state or federal prisons or local jails, just under 10% of the total prison and jail population (Correctional Association of New York, 2009; National Commission on Correctional Health Care, 1992). In 2006 over 4400 women were imprisoned in the United Kingdom, about 5.7% of the total prison population (HM Prison Service, 2010). Women account for 7% of the Australian prison population; at June 30, 2009 there were 2125 female prisoners, an increase of 9% from the previous year (Australian Bureau of Statistics, 2009). In many jurisdictions, the rate of increase in the female prison population is exceeding that for males (Australian Bureau of Statistics, 2009; Kendall, 2004). Women offenders with IDD have been described as *"situated within various networks of oppression"* (Kendall, 2004).

Assault-related offenses tended to predominate in a cohort of women offenders with IDD, whereas other offenses included serious charges such as murder and less serious offenses including prostitution-related crimes, assaults, breach of the peace, and theft (Lindsay, Smith et al., 2004). Twenty-two percent (22%) reoffended within a year with similar types of offenses. An Australian study found that 29.7% of a sample of women ex-prisoners had an IQ that placed them in the category of IDD (Lewis & Hayes, 1998). About 60% of women prisoners with IDD report having been the victim of sexual abuse (a significantly higher rate than their men counterparts), and about 40% report physical abuse (Alexander, Piachaud, & Gangadharan, 2005; Lindsay, Smith et al., 2004). These women offenders are likely to have engaged in self-harming behavior and physical violence toward others and to have a diagnosis of personality disorder (Alexander et al., 2005).

A long-term Swedish study found that the likelihood of a criminal conviction by age 30 for people with IDD was three times greater for men and four times greater for women compared with nondisabled peers. However, the disparity increased for violent offenses, with men having IDD being four times as likely as their nondisabled peers to have a criminal conviction, whereas women were 24 times more likely (Hodgins, 1992). A U.S. study found that murder defendants who were women were more likely than men to receive a diagnosis of IDD, possibly owing to reduced ability to manage major acute interpersonal conflicts that can lead to increased risk of violence (Dwyer & Frierson, 2006), which may also be the case for the cohort studied by Hodgins (1992).

Women with IDD in the criminal justice system are more likely than men, and more likely than women in the general population, to have a dual diagnosis of ID and mental health disorder or challenging behavior (Lewis & Hayes, 1997, 1998). Dual diagnosis rates for women offenders with IDD are as high as 67% (Lindsay et al., 2004), although Kendall (2004) warns that the high rate of psychiatric diagnoses may occur because women offenders tend to have their experiences pathologized owing to their violations of the law as well as the fact that they have failed to comply with cultural expectations of female passivity and innocence. Furthermore, some studies report high rates of psychiatric disorders among the female prison population generally (Australian Bureau of Statistics, 2004; Kesteven, 2002). As a result of poor verbal abilities and coping mechanisms, women can resort to maladaptive means of coping, such as self-harm, substance abuse, and eating disorders (Lewis & Hayes, 1998), which in turn may be diagnosed as psychiatric disorders or breaches of prison discipline or parole conditions (Kendall, 2004).

Concerning recidivism, female offenders with IDD reoffend less frequently than their male counterparts. This finding might be the result of female offenders with IDD receiving treatment for their psychological and mental health problems (Lindsay et al., 2004).

A small U.K. study found that fewer than half of women with IDD who had come to the attention of police were dealt with formally by the court, receiving outcomes such as probation with court-ordered treatment, or deferment of sentence for up to 2 years. Within this total group, 11% had no action taken after the police investigation, 38.3% were diverted to IDD services rather than proceeding through the criminal justice system, and 5.5% were placed in a high-security setting (not necessarily a prison). Women were more likely than their male counterparts to have no action taken against them (Allen, Lindsay, MacLeod, & Smith, 2001).

Generally, women offenders (with and without IDD) are not only overlooked by prison bureaucracies and community corrections, but usually lack a voice in prison reform advocacy groups. As such, although they face the same problems as men offenders with IDD, little is known specifically about women's situations of social deprivation, previous abuse and victimization, mental health, and needs (Hayes, 2007).

## TYPES OF CRIMINAL OFFENSES COMMITTED

People with IDD are more likely to be charged (in lower courts) with offenses against people, property, justice procedures, and good order. They are less likely to be charged with drugs, alcohol, or driving offenses, but in general the pattern of offenses differs little from that observed for offenders without disabilities (Cockram, 2005b; Sondenaa et al., 2008). They also tend to be on a par with their peers without disabilities for violent offense convictions, with the rate being about two out of three for both groups (Crocker et al., 2007). Although some professionals believe that this group is more prone than offenders without disabilities to commit arson and sexual offenses, more recent research appears to debunk this belief (Crocker et al., 2007; Holland et al., 2002; Sondenaa et al., 2008). As with offenders without disabilities, the IDD group tend to be versatile in their previous offenses with over 80% of both groups having previous convictions for more than one type of offense (Crocker et al., 2007).

Although there is a dearth of information concerning recidivism, some data suggest that people with IDD are rearrested at five times the rate of their peers without disabilities, and that a prior history of offending substantially increases the risk of subsequent offending (Cockram, 2005a). The rearrest rate raised questions about whether people with IDD may be more likely to be rearrested once they are known to police because aspects of their lifestyle, characteristics, and environment increase the likelihood of engaging in offending behavior. Of course, it is also possible that they receive less fair treatment by police (Cockram, 2005a).

## ISSUES RELEVANT TO COMPETENCY

Issues of competency occur at each stage when people with IDD enter the criminal justice system, including prior to or during police interviews, when making a confession, when determining competency or fitness to be tried, and when determining competency to plead, especially when pleading guilty (Baroff, Gunn, & Hayes, 2004). There are questions about whether the accused understood the police caution or Miranda warning and therefore, whether the confession can be introduced into evidence. Similarly, competency sentencing considerations arise in relation to deliberations about appropriate sentencing options and whether the person will be at risk in prison, can understand the conditions imposed by the court, and is likely to be violent and dangerous, perhaps as a consequence of intellectual disability or for related or unrelated reasons (Hayes, 2010). Furthermore, there may be questions as to whether the witness understands the oath or the obligation to tell the truth, and whether the witness is reliable. The basic principles underlying competency considerations arose from the concept of *mens rea*, that is, the ability to form an intent to commit a crime, which evolved into the capacity to distinguish right from wrong, as well as the capacity to participate effectively in one's own defence (Baroff et al., 2004; Hayes, 2010; Hayes & Craddock, 1992). The legal ramifications of incompetency at any of these stages differ between various jurisdictions. For example, the defendant may be committed to a secure forensic facility or the charges may be dropped if they are not serious. Alternatively, proceedings may be suspended for a determination about whether the defendant will become fit during the ensuing 12 months, and there may be a special hearing to determine whether the defendant performed the act of which they are accused (Baroff et al., 2004). In the United States, the various states have legislation addressing competency, although the major principles are those established in *Dusky v. United States* (1960)—the defendant needs to have the ability to consult rationally with an attorney to aid in his or her own defense and to have a rational and factual understanding of the charges.

In Canada, the criteria for competency are that the individual is presumed fit to stand trial unless, on account of mental disorder, the defendant is incapable of understanding the nature of object of the proceedings, understanding the possible consequences of proceedings, and communicating with counsel (Nussbaum, Hancock, Turner, Arrowood, & Melodick, 2008).

In Australia, the various states and territories have legislation establishing the procedure to be followed when an accused person may be unfit to be tried. In instances where the legislation is unclear, the common law definition, the so-called *Presser* formulation (*R. v. Presser*, 1958), tends to be accepted. The *Presser* formulation states that the accused person needs to 1) be able to understand the charge, 2) plead to the charge, 3) exercise the right to challenge potential jury members, 4) understand generally the nature of the proceedings as being an inquiry as to whether he or she did what he or she is charged with, 5) follow the proceedings in a general sense, and 6) understand the substantial effect of any evidence that may be given. In addition, the accused person must be able to make a defense or answer to the charge, as well as give counsel necessary instructions and let counsel know what his or her version of the facts. Additionally, the accused person must be able to decide what defense is to be relied on, and make the defense and the version of events known to the court and to counsel. In the United Kingdom, the leading case establishing the criteria for unfitness includes very similar concepts as the *Presser* formulation (*R. v. Pritchard*, 1836). It bears repeating that to arrive at their opinion, expert witnesses undertaking a fitness evaluation commonly work through all of the criteria applicable in their jurisdiction (Baroff et al., 2004).

Approximately 30% of IDD defendants in a United States study were found to be incompetent to stand trial, although the authors warn that rates may vary according to the severity and type of crime because competency becomes more significant for serious crimes, especially murder (Cochrane, Grisso, & Frederick, 2001).

Assessment of competence/fitness to stand trial can be assisted through the use of standardized instruments, such as the Competence Assessment to Stand Trial for Defendants with Mental Retardation (CAST-MR) (Everington, 1990) and the Nussbaum Fitness Questionnaire (Nussbaum et al., 2008), or through following the criteria established in the common law, such as the *Presser* and *Pritchard* criteria outlined previously.

The offender's competence to participate in a police interview involves issues such as comprehension of the police caution or warning and the right to remain silent, suggestibility during questioning, and lack of comprehension of the implications of making a false confession. Gudjonsson and colleagues have created an impressive body of research demonstrating that accused people with IDD in police interviews tend to be vulnerable to intimidation, deceit, or coercion and are more suggestible, more prone to confess, and unable to foresee the long-term consequences of their confessions (Clare & Gudjonsson, 1993; Gudjonsson, 1984; Gudjonsson, Clare, Rutter, & Pearse, 1993). Police exercise an important gate-keeping role in the criminal justice system before the accused appears in court by deciding whether to proceed with a complaint; making recommendations about probation, parole, or remand in custody; and deciding whether to pursue the matter by arresting or charging the individual (Mercier & Crocker, 2011). These authors note that influences on these decisions include involvement of the suspect with IDD services or other support networks, previous knowledge of the defendant by police, identification of the condition of IDD, and coexisting problems such as mental illness, homelessness, or substance abuse where alternative dispositions are available.

Mercier and Crocker (2011) recommended several possible improvements, including early screening for IDD, checkbox on the police event report form, and increased training for police and crown attorneys about IDD. Another suggestion was for summonsing the individual to appear in court rather than detaining the suspect pending a court appearance or extracting a promise to appear in court (which the suspect may forget about during the intervening time). Typically, a summons is sent to the person's place of residence and either the individual and/or a support person/caretaker will therefore be reminded about the court date. Other initiatives could include drawing up memorandums of understanding between police, legal agencies such as the crown attorney or legal aid, the judiciary, and community organizations offering services to people with IDD and/or mental disorders, as well as the establishment of more services aimed at diverting the people with IDD out of the criminal justice system into appropriate services (Mercier & Crocker, 2011).

The vulnerabilities of accused individuals with IDD are in turn germane to the issue of competency to plead guilty. It has been suggested that, given the significant outcomes of pleading guilty, such a plea should require a higher level of competency (Baroff et al., 2004). As Baroff points out, where separate tests exist for fitness to be tried and competence to plead guilty, accused people may find themselves in the invidious position of standing trial but being deemed not competent to plead guilty, thereby missing out on advantages which might accrue from a guilty plea.

The ability of the people with IDD to participate competently in every stage of the criminal justice system must be considered by all relevant service providers including police, defense lawyers, prosecutors, corrections staff, and probation and parole personnel. Family members and paid caretakers need to be aware of the pitfalls for the people with IDD during the legal process. They also must be mindful of their own role in assisting with understanding the issues and decision making, but not taking over the decision-making process. Otherwise, they could create an impression that people with IDD are competent to participate in the defense process when in reality they do not understand the issues at hand.

## Screening for Intellectual and Developmental Disabilities

Police forces in particular, but also other agencies in the criminal justice system—including corrective services, probation and parole, legal aid, and government attorneys or prosecutors—express the need for a simple, diagnostic screening instrument for IDD. The New South Wales (Australia) Law Reform Commission's report (New South Wales Law Reform Commission, 1996) concerning people with IDD in the criminal justice system included the following recommendations:

> Identification of intellectual disability is one of the most difficult issues for personnel in the criminal justice system... Nevertheless, without identification the police will not be able to implement any of the safeguards outlined in this chapter. Therefore the first issue which must be addressed in any Code of Practice is guidelines for identifying whether a person being questioned, whether suspect, victim or witness, may have an intellectual disability... It must be made clear that there is a difference between screening for intellectual disability through a series of tests or questions administered to all suspects, identification of the possibility of intellectual disability and expert assessment of intellectual disability. This recommendation only expects police to identify the possibility of intellectual disability; it does not expect police officers to screen for intellectual disability or to undertake assessments of intellectual disability in any formal sense. (pp. 107–108)

Screening instruments have been developed in response to needs expressed by police forces and other criminal justice system agencies, including the Hayes Ability Screening Index (HASI; the author of this chapter developed the HASI and declares an interest) (Hayes, 2000; Sondenaa et al., 2008; Sondenaa, Nottestad, & Bjorgen, 2007) and the Learning Disability Screening Index (LDSQ) (McKenzie & Paxton,

2006). The HASI is used in a variety of criminal justice system agencies such as police forces, corrective services, forensic mental health services, and legal aid offices in several nations including the United States, Canada, the Netherlands, Norway, the United Kingdom, Australia, and New Zealand. The HASI does not diagnose IDD, but indicates to police officers that a suspect may be vulnerable owing to possible IDD and may need the presence of a third party during a police interview. On the other hand, the HASI can indicate when a prisoner or accused person may need to be referred for further full diagnostic assessment within the prison system or prior to adjudication of their case.

## PREVENTIVE INTERVENTION

Preventing offending behavior is the Holy Grail of forensic sciences whether or not the offender has IDD. Strong evidence supports the effectiveness of early intervention strategies targeting behavioral disturbances and aimed at preventing involvement with crime. These strategies are cost effective for the potential offenders, families, victims, and the community (Rand Research Brief, 1997). Examples of effective early interventions are 1) training parents to better manage challenging behaviors, 2) giving incentives for young people to remain at and graduate from high school, 3) close supervision of young offenders by juvenile justice services, 4) early home-visit and day-care programs, 5) early intensive programs to identify and address behavioral difficulties that are occurring at pre-school age, and 6) preventing violence and abuse in families. However, demonstrating the cost effectiveness of early intervention and persuading politicians and bureaucrats about the wisdom of implementing programs do not go hand in hand. To illustrate, in the United States during 2001 prison operations consumed about 77% of state correctional costs, and the remaining 23% was spent on juvenile justice, probation and parole, community-based corrections, and central office administration (Bureau of Justice Statistics, 2004). Indeed the bulk of financial support in the criminal justice system continues to be poured into the endpoints of the courts and prisons (New South Wales Parliament, 1999).

## PRACTICE IMPLICATIONS AND RECOMMENDATIONS

Identifying people with IDD in the criminal justice system is the first hurdle to be overcome because if the presence of this condition is not noted, individuals are unlikely to be afforded the human and legal rights appropriate to their level of functioning. Service agencies need to establish screening protocols to determine if the individual requires special consideration because of the vulnerabilities associated with IDD or needs to be referred for full diagnostic evaluation in respect to IDD, mental health problems, and substance abuse disorders. Not every offender with IDD will be diverted out of the criminal justice system because suitable community-based secure services may not exist or the nature and severity of the crime may result in the person being charged, tried in court, and possibly imprisoned. Therefore, corrective, probation, and parole services must understand the size of the clientele with IDD if they are to establish rehabilitation programs that take into account the cognitive and adaptive behavior limitations and coexisting mental health issues of this cohort of offenders. This is an issue of concern in that people with IDD are unlikely to benefit from general rehabilitation programs, especially those that are highly verbally based (Allen et al., 2001; Barron, Hassiotis, & Banes, 2004; Glaser & Florio, 2004; Lindsay, Elliot et al., 2004; Lindsay et al., 2007). A rethink of the current allocation of government funding must occur, with more resources being devoted to early intervention and preventive programs, rather than being concentrated at the court and custodial end of the criminal justice system.

Early intervention relies on recognition of challenging behavior that places people with IDD at risk of entering the criminal justice system. Though seeming counterintuitive, community service agencies must clarify their criteria for evaluating violent and aggressive acts as being "offending" or "high-risk" behaviors and establish clear protocols for addressing the challenging behaviors rather than ignoring them.

Finally, an area of great need is training and education for criminal justice system personnel concerning the characteristics of people with IDD. The criminal justice system must consider the types of alternative dispositions that can be implemented for this group while continuing to respect the human rights of people with IDD and ensuring the safety and welfare of the community.

## FUTURE RESEARCH TO IMPROVE PRACTICE AND SERVICE DELIVERY

The previous discussion has established that there is not a "correct" prevalence of people with IDD in the criminal justice system, either within one jurisdiction or between many jurisdictions. However, in order to allocate resources, effective service delivery for offenders with IDD relies on governments collecting some data about prevalence in their local area. Therefore, local prevalence studies need to be undertaken, perhaps on a facility-by-facility basis, using standardized definitions of IDD, well-established psychometric tests for assessing intelligence and adaptive behavior, and adequate sampling methods and sample sizes. In addition, assessment must move towards a multidimensional framework for IDD which takes into account not only intellectual and adaptive behavior abilities, but also health, participation in society, and environmental and personal factors including ethnic, social, and family background, as well as analysing the types of support that an individual needs (American Association on Intellectual and Developmental Disabilities, 2010).

Other priority research areas include further analyses of the factors that determine an individual's involvement with the criminal justice system and the types of early or preventive interventions that are effective. This research focus should present evidence-based information about programs that can be replicated by other professionals in the field. It is encouraging that a small but growing body of research has demonstrated efficacy of therapeutic interventions for sexual and violent offenders (Beail, 2003; Lindsay et al., 2003; Lindsay, Elliot et al., 2004; Lindsay, Smith et al., 2004; Novaco & Taylor, 2008). This area warrants further research effort.

The socioeconomic deprivation suffered by many people with IDD and their families is emerging as an important factor that is related to rates of offending and prevalence of mental illness among this group (Hayes et al., 2008). Most certainly, it is vital for the link between IDD and poverty to receive further research and policy attention to alleviate the impact on families and the community and to improve the quality of life of this often-marginalized group in society.

## REFERENCES

Alexander, R., Piachaud, J., & Gangadharan, S. (2005). Letter: Response to Lindsay et al. (*Journal of Intellectual Disability Research*, 48, 580–590), Women with intellectual disability who have offended. *Journal of Intellectual Disability Research, 49,* 635.

Allen, R., Lindsay, W.R., MacLeod, F., & Smith, A. (2001). Treatment of women with intellectual disabilities who have been involved with the criminal justice system for reasons of aggression. *Journal of Applied Research in Intellectual Disabilities, 14,* 340.

American Association on Intellectual and Developmental Disabilities. (2010). *Intellectual disability: Definition, classification, and systems of supports.* Washington, DC: Author.

American Psychiatric Association. (2000). *Diagnostic and statistical manual of mental disorders* (4th ed. rev.). Washington, DC: Author.

Anno, B.J. (1991). *Prison health care: guidelines for the management of an adequate delivery system.* Washington, DC: National Institute of Corrections.

*Atkins v. Virginia*, 122 S.Ct. 2242 (June 20, 2002) (U.S. Supreme Court 2002).

Australian Bureau of Statistics. (2004). *Australian Social Trends, 2004. Crime and justice: women in prison* (No. 4102.0). Canberra, ACT: Author.

Australian Bureau of Statistics. (2009). *Prisoners in Australia, 2009* (No. 4517.0). Canberra, ACT: Author.

Baroff, G., Gunn, M., & Hayes, S.C. (2004). Legal issues. In W.R. Lindsay, J.L. Taylor & P. Sturmey (Eds.), *Offenders with developmental disabilities* (pp. 37–66). Chichester, UK: John Wiley and Sons Ltd.

Barron, P., Hassiotis, A., & Banes, J. (2004). Offenders with intellectual disability: a prospective comparative study. *Journal of Intellectual Disability Research, 48,* 69–76.

Beail, N. (2003). What works for people with mental retardation? Critical commentary on cognitive-behavioral and psychodynamic psychotherapy research. *Mental Retardation, 41,* 468–472.

Bureau of Justice Statistics. (2004). *State prison expenditures, 2001.* Washington, DC: U.S. Department of Justice, Office of Justice Programs.

Clare, I., & Gudjonsson, G. (1993). Interrogative suggestibility, confabulation, and acquiescence in people with mild learning disabilities (mental handicap): Implications for reliability during police interrogations. *British Journal of Clinical Psychology, 32,* 295–301.

Cochrane, R.E., Grisso, T., & Frederick, R.I. (2001). The relationship between criminal charges, diagnoses, and psycholegal opinions among Federal pretrial defendants. *Behavioral Sciences and the Law, 19,* 565–582.

Cockram, J. (2005a). Careers of offenders with an intellectual disability: The probabilities of rearrest. *Journal of Intellectual Disability Research, 49,* 525–536.

Cockram, J. (2005b). Justice or differential treatment? Sentencing of offenders with an intellectual disability. *Journal of Intellectual and Developmental Disability, 30,* 3–13.

Correctional Association of New York. (2009). *Women in prison fact sheet.* New York, NY: Women in Prison Project.

Crocker, A.G., Cote, G., Toupin, J., & St Onge, B. (2007). Rate and characteristics of men with an intellectual disability in pre-trial detention. *Journal of Intellectual & Developmental Disability, 32,* 143–152.

Crocker, A.G., & Hodgins, S. (1997). The criminality of non-institutionalized mentally retarded persons: Evidence from a birth cohort followed to age 30. *Criminal Justice and Behavior, 24,* 432–454.

Dekker, M.C., & Koot, H.M. (2003). *DSM-IV* disorders in children with borderline to moderate intellectual disability. II: Child and family predictors. *American Academy of Child and Adolescent Psychiatry, 42,* 923–931.

*Dusky v. United States*, 362 U.S. 402 (1960).

Dwyer, R.G., & Frierson, R.L. (2006). The presence of low IQ and mental retardation among murder defendants referred for pretrial evaluation. *Journal of Forensic Sciences, 51,* 678–682.

Emerson, E., & Hatton, C. (2005). *The socio-economic circumstances of families supporting a child at risk of disability in Britain in 2002*. Lancaster, UK: Institute for Health Research, Lancaster University.

Everington, C. (1990). The competence assessment for standing trial for defendants with mental retardation (CAST-MR): A validation study. *Criminal Justice and Behavior, 17,* 147–168.

Farrington, D.P. (2004). Childhood origins of antisocial behavior. *Clinical Psychology and Psychotherapy, 12,* 177–190.

Fazel, S., Xenitidis, K., & Powell, J. (2008). The prevalence of intellectual disabilities among 12,000 prisoners—A systematic review. *International Journal of Law and Psychiatry, 31,* 369–373.

Glaser, W., & Deane, K. (1999). Normalisation in an abnormal world: a study of prisoners with an intellectual disability. *International Journal of Offender Therapy and Comparative Criminology, 43,* 338–356.

Glaser, W., & Florio, D. (2004). Beyond specialist programmes: a study of the needs of offenders with intellectual disability requiring psychiatric attention. *Journal of Intellectual Disability Research, 48,* 591–602.

Gudjonsson, G. (1984). Interrogative suggestibility: comparison between "False Confessors" and "Deniers" in criminal trials. *Medicine, Science and Law, 24,* 56.

Gudjonsson, G., Clare, I., Rutter, S., & Pearse, J. (1993). *Interviews in police custody: The identification of vulnerabilities* (No. 12). London: Royal Commission on Criminal Justice Research Study.

Hall, T.S. (2002). Legal fictions and moral reasoning: capital punishment and the mentally retarded offender after Penry v. Johnson. *Akron Law Review, 35,* 327–370.

Hayes, S.C. (1993). *People with an intellectual disability and the criminal justice system: appearances before local courts. Research Report 4*. Sydney: New South Wales Law Reform Commission.

Hayes, S.C. (1996). *People with an intellectual disability and the criminal justice system: Two rural courts* (No. 5). Sydney: New South Wales Law Reform Commission.

Hayes, S.C. (2000). *Hayes Ability Screening Index (HASI) manual*. Sydney, Australia: University of Sydney, Department of Behavioural Sciences in Medicine.

Hayes, S.C. (2004). *The relationship between childhood abuse, psychological symptoms and subsequent sex offending*. Paper presented at the International Association for the Scientific Study of Intellectual Disability 12th World Congress, Montpellier, France.

Hayes, S. (2007). Women with learning disabilities who offend: What do we know? *British Journal of Learning Disabilities, 35,* 187–191.

Hayes, S.C. (2010). Intellectual disability. In I. Freckelton & H. Selby (Eds.), *Expert evidence*. Melbourne, Australia: Thomson Reuters.

Hayes, S.C., & Craddock, G. (1992). *Simply criminal,* 2nd ed. Sydney, Australia: Federation Press.

Hayes, S.C., Levy, M., Vanny, K., & Greenberg, D. (2008). *Dual diagnosis of intellectual disability and mental illness in a court sample*. Paper presented at the International Association for the Scientific Study of Intellectual Disability, 13th World Congress.

Hayes, S.C., Shackell, P., Mottram, P., & Lancaster, R. (2007). Prevalence of intellectual disability in a major UK prison. *British Journal of Learning Disabilities, 35,* 162–167.

HM Prison Service (2010). *Female prisoners*. Retrieved from http://www.hmprisonservice.gov.uk/adviceandsupport/prison_life/femaleprisoners/

Hodgins, S. (1992). Mental disorder, intellectual disability and crime: Evidence from a birth cohort. *Archives of General Psychiatry, 49,* 476–483.

Hodgins, S., Mednick, S.A., Brennan, P.A., Shulsinger, F., & Engberg, M. (1996). Mental disorder and crime: Evidence from a Danish birth cohort. *Archives of General Psychiatry, 53,* 489–496.

Holland, A.J. (2004). Criminal behaviour and developmental disability: an epidemiological perspective. In W.R. Lindsay, J.L. Taylor, & P. Sturmey (Eds.), *Offenders with developmental disabilities* (pp. 23–34). Chichester, UK: John Wiley & Sons Ltd.

Holland, T., Clare, I.C.H., & Mukhopadhyay, T. (2002). Prevalence of "criminal offending" by men and women with intellectual disability and the characteristics of "offenders": Implications for research and service delivery. *Journal of Intellectual Disability Research, 46*(Suppl. I), 6–20.

Holland, A.J., & Koot, H. (1998). Mental health and intellectual disability: an international perspective. *Journal of Intellectual Disability Research, 42,* 505–512.

Jones, J. (2007). Persons with intellectual disabilities in the criminal justice system. Review of issues. *International Journal of Offender Therapy and Comparative Criminology, 51,* 723–733.

Kendall, K. (2004). Female offenders or alleged offenders with developmental disabilities: A critical overview. In W.R. Lindsay, J.L. Taylor, & P. Sturmey (Eds.), *Offenders with developmental disabilities* (pp. 265–303). Chichester, UK: John Wiley & Sons Ltd.

Kesteven, S. (2002). *Women who challenge: women offenders and mental health issues*. London: National Association for the Care and Resettlement of Offenders (NACRO).

Keyes, D., Edwards, W., & Perske, R. (2002). People with mental retardation are dying, legally: At least 44 have been executed. *Mental Retardation, 40,* 243–244.

Klimecki, M.R., Jenkinson, J., & Wilson, L. (1994). A study of recidivism among offenders with an intellectual disability. *Australia and New Zealand Journal of Developmental Disabilities, 19,* 209–219.

Lewis, K., & Hayes, S.C. (1997). Health of women ex-prisoners. *Psychiatry, Psychology and Law, 41,* 55–64.

Lewis, K., & Hayes, S.C. (1998). Intellectual functioning of women ex-prisoners. *Australian Journal of Forensic Sciences, 30*(1), 19–27.

Lindsay, W.R., Allan, R., Macleod, F., Smart, N., & Smith, A.H.W. (2003). Long term treatment and management of violent tendencies of men with intellectual disabilities. *Mental Retardation, 41,* 47–56.

Lindsay, W.R., Elliot, S.F., & Astell, A. (2004). Predictors of sexual offence recidivism in offenders with intellectual disabilities. *Journal of Applied Research in Intellectual Disabilities, 17,* 299–305.

Lindsay, W.R., Hastings, R.P., Griffiths, D.M., & Hayes, S.C. (2007). Trends and challenges in forensic research on offenders with intellectual disability. *Journal of Intellectual and Developmental Disability, 32,* 55–61.

Lindsay, W.R., & Holland, A. (2000). Changing services for offenders with intellectual disability. *Journal of Intellectual Disability Research, 44,* 367–368.

Lindsay, W.R., Holland, T., Wheeler, J.D.C., O'Brien, G., Taylor, J.L., Steptoe, L., Young, S. J. (2010). Pathways through services for offenders with intellectual disability: A one- and two-year follow-up study. *American Journal on Intellectual and Developmental Disabilities, 115,* 250–262.

Lindsay, W.R., Law, J., Quinn, K., Smart, N., & Smith, A. (2001). A comparison of physical and sexual abuse: Histories of sexual and non-sexual offenders with intellectual disability. *Child Abuse and Neglect, 25,* 989–995.

Lindsay, W.R., Smith, A.H.W., Quinn, K., Anderson, A., Smith, A., Allan, R., & Law, J. (2004). Women with intellectual disability who have offended: characteristics and outcome. *Journal of Intellectual Disability Research, 48,* 580–590.

Lunsky, Y. (2004). Suicidality in a clinical and community sample of adults with mental retardation. *Research in Developmental Disabilities, 25,* 231–243.

Lunsky, Y., & Palucka, A.M. (2004). Depression in intellectual disability. *Current Opinion in Psychiatry, 17,* 359–363.

McKenzie, K., & Paxton, D. (2006). Promoting access to services: the development of a new screening tool. *Learning Disability Practice, 9,* 17–21.

Mercier, C., & Crocker, A.G. (2011). The first critical steps through the criminal justice system for persons with intellectual disabilities. *British Journal of Learning Disabilities, 39*(2), 130–138.

Murphy, M., Harrold, M., Carey, S., & Mulrooney, M. (2000). *A survey of the level of learning disability among the prison population in Ireland.* Dublin: Irish Department of Justice, Equality and Law Reform.

Myers, F. (2004). *On the borderline? People with learning disabilities and/or autistic spectrum disorders in secure, forensic and other specialist settings.* Edinburgh, Scotland: Scottish Executive Social Research.

National Commission on Correctional Health Care. (1992). Mental health in correctional settings. Retrieved 27 September 2010 from http://www.ncchc.org/resources/statements/mentalhealth.html

New South Wales Law Reform Commission. (1996). *People with an intellectual disability and the criminal justice system* (No. 80). Sydney: New South Wales Law Reform Commission.

New South Wales Parliament. (1999). *First report of the inquiry into crime prevention through social support.* Sydney, Australia: NSW Parliamentary Standing Committee on Law and Justice.

Novaco, R.W., & Taylor, J.L. (2008). Anger and assaultiveness of male forensic patients with developmental disabilities: Links to volatile parents. *Aggressive Behavior, 34,* 380–393.

Nussbaum, D., Hancock, M., Turner, I., Arrowood, J., & Melodick, S. (2008). Fitness/competency to stand trial: A conceptual overview, review of existing instruments, and cross-validation of the Nussbaum Fitness Questionnaire. *Brief Treatment and Crisis Intervention, 8,* 43–72.

Parton, F., Day, A., & White, J. (2004). An empirical study on the relationship between intellectual ability and an understanding of the legal process in male remand prisoners. *Psychiatry, Psychology and Law, 11,* 96–109.

Petersilia, J.R. (1997a). *Criminal justice policies toward the mentally retarded are unjust and waste money. RAND Research Brief 4011. RAND Public Safety and Justice.* Retrieved from http://www.rand.org/pubs/research_briefs/RB4011.html

Petersilia, J.R. (1997b). Justice for all? Offenders with mental retardation and the California Corrections System. *Prison Journal, 77*(4), 358–380.

*R. v. Presser,* VR 45 (1958).

*R. v. Pritchard,* 7 C & P 303 (1836).

Raina, P., & Lunsky, Y. (2010). A comparison study of adults with intellectual disability and psychiatric disorder with and without forensic involvement. *Research in Developmental Disabilities, 31,* 218–223.

Salekin, K.L., Olley, J.G., & Hedge, K. (2010). Offenders with intellectual disability: Characteristics, prevalence, and issues in forensic assessment. *Journal of Mental Health Research in Intellectual Disabilities, 3,* 97–116.

Shaffer D, Fisher P, Lucas C, Comer J. (2000). *Scoring Manual diagnostic interview Schedule for Children (DISC-IV).* New York, NY: Columbia University, New York State Psychiatric Institute.

Simons, K. (2000). *Life on the edge. The experiences of people with learning disability who do not use specialist services.* Brighton, UK: Pavilion Publishing/Joseph Rowntree Foundation.

Simpson, M.K., & Hogg, J. (2001). Patterns of offending among people with intellectual disability: A systematic review. Part II: Predisposing factors. *Journal of Intellectual Disability Research, 45,* 397–406.

Sondenaa, E., Nottestad, J., & Bjorgen, T.G. (2007). Validation of the Norwegian version of Hayes Ability Screening Index for mental retardation. *Psychological Reports, 101,* 1023–1030.

Sondenaa, E., Rasmussen, K., Palmstierna, T., & Nottestad, J. (2008). The prevalence and nature of intellectual disability in Norwegian prisons. *Journal of Intellectual Disability Research, 52,* 1129–1137.

Taylor, P.J., Leese, M., Williams, D., Butwell, M., Daly, R., & Larkin, E. (1998). Mental disorder and violence. A special (high security) hospital study. *British Journal of Psychiatry, 172,* 218–226.

Vanny, K., Levy, M.H., Greenberg, D.M., & Hayes, S.C. (2009). Mental illness and intellectual disability in Magistrates Courts in New South Wales, Australia. *Journal of Intellectual Disability Research, 53,* 289–297.

Vanny, K., Levy, M., & Hayes, S. (2008). People with an intellectual disability in the Australian criminal justice system. *Psychiatry, Psychology and Law, 25,* 261–271.

# The Death Penalty, the Courts, and Intellectual Disabilities

**CHAPTER 13**

*J. Gregory Olley*

In 2002, the U.S. Supreme Court in *Atkins v. Virginia* found in a 6–3 decision that the execution of people with intellectual disability (ID, still known in most state statutes as mental retardation) violates the Eighth Amendment's prohibition of cruel and unusual punishment. Although this decision was widely praised in the disability community and widely debated in the legal community, courts of the 37 states, the federal government, and the U.S. military, which have capital punishment, faced a need to clarify the standards by which the decision would be implemented. Since the *Atkins* decision, many psychologists, psychiatrists, and other experts in developmental disabilities have worked as individuals and in collaboration with other individuals and organizations to clarify the scientific and clinical basis on which expert witnesses could testify to the diagnosis of mental retardation in *Atkins* hearings. This chapter reviews the progress that has been made by the field of psychology and related disciplines in this effort.

In *Atkins*, Justice John Paul Stevens wrote for the majority. His statement describing the basis for the majority decision is a good summary of the characteristics of ID that led the court to its decision: "they have diminished capacities to understand and process information, to communicate, to abstract from mistakes and learn from experience, and engage in logical reasoning, to control impulses, and to understand the reactions of others" (*Atkins v. Virginia*, 2002).

It is emphasized that this decision simply removed the death penalty from consideration, and people with ID are still responsible for their actions. If convicted of a capital crime, most individuals will serve life in prison. Although the *Atkins* decision was in some ways groundbreaking, for many years people with ID have been regarded as less culpable for their crimes. In Wickham's (2002) article, "Conceptions of Idiocy in Colonial Massachusetts," she noted that the colonial law absolved "idiots" of guilt in capital cases and that this law was "traced directly to English statute...." She further cited Walker (1968) who noted that "English laws have incorporated modifications that take into account a criminal offender's mental state as far back as the tenth century. What might be the earliest record of a case brought before the king was described as 'an idiot who [in 1212] is in the prison

This chapter is an expanded and significantly adapted version of Olley (2010).

because in his witlessness he confessed that he is a thief, although in fact he is not to blame'" (p. 939).

Before *Atkins*, 18 states had statutes banning the death penalty for people with mental retardation. In the remaining states that had a death penalty, ID could be presented as a potentially mitigating factor in the sentencing phase of a capital trial. Thus, *Atkins* served to codify views that had become increasingly common in state legislatures and in the courts.

In 2005, the Division on Intellectual and Developmental Disabilities of the American Psychological Association formed a Committee on Mental Retardation and the Death Penalty. The committee's members and other scholars and expert witnesses responded to *Atkins* in several ways. They wrote articles and presented at meetings of attorneys, forensic psychologists, and colleagues specializing in developmental disabilities. They also conducted evaluations of individual defendants, which led to court testimony regarding their diagnoses. The testimony and the resulting court decisions have contributed to progress in clarifying the validity of procedures for making this diagnosis in capital cases. However, there is much to be done.

This chapter summarizes progress in three categories. First, psychologists have a large body of research and clinical findings on ID that go back far before the *Atkins* decision. In other words, a great deal of relevant information existed before *Atkins*, and that information should be applied in *Atkins* hearings. Second, *Atkins* hearings have pushed some issues into the spotlight that might otherwise have received less attention. The following pages summarize what has been learned so far from *Atkins*. Third, there is much that needs to be learned, and the final section emphasizes the challenges that remain.

## WHY ARE *ATKINS* CASES SO CHALLENGING?

Although there are decades of psychological research on the nature of mild ID, established clinical procedures for diagnosis, and a definition of ID that is widely accepted, translating what is known in customary research and clinical settings to the adversarial setting of the courtroom can be very difficult. Most clinical assessment procedures are used to determine the best services for the individual. These procedures are employed to examine strengths, weaknesses, and preferences and to present complex findings.

Clinicians and researchers work collaboratively and openly. Science shares objective information and usually progresses in small increments. Researchers acknowledge positive and negative findings and live comfortably with shades of gray.

Courtroom testimony, however, is presented in the adversarial context of defense and prosecution, and the court must produce a decision. It is a world of black and white with little tolerance for gray. The expert in ID who offers expert court testimony may present information using the same approach he or she would use to present clinical or research findings and fail to appreciate the court's rules of evidence. On the positive side, the court does welcome scientific evidence. Different states embrace either the *Daubert* (*Daubert v. Merrell Dow Pharmaceuticals*, 1993) or *Frye* (*Frye v. United States*, 1923) standard for evidence presented by experts. The *Frye* standard requires that the evidence be widely accepted in the field. The more stringent *Daubert* standard requires that the evidence be supported by scientific findings.

## Information Already Known

Whether the expert is hired by the prosecution or the defense, it is his or her ethical responsibility to present information objectively (Committee on the Revision of the Specialty Guidelines for Forensic Psychology, 2011). Thus, it is essential that one knows and relies upon the established research on ID. The list of established findings that are relevant to *Atkins* is long, but a few examples may make the point.

First, psychological research over many years has identified numerous characteristics that are common, although not universal, in individuals with mild ID (Snell & Luckasson, 2009). I emphasize this group because they are the people who are most vulnerable to engaging in criminal activities. They are the most likely to be receiving no supports or services or to have never received a diagnosis of ID. They are the people who received special education services while in school but became invisible to human services providers as soon as they left school. They are the people who qualified for school services in the category of educable mental retardation but instead were classified as students with learning disabilities due to legal and social pressure on school systems.

Nevertheless, they are likely to have the characteristics of impulsiveness, responsiveness to immediate rather than long-term consequences, naïveté, gullibility, poor problem solving, and, of course, low intelligence. In addition, they are likely to come from backgrounds of social and economic deprivation and families with generations of similar problems.

Second, the work of Siperstein and his colleagues (Siperstein, Norins, Corbin, & Shriver, 2003) has shown that in many countries, including the United States, the public generally misunderstands mild ID and expects that such individuals are easy to identify by their physical appearance, their speech, or other readily apparent characteristics. This misunderstanding is common in court, and the expert witness must clarify for the court the fact that mild ID typically presents no obvious physical signs and that such individuals have many areas of competence to accompany areas of impairment (American Association on Intellectual and Developmental Disabilities, 2010).

Third, the most widely accepted definitions of ID are quite similar. The American Association on Intellectual and Developmental Disabilities (2010) and the American Psychiatric Association (2000) definitions require the same elements for a diagnosis: significant impairment in intelligence and adaptive functioning, both of which originate in childhood. Although there are differences in their descriptions of areas of adaptive behavior, the definitions are conceptually similar.

Fourth, there are well-established standards for the administration and interpretation of intelligence tests and related measures (American Educational Research Association, American Psychological Association, & National Council on Measurement in Education, 1999). These standards help to specify the reliability and validity of tests that may be relied on for diagnosis and guide us in interpretation by taking into consideration factors such as the standard error of measurement of the test and the possible influence of the practice effect. Reliance on such standards is important, because the states affected by the *Atkins* decision often do not have sufficiently detailed statutes that specify standards for test administration.

Fifth, clinicians and others who have personal experience with people with mild ID readily find that these individuals eschew the label of mental retardation. The anthropologist Robert Edgerton (1967, 1993) has called this phenomenon of attempting to hide one's limitations the "cloak of competence." This finding is very important in *Atkins* cases because those not familiar with it may assume that people will eagerly try to fake the condition of mental retardation in order to avoid the death penalty. In fact, this author has found that even with their lives at stake, many defendants will try to do their best on tests and often to exaggerate their accomplishments in order to avoid the stigma of mental retardation.

Sixth and related to the point cited, research has identified many pitfalls in interviewing people with ID (Finlay & Lyons, 2001, 2002; Perry, 2004). Although an interview of the defendant is a customary part of an *Atkins* evaluation or any evaluation related to the diagnosis of ID, one must be aware of many ways in which the self-report of the defendant may be inaccurate. Interviews may be influenced by the communication limitations of the defendant (e.g., difficulty understanding the questions, particularly those of a conceptual nature, or difficulty responding to open-ended questions) or the tendency to try to hide one's limitations (i.e., the cloak of competence).

Seventh, the relationship between the conditions of poverty and mild ID are well established (Hurley, 1969), especially when such conditions are experienced in early childhood (Center on the Developing Child, 2008). Investigation of the background and history of *Atkins* defendants can be tragically sad as one documents the environmental deprivation and family history of limited education, unemployment, criminal activity, neglect, and abuse. These conditions contribute to ID. A failure to understand this relationship sometimes leads to misguided court testimony in which it is argued that these conditions are the cause of the defendant's limitations, and, thus, the diagnosis of mental retardation cannot be made. In fact, these conditions are such a familiar pattern that mild ID has historically been referred to as "cultural familial mental retardation."

Eighth, ID can coexist with mental health problems. Awareness of these "dual diagnoses" has increased in recent years leading to the publication of a diagnostic manual (Fletcher, Loschen, Stavrakaki, & First, 2007) and the *Journal of Mental Health Research in Intellectual Disabilities*. An understanding of dual diagnoses is important because it may be mistakenly argued in court that the defendant has a mental illness diagnosis that rules out mental retardation.

Ninth, Stephen Greenspan has argued for many years that a central characteristic of ID is naïveté or gullibility (e.g., Greenspan, Loughlin, & Black, 2001). Thus, people with mild ID are easily led into criminal activities and are very limited in their ability to deal with the criminal justice system. It is shocking to learn how poorly the general public understands their *Miranda* rights (Rogers, 2008) and how readily police interrogation techniques can induce innocent people to confess to murder (Kassin, 2005; Kolker, 2010). These vulnerabilities are even greater for people with ID (Perske, 2008).

Tenth, it is important to note that a clinical evaluation emphasizes strengths in order to plan services that capitalize upon those strengths to promote success. An evaluation for the court is focused on deficits because its purpose is to determine a diagnosis, and an ID is, by definition, a condition characterized by deficits. As noted earlier, people with mild ID are a heterogeneous group with individual profiles of relative strengths and weaknesses. One cannot argue that the presence of a particular strength rules out ID, particularly if it is a strength shared with others with ID. In fact, the American Psychiatric Association (2000) definition of mental retardation specifically stated that there is no exclusion criterion for the diagnosis. Thus, neither having a mental illness, nor a learning disability, nor antisocial personality disorder, nor various other diagnoses excludes a diagnosis of ID. In a similar way, accomplishments such as driving a car, having a job, being married, and having friends do not rule out ID, although these arguments, and many others, have been made in court.

A final example of established knowledge that is relevant to *Atkins* comes not from the literature on developmental disabilities but from a classic book on social psychology research. Webb, Campbell, Schwartz, Sechrest, and Grove (1981) addressed the problem of research that relies on only one method. They specifically noted the limitations of interview and questionnaire methods and encouraged data collection using "nonreactive" methods. In light of the dependence on interviews in *Atkins* evaluations, Webb et al.'s warning should be carefully examined. "Interviews … intrude as a foreign element into the social setting they would describe, they create as well as measure attitudes, they elicit atypical roles and responses, they are limited to those who are accessible and will cooperate, and the responses obtained are produced in part by dimensions of individual differences irrelevant to the topic at hand" (p. 1). Their proposed solution is one very applicable to *Atkins* evaluations. "No research method is without bias. Interviews … must be supplemented by methods testing the same social science variable but having different methodological weaknesses" (p. 1).

## THINGS LEARNED FROM *ATKINS* HEARINGS

*Atkins* hearings have brought increased attention to some issues that had previously seemed less important. A few examples follow.

### The Flynn Effect

The best example of this increased attention is the Flynn effect. Flynn (1984, 2007) pointed out the rise of IQ scores over many years in countries around the world. The existence of this phenomenon is not particularly controversial. After all, norms do become out of date, and IQ tests are renormed every 10 or 15 years to make current scores more reflective of the general population. The issue that is often argued in court is whether the Flynn effect should be taken into consideration when interpreting the scores of individuals. The literature on this topic indicates that on average scores rise about 0.3 points per year. Therefore, for an IQ test normed 10 years ago, the mean score for the population is now 103, rather than 100. Many courts have accepted Flynn's (2009) argument that inferring from the general population to an individual is something that psychological testing does regularly and that, although it is an approximation, applying the Flynn effect to the score of an individual leads to a more accurate understanding of the person's general intelligence.

Given the adversarial nature of court proceedings, it is not surprising that this issue continues to spark debate in the courtroom and in professional journals. For example, Hagan, Drogin, and Guilmette (2008, 2010) have acknowledged that the Flynn effect is a valid scientific finding but have argued that adjusting IQ scores to take this phenomenon into account is not customary practice and is too imprecise to be appropriate in court. They have taken the position that the Flynn effect varies depending upon the test used, the age of the test taker, and other factors. Cunningham and Tassé (2010) have supported taking the Flynn effect into consideration and cited studies showing that the effect holds in the range of scores that are most often at issue in *Atkins* cases (about IQ 70–80). Some of these differences may be semantic, because Hagan et al. (2008, 2010) and Cunningham and Tassé (2010) agreed that rising test scores should be considered but disagree regarding the terms score "adjustment" or "correction."

Kevin McGrew has created a blog that is a remarkable resource for information on *Atkins* cases and the associated literature. Among other topics, he has compiled a nearly complete bibliography of articles on the Flynn effect and has written several blog posts on this topic (http://www.atkinsmrdeathpenalty.com).

## Malingering

Supreme Court Justice Antonin Scalia, in his dissenting opinion in *Atkins*, expressed concern "that the symptoms of this condition can readily be feigned" (*Atkins v. Virginia*, 2002) and that the decision would result in a flood of appeals by death row inmates. With regard to his first concern, research by Salekin and Doane (2009) has shown that the few instruments used to identify malingered ID lack acceptable validity. Considering this limitation and the general reluctance of people with low intelligence to embrace the label "mental retardation," the prevalence of malingering in *Atkins* cases is unknown. Fortunately, the requirement that the characteristics of ID be present in childhood serves to identify people who feign ID in adulthood but lack a history of impaired functioning.

With regard to Justice Scalia's second concern, Blume, Johnson, and Seeds (2009) reviewed the *Atkins* cases that had been ruled on in the 6 years following the 2002 decision. They found that only about 7% of death row inmates filed *Atkins* claims, and nearly 40% resulted in a decision supporting those claims (although the success rate has varied widely among states). Thus, contrary to Justice Scalia's prediction, *Atkins* has not resulted in a flood of frivolous claims.

As a practical matter, an *Atkins* evaluation must consider the possibility of malingering, but the best way to do that is unclear. One can cite Salekin and Doane (2009) and argue not to use tests that have been shown to be invalid for this purpose. In this case, one must rely on the defendant's history of functioning since childhood and trust the examiner's judgment about how much effort the defendant put into testing. As an alternative, the examiner may use an instrument such as the Test of Memory Malingering (Tombaugh, 1996), a test of memory for pictures. Research by Hurley and Deal (2006) suggested that most people with mild ID should score very high on this test, indicating that they are showing good effort. On the other hand, some people with mild ID are genuinely deficient in their memory for pictures, and a low score could be mistakenly identified as malingering or intentional lack of effort.

### Retrospective Evaluation

*Atkins* evaluations are, by their nature, retrospective. Experts are being asked to determine intellectual functioning in childhood, at the time of the crime, and, in some cases, currently. Perhaps the most extreme example of retrospective assessment came quite recently. On January 7, 2011, Governor Bill Ritter of Colorado granted a full and unconditional posthumous pardon to Joe Arridy who was convicted of killing a 15-year-old girl, sentenced to death, and executed by lethal gas 7 decades ago. The governor's press release indicated that

> Arridy, who had an I.Q. of 46 and behaved more like a child than a man, confessed to the 1936 sexual assault and murder of Dorothy Drain in Pueblo. Drain and her sister were found in their home, both having been attacked with a hatchet. But an overwhelming body of evidence indicates the 23-year-old Arridy was innocent, including false and coerced confessions, the likelihood that Arridy was not in Pueblo at the time of the killing, and an admission of guilt by someone else (Office of Governor Bill Ritter, Jr., 2011).

The treatment of people with ID by our justice system has progressed greatly since 1936, but it is still a challenge to look back in time to diagnose this disability.

### Intelligence

Retrospective assessment of intelligence depends on the availability of good records. If no earlier testing took place, or if school records are missing or incomplete, a valid IQ from childhood cannot be obtained. It is fortunate that the diagnostic criteria of the American Association on Intellectual and Developmental Disabilities make clear in the current (2010) manual and in earlier manuals that a measured IQ is not necessary for diagnosis. It is sufficient to demonstrate that the individual showed impaired functioning in childhood. Reschly (2009) described many of the complexities of establishing impaired functioning in childhood.

Even if IQ scores from childhood can be found in school or other records, recent experience in *Atkins* hearings has placed greater scrutiny on specific tests, circumstances of their administration, and qualifications of the examiner. Furthermore, although the Wechsler scales continue to be the most widely used individually administered intelligence tests, the *Atkins* decision has called attention to the theory of intelligence that underlies such tests. In all contemporary IQ tests, the Cattell–Horn–Carroll theory has influenced test construction, and the extent to which the test reflects this theory provides evidence for the acceptability of the test (Benson, Hulac, & Kranzler, 2010). McGrew's blog, noted earlier, is an excellent source of information for assessing the psychometric strength of intelligence tests.

### Adaptive Functioning

Perhaps because intelligence can be assessed with reasonable validity in a matter or minutes, the second requirement for a diagnosis of ID, impaired adaptive functioning, has taken a back seat to IQ in most discussions of ID diagnosis. Nevertheless, ID cannot be diagnosed without evidence of impairment in everyday functioning. Rating scales of adaptive behavior, such as the Adaptive Behavior Assessment System, Second Edition (Harrison & Oakland, 2003) are the most common method for assessing adaptive behavior. Although tests of adaptive behavior are reasonably correlated with practical skills, such as employment (Su, Lin, Wu, & Chen, 2008) and community independence (Woolf, Woolf, & Oakland, 2010), they should be supplemented with other information in *Atkins* evaluations (Olley & Cox, 2008). Missing IQ scores or scores that fall very close to the IQ 70 cutoff shift the emphasis of the evaluation to adaptive behavior. It is emphasized that impairment in adaptive behavior is not the same as the maladaptive behavior that is the focus of this volume. The American Association on Intellectual and Developmental Disabilities diagnostic manual (2010) makes clear that the two types of behavior are poorly correlated and maladaptive behavior should not be used to prove deficits in adaptive behavior.

On a similar note, the assessment of adaptive deficits is about deficits. As noted earlier, evidence of isolated examples of adaptive functioning does not disprove ID. Although the American Association on Intellectual and Developmental Disabilities manual (2010) clearly stated that people with mild ID are likely to have areas of adequate functioning, courts have mistakenly accepted examples of competent functioning to show that the defendant does not have an ID. Examples include knowing what days of the week the defendant could have visitors, having long-term gainful employment, being able to drive, passing the driver's test, and even being able to steal a television. As an even more extreme example, judges have relied on their own ability to diagnose ID on the basis of what they observe in court. In the case of James Lee Henderson, "The trial judge also explicitly relied upon his personal knowledge and recollection of Henderson's in-court demeanor during both the trial and [the state court] *habeas* hearing" (*Henderson v. Quarterman*, 2008).

The customary instruments used for diagnosis of ID are designed to assess current functioning. Thus, in looking back in time, the advice of Webb et al. (1981) to rely on as many sources as possible will help achieve consensual validity. Many *Atkins* evaluations in the first years after the decision relied on the available records, an interview of the defendant, and little else. More recent evaluations have been, in my experience, much more comprehensive. This is a good trend, but it raises a question of which sources of information are most valid. For instance, is information gathered in prison valid for a diagnosis of current or past functioning? The definition of adaptive behavior (American Association on Intellectual and Developmental Disabilities, 2010) is functioning in one's community, so functioning in the restricted circumstances of prison would appear to have limited value. Tests of knowledge administered in jail or prison have similar limitations. There is no assurance that knowledge of adaptive functioning results in adaptive community behavior.

Is the self-report of defendants with known low intelligence a valid source? As noted earlier, substantial research on interviewing people with low intelligence should make one very cautious in interpreting this information (Finlay & Lyons, 2001, 2002; Perry, 2004).

Parents are the most common source of adaptive behavior information. Are parents automatically biased and assumed to provide false information indicating low functioning, or do parents show bias toward exaggerated accomplishments and want their children and their family to appear in the best light? Or is every case different, and is the clinical experience of the expert an essential component of a valid evaluation? This author votes for the latter.

Although the best source of information is not always clear, sometimes the worst source is. It is inappropriate and clearly invalid to ask a family member, friend, or other lay witness, "Do you think he has mental retardation?"

## Interpreting Multiple Scores

*Atkins* cases typically offer mixed evidence for a diagnosis of ID, including a history of several IQ tests and academic achievement tests at different periods and with variable scores. Looking at this information from its black-or-white viewpoint, the court wants to know, which is the "true IQ" or the "true" level of academic functioning? Although academic performance would be expected to go up with each year of schooling, IQ is generally regarded as a stable trait. Nevertheless, scores can vary in puzzling ways.

The gray world of science acknowledges that there are many reasons that scores vary. Whitaker (2008) provided a clear discussion of the many factors influencing IQ score variability and noted that variability is greater in low IQ ranges than in the average range. In his meta-analysis of studies of the stability of low IQ, he found that for most individuals IQ remained fairly stable, but "14% of IQs changed by 10 points or more" on retesting. In a later study of people with low IQ, Whitaker (2010) concluded that "for low Full Scale IQs the WAIS-III can only be considered accurate to within 18 points above the measured IQ and 28 points below, and the WISC-IV to 16 points below the measured IQ and 25 points above it" (p. 517). This range is considerably larger than the standard error of measurement associated with IQ tests. These findings make it very difficult to assess IQ retrospectively in *Atkins* cases.

The exact reason(s) for score variability in any single case may not be certain, but taking the mean of several IQ scores is statistically inaccurate, although it has been done and accepted by courts in several *Atkins* cases.

## Evaluating Non–English-Speaking Defendants

Awareness of cross-cultural factors in research and clinical practice has greatly increased in recent years (Byrne et al., 2009). However, in *Atkins* cases, the evaluation of non–English-speaking defendants presents several challenges with regard to both IQ and adaptive functioning. For a person who lived most of his or her life in another country and culture, what norm group should be used to judge an adaptive functioning deficit? For IQ measurement, it is clear that an IQ test should be administered in the defendant's native language and not in English or with an interpreter. However, what is the appropriate test and norm group? Most non–English-speaking defendants in *Atkins* cases have been Spanish speaking, and there are several IQ tests in Spanish. Suen and Greenspan (2009) pointed out problems with the use of the Mexican WAIS. Kevin McGrew, mentioned earlier, is one of the authors of a more appropriate test, the Batería III Woodcock-Muñoz (Woodcock, Muñoz-Sandoval, McGrew, & Mather, 2010), which includes in its normative sample individuals living in the United States but raised in various Spanish-speaking countries.

## MORE INFORMATION IS NEEDED

Although psychologists and other experts in ID have successfully translated some of the extensive research and clinical base to the unfamiliar territory of the courtroom and have used the timely circumstances of *Atkins* to clarify new issues, much work remains. For instance, Haney and Specter (2001) have pointed out the special challenges in adjustment to prison life faced by people with developmental disabilities, but little is known about the specific, long-term effects of incarceration on people of low intelligence. For example, is there impairment or improvement in IQ? Is it possible that the environment of prison with healthy meals, access to exercise, social interaction, and the absence of street drugs and alcohol is actually an intellectually beneficial setting?

Perhaps the years since the *Atkins* decision have produced more questions than answers regarding the best implementation of this landmark case. The challenges will continue, but this author is confident that psychologists will provide leadership to assist the courts in the best application of science and clinical practice in *Atkins* decisions. Toward this end I recommend that information and skills related to forensic practice be a part of the training for all psychologists, especially those in applied areas. Few psychologists anticipate testifying in court, but the reality is that nearly all will testify at some time. They must be prepared to present the best science and practice to assist the court and to understand the role that they will play in the courtroom and the ways in which it differs from the customary clinical or research role. The specific skills needed for testimony in *Atkins* cases should be addressed in continuing education opportunities for psychologists and are described more fully in Olley (2009).

## REFERENCES

American Association on Intellectual and Developmental Disabilities. (2010). *ID: Definition, classification, and systems of supports* (11th ed.). Washington, DC: Author.
American Educational Research Association, American Psychological Association, & National Council on Measurement in Education. (1999). *Standards for educational and psychological testing*. Washington, DC: AERA.

American Psychiatric Association. (2000). *Diagnostic and statistical manual of mental disorders* (4th ed., text rev.). Washington, DC: Author.

*Atkins v Virginia*, 536 U.S. 304 (2002).

Benson, N., Hulac, D.M., & Kranzler, J.H. (2010). Independent examination of the Wechsler Adult Intelligence Scale–Fourth Edition (WAIS-IV): What does the WAIS-IV measure? *Psychological Assessment, 22,* 121–130.

Blume, J.H., Johnson, S.L., & Seeds, C. (2009). An empirical look at *Atkins v. Virginia* and its application in capital cases. *Tennessee Law Review, 76,* 625–639. Retrieved September 15, 2010, from the Social Science Research Network Web site: http://ssrn.com/abstract=1473806

Byrne, B.M., Oakland, T., Leong, F.T.L., van de Vijver, F.J.R., Hambleton, R.K., Cheung, F.M., & Bartram, D. (2009). A critical analysis of cross-cultural research and testing practices: Implications for improved education and training in psychology. *Training and Education in Professional Psychology, 3,* 94–105.

Center on the Developing Child. (2008). In brief: The impact of early adversity on children's development. Cambridge, MA: Harvard University. Retrieved September 15, 2010, from the Harvard Center on the Developing Child Web site: http://www.developingchild.harvard.edu/content/downloads/inbrief-adversity.pdf

Committee on the Revision of the Specialty Guidelines for Forensic Psychology. (2011). Specialty guidelines for forensic psychology. Retrieved September 9, 2011, from American Psychology-Law Society Web site: http://www.ap-ls.org/aboutpsychlaw.SGFP_Final_Approved_2011.pdf

Cunningham, M.D., & Tassé, M.J. (2010). Looking to science rather than convention in adjusting IQ scores when death is at issue. *Professional Psychology: Research and Practice, 41,* 1–7.

*Daubert v. Merrell Dow Pharmaceuticals*, 509 U.S. 579 (1993).

Edgerton, R.B. (1967). *The cloak of competence: Stigma in the lives of the mentally retarded*. Berkeley: University of California Press.

Edgerton, R.B. (1993). *The cloak of competence: Revised and updated*. Berkeley: University of California Press.

Finlay, W.M.L., & Lyons, E. (2001). Methodological issues in interviewing and using self-report questionnaires with people with mental retardation. *Psychological Assessment, 13,* 319–335.

Finlay, W.M.L., & Lyons, E. (2002). Acquiescence in interviews with people who have mental retardation. *Mental Retardation, 40,* 14–29.

Fletcher, R., Loschen, E., Stavrakaki, C., & First, M. (Eds.). (2007). *Diagnostic manual—ID (DM-ID): A textbook of diagnosis of mental disorders in persons with ID*. Kingston, NY: NADD Press.

Flynn, J.R. (1984). The mean IQ of Americans: Massive gains 1932 to 1978. *Psychological Bulletin, 95,* 29–51.

Flynn, J.R. (2007). *What is intelligence?* New York: Cambridge University Press.

Flynn, J.R. (2009). The WAIS-III and WAIS-IV: Daubert motions favor the certainly false over the approximately true. *Applied Neuropsychology, 16,* 98–104.

*Frye v. United States 293 F.* 1013 (DC Cir. 1923).

Greenspan, S., Loughlin, G., & Black, R.S. (2001). Credulity and gullibility in persons with developmental disorders: A framework for future research. In L.M. Glidden (Ed.), *International review of research in mental retardation* (vol. 24, pp. 101–135). San Diego: Academic Press.

Hagan, L.D., Drogin, E.Y., & Guilmette, T.J. (2008). Adjusting IQ scores for the Flynn Effect: Consistent with the standard of practice? *Professional Psychology: Research and Practice, 39,* 619–625.

Hagan, L.D., Drogin, E.Y., & Guilmette, T.J. (2010). Science rather than advocacy when reporting IQ scores. *Professional Psychology: Research and Practice, 41,* 420–423.

Haney, C., & Specter, D. (2001). Vulnerable offenders and the law: Treatment rights in uncertain legal times. In J. Ashford, B. Sales, & W. Reid (Eds.), *Treating adult and juvenile offenders with special needs* (pp. 51–79). Washington, DC: American Psychological Association.

Harrison, P.L., & Oakland, T. (2003). *Adaptive Behavior Assessment System* (2nd ed.). San Antonio, TX: Psychological Corporation.

*Henderson v. Quarterman*, U.S.D.C, E.D. Tex., Civil Action No. 1:06-CV-507 (filed Mar. 31, 2008), slip op. at pg. 10.

Hurley, K.E., & Deal, W.P. (2006). Assessment instruments measuring malingering used with individuals who have mental retardation: Potential problems and issues. *Mental Retardation, 44,* 112–119.

Hurley, R.L. (1969). *Poverty and mental retardation: A causal relationship*. New York: Vintage.

Kassin, S.M. (2005). On the psychology of confessions: Does innocence put innocents at risk? *American Psychologist, 60,* 215–228.

Kolker, R. (October 3, 2010). "I did it." Why do people confess to crimes they didn't commit? *New York Magazine*. Retrieved November 10, 2011, from Downloaded 11-10-2010 from http://nymag.com/news/crimelaw/68715

Office of Governor Bill Ritter, Jr. (2011, January 7). *Gov. Ritter grants posthumous pardon in case dating back to 1930s* [Press release]. Retrieved from http://www.scribd.com/doc/46754541/Arridy-Press-Release

Olley, J.G. (2010, Fall). The death penalty, the courts, and what we have learned about intellectual disability. *Psychology in Intellectual and Developmental Disabilities, 36*(2), 2-5.

Olley, J.G. (2009). Knowledge and experience required for experts in *Atkins* cases. *Applied Neuropsychology, 16,* 135–140.

Olley, J.G., & Cox, A.W. (2008). Assessment of adaptive behavior in adult forensic cases: The use of the Adaptive Behavior Assessment System-II. In T. Oakland & P.L. Harrison (Eds.), *Adaptive Behavior Assessment System-II: Clinical use and interpretation* (pp. 381–398). San Diego: Elsevier.

Perry, J. (2004). Interviewing people with intellectual disabilities. In E. Emerson, C. Hatton, T. Thompson & T.R. Parmenter (Eds.), *International handbook of applied research in intellectual disabilities* (pp. 115–131). West Sussex, England: Wiley.

Perske, R. (2008). False confessions from 53 persons with intellectual disabilities: The list keeps growing. *Intellectual and Developmental Disabilities, 46,* 468–479.

Reschly, D.J. (2009). Documenting the developmental origins of mild mental retardation. *Applied Neuropsychology, 16,* 124–134.

Rogers, R. (2008). A little knowledge is a dangerous thing...Emerging *Miranda* research and professional roles for psychologists. *American Psychologist, 63,* 776–787.

Salekin, K.L. & Doane, B.M. (2009). Malingering ID: The value of available measures and methods. *Applied Neuropsychology, 16,* 105–113.

Siperstein, G.N., Norins, J., Corbin, S., & Shriver, T. (2003). *Multinational study of attitudes toward individuals with intellectual disabilities: General findings and call to action.* Washington, DC: Special Olympics.

Snell, M.E., & Luckasson, R., Borthwick-Duffy, S., Bradley, V., Buntinx, W.H.E., Coulter, D.L., . . . Yeager, M.H.. (2009). Characteristics and needs of people with ID who have higher IQs. *Intellectual and Developmental Disabilities, 47,* 220–233.

Su, C.Y., Lin, Y.H., Wu, Y.Y., & Chen, C.C. (2008). The role of cognition and adaptive behavior in employment of people with mental retardation. *Research in Developmental Disabilities, 29,* 83–95.

Suen, H.K., & Greenspan, S. (2009). Serious problems with the Mexican norms for the WAIS-III when assessing mental retardation in capital cases. *Applied Neuropsychology, 16,* 214–222.

Tombaugh, T.N. (1996). *Test of Memory Malingering.* Tonawanda, NY: Multi-Health Systems.

Walker, N. (1968). Crime and insanity in England: The historical perspective (vol. 1). Edinburgh, Scotland: University Press. Cited by Wickham (2002).

Webb, E.T., Campbell, D.T., Schwartz, R.D., Sechrest, L., & Grove, J.B. (1981). *Nonreactive measures in the social sciences* (2nd ed.). Boston: Houghton Mifflin.

Whitaker, S. (2008). The stability of IQ in people with low intellectual ability: An analysis of the literature. *Intellectual and Developmental Disabilities, 46,* 120–128.

Whitaker, S. (2010). Error in the estimation of intellectual ability in the low range using the WISC-IV and WAIS-III. *Personality and Individual Differences, 48,* 517–521.

Wickham, P. (2002). Conceptions of idiocy in colonial Massachusetts. *Journal of Social History, 35,* 935–954.

Woodcock, R.W., Muñoz-Sandoval, A.F., McGrew, K.S., & Mather, N. (2010). *Batería III Woodcock-Muñoz.* Rolling Meadows, IL: Riverside Publishing Co.

Woolf, S., Woolf, C. M., & Oakland, T. (2010). Adaptive behavior among adults with intellectual disabilities and its relationship to community independence. *Intellectual and Developmental Disabilities, 48,* 209–215.

# SECTION VI

# Therapeutic (Physical) Restraint

# Therapeutic Implementation of Physical Restraint

*James K. Luiselli*

CHAPTER

Physical restraint (PR) is sometimes required with people who have intellectual and developmental disabilities (IDD) (Harris, 1996; Luiselli, 2009; Matson & Boisjoli, 2009). Different names have been used to describe PR, for example, movement suppression (Rolider, Williams, Cummings, & Van Houten, 1991), response immobilization (Bitgood, Crowe, Suarez, & Peters, 1980), and protective holding (Luiselli, Dunn, & Pace, 2005). Regardless of terminology, PR is applied in the same way: one or more people, typically trained care providers, restrict another person's movement contingent on behaviors that pose a threat to self (self-injury), others (aggression), and the environment (property destruction). Care providers implement PR by holding a person's arms, legs, and torso in a standing, sitting, or supine position. Of note, prone, or "face-down" PR, has been prohibited in many settings because it has been linked to deaths caused by positional asphyxia and ventilation compromise (Mohr & Mohr, 2000; O'Halloran & Frank, 2000; Weiss, 1998).

One indication for using PR in a clinical context is to control and manage crisis events. For example, an adolescent with IDD may occasionally have a disruptive episode in which he hits care providers, throws objects, and seriously upsets his surroundings. Because the episode was dangerous and unexpected, care providers may have to apply PR as an *emergency* intervention to keep the adolescent safe and to stop the disruptive episode. Many professionals and regulatory agencies, in fact, advocate that PR should only be permitted in emergency situations (see Chapter 16, this volume).

However, PR can also be considered a strategic intervention procedure that, when implemented as one component of a comprehensive behavior support plan (BSP), is intended to have a therapeutic effect (Federal Statutes, Regulations, and Policies Governing the ICF/MR Program, 2003). If incorporated in a BSP, care providers are trained to implement PR when, and only when, a person displays specific and operationally defined problem behaviors. Similar to applying emergency PR, planned PR should be reserved for the most serious at-risk behaviors. Planned PR would be judged to have a therapeutic effect when the behaviors that produce restraint decrease in frequency over an extended period of time or, ideally, are eliminated. Compared to emergency PR, planned implementation of PR as prescribed in a BSP eliminates subjective decision making by care providers. Also, injuries are more likely to be sustained with emergency PR than planned PR (Spreat, Lipinski, Hill, & Halpin, 1986; Williams, 2009).

Whether PR is applied as an emergency or planned intervention procedure, it potentially can be misapplied, posing a physical risk to the recipient and implementer (Hill & Spreat, 1987), and in some cases, can function as positive reinforcement (Favell, McGimsey, & Jones, 1978). Restraining children, adolescents, and adults, whether or not they have IDD, may also be seen as an overly restrictive impediment to personal freedom. A related concern when instituting PR on an organizational level is the need for comprehensive staff training and clinical supervision, a demand that exceeds the professional resources of some service settings. Finally, most care providers do not approve of PR (Cunningham, McDonnell, Easton, & Sturmey, 2003; McDonnell & Sturmey, 2000)—in consequence, there could be a threat to intervention integrity if they are reluctant to implement PR as intended and according to behavior-specific criteria.

This chapter focuses on therapeutic implementation of PR with people who have IDD. The intent is to present and review several key considerations for designing, applying, and evaluating PR as a planned intervention procedure to reduce and eliminate high-risk behaviors. The premise for the chapter is twofold. First, it is believed desirable to never use PR. However, this author's clinical experiences indicate that this objective is difficult to achieve and that there are occasions when PR is a justified intervention. Accordingly, the second premise is that there are critical steps and necessary guidelines that should be followed when adopting PR therapeutically. Equally important, and also reviewed in the chapter, is that there are methods that can effectively reduce and eliminate PR.

## CLINICAL JUSTIFICATION FOR PHYSICAL RESTRAINT

The Association for Behavior Analysis International (ABAI) Statement on Restraint and Seclusion (Vollmer, Hagopian, Baily, Dorsey, Hanley, Lennox, et al., 2011) sets forth several guiding principles when selecting intervention procedures. First, "clinical decisions should be made based upon the professional judgment of a dually formed treatment team that demonstrates knowledge of the broad research base and best practice" (p. 104). Underlying any intervention planning is the welfare of the person being served and his or her family. A second critical feature is that people requiring intervention and their families have "rights" to effective treatment and should be allowed to choose those methods with guidance and direction from responsible professionals. Finally, the ABAI (2011) statement endorses the principle of least restrictiveness—that is, selecting intervention "that affords the most favorable risk to benefit ratio, with specific consideration of probability of treatment success, anticipated duration of treatment distress cause by procedures, and distress caused by the behavior itself" (p. 104).

Relative to the aforementioned guiding principles, the clinical justification for PR should be that a person continues to demonstrate high-risk challenging behaviors despite intervention efforts that have incorporated least restrictive procedures and were subjected to data-based evaluation. Furthermore, clinicians who have requisite expertise (ideally, licensed psychologists and board-certified behavior analysts) must verify that without PR, the person with high-risk challenging behaviors will continue to pose a threat to self, others, and the environment. These same clinicians should be responsible for formulating intervention with PR, supervising care providers, and evaluating outcomes.

As a planned intervention procedure, PR must be described in a written BSP. The BSP may have been designed and implemented before adding PR, or PR may be one of the procedures included in a new BSP that has not yet been introduced. Minimally, the BSP should include the following components:

1. All of the challenging behaviors targeted by the BSP and those that will receive PR are defined clearly to permit unambiguous detection by care providers. Conducting regularly scheduled interobserver agreement (IOA) assessments is one way to ensure reliable data recording and accurate implementation of PR (Kleinmann et al., 2009).

2. The BSP indicates the hypothesized function of the challenging behaviors. Functional behavioral assessment (FBA) and functional analysis (FA) are the recommended methods for isolating the antecedent and consequence conditions that set the occasion for and maintain challenging behaviors respectively (Hanley, Iwata, & McCord, 2003).

3. The BSP has antecedent, positive reinforcement, and skill-building intervention procedures. *Antecedent* procedures have the goal of preventing challenging behaviors by eliminating behavior-provoking conditions (Luiselli, 2006; 2008a). *Positive reinforcement* procedures specify consequences that care providers should provide when the people with IDD do not either display challenging behaviors or demonstrate functionally equivalent but alternative responses (Kern & Kokina, 2008). The *skill-building* procedures should concentrate on care providers teaching the people meaningful behaviors to help them as they communicate more effectively, perform self-care and daily living routines, occupy leisure time, and socialize with peers.

4. Only approved methods of PR are specified in the BSP and only appropriately trained care providers should implement them. Typically, organizations have an accredited outside agency conduct training with staff (see Chapter 16, this volume). In addition to the behaviors that call for PR, the BSP also defines the conditions under which PR is permitted and those, if any, where it is not sanctioned.

5. All care providers responsible for implementing the BSP are trained in the constituent procedures. The rationale for the BSP, how the plan was formulated, and the purpose of including PR should be explained. Training usually begins through simulation with a clinical supervisor, who demonstrates BSP procedures, observes care providers implementing the procedures during behavioral rehearsal sessions, and delivers performance feedback to the providers. After simulated training, care providers should have frequent supervision of BSP and PR implementation during their routine interactions with clients.

6. A final step linked to developing, training, and implementing a BSP is securing informed consent from the legal guardian of the people with IDD. The supervising clinician should meet with the guardian, present the written BSP, explain

all procedures, review the method of PR, and answer questions. A guardian's consent or nonconsent should be indicated by signature on a form that summarizes the reasons for including PR in the BSP and potential risk factors. The form should also stipulate that the guardian can withdraw consent at any time.

A further suggestion is that the clinical justification for PR be augmented by having a physician evaluate the person with IDD to rule out medical risk factors that contraindicate restraint. Chronic health problems, orthopedic limitations, cardiovascular conditions, prior surgeries, and neurological status are just some of the areas that demand physician screening. If applicable, a person's current medication regimen should also be scrutinized.

## MEASUREMENT

The therapeutic effectiveness of planned PR can only be judged by measuring how often it is implemented. There are other critical data sources as well such as the duration of PR per application, clinical context in which PR was applied, behavior of the person when restrained, and any untoward consequences of PR (Luiselli, Sperry, & Magee, 2011). The Clinical Incident Report Form for Recording Physical Restraint is an example of a data sheet for documenting these measures. In effect, care providers complete the form every time PR is implemented. Supervising clinicians must then summarize and interpret the recorded information.

As seen in the Clinical Incident Report Form for Recording Physical Restraint on the next page, frequency and duration of PR are fundamental data for evaluating intervention effectiveness. Different trends in frequency and duration are often encountered. For example, it is possible that a person with IDD could have progressively fewer applications of PR over consecutive weeks but the average duration per PR does not change. Additional intervention procedures, discussed later in the chapter, might then be implemented to reduce restraint duration. Or, data might show that physical restraint frequency and average duration are high on some days, followed by consecutive "zero-restraint" days. This pattern suggests the influence of stimulus control over the behaviors that provoke PR and the need for alternative intervention. As seen in these examples, continuous measurement of PR frequency and duration allows for data-derived clinical decision making.

It was indicated previously that the context in which PR is implemented is another valuable data source. To illustrate, Luiselli and colleagues (Luiselli et al., 2005; Luiselli, Pace, & Dunn, 2003) conducted antecedent assessment analyses of planned PR with children and adolescents who had acquired brain injury and challenging behaviors. Using standardized recording forms, care providers documented one or more conditions that preceded each restraint. The results of Luiselli et al. (2003), revealed that two antecedent conditions, a staff directive and staff intervention, were the recorded antecedents for 69% of restraints. Similarly, Luiselli et al. (2005) found that specific activities, such as seated desk work and leisure time, were associated with implementation of PR. The conclusion from these studies is that certain interactions and situations may reliably "trigger" challenging behaviors that require PR. If so, "By

# Clinical Incident Report Form
## for Recording Physical Restraint (PR)

Name of person receiving PR _____

Date of PR _____

Location (setting) of PR _____
_____

Duration of PR _____ (start time) _____ (stop time)

Type of PR _____

Staff (names) implementing PR _____

_____     _____

_____     _____

_____     _____

Situation(s) associated with PR (check and describe)

[ ]    During instruction/training routine:
[ ]    During meal:
[ ]    During play/leisure activity:
[ ]    During an ambulatory transition:
[ ]    During free-time:
[ ]    Other:

Injury sustained during PR

[ ]    No
[ ]    Yes (describe)

Staff person completing report _____

Date that report was submitted to supervisor _____

Supervisor review _____

Date _____

Comments _____
_____
_____
_____
_____
_____
_____
_____
_____
_____
_____
_____
_____

isolating relevant antecedents, it should be possible to modify their influence in such a way that challenging behaviors do not occur, thereby eliminating the need for an invasive procedures such as therapeutic restraint" (Luiselli et al., 2003, p. 263).

It is not uncommon for people with IDD to struggle against and resist PR. A person's behavior during restraint itself is a critical measure of therapeutic effectiveness. That is, PR should not worsen a person's distress or induce counter-reactions that could cause injury. The Physical Restraint Resistance Recording Form on page 249 was created to measure a person's behavior during PR to determine the overall "intensity" of application and if necessary, evaluate resistance-reducing procedures. For example, a fixed-time release (FTR) criterion from PR, reviewed later in the chapter, is one strategy for lessening resistant behaviors by decreasing the total time a person is restrained.

## PHYSICAL RESTRAINT REDUCTION AND ELIMINATION

Acknowledging the controversy about and limitations of PR, even as therapeutic intervention, few studies have addressed the topic of restraint reduction and elimination (Luiselli, 2009; Sturmey & McGlynn, 2002). This lack of research may be the result of professionals avoiding PR or perhaps more reasonably, constraints in carrying out controlled studies within applied settings. In the past 10 years, this author has pursued a program of clinical research with several colleagues, the focus of which has been evaluating methods for reducing PR within human services organizations serving children, adolescents, and adults with IDD.[*] The following section describes this research and two strategies we have found to be effective: 1) antecedent intervention for decreasing challenging behaviors that lead to PR, and 2) FTR for reducing the duration of time a person is exposed to PR.

### Antecedent Intervention

Luiselli, Kane, Treml, and Young (2000) conducted a study with two male students, 14 and 15 years old, who had pervasive developmental disorder (PDD) and attended a residential school. Both students hit, bit, scratched, and kicked peers and care providers. During a 1-month baseline phase, the care providers implemented several procedures, including PR, according to student-specific BSPs. The plans had care providers deliver pleasurable consequences to the students when they demonstrated positive behavior and did not exhibit aggression. The care providers applied PR to the students when they determined that aggression was unmanageable. Next, intervention was changed so that PR was implemented according to behavior-specific criteria and not arbitrarily determined by the care providers. A second intervention phase subsequently was evaluated in which several antecedent control procedures were introduced, each designed to reduce the escape function of aggression and, in consequence, produce less frequent PR. For one of the students (Glenn), care

[*]I acknowledge research collaboration with Erin K. Dunn, Ph.D., Ava E. Kleinmann, Ph.D., Gary M. Pace, Ph.D., BCBA-D., James M. Sperry, M.S., and Tania Tremel, Med., BCBA. Portions of this section are adapted from Luiselli (2009).

# Physical Restraint (PR) Resistance Recording Form

Instructions: Complete this form following each application of PR with the designated person. Record the highest level of resistance that was observed during the restraint.

Name of person receiving PR _____

Date of PR _____

| Ratings and descriptions | Resistance (✓) during restraint |
|---|---|
| 0: No resistance: The person remains passive during implementation of protective holding and does not demonstrate resistance. There is an absence of agitation and distress. | |
| 1: Minimal resistance: The person may tug or pull gently against the physical contact, usually for 1–3 seconds, several times during restraint but staff does not have to apply more intense pressure to maintain contact. There are no discernable signs of agitation and distress. | |
| 2: Mild resistance: The person pulls and tugs against the physical contact, staff occasionally must apply more intense pressure to maintain restraint, and resistance occurs for durations not exceeding 5 seconds. The person may demonstrate low-level and infrequent agitation and distress. | |
| 3: Moderate resistance: The person pulls and tugs against the physical contact, staff must apply more intense pressure to maintain restraint, and resistance occurs for durations lasting 5–10 seconds. Such resistance may occur several times when restraint is applied. The person may break contact, requiring re-implementation by staff. The child or adult demonstrates periodic agitation and distress. | |
| 4: Extreme resistance: The person pulls and tugs against the physical contact, staff must apply more intense pressure to maintain restraint, and the resistance occurs for durations that exceed 10 seconds. Such resistance may occur several times when restraint is applied. The person breaks contact, one or more times, requiring re-implementation by staff. The child or adult demonstrates frequent and lengthy periods of agitation and distress. | |

Comments _____

_____

_____

_____

_____

_____

_____

_____

_____

_____

*The Handbook of High-Risk Challenging Behaviors in People with Intellectual and Developmental Disabilities,* edited by James K. Luiselli
Copyright © 2012 by Paul H. Brookes Publishing Co., Inc. All rights reserved.

providers were taught to detect behavior indicating he was becoming upset and often predicted aggression. Upon observing these precursor behaviors, they directed the student to take time away from his group until he was composed. Functional communication training also was provided so that he could request a break from instruction. With the second student (Paul), the antecedent procedures were giving him more access to novel activities, reducing sedentary tasks in favor of more preferred interactions and placing him strategically within groups so that he had less proximity to peers.

For both students, implementing behavior-specific criterion for PR as the first intervention was ineffective. However, PR decreased and remained at near-zero frequency when the same criteria were maintained in conjunction with student-specific antecedent intervention procedures. Again, the key element to this PR–reduction approach was to eliminate situations that were associated with the challenging behaviors that required restraint.

In another antecedent intervention study, Luiselli et al. (2005) focused on a 15-year-old female, Betty, who had brain injury (Grade IV intraventricular hemorrhage at birth secondary to hydrocephalus and hepatitis). She attended a residential school where she received PR as a therapeutic intervention procedure in a BSP that addressed aggressive behavior. Antecedent assessment data revealed that nearly 50% of Betty's PR was implemented contingent on aggression during deskwork activities in the classroom. We hypothesized that these activities were too "demanding" for Betty and that her aggressive behavior functioned to escape them. In an attempt to reduce the demand features of deskwork instruction so that aggression-provoked PR would be implemented less frequently, we evaluated the following antecedent intervention phases.

### Intervention I

Betty's daily schedule was changed to include "preferred" activities that were performed outside of the classroom. The revised schedule had her spend less time in the classroom doing deskwork activities and more time ambulating throughout the school building, working on more functional activities of daily living. Activities were depicted in a picture schedule that provided Betty with a visual representation of her day. She was allowed to choose the activities available to her and could engage in them for any duration. Therefore, in this phase, "demands" essentially were eliminated.

### Intervention II

All Intervention I procedures remained in effect, but the daily schedule was adjusted so that Betty could select 75% of activities in her schedule. Her care providers selected the remaining 25% of activities.

### Intervention III

Care providers presented Betty with 100% of activities comprising her daily schedule. However, she was able to choose from two to three activities available at each selection opportunity. Thus, as compared to Interventions I and II, Betty was allowed to make activity choices but only from those that her care providers offered.

### Intervention IV

Betty no longer selected activities in her daily schedule. Instead, care providers identified the activities and she was expected to participate in them. When she completed a criterion number of activities successfully, care providers gave her a "walk pass" that allowed her to move about the school building (with supervision) for 5–10 minutes, visiting and conversing with students and other personnel. She also had three "free" passes each day that were independent of activity participation and could be requested at any time.

### Intervention V

Care providers continued to present Betty with 100% of daily activities but she could choose the order in which they were performed. For example, she might be informed that there were three activities to complete from 10:00 a.m. to 10:30 a.m. and was then allowed to pick the sequence. Contingent and free access to walks remained components of her BSP.

During the initial baseline phase Betty required PR on average more than three times per week. Frequency of PR decreased with Interventions I and II, increased to preintervention levels during a one-week reversal-to-baseline phase, and decreased again when Intervention II was reintroduced. There was a slight increase in PR frequency during Intervention III. A second reversal-to-baseline phase was associated with an increase in PR. Frequency of PR decreased once again during the initial weeks of Intervention IV but subsequently, there was an increasing trend. The most dramatic and stable reduction in PR occurred during Intervention V, and these results were maintained over a 6-month follow-up period.

## Summary of Antecedent Intervention

Although few in number, studies suggest that PR among people with IDD can be reduced and potentially eliminated by preventing challenging behaviors that require restraint. The first step in this process is to assess the antecedent conditions that reliably precede challenging behaviors. Typically, the assessment data point toward a broad class of antecedent influences that subsequently require a more fine-grained analysis. For example, "instructional demands" as an antecedent condition might include the types of tasks, response effort needed for task completion, duration of instruction, ratio of mastered versus novel tasks, and so on. Similarly, challenging behaviors and associated PR during "activity transitions" could be influenced by the preference value of activities, complexity of the transition (e.g., having to walk a long distance), and response expectations. The more precise the assessment, the more likely the relationship of antecedent > challenging behaviors > PR can be identified and manipulated for therapeutic effect.

## Fixed-Time Release

FTR refers to terminating PR when a predetermined duration of time elapses independent of the person's behavior during restraint. Typically, PR is maintained according to a behavior-contingent release (BCR) criterion—the person is not released from restraint until she or he is calm and nonagitated for a defined period, say, 60 consecutive seconds. The basis for BCR, borrowed from an earlier literature concerning time-out (MacDonough & Forehand, 1973), is to ensure that restraint-induced problem behaviors such as struggling, agitation, and resistance are not negatively reinforced. However, a BCR criterion can lead to lengthy PR applications if a person is not able to calm quickly. Therefore, FTR may be clinically advantageous as a strategy for decreasing total time in restraint.

The impetus for our research on FTR was a study by Mace, Page, Ivancic, and O'Brien (1986) comparing two time-out release contingencies with children who displayed challenging behaviors. With contingent delay, time-out was maintained until the children were not disruptive for 15 seconds after they spent a minimum of 1 minute and 45 seconds in time-out. During a no-contingent delay, time-out ended as soon as 2 minutes elapsed. The contingent-delay and no-contingent delay contingencies were equally effective in reducing challenging behaviors. The added benefit of no-contingent delay, of course, was that the children experienced fewer minutes in time-out.

In a pilot study of BCR and FTR from PR, Luiselli, Treml, Kane, and Young (2004) reported the case of a 17.5-year-old female student who had PDD, aggressive behaviors, and frequent applications of PR at a community based residential school. Under baseline conditions in an AB design (A = baseline, B = intervention), care providers implemented PR contingent on aggression and terminated PR when the student stopped struggling and screaming for 60 seconds. With this BCR criterion, the average duration of PR was 5.6 minutes. Intervention to reduce total time in PR featured a 60-seconds FTR criterion. That is, PR terminated as soon as 60 seconds elapsed. For clinical reasons, if care providers judged that they could not safely terminate PR after 60 seconds, they maintained physical contact with the student until the BCR criterion was achieved for 15 seconds. The results of this preliminary study were that the FTR criterion reduced average PR duration to 3.1 minutes. Although unanticipated, the frequency of aggression resulting in PR also decreased from 3.2 per week with BCR to .67 per week with FTR. Thus, we concluded that there may be a therapeutic advantage to terminating PR based on the passage of time instead of a criterion linked to behavior.

In related research, Luiselli, Pace, and Dunn (2006) compared BCR and FTR from PR in multiple baseline and reversal designs with 3 students, ages 11–14 years old, who had IDD resulting from brain injury and lived at a community-based residential school. Each student's BSP included PR as a consequence for aggression and self-injury. During a BCR phase, PR was maintained until the students did not resist for individually determined durations of 15 to 120 seconds. The criterion for release from PR then was changed to FTR by computing 60 % of the average duration recorded with BCR. For the three students, the FTR criteria were 2 minutes, 3 minutes, and 5 minutes respectively. The experimental designs verified that shifting to a FTR criterion was associated with less frequent PR. Regarding the total time exposed to PR, one student spent an average of 14.2 minutes each week with BCR and 3.8 minutes each week with FTR; the second student spent an average of 5.1 minutes each week with BCR and 1.4 minutes each week with

FTR; and the third student spent an average of 11.2 minutes each week with BCR and 3.0 minutes each week with FTR. In summary, although the results of Luiselli et al. (2006) were that PR continued to be required with the students, a worthy clinical benefit was realized by reducing the cumulative time they were restrained.

Finally, Luiselli (2008b) explored the possibility of *FTR-fading* to eliminate PR, not just reduce the time in restraint. The participant was a 13-year-old boy with Autistic Disorder and Pervasive Development Disorder-Not Otherwise Specified diagnoses. He slapped, pinched, bit, and pulled the hair of care providers, resulting in a BSP that had aggression-contingent PR. In an initial (prefading) intervention phase, care providers released the boy from PR after 60 seconds. During subsequent phases, the FTR criterion was decreased from 60 seconds to 30 seconds, 15 seconds, and 7 seconds, respectively, based on a deceasing frequency of PR and, by default, reduced duration. Upon reaching the FTR 7-seconds criterion, PR was successfully eliminated by having a care-provider move behind the boy as if to implement restraint, touch him gently on the shoulder, and instruct him to "sit down." When he complied, the care provider stepped back, waited a few seconds, and then had the boy stand up.

## Summary of Fixed-Time Release

FTR appears to be a promising approach toward reducing PR. Shorter durations of PR should decrease the risk of injury to those who receive and apply PR. Intervention integrity by staff also may improve with FTR because as compared to BCR, it is less strenuous and easier to apply. Similar to the previously reviewed studies, FTR can be instituted as an alternative to BCR or as the initial criterion for new BSPs that include PR. Another consistent finding is that with FTR, frequency of PR has not increased and, on occasion, may actually decrease. As shown by Luiselli (2008b), PR can be eliminated in some cases by systematically fading the FTR criteria.

## ORGANIZATIONAL AND SYSTEMS-LEVEL SUPPORT

To ensure that PR is implemented therapeutically, care providers are trained properly, and intervention effectiveness is evaluated, human services and behavioral healthcare organizations should adopt systems-level supervision and oversight (Donat, 1998; Luiselli & Russo, 2005; Singh, Singh, Davis, Latham, & Ayers, 1999). Fundamentally, an organization must have clearly articulated policies governing PR. It is essential that the policies state the rationale for PR as an emergency and planned intervention. In addition, the organization should stipulate the types of PR that are permitted and prohibited. As well, there should be information about the care provider training program and the process for obtaining informed consent from guardians.

Clinical supervision of PR should follow a model of continuous quality improvement. Procedures for measuring and reporting use of PR, conducting contextual analyses, and aggregating data for evaluation were outlined previously. These procedures form the basis of reasonable clinical management but there are other considerations. For example, injuries to clients and care providers during PR must be documented to implement injury reduction and prevention programs (Luiselli, 2011; Urban, Luiselli, Parenteau, & Child, 2011; Williams, 2009). In particular, behavior-based safety (BBS) offers a useable framework for instituting occupational risk management protocols, especially applicable to PR safety (Geller, 2005).

Clinical supervision of care providers implementing PR demands routinely scheduled observations that feature *intervention integrity assessment* (DiGennaro, Martens, & Kleinmann, 2007; Reed, Fienup, Luiselli, & Pace, 2010). Intervention integrity refers to the accuracy of procedural implementation—do care providers intervene correctly according to written guidelines? Integrity is particularly important when PR is a component of a BSP. Through intervention integrity assessment, clinical supervisors are able to ascertain whether care providers properly implement the approved type of PR, other procedures comprising the BSP, and required data recording. Absent such assessment it is not possible to evaluate convincingly the therapeutic effects of PR.

*Competency-based training* is another essential element of clinical supervision (Ricciardi, 2005). Such training enables supervisors to give care providers immediate performance feedback following observations. Feedback can occur as *positive reinforcement* (e.g., "that's great, you gave Bill a verbal reminder before holding his arm") or *behavior correction* (e.g., "remember, you have to release Bill from restraint 20 seconds after you implement it"). The advantages of competency-based training are that it is informed by behavior-specific criteria, conducted in vivo, time efficient, and skill focused. When conducting competency-based training, a supervisor usually records performance on a rating checklist. The checklist data can then be used as additional feedback by showing graphic results to care providers and reinforcing their documented improvement.

Finally, most care providers do not approve of PR, although the social validity (acceptability and satisfaction) assessment research on this topic is limited (Cunningham et al., 2003; McDonnell & Sturmey, 2000). Practitioner acceptability, and therefore adherence to a BSP, especially impacts implementation of therapeutic PR in that care providers are expected to intervene according to clinically determined guidelines. Therefore, human services and behavioral healthcare organizations would benefit from periodically assessing care-provider opinions about PR. Such assessment could focus on their satisfaction with and acceptance of the training they received, clinical supervision, circumstances associated with PR, risk factors, and efforts to reduce and eliminate PR intervention. Learning what care providers think about PR and its implementation will not only improve clinical services but will also demonstrate to staff that their opinions matter, are taken seriously, and help inform organizational policy.

## SUMMARY

PR is not a desirable intervention procedure but may have to be included in a therapeutic approach with people who have IDD and high-risk challenging behaviors. It is first necessary to have sound clinical justification for implementing

PR. Planned PR should be specific and defined in a written BSP. In turn, the BSP should be formulated from functional behavioral assessment data. Measurement of PR effectiveness includes frequency, duration, and possible untoward intervention effects. Measurement must also capture contextual influences associated with PR implementation. Two research-supported methods for reducing PR are antecedent intervention and FTR. It behooves human services and behavioral health care organizations to emphasize competency-based training of care providers, support clinical supervision models that feature intervention integrity assessment, and solicit social validity measures from the people required to implement PR. Ultimately, a sophisticated, well-conceived, research-directed, and rigorously monitored approach to therapeutic PR will greatly curtail and possibly do away with such intervention.

## REFERENCES

Bitgood, S.C., Crowe, M.J., Suarez, Y., & Peters, R.D. (1980). Immobilization effects and side effects on stereotyped behavior in children. *Behavior Modification, 4,* 187–208.

Cunningham, J., McDonnell, A., Easton, S., & Sturmey, P. (2003). Social validation data on three methods of PR: Views of consumers, staff, and students. *Research in Developmental Disabilities, 24,* 307–316.

DiGennaro, F.D., Martens, B.K., & Kleinmann, A.E. (2007). A comparison of performance feedback procedures on teachers' treatment implementation integrity and students' inappropriate behavior in special education classrooms. *Journal of Applied Behavior Analysis, 40,* 447–461.

Donat, D.C. (1998). Impact of a mandatory behavioral consultation on seclusion/restraint utilization in a psychiatric hospital. *Journal of Behavior Therapy & Experimental Psychiatry, 29,* 13–19.

Favell, J.E., McGimsey, J.F., & Jones, M.L. (1978). The use of PR in the treatment of self-injury and as positive reinforcement. *Journal of Applied Behavior Analysis, 11,* 225–241.

*Federal statutes, regulations, and policies governing the ICF/MR program.* (2003). Retrieved from http://cms. hhs.gov/medicaid/icfmr/icfregs.asp

Geller, E.S. (2005). Behavior-based safety and occupational risk management. *Behavior Modification, 29,* 539–561

Hanley, G.P., Iwata, B.A., & McCord, B.E. (2003). Functional analysis of problem behavior: A review. *Journal of Applied Behavior Analysis, 36,* 147–185.

Harris, J. (1996). PR procedures for managing challenging behaviors presented by mentally retarded adults and children. *Research in Developmental Disabilities, 17,* 99–134.

Hill, J. & Spreat, S. (1987). Staff injury rates associated with the implementation of contingent restraint. *Mental Retardation, 25,* 141–145.

Kern, L. & Kokina, A. (2008). Using positive reinforcement to decreased challenging behavior. In J.K. Luiselli, D.C. Russo, W.P. Christian, & S.M. Wilczynski (Eds.), *Effective practices for children with autism: Educational and behavioral support interventions that work* (pp. 413–432). New York: Oxford University Press.

Kleinmann, A.E., Luiselli, J.K., DiGennaro, F.D., Pace, G.M., Langone, S.R., & Cochran, C. (2009). Systems-level assessment of interobserver agreement (IOA) for implementation of protective holding (therapeutic restraint) in a behavioral healthcare setting. *Journal of Developmental and Physical Disabilities, 21,* 473–483.

Luiselli, J.K. (2006). *Antecedent assessment and intervention: Supporting children and adults with developmental disabilities in community settings.* Baltimore, MD: Paul H. Brookes Publishing Co.

Luiselli, J.K. (2008a). Antecedent (preventive) intervention. In J.K. Luiselli, D.C. Russo, W.P. Christian, & S.M. Wilczynski (Eds.), *Effective practices for children with autism: Educational and behavioral support interventions that work* (pp. 393–412). New York: Oxford University Press.

Luiselli, J.K. (2008b). Effects of fixed-time release (FTR) fading on implementation of PR. *Mental Health Aspects of Developmental Disabilities, 11,* 1–6.

Luiselli, J.K. (2009). PR of people with intellectual disability: A review of implementation and reduction procedures. *Journal of Applied Research in Intellectual Disabilities, 22,* 126–134.

Luiselli, J.K. (2011). *Behavioral systems analysis and intervention for staff injury reduction and prevention.* Manuscript submitted for publication.

Luiselli, J.K., Dunn, E.K., & Pace, G.M. (2005). Antecedent assessment and intervention to reduce PR (protective holding) of children and adolescents with acquired brain injury. *Behavioral Interventions, 20,* 51–65

Luiselli, J.K., Kane, A., Treml, T., & Young, N. (2000). Behavioral intervention to reduce PR of adolescents with developmental disabilities. *Behavioral Interventions, 15,* 317–330.

Luiselli, J.K., Pace, G., & Dunn, E.K. (2003). Antecedent analysis of therapeutic restraint in children and adolescents with acquired brain injury: A descriptive study of four cases. *Brain Injury, 17,* 255–264.

Luiselli, J.K., Pace, G.M., & Dunn, E.K. (2006). Effects of behavior-contingent and fixed-time release contingencies on frequency and duration of therapeutic restraint. *Behavior Modification, 30,* 442–455.

Luiselli, J.K., & Russo, D.C. (2005). Clinical peer review: Description of a model in behavioral healthcare. *Behavior Modification, 29,* 470–487.

Luiselli, J.K., Sperry, J.M., & Magee, C. (2011). Descriptive analysis of PR (protective holding) among community living adults with intellectual disability. *Journal of Intellectual Disabilities, 15,* 93–99.

Luiselli, J.K., Treml, T., Kane, A., & Young, N. (2004). PR intervention: Case report of an implementation-reduction strategy and long term outcome. *Mental Health Aspects of Developmental Disabilities, 7,* 91–96.

MacDonough, T.S., & Forehand, R. (1973). Response-contingent time-out: Important parameters in behavior modification with children. *Journal of Behavior Therapy & Experimental Psychiatry, 4,* 231–236.

Mace, F.C., Page, T.J., Ivancic, M.T., & O'Brien, S. (1986). Effectiveness of brief time-out with and without contingent delay: A comparative analysis. *Journal of Applied Behavior Analysis, 19,* 79–86.

Matson, J.L., & Boisjoli, J.A. (2009). Restraint procedures and challenging behaviors in intellectual disability: An analysis of causative factors. *Journal of Applied Research in Intellectual Disabilities, 22,* 111–117.

McDonnell, A.A., & Sturmey, P. (2000). The social validation of three PR procedures: A comparison of young people and professional groups. *Research in Developmental Disabilities, 21,* 85–92.

Mohr, W.K. & Mohr, B.D. (2000). Mechanisms of injury and death proximal to restraint use. *Archives of Psychiatric Nursing, 14,* 285–295.

O'Halloran, R.L. & Frank, J.G. (2000). Asphyxial death during prone restraint revisited: A report of 21 cases. *American Journal of Forensic Medicine and Pathology, 21,* 39–52.

Reed, D.D., Fienup, D.M., Luiselli, J.K., & Pace, G.M. (2010). Performance improvement in behavioral healthcare: Collateral effects of planned treatment observations as an applied example of scheduled induced responding. *Behavior Modification, 34,* 367–385.

Ricciardi, J.N. (2005). Achieving human service outcomes through competency-based training: A guide for managers. *Behavior Modification, 29,* 488–507.

Rolider, A., Williams, L., Cummings, A., & Van Houten, R. (1991). The use of a brief movement restriction procedure to eliminate severe inappropriate behavior. *Journal of Behavior Therapy & Experimental Psychiatry, 22,* 23–30.

Singh, N.N., Singh, S.D., Davis, C.M., Latham, L.L., & Ayers, J.G. (1999). Reconsidering the use of seclusion and restraints in inpatient child and adult psychiatry. *Journal of Child & Family Studies, 8,* 243–253.

Spreat, S., Lipinski, D., Hill, J., & Halpin, M.E. (1986). Safety indices associated with the use of contingent restraint procedures. *Applied Research in Mental Retardation, 7,* 475–481.

Sturmey, P., & McGlynn, A.P. (2003). Restraint reduction. In D. Allen (Ed.), *Ethical approaches to physical interventions: Responding to challenging behaviour in people with intellectual disabilities* (pp. 203–218). Plymouth, UK: BILD Publications.

Urban, K.D., Luiselli, J.K., Parenteau, R., & Child, S.N. (in press). Effects of protective equipment on frequency and intensity of aggression-provoked staff injury. *Journal of Developmental and Physical Disabilities.*

Vollmer, T.R., Hagopian, L.P., Bailey, J.S., Dorsey, M.F., Hanley, G.P., Lennox, D., et al (2011). The Association for Behavior Analysis International position statement on restraint and seclusion. *The Behavior Analyst, 34,* 103–110.

Weiss, D.M. (1998, October 11–15). Deadly restraint. *Hartford Courant,* 11–15.

Williams, D.E. (2009). Restraint safety: An analysis of injuries related to restraint of people with intellectual disabilities. *Journal of Applied Research in Intellectual Disabilities, 22,* 135–139.

# 15

**CHAPTER**

# Regulatory Governance of Physical Restraint in Schools

*Joseph B. Ryan and Reece L. Peterson*

Given the increasing number of violent incidents that take place within U.S. schools each year, there is a growing safety concern for both students and staff members alike. Physical restraint is one intervention that many schools or individual staff members have used to manage aggressive student behavior. Physical restraint, or what is sometimes referred to as ambulatory restraint, occurs when one or more staff members use their bodies to restrict an individual's voluntary movement as a means for reestablishing behavioral control and establishing and maintaining safety for the individual, other students, and staff (Ryan, Robbins, Peterson, & Rozalski, 2009).

Although traditionally restraint procedures have been limited to more restrictive placement settings such as hospitals and residential treatment centers, they have become increasingly more common within public schools. Some researchers posit this increased use of restraints in public schools is the result of providing educational treatment of students with disabilities in the least restrictive environment, or what is commonly referred to as LRE (Ryan & Peterson, 2004). That is, for several decades there has been a strong push at both the federal and state levels to educate students with all disabilities—including those with emotional and behavioral disorders (EBD), autism, and cognitive disabilities—in the general education environment and in regular classroom settings. As a result, children who had in years past been served in specialized educational settings such as residential or special day schools may now be educated in public school settings. The behavioral interventions that were traditionally limited to more restrictive settings have migrated with these students to U.S. public schools. School administrators have also had to face the possibility of violence occurring in schools, and the need to protect the safety of students and staff. In these situations physical restraint may also be viewed as a tool to manage or prevent violence. As a result of these influences, physical restraint procedures may now be used more broadly with all students who display aggressive behaviors in school, whether or not they have a disability.

## FREQUENCY OF PHYSICAL RESTRAINT IN SCHOOLS

Unfortunately, there are no standardized reporting procedures for using restraint procedures across states and school districts, making it difficult to acquire prevalence statistics within schools today. However, a report released by the U.S. Government

Accountability Office (2009) found two states (California and Texas) that do track the use of restraint procedures in schools. In these two states, schools had used the procedure over 33,000 times during the course of the 2007/2008 school year. Because these two states represent approximately 20% of the U.S. student population, one could surmise that restraints may be implemented as many as 165,000 times each year on students across the nation.

## EFFECTIVENESS OF PHYSICAL RESTRAINT IN SCHOOLS

Although the use of restraint in schools has apparently increased over the last decade, little is actually known about the efficacy of restraint procedures due to a lack of research (Persi & Pasquali, 1999; Ryan & Peterson, 2004). A few of the early proponents of physical restraint attempted to justify its use through the attachment theory developed during the early to mid-1970s (Bowlby, 1973; Cline, 1979; Zaslow & Menta, 1975). However, Day (2002) reviewed the research supporting these theories and, for the most part, debunked them because they were poor quality (e.g., case reports, anecdotal evidence) and unverifiable.

Today, knowledgeable school administrators view physical restraint as an emergency procedure to prevent injury to the student or others when a student is in crisis and displays physical aggression. Although this standard has been commonly accepted, it is also difficult to define "emergencies" and implementation criteria. There is also some evidence that restraint may in practice be used for behavioral crises that do not meet this standard, such as student noncompliance or running away (Ryan, Peterson, Tetreault, & Van der Hagen, 2004). Overall, however, there is little empirical evidence about restraint use for any purpose and, accordingly, it is difficult to draw conclusions about its effectiveness.

## REGULATING PHYSICAL RESTRAINT IN SCHOOLS

Due to the number of injuries and deaths associated with the use of restraint procedures in schools that have occurred during the past decade, professional organizations (e.g., Council for Children with Behavior Disorders [CCBD], 2009; Council for Exceptional Children, 2009), and advocacy groups (e.g., Child Welfare League of America, 2000) have recently called for either federal or state legislation to prevent injuries and deaths associated with restraint and to protect the rights of students. These groups emphasize that restraint procedures need to be regulated because they 1) pose a risk of injury and death for both students and staff alike, 2) are frequently used inappropriately by staff, 3) continue to be used despite being ineffective in reducing aggressive behavior, and 4) are often used without adequate oversight, training, or proper implementation. Each of these concerns is addressed in more detail in the sections that follow.

### Dangers of Restraint

The risk of injury and death associated with the use of restraint procedures has been widely recognized (Sturmey, Lott, Laud, & Matson, 2005). Although poor reporting procedures impede reliable data collection on the number of deaths and injuries that occur each year due to improperly performed restraint procedures, advocacy agencies estimate that as many as 8 to 10 individuals die each year across agencies and settings due to these interventions (Child Welfare League of America, 2000). A review of the medical causes associated with deaths resulting from restraint found most fatalities were caused by 1) positional asphyxia (suffocation) during a prone (face down) floor restraint caused by staff members placing their body weight on an individual's back or chest, 2) aspiration (choking) during a supine (face-up) floor restraint, and 3) blunt trauma to the chest in which the individual hits something (e.g., desk) hard during the "takedown" or initiation of restraint procedure, resulting in cardiac arrhythmia leading to sudden death (Mohr, Petti, & Mohr, 2003). Individuals taking certain psychotropic medications (e.g., neuroleptic drugs) are also at an increased health risk, as these drugs make them more susceptible to respiratory or heart conditions that can lead to sudden death.

In addition to the risks of physical injury caused by restraint, there are also serious concerns about associated psychological trauma, particularly with children who have experienced prior physical and/or sexual abuse as well as those who are unable to understand language and communicate fluently (Adams, 2010). Advocates of "trauma-informed care" suggest that physical restraint may exacerbate the negative effects of this prior trauma and actually increase the child's aggressive or violent behaviors. Recent attention has focused on the psychological affects on students who are restrained, as well as the staff members who conduct restraints who may be traumatized by these situations. These effects may be short-term effect, such as fear and an adrenaline rush of physical confrontation, or long-term effect, such as post-traumatic stress disorder. Although there are little research data to support this hypothesis, it is both plausible and supported by numerous anecdotal reports from people who have been restrained or restrained others (CCBD, 2009).

## Inappropriate Use of Restraint

Many parents and advocacy groups have expressed concerns that schools often implement restraint procedures for reasons other than physical safety. Ryan et al. (2008) found that even well trained staff members frequently implemented restraint procedures in a special day school predominantly for reasons other than what school policy stipulated (i.e., student posed a danger to themselves or others). When analyzing incident reports, Ryan et al. (2008) found staff reported "noncompliance" (48.4%) and "leaving the assigned area" (19.4%) were the leading precipitators of restraint. Other reasons mentioned by staff members for implementing restraint included "property misuse/destruction" (7.3%), "disrespect" (7.3%), "disrupting the class" (6.5%), "threatening" (3.2%), "physical aggression" (3.2%), "horseplay" (3.2%), and "harassment" (0.8%). Hence, nearly all (over 90%) of physical restraint procedures were performed for reasons other than what was permissible in accordance with school policy. Similarly, Sellman (2009) interviewed students in a special school for students with social, emotional, and behavioral difficulties and found that although students stated they understood the need for restraint procedures, they thought staff members often used the restraint procedures inappropriately and inconsistently. Students also reported that prior to and even during restraints, the staff members used antagonistic language toward them. Obviously these types of staff behaviors are more likely to result in escalating a student's behavior as opposed to de-escalating the situation as desired (see also Luiselli, Bastien, & Putnam, 1998).

## Overreliance on Restraint Even When Ineffective

Perhaps the most alarming aspect of schools implementing restraint is applying it with specific students without reducing aggressive or dangerous behavior. Often restraint procedures are used repetitively on a student who has a history of displaying aggressive behaviors throughout a school year. Research has shown some students may be restrained as often as 60 times within an academic school year (Ryan et al., 2008). In such cases, staff members are applying an ineffective intervention. The CCBD, (2009) cautions that repeated use of physical restraints for any one student or multiple physical restraints across different students should be viewed as failed educational programming. It is important that schools conduct a functional behavioral assessment (FBA) to properly identify the underlying purpose or function of a student's maladaptive behavior, and to consider other measures that might provide more effective or intensive behavioral intervention.

## Lack of Oversight

Although the behavioral practices of physical restraint migrated to our nation's public schools from more restrictive settings, the federal legislation (Children's Health Act, 2000) and related state regulations applicable to hospital and residential treatment settings do not apply to schools. Oversight of public and private schools are typically provided by state education agencies. The legal and licensing standards that govern the use of restraints within several other professions such as medicine, psychiatry, and law enforcement do not apply to these educational settings. When state or local policies do exist, they typically vary greatly in content, and are often advisory in nature (Ryan et al., 2009; U.S. GAO, 2009). The lack of these commonly accepted written state standards for school districts regarding restraint has left schools more susceptible to misunderstanding, improper implementation, and abuse of these types of procedures. However, as a result of the proposed federal legislation pending in Congress (HR 4247), many states and local school districts are currently creating or revising their policies and procedures. It is still unclear whether there will be federal standards on these procedures for schools, but state and local district policies will likely be more complete and updated, if not standardized as a result.

The recent focus on developing district level policies and procedures should also result in more consistent training related to the use of physical restraint in schools. Some districts have provided clear training to the staff members who are most likely to use these procedures, but others have not (see Chapter 17, this volume). As a result of proposed federal legislation, when training is provided now in schools, it typically focuses on the only accepted rationale for the use of these procedures (safety of students and staff), may be more prevention oriented (de-escalation of inappropriate behaviors), and is provided to all school staff.

## COURT RULINGS AFFECTING THE USE OF PHYSICAL RESTRAINT

For several decades numerous court rulings have helped establish precedent for using restraint procedures as an intervention for individuals with aggressive behavior. Several critical areas the courts have ruled on to date include 1) permissibility, 2) required staff training, and 3) professional judgment. A brief overview of each is provided as follows.

### Permissibility of Restraint in Schools

The courts, state educational agencies, and the Office for Civil Rights (U.S. Department of Health and Human Services) have consistently found that physical or ambulatory restraint is an acceptable means for staff to safely deal with a student's aggressive behavior when implemented appropriately (*Brown v. Ramsey*, 2000). Furthermore, restraint does not violate a student's Individuals with Disabilities Education Act (IDEA) rights (*Melissa S. v. School District of Pittsburgh*, 2006), is not considered to be cruel and unusual punishment when implemented in accordance with professional practices (*Garland Independent School District v. Wilks*, 1987), and does not qualify as corporal punishment (*Florence (SC) County No. 1 School District*, 1987). Note, however, that the courts have ruled that schools cannot use excessive force and appreciable physical pain on a student (*Metzger v. Osbeck*, 1988), must provide parents and/or legal guardians written notice if physical restraint is being implemented on a regular basis (*Waukee Community School District v. Douglas and Eva L.*, 2008), and cannot use restraint as a form of punishment (*Converse v. Nelson*, 1995). The Office of Special Education Programs (OSEP, U.S. Department of Education) has clarified that IDEA does not prohibit physical restraint for individuals with disabilities; however, it may be limited by either state law or the student's Individualized Education Plan (Letter to Anonymous, 2008, OSEP, U.S. Department of Education).

### Required Staff Training

In *Wyatt v. King* (1992) the U.S. Circuit Court ruled that staff working with individuals with mental illness require specific training regarding behavioral interventions that are unique to their care. The Court ruled that this professional training should entail psychopharmacology, psychopathology, and psychotherapeutic interventions, as well as interviewing and assessment procedures for determining a patient's mental status. Although this specific case dealt with treatment in psychiatric settings, the need for adequate staff training in any setting, including schools, is implied.

### Importance of Professional Judgment

Over a quarter century ago, the Supreme Court ruled in *Youngberg v. Romeo* (1982), that the judicial system should not invade the province of those whose job it is to make medical and custodial decisions. The case set precedent for the establishment of procedures used to determine whether restraint was considered reasonable and hinged upon whether staff properly exercised "professional judgment." The Court ruled that professional judgment was considered to be presumptively valid. This presumption effectively shifted the burden of proof from the caretaker (e.g., staff) to the individual patient (e.g., parent) alleging that restraint was unreasonable (Kennedy & Mohr, 2001). Although this ruling did not directly pertain to schools, it could place the burden of proof upon parents claiming the use of restraint procedures violated the rights of their child, and not upon the school to defend its use of the procedure. A recent 11th circuit court ruling has reinforced this position (*T.W. v. School Board of Seminole County, Florida*, 2010).

## FEDERAL AND STATE REGULATION

Because physical restraint is an invasive and controversial procedure that has resulted in numerous deaths and injuries from being used inappropriately, there are now an increasing number of proposed federal, state, and local policies governing its use in educational settings. The intent of most all of these policies is to 1) protect children from the dangers of misapplication, 2) identify appropriate uses of restraint, and 3) ensure staff members are properly trained.

Although there has been federal legislation governing restraint in hospital and residential treatment settings since 1990 (Children's Health Act, 1990), there is currently no applicable federal law in schools. Following a series of congressional hearings and briefings held during the spring and summer of 2009, both the U.S. U.S. House of Representatives and Senate proposed almost identical federal legislation mandating that schools nationwide implement policies that regulate physical restraint. The intent of the federal legislation is to protect students from physical or mental abuse from the inappropriate use of restraint procedures imposed solely for purposes of discipline or convenience. While the U.S. House of Representatives bill (H.R. 4247) was passed successfully, the Senate's version (S. 2860) died in committee and the bill never became a law. On March 6, 2011, Rep. George Miller (D-CA), ranking member of the Education and Workforce Committee in the House of Representatives reintroduced the bill as "Keeping All Students Safe Act."

State policy may consist either of legislation, administrative rules, or guidelines (often identified as technical assistance documents) designed to promote best practices and clarify essential principles of restraint procedures within schools. These policies represent a continuum in that laws and regulations provide compulsory procedures that schools must follow, whereas guidelines generally are not compulsory. A recent examination of existing state policies found that many states have neither a regulation or guideline governing restraint procedures in school settings, and that those states that do have some policies or guidelines vary tremendously in their content (Ryan et al., 2009). However, the U.S. Secretary of Education, Arne Duncan (2009), has called on states in the United States to create or revise their policies on this topic. As a result, many states have begun to implement new or revised policies on these topics, and the number of states that may have policies in this area is expected to change quickly.

In addition to federal or state policy, local school boards may also create their own regulatory policies. For example, a school district or school board policy may indicate the overall philosophy about why restraint should be used (e.g., threat to injury), how it should be implemented, and what training is required for staff members. Policies at this level might also emphasize the need for positive behavior supports within schools to prevent restraint.

A second type of local school policy is the student/parent "handbook," a document generally used to inform students and parents about many policies and operating procedures, including restraint implementation. Finally, many schools may also have detailed written procedures which provide guidance for educators on various topics such as safe application of restraints in schools, non-restrictive behavior supports, and safety plans. Unfortunately, there are virtually no data about the number of school districts that have these types of policies, and no information about the nature or content of these policies where they do exist at the school district level.

## ESSENTIAL COMPONENTS OF NEW FEDERAL, STATE, OR LOCAL POLICY

The bills proposed in the U.S. Congress generally reflect what others have identified as good professional practice regarding physical restraint (CCBD, 2009). These bills, as well as other policies, include several key components that should be addressed in policy and practice when restraint procedures are used in the schools.

### Criteria for Using Physical Restraint

As discussed previously, physical restraint has been used across many professions, including law enforcement, mental health, and education. In all of these professions, the purpose of physical restraint is consistent, primarily to control the behavior of an individual in an emergency situation to prevent immediate danger or possible injuries to themselves or others in the environment. Although there continues to be arguments that physical restraint may be implemented as a therapeutic procedure for some children, the supportive research data are equivocal (Day, 2002; Luiselli, 2009).

### Terminology and Use of Restraint

Perhaps the most critical component of a policy is that it accurately describes restraint and proper application. Currently some state policies only categorize a restraint as a procedure that lasts for over 30 seconds. Other states only recognize a restraint as occurring once, despite how many times it was actually implemented during a day. The recommended use of restraint, as we have emphasized, is that it be applied to control behavior only under the following emergency circumstances and only if all four of these elements exist, including 1) student's actions pose a clear, present, and imminent physical danger to him or her or to others, 2) less restrictive measures have not effectively de-escalated the risk of injury, 3) restraint should last only as long as necessary to resolve the actual risk of danger or harm, and 4) degree of force applied may not exceed what is necessary to protect the student or other persons from imminent bodily injury (CCBD, 2009). These four components define the circumstances and limits of using restraint. Proper implementation of restraint demands professional judgment by individuals within the school who have specific training. As noted earlier in the chapter, physical restraint should never be used for the purpose of managing student behavior, punishment, addressing noncompliance, or responding to students running away unless there is imminent risk of injury related to that flight.

## Mandatory Staff Training

All personnel who work with students demonstrating aggressive behaviors require the necessary tools, training, and support to ensure the safety of all students and all school personnel. Unfortunately, many school staff are not trained in effective behavioral interventions necessary to prevent emotional outbursts typically associated with students who have severe behavioral problems (Moses, 2000). Such interventions are critical in preventing student behavior from escalating to potentially dangerous levels where restraint may be needed. Hence, a critical component of any policy should focus on training requirements for staff members who are authorized to implement physical restraint procedures.

Training should result in some form of certification or credential for each individual staff member and overall certification or credential for the school district, agency, or school. Wherever possible, only staff trained in physical restraint should implement the procedure. Training should include recognition of the various phases of the cycle of aggression, verbal de-escalation strategies, counseling procedures, and specific restraint methods. Staff should also be certified in first aid and cardio-pulmonary resuscitation in the event of an emergency related to restraint. Training should be recurrent with annual updates at a minimum, be appropriate to the type of school setting and consistent with the developmental level of students. Training should also cover positive, instructional, and preventive methods for addressing student behavior. Other training components would be conflict prevention, de-escalation, conflict management, and evaluation of risks of challenging behavior. For safety purposes staff should learn multiple methods for monitoring a student's well-being (e.g., breathing, pulse oximeters) during a restraint.

## Certification of Staff to Perform Restraint Procedures

In most medical, psychiatric, and law enforcement applications, strict standards govern use of physical restraint and seclusion. For example, agencies such as the Joint Commission on Accreditation of Healthcare Organizations, the National Association of Psychiatric Treatment Centers for Children (Cribari, 1996), and the American Academy of Pediatrics Committee on Pediatric Emergency Medicine (1997) regulate restraint. These requirements have resulted in widespread training and certification of staff in the medical and psychiatric programs that employ physical restraints, and many of these programs have attempted to reduce drastically their use of these procedures as a result of the deaths and injuries related to their use. Similarly, many schools employ Crisis Intervention Training from private vendors that offer such certification (Couvillon, Peterson, Ryan, Scheuermann, & Stegall, 2010).

## Documentation Procedures

Appropriate documentation of restraint use is essential. Any time restraint is implemented, schools should record 1) student information, 2) day/time of occurrence, 3) names of those staff members involved, 4) circumstances surrounding use of restraint, and 5) any injuries incurred. This information must be documented immediately following a restraint, with a copy placed in the student's record and provided to the parent. Be aware that state advocacy and protection agencies can request access to all school records of restraint to investigate the possibility that abuse is occurring. If schools do not maintain accurate records there could be a partial basis for a finding against the school. It behooves state or provincial department of education to provide oversight of this data much in the way that it now does for school discipline data.

## Individualized Education Plans and Individual Safety Plans

Proposed federal legislation states that in the case of a student with a disability, restraint procedures *should not* be written into her or his individualized education plan, individual safety plan, or behavioral intervention plan. There was serious debate about whether restraints should be included in these documents, with a clear divide between school administrators, who called for their inclusion, and parent advocacy groups, who argued vehemently for excluding them in individualized plans. Many parents believe that having restraint procedures within these documents implies tacit approval of their use, and may legitimize their use on a more routine basis than would otherwise be the case. On the other hand, many school administrators contend that inclusion of restraint procedures in these documents is one way to inform parents about their potential use and may make staffing and training issues more clear.

## Safety Procedures

Only trained personnel should implement physical restraint. A restraint should not be applied without at least one additional staff member present and in line of sight. This is a safety precaution for the student restrained, the staff implementing restraint, and other students. In the case of floor restraint that places pressure or weight on the chest, lungs, sternum, diaphragm, back, neck, or throat, staff members should use extreme caution when using either prone (face down) or supine (face up) restraints. No restraint should be administered in such a manner that prevents a student from breathing or speaking.

As we discussed earlier, repeated use of physical restraints for any one student or multiple physical restraints across different students should be viewed as the failure of educational programming and the likelihood that supports, educational methodologies, and other interventions for the students are inadequate and should be modified. As an emergency procedure, restraint should only be used if there is a threat of imminent physical danger to the student or others. We reiterate that a large number of "emergencies" is a clear sign that the normal educational or behavioral programming is failing and should be revised. For students with disabilities in special education, such data should trigger an individualized education plan team review of the individual student's programs and placement as well as overall school evaluation of its behavior support plans and programs serving students with behavioral needs.

## Notification Procedures

All schools should have procedures for reporting when restraint procedures are used. Following a physical restraint, a designated staff member should verbally notify either the program supervisor or building administrator as soon as possible, and file a written incident report within 24 hours. Parents or guardians should be informed immediately after each and every use of restraint, and should be provided a copy of all documentation as soon as it is created.

## Monitoring Procedures

Due to the risk of shock, potential delayed effects, or possible injury from restraint, the physical well-being of the student who was restrained should be monitored for the remainder of the school day. Similarly, the physical well-being of the team who conducted the restraints should also be monitored.

## Compliance Procedures

Compliance with district and school policies should be mandatory for all school staff with clear lines of responsibility and oversight identified. In any school where physical restraint is used, there should be written policies and the possibility of emergency use of physical restraint procedures should be clearly stated. Schoolwide or general safety plans or policies must identify if physical restraint might be employed in emergency situations within a school setting. District and school polices should be made known to all staff, and they should be disseminated to parents of all students in that school. It is incumbent upon senior administrators (e.g., school principal) to ensure the implementation of these policies.

## Contentious Issues Regarding Regulations in Education

Despite the guidance that the proposed federal restraint legislation provides schools, there are still many unanswered questions, as considered in the following section.

### Who Should Be Trained?
Perhaps the first issue administrators need to address is which staff should be trained in de-escalation and restraint procedures. Should all staff members be trained or

only those who directly interact with challenging students? An alternative we recommend is that all staff members become trained in basic de-escalation strategies to help reduce the potential of a crisis situation, and only a core group of staff members be trained in conducting restraint procedures. This option would be a more cost effective means to training staff, and ensure the members that actually conduct restraint procedures are trained to a higher degree and maintain higher levels of proficiency.

### What Comprises an Effective Training Program?

Being able to determine the need for physical intervention, and how to correctly and appropriately implement restraint in emergency situations, requires staff training. Selecting a training program that provides sufficient evidence-based information about the broad range of variables that are important to prevention of behavioral crises (e.g., variables related to curriculum, instruction, behavior management, or verbal interactions) is an important task for school and agency administrators. The reader is referred to Couvillon et al. (2010), who reviewed 13 commercial crisis de-escalation training programs and compared them based on course content, duration, and type of instruction. Chapter 17, this volume, also provides a detailed analysis of restraint training programs.

### Costs of Implementation

In today's financial climate of budget cuts and teacher furloughs, administrators must consider the costs of teacher training. Many school districts have already cried that the pending federal legislation is essentially yet another unfunded federal mandate that states will be required to implement without requisite funding. Current federal legislation proposes that grants be awarded to state educational agencies for 1) establishing, implementing and enforcing restraint policies, 2) collecting and analyzing restraint data, and 3) implementing positive behavioral supports. Another potential cost saving measure is to utilize commercial "train the trainer" programs, in which a school district sends one or a few members for advanced training in de-escalation and restraint procedures. These individuals are then tasked with training other district personnel on their return.

### How Can Data Be Gathered and Provided to Outside Agencies?

A consistent problem in researching the prevalence of restraint procedures used in schools nationwide is the lack of consistent data reporting procedures. As the US GAO (2009) recently reported, they could not identify a single web site, federal agency, or other entity that collects comprehensive information on the use of restraints in public schools. Although certain agencies (e.g., Department of Education's Office of Civil Rights) are responsible for processing complaints about the inappropriate use of restraint on children with disabilities, their data collection system does not permit them to identify these specific incidents. Hence, it is critical that data collection procedures be handled in a standardized manner across states to accurately track prevalence rates and injuries associated with the use of restraint in school systems.

## FUTURE RESEARCH

To date, almost no research has been conducted on the prevalence and effectiveness of restraint procedures in educational settings. We do not know how widely physical restraint is used in the schools, the extent or nature of injuries occurring when it has been used, or its success in achieving desired outcomes. It is apparent there is a strong need for additional research regarding implementation procedures, evaluation of the efficacy of restraint on reducing aggressive behaviors and impact of differing policies/procedures on the use of restraint within schools. Research about these procedures is needed and would permit better understanding of both negative and positive outcomes of the use of restraint procedures. Recommended areas for future research include but are not limited to 1) extent to which schools currently employ physical restraint, 2) types of restraint procedures used, 3) nature of antecedents or behavior that precipitate restraint, 4) characteristics of students restrained, 5) intended purposes or goals of restraint, 6) efficacy of restraint procedures in reducing aggressive behavior, 7) side effects both physical (e.g., injuries) and emotional (e.g., stress) experienced by both students and staff members involved, 8) training level of staff members, and 9) alternatives to restraint. Finally, there is also a need for new and updated research on the policy content, implementation, costs, and impact at federal, state and district levels regarding the use of restraint procedures.

## CONCLUSIONS

Increased levels of violence across schools nationwide have created a sense of urgency for school systems to be able to safely protect students and staff alike. Greater reliance on restraint may also be the result of more students with developmental disabilities and serious challenging behaviors receiving educational services in their local schools as opposed to more restrictive settings. The adoption of restraint procedures by many schools to manage aggressive behaviors has unfortunately resulted in a number of injuries and fatalities. The resulting media attention and litigation has prompted federal legislation to monitor restraint procedures in schools. However, with limited research on prevalence, appropriate applications, and efficacy, restraint, continues to be adopted by school systems nationwide. If schools elect to use restraint procedures to address aggressive behaviors, regulation at the federal or state levels is essential to ensure restraint procedures are utilized in a safe and efficacious manner. Restraint procedures should be reserved for only those situations where there is a threat to safety of students or staff. It is also imperative that all staff members who implement restraints be trained in de-escalation techniques as well as proper restraint techniques. Although, ideally, all staff members should be trained, schools should at least establish and train teams designated to serve as crisis prevention and intervention. Furthermore, procedural guidelines regarding documentation and notification should be implemented. We recommend that a system of documentation include a periodic monitoring procedure by administrators or intervention teams to ensure proper techniques are being implemented, and to examine the effectiveness of the practice for individual students.

Because restraint in schools is not an evidence based procedure, research is needed to investigate the effects of regulations and context of training and resources needed to evaluate regulations. Although federal policy on these topics remains in flux, there is an increased level of importance for state and local policies to be put in place in order to address the critical safety issues addressed within this chapter.

## REFERENCES

Adams, E. (2010, July). *Healing invisible wounds: Why investing in trauma-informed care for children makes sense.* Washington, DC: Justice Policy Institute. Retrieved from http://www.justicepolicy.org/

American Academy of Pediatrics Committee on Pediatric Emergency Medicine (1997). The use of physical restraint interventions for children and adolescents in the acute care setting. *Pediatrics, 99*(3), 497–498.

Bowlby, J. (1973). *Attachment and loss: Vol. 2. Separation, anxiety and anger.* New York, NY: Basic Books.

*Brown v. Ramsey*, 121 F. Supp. 2d 911, 923–925 (E.D. Va. 2000).

Child Welfare League of America (2000). *Advocacy: Seclusion and restraints: Fact sheet*, 1–2. Retrieved from http://cwla.org/advocacy/seclusionrestraints.htm

Children's Health Act of 2000 (P.L. 106-310), 42 U.S.C. 201, Title 32, Section 59. (Amends Title V of the Public Health Service Act [42 U.S.C. 290aa et seq.]

Cline, F.W. (1979). *What shall we do with this kid? Understanding and treating the disturbed child.* Evergreen, CO: Evergreen Consultants.

*Converse v. Nelson*, No. 95-16776 (Mass Superior Ct., July 1995).

Council for Children with Behavior Disorders. (2009). CCBD's position summary on the use of physical restraint procedures in school settings. *Behavioral Disorders, 34*(4), 223–234.

Council for Exceptional Children. (2009, September). CEC's policy on physical restraint and seclusion procedures in school settings. Reston, VA: Author.

Couvillon, M., Peterson, R.L., Ryan J.B., Scheuermann, B.K., & Stegall, J. (2010). A review of crisis intervention training programs for schools. *Teaching Exceptional Children, 42*(5), 6–17.

Cribari, L. (1996). Facilities rethink policies on use of physical restraint. *Brown University Child & Adolescent Behavior Letter, 12*(8), 1–3.

Day, D.M. (2002). Examining the therapeutic utility of physical restraint and seclusion with students and youth: The role of theory and research in practice. *American Journal of Orthopsychiatry, 72,* 266–278.

Duncan, A. (2009, July 31). *Letter to chief state school officers regarding policies on physical restraint and seclusion.* Washington, DC: Secretary of Education, U.S. Department of Education.

Florence (SC) County No. 1 School Dist., EHLR 352:495 (OCR 1987).

*Garland Independent School District v. Wilks*, 657 F. Supp. 1163 (N.D. Tex. 1987).

Kennedy, S.S., & Mohr, W.K. (2001). A prolegomenon on restraint of children: Implicating constitutional rights. *American Journal of Orthopsychiatry, 71*(1), 26–37.

Letter to Anonymous, 50 IDELR 228 (OSEP 2008), U.S. Department of Education.

Luiselli, J.K. (2009). Physical restraint of people with intellectual disability: A review of implementation reduction and elimination procedures. *Journal of Applied Research in Intellectual Disabilities, 22,* 126–134.

Luiselli, J.K., Bastien, J.S., & Putnam, R.F. (1998). Behavioral assessment and analysis of mechanical restraint utilization on a psychiatric child and adolescent inpatient setting. *Behavioral Interventions, 13,* 147–155.

*Melissa S. v. School District of Pittsburgh*, 183 Fed Appx. 184, 2006 WL 1558900 (3rd Cir. 2006).

*Metzger v. Osbeck*, 841 F.2d 518 (3rd Cir. 1988).

Mohr, W.K., Petti, T.A., & Mohr, B.D. (2003). Adverse effects associated with physical restraint. *Canadian Journal of Psychiatry, 48*(5), 330–337.

Moses, T. (2000). Why people choose to be residential child care workers. *Child and Youth Care Forum, 29*(2), 113–126.

Persi, J., & Pasquali, B. (1999). The use of seclusion and physical restraints: Just how consistent are we? *Child and Youth Care Forum, 28*(2), 87–103.

Ryan, J.B., Peterson, R.L., Tetreault, G., & Van der Hagen, E. (2004). Reducing the use of seclusion and restraint in a day school program. In M.A. Nunno, L. Bullard, & D.M. Day (Eds.), *For our own safety: Examining the safety of high-risk interventions for children and young people* (pp. 201–216). Washington, DC: Child Welfare League of America.

Ryan, J.B., Robbins, K., Peterson, R.L., & Rozalski, M. (2009). Review of state policies concerning the use of physical restraint procedures in schools. *Education and Treatment of Children, 32*(3), 487–504.

Ryan, J.B., & Peterson, R.L. (2004). Physical restraint in school. *Behavioral Disorders, 29*(2), 154–168.

Sellman, E. (2009). Lessons learned: Student voice at a school for pupils experiencing social, emotional and behavioral difficulties. *Emotional and Behavioural Difficulties, 14*(1), 33–48.

Sturmey, P., Lott, J.D., Laud, R., & Matson, J.L. (2005). Correlates of restraint use in an institutional population: A replication. *Journal of Intellectual Disability Research 49*(7), 501–506.

*T.W. v. School Board of Seminole County, Florida,* aff'd, No. 09-12623, (11th Cir. June 29, 2010).

U.S. Government Accountability Office. (2009). *Seclusions and restraints: Selected cases of death and abuse at public and private schools and treatment centers.* (Publication No. GAO-09-719T). Retrieved from http://www.gao.gov/

*Waukee Community School District v. Douglas and Eva L.,* 51 IDELR 15 (S.D. Ia. 2008).

*Wyatt v. King, 793 F. Supp. 1058,* 1077–79 (1992).

*Youngberg v. Romeo,* 457 U.S. 307, 323, 321 (1982).

Zaslow, R.W., & Menta, M. (1975). *The psychology of the Z process: Attachment and activation.* San Jose, CA: San Jose State University Press.

**16**

CHAPTER

# Emergency Physical Restraint

## Considerations for Staff Training and Supervision

*David Lennox, Mark A. Geren, and David Rourke*

Of all the skill areas in which staff members require training to effectively, safely, and ethically provide services to individuals who exhibit high-risk challenging behaviors, the use of emergency physical interventions is perhaps the most difficult, controversial, and problematic. A primary goal of emergency intervention (EI) training is to train staff in methods to prevent and avoid their use. Staff is then trained to precision in implementing those strategies. Thus, the trainer's task is somewhat contradictory: "I've trained you how to do this; now don't do what I've just trained you to do!" This is, however, the state of affairs many organizations face when considering the high-risk challenging behavior exhibited by individuals they serve—make sure everyone is safe while avoiding restraint whenever possible.

Although we agree with the general consensus that the use of physical restraints is undesirable, training in EI skills is important and essential for numerous reasons. First, despite efforts to prevent, assess, and treat high-risk behaviors more effectively, such behaviors do happen. Because they do, properly trained physical restraint techniques are considered a necessary, appropriate, and justifiable response to limit, dangerous, high-risk behaviors (American Psychological Association, 1994; Association of Professional Behavior Analysts, 2010; Luiselli, Kane, Treml, & Young, 2000; Matson & Boisjoli, 2009; Tilli & Spreat, 2009; Vollmer et al., 2010). Second in the absence of formal training in safe, effective and ethical management strate gies, other less desirable, dangerous, or abusive management techniques are possi if not likely.

From a regulatory perspective, it is the responsibility of any provider to clients free from harm. To date, however, neither federal regulations nor mo regulations sufficiently specify the allowable parameters around which to tr in using restraint. A recently completed U.S. Government Accountabilit (GAO) report (2009) focusing exclusively on school settings found that t "...no federal laws restricting the use of seclusion and restraints in private schools and widely divergent laws at the state level" with up to nineteen states specifying no regulations at all governing the use of restraint in schools. In settings other than schools, use of restraint is probably more regulated; however, in 1998 the GAO did report states have varying degrees of regulation and oversight for restraint, with some states having different standards for their state-run facilities and private providers across a wide variety of treatment populations.

Although a review of regulations, efficacy, and ethical issues governing the use of physical restraint is available elsewhere (Ryan & Peterson, 2004; Ryan & Peterson, 2012; U.S. Department of Education, 2010; U.S. Government Accountability Office, 2009), the minimal or, in some cases, nonexistent, regulatory consideration of restraint with high-risk challenging behavior is noteworthy and highly relevant to any discussion about training and supervision of restraint implementation.

This chapter 1) reviews the critical components of a comprehensive EI training program, 2) describes conventional and evidence-based methods for training staff in restraint prevention and implementation, 3) makes recommendations for the implementation of such training programs across education and habilitation settings, and 4) considers issues of maintenance and supervision of restraint prevention and restraint strategies.

## COMPONENTS OF EMERGENCY INTERVENTION TRAINING CURRICULA

There are dozens of commercially available EI training programs available to providers serving individuals with high-risk behaviors, as well as numerous additional "in-house" training programs developed by providers. Although some organizations may develop their own in-house EI training program or mix and match from multiple programs, the authors do not recommend this. It is also prohibited under some regulatory schemes (e.g., Rhode Island Department of Children, Youth, and Families). There are also several published articles that have reviewed content and other characteristics of EI training programs (Couvillon, Peterson, Ryan, Scheuermann & Stegall, 2010; Doughty, 2005; Farrell & Cubit, 2005; Morrison & Love, 2003). In addition, there are regulations in (a surprisingly) few number of states that either dictate minimum content, duration, and other standards for the training of physical restraint procedures (see U.S. Department of Education, 2010, for a review of states' regulations) or require the use of approved selected commercially available training programs.

## GOALS OF EMERGENCY INTERVENTION TRAINING PROGRAMS

Before implementing an EI training program, goals should be clearly stated and consistent with standards of practice, regulations, organizational policies and procedures, and any other governing influences. Generally speaking, most EI training programs begin with some variation of the following goals (for detail, see the corresponding content outlined in the first three columns of Table 16.1): 1) prevent high-risk behaviors from occurring, 2) reverse the momentary escalation and intensity of high-risk behaviors, 3) safely and therapeutically manage high-risk behaviors without injury or trauma, and 4) terminate the high-risk situation as quickly as possible.

**Table 16.1.** Emergency intervention training content areas

| Content area | General content | Specific content | ABA enhancements |
|---|---|---|---|
| Understanding causes of high-risk behavior | Conditions that may cause or contribute to such behaviors including medical and health conditions, various contributing diagnostic conditions (neurologic, psychiatric), as well as skill and sensory impairments, and social and abuse histories. | Goals of safety management<br>Interdisciplinary treatment<br>General regulatory issues<br>Ethical issues and constraints<br>Contributors to high-risk behavior | Inadvertent reinforcement of high-risk behavior<br>Motivational variables and operations |
| Prevention strategies | Environmental, social, scheduling, and structural recommendations for preventing the occurrence of high-risk behavior. Such recommendations as reducing sources of stimulation, "engineering" a safer environment, general staff-to-consumer interaction suggestions, and general safety habits are often included. | Creating a safe and therapeutic environment<br>Safety habits | Noncontingent reinforcement<br>Differential reinforcement |
| Minimization strategies | Recommendations designed to train staff to be sensitive to and detect the wide array of possible antecedents and precursors and engage in strategies to minimize or prevent subsequent high-risk behavior(s). | Detecting antecedents and predicting behavior<br>• Environmental antecedents<br>• Behavioral antecedents<br>Safety stance and sitting<br>Calling for assistance<br>Leadership and teamwork<br>De-escalation<br>• Safety during de-escalation<br>• Avoidance of power struggles<br>• The de-escalation process | Antecedent interventions<br>Behavioral de-escalation procedures<br>• Functional communication<br>• Behavioral momentum<br>• Differential reinforcement<br>• Planned ignoring |

(continued)

**Table 16.1.**  *(continued)*

| Content area | General content | Specific content | ABA enhancements |
|---|---|---|---|
| Management strategies | Evasive and release techniques for avoiding, escaping, and managing high-risk physical behavior (e.g., aggression) to avoid contact and harm. Strategies include a wide range of methods for physically holding (restraining) a consumer from whom high-risk behavior is either imminent or is occurring, as well as methods for release from a hold. | Management of weapons<br>Basic physical safety skills<br>The protective stance and evasion<br>Blocking, response interruption, guiding<br>Release (wrist, choke, hair)<br>Bite prevention and release<br>When to use physical management<br>Minimizing risk of procedures<br>Standing holds<br>Escort procedures<br>Seated/floor holds | Using reinforcement during release |
| Postmanagement considerations | Critical activity to understanding the previous crisis event, from which potentially effective changes in prevention, minimization, and management strategies specific to the consumer may be derived. | Releasing from physical management<br>Physical examination of the client<br>Documentation of intervention | Functional assessment account of antecedent events, high-risk behavior, interventions<br>Behavioral consultation |

*Key:* ABA, applied behavior analysis.

Beyond these typical goals, we believe that EI training programs have mistakenly focused primarily and, in some cases, exclusively on *suppression* of high-risk behaviors. By doing so, the opportunity and efficacy of evidence-based *behavior change* procedures have been omitted, even though these procedures provide the most effective preventive strategies for high-risk behaviors (e.g., Donat, 1998). In other words, within the context of training prevention and emergency interventions, evidence-based behavior change procedures are often not even considered.

This phenomenon, unfortunately, often leads to two separate and distinctly different staff training programs in many treatment and educational settings: one training program involving the organizationally mandated EI training course; and one training program including behavior change procedures. In fact, additional (or separate) training in techniques for teaching clients alternative appropriate behaviors with behavior analytic procedures has been an approach recommended by many authors publishing in the area of restraint practices (Spreat & Baker-Potts, 1983; Tilli & Spreat, 2009; Williams, 2010). Having separate training programs is understandable because of the historical and developmental factors of EI training programs and because of the general goal of EI training: preparing staff for unpredictable high-risk challenging behavior for which a treatment intervention has not yet been developed (Williams, 2010).

We contend, however, that behavior change procedures and EI procedures are not and should not be considered two separate repertoires trained in two separate programs. Instead, applied behavioral research and technology lends itself particularly well to integration into EI training programs. (One such program that exemplifies the integration of applied behavior analytic strategies and emergency interventions is the Safety-Care™ Behavioral Safety Training Program by QBS Inc., 2010.[1]) The integration of behavior change procedures, particularly behavior analytic strategies into EI training, may make it more likely that these strategies will be used before "last resort" EI procedure, potentially making those procedures unnecessary. It is not unreasonable to hypothesize that if trained in the same context, within the same scenarios, and afforded the same "weight," the procedures may be more likely to be implemented correctly. A combined training may also require shorter overall training time for staff to acquire both behavioral and EI skills, a practical concern with any training program (Matson & Boisjoli, 2009). Utilizing behavior analytic procedures that evoke and generate reinforced alternative responses to high-risk behaviors, under the stimulus conditions present at the time of the high-risk behaviors, allows for training to occur under the strongest motivational conditions possible—those that actually produce the high-risk behavior. Moreover, many professionals have lamented to us that EI training programs often train prevention and EI strategies that are not only different from, but incompatible with functionally-based interventions that are also recommended. Anecdotally, numerous trainers from a behavior analytic background, when discussing training of EI training skills to their staff, have reported saying to their staff, "I know I just trained those procedures, but please don't use them." We believe this sentiment reflects a number of concerns with nonbehavior-analytic curricula including the potentially reinforcing effects of emergency interventions on the high-risk behavior being managed (e.g., Favell, McGimsey, & Jones, 1978).

---

[1]Safety-Care is a trademark of QBS, Inc.

Some of the most relevant applied behavior analytic content we recommend for inclusion in EI training programs is summarized in column 4 of Table 16.1. These enhancements permit the addition of two goals to EI training programs: 1) teach and strengthen behaviors that are incompatible with high-risk behaviors and 2) decrease the future likelihood of high-risk behaviors.

## Additional Content Comments and Considerations

Although much of the specific content in Table 16.1 is common to many EI training programs, there are several possible areas needing clarification or elaboration. First, as noted above, there are selected antecedent and operant procedures that integrate well into an EI training program and provide a more evidence-based foundation. For instance, de-escalation procedures are often a combination of ambiguous counseling strategies, choice offerings, limit setting, and/or warning systems that may or may not be derived from any particular theoretical and/or research foundation. As noted earlier, however, the integration of selected behavior analytic procedures, particularly those that are relatively "function-neutral" (with respect to the reinforcement and motivational characteristics of the behavior), provides for evidence-based skills that can be specifically trained and evaluated for competency. (It is somewhat interesting that although de-escalation strategies are included in most every EI training program known to the current authors, few actually require demonstration of mastery in what is arguably one of the most important content areas contributing to restraint prevention.)

A second consideration is relevant to the scope or breadth of the EI training program content. When working with high-risk individuals, it is generally accepted that no single curriculum will account for all possible scenarios that may arise. For instance, it may be entirely reasonable to expect that a client would not limit their method of grabbing a staff member at the wrist or hair in the manner taught by a particular EI training program, instead grasping a staff member by the legs. Similarly, a client may be so large as to limit a particular staff member's ability to conduct a safety hold as prescribed. Additionally, some EI procedures may be substantially more dangerous to the staff or client than other common procedures. In consequence, these procedures may only be trained to select staff, or be considered an "optional" offering, to limit its use only to those organizations for which it is considered absolutely necessary. Therefore, when selecting an EI training curriculum, the desired scope and comprehensiveness of the content should be guided by a combination of the factors specific to the organization including, but not limited to

- Regulations under which an organization operates.
- Intensity and severity of behaviors with whom the procedures will be applied.
- Physical skills and limitations of the staff implementing procedures.
- Number and ratio of available staff during emergency interventions.
- Staff supervision practices and processes when interventions might be implemented.
- Medical, physical, and other impairments of the clients.
- The variety of contexts, settings, and situations in which the procedures may be applied.

- The difficulty and vulnerability of misuse and misapplication of a particular procedure.
- Number of staff to train, available training time, costs, and scheduling logistics.

The concept of "abuse potential," often used in describing medication characteristics, is useful here to describe the risks of misuse, inaccurate implementation, and application to an individual for whom the procedure may be dangerous. For instance, the abuse potential of a prone floor hold is usually considered quite high, as it could result in compression asphyxia, injury, or death when misused, even marginally inaccurately implemented, or implemented with clients who have respiratory, cardiac, or other identified medical conditions. This relatively high abuse potential and the resulting consequences have led many states to ban prone floor holds in many settings.

It is often the case that organizations use commercially available programs that omit desired content or include content that is inconsistent or incompatible to the procedure, policies, or philosophy of the organizations. In these cases, there are options available since simply changing the current curriculum is typically forbidden. One option, of course, is to switch to a curriculum that better matches the organization's philosophy. If this is considered too costly or cumbersome, another option is to deemphasize the less desirable or incompatible content during training, then provide additional alternative training that supersedes the curriculum. A third option is to ensure that individual behavior support plans for individuals contain more specific and individualized interventions that, in all cases, preclude or supersede the general intervention training.

A final content consideration is educating and training staff about the limited conditions under which emergency restraint is to be implemented. General consensus, many regulations, and most EI curricula specify that restraint should be implemented only 1) if there is serious and imminent risk of self-injury or harm to others, 2) as a last resort, after less restrictive procedures have failed, 3) as long as imminent risk is present, 4) by staff who are trained in prevention and restraint procedures, and 5) as a behavior management strategy and never as punishment, convenience, or because of low staffing ratios.

## TRAINING PROCEDURES AND PROCESSES

Once the scope and content of the curriculum has been determined, training of the concepts and skills can be initiated. Most EI training courses focus on teaching new skills individually and in a slow, accurate fashion, typically following a stepwise sequence of simple to complex. This approach is reasonable and advisable, but not necessarily adequate without ensuring that effective instructional techniques are being used. We recommend that a combination of several evidence-based strategies make up the teaching approach for teaching of specific skills that staff will be expected to perform when working with clients.

First, strategies within the errorless teaching literature (Cooper, Heron, & Heward, 1987; Jerome, Frantino, & Sturmey, 2007; Touchette, 1968) can be efficient and cost effective in training many skills. Although there is little empirical support for errorless procedures in teaching staff to implement restraint and escort methods, they are accepted widely, although not labeled as such, for teaching motor skills (e.g., Luyben, Funk, Morgan, Clark, & DeLulio, 1986). Given the importance of teaching EI procedures accurately, errorless procedures are recommended.

For training EI skills, we recommend the following errorless teaching strategies, many of which transfer stimulus control from the instructor to appropriate and relevant circumstances:

1. Provide step-by-step demonstrations of the skill.
2. Present step-by-step instructions to the participant, essentially narrating her or him through a slow-motion demonstration of the procedure.
3. Provide physical guidance and/or other stimulus prompts if applicable and necessary to ensure additional correct responding.
4. Praise correct responding whether prompted or independent.
5. Over the course of to to three trials, gradually fade the vocal, physical guidance (to shadowing), and/or other stimulus prompts, eventually allowing independent responding.
6. If errors occur during or after fading guidance, terminate the trial, offer specific corrective feedback and provide significantly enhanced verbal, modeling, and/or manual guidance through the next trial.

Errorless training procedures present several benefits (Cooper et al., 1987; Martin & Pear, 1983). First, they prevent incorrect responses such as inaccurate hand placement and unstable body positioning that may emerge during or after training. Second, fewer or no errors reduces instruction time—an important factor for most organizations. Errorless learning strategies also limit the need for corrective feedback that can adversely affect a participant's learning if perceived as negative or functioning as a distraction.

The second collection of strategies used in EI training is derived from the active student responding (ASR) literature. The research is reasonably clear on the importance of ASR (Barbetta, Heron, & Heward, 1993; Kellum, Carr, & Dozier, 2001) when teaching conceptual information to diverse populations. Some forms of ASR that can easily be employed in EIT programs include requiring participants to fill in blanks in the participant manual at key points (e.g., minimum criteria for employing restraint) during the lecture, engage in choral responding corresponding to the steps of the procedure, and answering questions about content and demonstrations. In addition, frequent, random querying of individuals about immediately preceding critical material will likely improve verbal command of the material. At a minimum, a short vocal quiz should be given to the participants at the end of each major section of the training, addressing all key points of that section. We suggest using ASR throughout the course of training.

A third set of strategies involves generating response fluency. Fluency, best described as accurate *and* fast responding, is most often implemented to improve reading skills (Binder, 1996) but has been evaluated as a training technique to improve employee performance in several areas (Binder, 1996; Binder & Bloom, 1989; Binder & Sweeney, 2002). Although rarely mentioned within the context of training curricula for physical restraint, obtaining fluency in all EI skills may be perceived as impractical due to the time typically allotted for most courses. Nevertheless, because fluency may be an essential characteristic of participant performance in order for the skills to be exhibited readily in the natural setting, training skills to fluency through repeated trials, numerous role-plays, and other methods should be considered when designing or teaching a course that includes physical restraint.

Finally, the educational research has also demonstrated the value in conducting interspersed and spaced trials during skills training for generating acquisition, generalization, and maintenance of the skills trained (Browder & Shear, 1996; Koegel & Koegel, 1986; Neef, Iwata, & Page, 1977, 1980; Rowan & Pear, 1985; Volkert, Lerman, Trosclair, Addison, & Kodak, 2008). The strategies involve interspersing previously mastered tasks with instruction of new or unknown tasks. Therefore, once a skill has been trained and is fluent, introducing additional interspersed and spaced practice—opportunities for staff to practice multiple, previously learned skills in the training context—is strongly recommended. Beyond improving acquisition, generalization, and maintenance, there are additional benefits of interspersing and spacing practice of previously learned skills. First, as when teaching nonphysical strategies, interspersing and spacing provide the opportunity to observe and correct participant behavior should errors arise. Just as important, however, doing so allows instructors to teach staff to make correct (or at least reasonable) choices for when to implement specific emergency procedures of the *appropriate* level of restrictiveness. Indeed, this process may be the most difficult aspect of the training.

It seems obvious that participants should be able to exhibit the physical skills necessary to address crisis situations both accurately and quickly. For example, waiting too long to physically escort a client who is about to assault another client may lead to an otherwise avoidable assault. Therefore, being able to implement a physical procedure quickly and accurately in training is likely necessary for accurate responding in the natural context. For all these reasons we advise that participants demonstrate critical skills at normative speeds and within simulated contexts (e.g., role-play, fast drills) during training that approximate the actual environment in which they are to be used. Concerning generalization of acquired skills, multiple trainers should conduct instruction and they should incorporate scenarios that approximate situations that the participants will encounter.

## Implementing the Training Sequence

Combining the foregoing strategies provides a logical and natural training sequence involving four steps, as listed in Table 16.2 and illustrated in Figure 16.1. First, a new skill or concept is introduced establishing the foundation, conditions for its use, and alternatives for the skill to be trained. Next, the skill is demonstrated to a group of participants, requiring both choral and written responding (ASR) and vocal fluency, as well as discussion of examples and nonexamples of use of application.

**Table 16.2.**   Detailed training process

| Area | Training steps |
|---|---|
| Introduction of skill | 1. Introduce a single concept or skill in the order it appears in the training sequence (e.g., single-person hold) and briefly describe the purpose of and circumstances in which to use the technique along with the less restrictive alternatives that should have been considered first. |
| | 2. Avoid details such as all exceptions and variations to procedure (e.g., client sits during restraint), and reserve this for after all staff have demonstrated competency with basic version of procedure. |
| | 3. Discuss common errors and actions to avoid (e.g., moving hands outward in a manner that might lead to striking client). |
| | 4. Keep this introduction under 1–3 minutes, depending on the complexity of procedure. |
| Demonstration of skill | 5. Obtain a willing and cooperative participant on whom to demonstrate technique slowly so that all staff can see the steps and can see the desired end state of the procedure. Repeat this two or three times, changing your position so that participants can see it from different perspectives. |
| | 6. Have participants read the steps from their manual (en masse or individually) while you simultaneously demonstrate the steps. This will help to maintain attention to critical aspects of the skills and may help to bring the behavior under self-instructional stimulus control prior to participants having to demonstrate the task. |
| Training individual participants in skill | 7. Instruct one participant (or multiple for procedures requiring multiple participants) to demonstrate the technique. (It can be helpful to demonstrate the technique once more, slowly.) |
| |    a. Provide step-by-step instruction, essentially guiding participant through a slow-motion demonstration of procedure. Provide physical guidance if applicable and necessary. |
| |    b. Over the course of two or three trials, gradually fade vocal, physical guidance, and/or other prompts. |
| |    c. If the participant demonstrates the technique independently, provide praise. If errors occur during or after fading guidance, terminate the trial, provide specific feedback on what needs to be corrected and provide significantly enhanced verbal, modeling, and/or manual guidance through the next trial. |
| | 8. If a participant continues to demonstrate inaccuracies through several trials, additional instructional strategies may be required including, but not limited to |
| |    a. Observing several others before trying to demonstrate it again. |
| |    b. Pantomiming the action while you demonstrate the technique. |
| |    c. Physical guidance as they slowly attempt the procedure. Repeat over two or three trials, reducing your guidance as they show improved performance. |
| |    d. Individualized instruction, which may involve more description, practice of component skills in isolation, chaining learned components under fully prompted control, fade prompts over successive trials, all the while reinforcing aspects of the performance that are correct. In rare instances, a participant may not be able to acquire necessary skills *in the allotted time*, in which case training remedial training at a later date is appropriate. |
| | 9. Repeat (7) with all participants. Once all participants have demonstrated the technique to competency, select the next technique in the curricular sequence and teach it in a similar fashion. |
| Role-play of skill | 10. When several (e.g., two or three) of the techniques from the curriculum have been trained to all participants, introduce role-played practice. |

| Area | Training steps |
|---|---|
| | *For example,* |
| | Participants have learned to demonstration a simple DRO; several new de-escalation strategies (identifying antecedents, FCT, behavioral momentum, and planned ignoring), and safe body positioning. The trainer would then present one or two participants at a time with a hypothetical situation such as "I'm a moderately agitated individual in the day habilitation program who is likely to exhibit antecedent behaviors like pacing and groaning. These behaviors rarely lead to aggression, but I can sometimes hit myself and break furniture...." Instruct participants to practice de-escalation. Stop the role-played practice and provide feedback if a significant error is happening such as the participant continues to stand too close, then resume. As the participants implement procedures correctly, simulate de-escalation of the client. Modulate the intensity of the client's behavior in order to differentially reinforce the participants' correct implementation of the strategies. When participants have effectively demonstrated de-escalation, complete a short debriefing, describing to participants what was done correctly and what needs improvement. |
| | 11. Repeat with another one or two participants until all have participated in the role-played practice and engaged in multiple strategies of those trained up to this point. |
| | 12. Introduce and train (Steps 1–11) the next two or three skills until all skills have been trained. |
| Comprehensive role-play | 13. Once all the strategies and concepts in the curriculum have been trained, a more comprehensive role-played practice should be completed in which several staff participate, giving them a chance to practice all techniques with the trainer(s) serving as the client in order to insure safe practice. It also gives an opportunity for participants to operate cooperatively and to establish clear direction during an incident. |
| |     a. All role-played practice should begin with clear statements regarding safety. At a minimum, this should include a statement that participants are not to engage in risky behavior such as actual hitting or breaking things. It should clearly describe a safe way of simulating aggression or self-harm (e.g., "I will reach my hand towards you and say 'punch'"). There should be clear signals for when and how to end the role play. All participants should be informed that they are to terminate the practice if they see anything unsafe happening (e.g., another participant is holding in an unsafe manner) or someone is experiencing pain. It is strongly advised that there be a "code word" to end the practice such as "break." |
| |     b. Participants should be provided enough information about the client and the situation to effectively plan and execute interventions. Trainer should start role-play after all the participants indicate and understanding the hypothetical situation. A scenario might involve a student who exhibits a clear set of antecedent behaviors (e.g., pacing, whining, dropping) when presented with tasks in the hour preceding lunch. A hint might be provided that being hungry might be a factor in the escalation. Provide participants with the upper limit on the severity of the "client's" behavior. As role play progresses, test staff on their ability to implement de-escalation strategies as well as any physical management techniques that might be necessary, modulating behavior in order to differentially reinforce participants' correct responses. |

*Key:* DRO, differential reinforcement of other behavior; FCT, functional communication training.

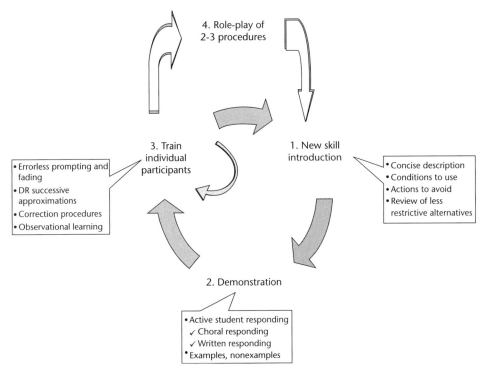

**Figure 16.1.** Strategies providing a logical and natural training sequence involving four steps. (*Key:* DR, differential reinforcement.)

Training on the single skill is then conducted sequentially with individual participants in an errorless fashion using vocal instruction, stimulus prompting techniques (gestural, pictorial, graduated guidance), prompt fading, successive approximations, and correction procedures should errors occur. Once two or three skills have been trained across all participants, role-play should be conducted requiring the participants to demonstrate recently and previously trained skills.

The foregoing instructional sequence is repeated until all skills are trained and acquired. Finally, a series of comprehensive role-plays are conducted allowing for more naturalistic demonstration and combinations of skills by one or more participants.

## Tracking Progress

It is essential to track the progress for all participants as the course proceeds by recording a "pass or fail" for each competency (physical or nonphysical technique) when there is a well-defined, observable skill to be trained (actual competency). For didactic or lecture portions of the EI course, as when a concept is introduced and no actual competency is required, the participants' ability to respond to vocal queries or to engage in choral responding can be used as a criterion for recording a "pass." See Figure 16.2 for an example of a simple tracking sheet that we use.

**QBS, Inc.**

version 5.4

## Safety-Care™ Specialist Training Checklist

Trainee _____ Date(s) _____ Location _____ Pass/Fail _____

| Topic | Reviewed (✓) | Competency Pass, Fail, Restriction (P/F/R) |
|---|---|---|
| About: Safety-Care, Important Points, Ground Rules, Goals, Interdisciplinary Treatment, Regulatory Issues | | |
| Understanding Challenging Behavior | | |
| Reinforcement of Challenging Behavior | | |
| Creating a Safe and Therapeutic Environment | | |
| Elbow Check | | |
| Safety Habits | | |
| Staff Behavior and Emotional Reactions | | |
| How to Reinforce Effectively | | |
| Differential Reinforcement | | |
| Detecting Antecedents & Predicting Behavior | | |
| Safety Stance | | |
| Calling for Assistance | | |
| Leadership and Teamwork | | |
| De-Escalation | | |
| Management of Dangerous Objects | | |
| Protective Stance | | |
| Safety Shuffle | | |
| Shoulder Check | | |
| Supportive Guide | | |
| Wrist Grab Release | | |
| Stripping a Grab | | |

| Topic | Reviewed (✓) | Competency Pass, Fail, Restriction (P/F/R) |
|---|---|---|
| Hair Pull Release | | |
| Choke Release | | |
| Bite Release | | |
| Physical Management | | |
| 1-Person Stability Hold | | |
| 2-Person Stability Hold | | |
| Forward Escort | | |
| Reverse Escort | | |
| Seated 1-Person or 2-Person Stability Hold | | |
| Chair Stability Hold | | |
| Leg Wrap | | |
| Post-Incident Procedures | | |
| Written Test | | |
| Role-Play | | |
| **Advanced Modules** | | |
| | | |
| | | |
| | | |
| | | |
| | | |
| | | |

**QBS Certified Safety-Care Trainer** _____ Date ____/____/____

**Figure 16.2.** Training Checklist for Safety-Care™ Behavioral Safety Training. (QBS, 257 Turnpike Road, Suite 230, Southborough, Massachusetts. Used with permission.) (Safety-Care is a trademark of QBS, Inc.)

## Dealing with Problems During Training

Training should remain on topic and on schedule to ensure that all the material will be covered and taught to a minimum standard. Redundancies and actual treatment planning should be avoided during the course. Participants may come laden with endless "what if" scenarios, and an effective trainer will be ready to field the questions quickly and redirect the discussion to the topic at hand or preclude it altogether with clear ground rules. Training can be made more effective when common concerns are anticipated, perhaps by way of giving examples at opportune times (not when introducing a topic) that address those concerns.

Even when errorless learning strategies are implemented during training there will be variability in the ability of participants to efficiently acquire the physical skills. Some participants may have difficulty with the physical aspects of the training; some may have difficulty with other strategies, such as de-escalation. Others may be hesitant to demonstrate procedures in front of their peers, making it difficult to ascertain their skill level. It is important to anticipate these problems. One suggestion is that prior to initiating training, a trainer explicitly state that discussion on individual cases will be limited and, although examples are encouraged, spiraling "what if" scenarios will be truncated.

If verbal and visual cues are not effective during training, physical guidance may be required so that the participant completes the action. Of note, all these methods may be unfamiliar to the participants, so it is necessary to clarify them at the beginning of the training so that participants will not be offended or resistant.

## ROLLING OUT THE TRAINING ACROSS AN ORGANIZATION

Once a curriculum and methods for staff training are selected, an organizational dissemination plan must be developed. There are some potential risks, should this process be mismanaged. These include 1) confusion among direct care and supervisory staff about which procedures are "official policy" and which are not, 2) staff trained in different procedures attempting to respond to crisis situations using incompatible approaches, 3) staff responding to inconsistencies in communication by utilizing the most restrictive of potential options, 4) failure to use preventive strategies, leading to increased crisis events, 5) overuse of restrictive procedures when other options are available, and 6) underuse of procedures necessary for safety. Any rollout plan should be designed to minimize these issues.

Apropos to the preceding discussion, it is important to implement training thoughtfully with clear communication about expectations, policies, and timelines. In developing such a plan, the organization's administrative team must consider several practical issues including, but not limited to, the size of the organization, characteristics of the people served, staff experience, previous training curriculum, treatment team processes, and anticipated time frame for training. We recommend that the planning process include representatives from various hierarchical levels of the organization and from each departmental group that might be called on to implement the training. Such an interdepartmental team is most likely to anticipate the range of problems that might be encountered.

Perhaps the most common and practical model for rollout is that a group of staff are chosen to be trained as trainers in the selected behavioral safety curriculum. This type of pyramidal training model in which peers serve as trainers (e.g., within an organization) is well established and has been shown to be effective, acceptable to participants, and, importantly, facilitate the maintenance of the skills of those peers serving as trainers (Kuhn, Lerman, & Vorndran, 2003; Neef, 1995; Page, Iwata, & Reid, 1982; van den Pol, Reid, & Fuqua, 1983). A small organization may be able to rely on outside trainers, but this is typically cost-prohibitive for larger organizations. There are also additional potential advantages in having a certified trainer on-site, as this assists with follow-up feedback, retraining, and troubleshooting and reduces costs of soliciting repeated training services from an outside source.

If in-house trainers are used, the selection process for identifying the trainer(s) should be systematic. Optimally, the number of trainers selected should allow small trainer-to-participant ratios during initial training (many training curricula specify maximum ratios or other limits). Trainers usually have other job responsibilities, placing a practical limit on the amount of training that can reasonably be conducted by one trainer. At the same time, too many trainers may result in each having too few opportunities to conduct training and potential degradation of training skills.

In addition to the foregoing considerations, trainers should be physically fit and have normal range of motion in major joints, sufficient endurance to complete training, and sufficient strength to demonstrate physical restraint procedures effectively. Trainers should have enough experience with the relevant client population and high-risk behaviors to be able to provide relevant examples during training and answer questions effectively. As noted, it is helpful to include trainers from a range of hierarchical levels in the organization in order to demonstrate both commitment from middle to upper management and involvement of experienced direct care staff. It is also essential that trainers have previous experience with teaching or training and are comfortable speaking in front of an audience.

In general, it is best if no staff expected to implement safety procedures is geographically or hierarchically distant from all available trainers. A plan, in which a distant training department provides training to staff from other departments and, subsequently, has no contact with those staff until recertification time months or years later, is not recommended. If providing off-site instruction is necessary, trainers should frequently be available in the settings where the trained skills are most likely to be implemented. This allows trainers to provide direct support, problem-solving, remedial teaching, and review with staff that may be having difficulty with minimal delay between crisis incidents and on-site supplemental training. If staff perceive trainers as respected individuals who understand the characteristics and complexities of the staff's job, then this additional training is more likely to occur and to be effective.

## Developing the Training Plan

Whether implementing a training curriculum for the first time or transitioning to a new curriculum, it is best to create a detailed written plan describing how the training will be conducted. It should answer a number of questions:

*What is the date by which all staff must be trained?* Optimally, the core training happens over weeks, not months, for all staff. The less time between the start of training and the completion of training for current staff, the better. If training is spread out over more than 2–3 weeks, consider scheduling a refresher session for staff that may have had the training but have not used it for a period of time.

*Who will do the training for which groups of staff?* If multiple trainers are available, decide how they will be deployed. If trainers are new to this particular staff training program, it is generally best to train in pairs, for at least the first few sessions. Many training programs specify a ratio of trainers to trainees. These ratios should not be exceeded. If possible, the first session for each trainer should not maximize the number of allowed trainees.

*Where will the training be conducted?* Make sure the training space is appropriate to both didactic and role-play instruction. Also consider how staff will be assigned and notified about training as well as what they should wear.

Once the training has been implemented, a number of additional questions must be anticipated. For example, what is the plan in the event that a staff person does not pass the training or cannot pass because of physical restrictions or limitations? Depending on the setting and the specific job role, such restrictions might not be considered a requirement for employment. If not, it may be possible to make accommodations such as limiting the client groupings to which that person is assigned. Also, what is the plan for ensuring retention of trained skills or to train newly hired staff? In this regard, most programs require routine (i.e., annual) recertification training.

## Starting from Scratch

If the organization has no previous EI training curriculum in place and is starting with a new program from scratch, it is important to clearly communicate to all staff what the new curriculum is expected to accomplish and how it relates to job roles. If possible, identify specific teams of staff who work together and roll out the training one team at a time. This approach facilitates working and supporting each other with new procedures and concepts. Make sure that trainers are available to answer questions and provide quick review of specific skills.

## Making the Transition from a Previously Trained Curriculum

If the organization currently uses another behavioral safety training curriculum and the goal is to replace it with a new one, the transition must be carefully planned. The training plan should first identify a rollout date. There certainly can be one date for the entire organization, but in some cases it is more practical to have a separate date for each specific team of staff who work on a particular unit, building, or classroom. Staff that participates in training of the new plan should be clearly informed of the date on which newly trained procedures are to be used. The time from the start of training to rollout should be minimized. It is best not to spread training out over more than a month. If that is not possible, weekly review sessions should be conducted leading up to rollout. Also, be prepared for resistance to change. It is inevitable that some staff may prefer the old program, in part because they have used it many times and know exactly how to make it work. Those concerns are understandable, and trainers should be available to answer questions, respond to concerns, and role-play potentially challenging scenarios. It is important to state unequivocally, however, that as of a specific date, the new program will be the only approved curriculum for prevention, minimization, and management of behavioral crises. Staff must clearly understand that it is unacceptable to mix and match between the old program and the new one. Finally, once the program has been rolled out, trainers should be made available to answer staff questions and provide quick review of specific skills as needed.

## Multiple or Coexisting Behavioral Safety Training Systems

Some organizations may find it necessary to train some staff in one training system and some staff in another. This is generally not recommended as it increases both the chances for miscommunication and injury, as well as the increased burden of training. If this approach is taken, then certain cautions must be observed. The most serious concern is that a behavioral crisis could occur and staff trained in two different courses must work together. If it is necessary for multiple staff to implement a physical hold, differences in procedures can create a particularly dangerous situation. Less dangerous, but also potentially problematic, is if staff trained in two different programs are trying to work together to prevent or manage a behavioral crisis. There is the possibility that they might miscommunicate or work at cross-purposes, increasing the likelihood of serious behavioral escalation.

Therefore, it is best to separate programs—organizationally and geographically—that use different curricula. Staff working in one location, and those called to assist, should all be trained in a common set of concepts, skills, and procedures as close in time as is feasible. Staff that are not trained in the locally approved program who arrive to assist should be instructed (in advance) to help manage other clients, remove dangerous items, and the like but should avoid intervention if possible.

## Supervision After Training

Once staff are trained to competency, generalization and maintenance of the skills are of critical concern, particularly with procedures that involve physically restraining the client. Although more research is clearly needed to evaluate the maintenance of EI skills after training, recent findings have shown that significant variability occurs after training has been completed (Busch & Shore, 2000; Carpenter, Hannon, McLeery, & Wanderling, 1988a, 1988b; Persi & Pasquali, 1999; Ray & Rappaport, 1995). In some cases, significant performance decrements in such skills occur as early as 6 months after training, even with staff who work in environments in which the skills are required (Shapiro, Cameron, & Geary, 2005).

If there is poor maintenance of EI skills, it seems likely that inaccurate implementation will lead to increased risk, injury, and abuse, although research is lacking in this area. A notable exception to this lack of research is that several studies have revealed that unplanned physical restraint—essentially utilized as an EI—is more likely to result in injuries to both the staff and client (Hill & Spreat, 1987; Spreat, Lipinski, Hill, & Hagopian, 1986; Tilli & Spreat, 2009). Even then, the rate of injury has been found to be low with less than 3% of applications resulting in injury (Williams, 2009). Regardless, it is critical that both prevention and management (i.e., restraint) skills are implemented accurately outside the training environment within treatment, educational, and residential settings.

There should be no expectation that skills acquired in classroom training will automatically either generalize to the job setting or maintain over time. Barriers to generalization and maintenance include the dissimilarity between the training setting and the job setting (place, presence of clients, private emotional events such as anger and fear, and antecedent and maintaining events for alternative responses to client behavior), forgetting seldom-used procedures over time, and poor implementation integrity. To a large degree, these are the same issues that affect any set of training and behavioral expectations for staff in a direct care setting. Intervention integrity has been shown to be critical to the efficacy of some type of behavioral treatment procedures while not so critical to others (McIntyre, Gresham, DiGennaro, & Reed, 2007). With respect to EI, however, the potential consequences of poor integrity (inaccurate implementation) generate concerns well beyond efficacy, impacting the safety of clients and staff. Typically, staff has been trained in a large number of policies and skills and are expected to implement them. In addition, there are certain differences between some procedural expectations for staff and those related to EI skills. Effective responses to aggression and self-injury may require physical agility and emotional self-management in response to danger, in addition to accurately recalling the procedures. Staff that consistently follow other organizational protocols and training may find it difficult to do so in response to high levels of client agitation. Therefore, implementation integrity should be addressed by using a standardized checklist that allows performance to be continuously monitored and improved.

To facilitate generalization and maintenance of EI skills, staff retraining and recertification should occur at least annually. Although, as pointed out earlier, performance decrements are detected as early as 6 months after training. All critical components of the training curriculum should be reviewed and staff should demonstrate continued competency in each procedure, with correction whenever performance is not as specified. We also recommend scheduling frequent opportunities for staff to practice, review, and problem solve. Trainers should make them-selves available to staff regularly as well as during formal review sessions in which specific techniques are practiced. One strategy we encourage is called "Technique of the Week," wherein a procedure is reviewed every week with trainers or peers. Including all staff in this process of reviewing with their peers may also improve competence by both participants (Alvero & Austin, 2004; van den Pol et al., 1983).

Meetings involving trainers should also provide staff with time to ask questions and devise solutions to problems. Clear communication to staff about acceptable and unacceptable practices—especially in response to unanticipated crisis events—will also support generalization and maintenance. Finally, we advise training supervisors to conduct observations of staff and record data on the implementation of EI procedures, as well as provide "in the moment" feedback for staff, particularly during crisis events.

Procedures can be developed to facilitate trainer and supervisor feedback. For example, the practice of touching a staff person on the shoulder and speaking quietly and calmly near the ear of the participant can be used as a method for giving feedback even in the midst of a fast-moving crisis event. Another focus of training supervisors is how to intervene during a crisis when staff is not implementing procedures accurately. Supervisors should know how and when to remove a staff member who is performing outside of expectations and making a crisis event more dangerous than necessary. A predetermined code phrase that allows staff to be removed from a crisis, such as "you have a phone call," can be helpful. Additional considerations include debriefing procedures that involve an analytic account of the sequence of events leading to the crisis, a clear system to refer staff for additional training, review, and problem solving, and reasonable and consistent disciplinary policies for staff who do not comply with expectations.

## A FINAL COMMENT ON RESTRAINT REDUCTION

Although research on the topic of physical restraint has been conducted for some time, efforts at reducing emergency interventions have taken on recent importance. Toward that end, several studies have reported both analyses of organizational, staff, and consumer characteristics associated with restraint (Carpenter et al., 1988a, 1988b; Crenshaw & Francis, 1995; Forquer, Earle, Way, & Banks, 1996; Way & Banks, 1990), as well as successful restraint reduction interventions (Donat, 1998; Forster, Cavness, & Phelps, 1999; Luiselli, 2009; Luiselli, Dunn, & Pace, 2005; Luiselli et al., 2000; Luiselli, Pace, & Dunn, 2006; Masker, 2001; Singh, Singh, Davis, Latham, & Ayers, 1999).

Seemingly lacking, however, has been discussion or investigation of the motivational variables supporting the use of restraint by staff. An argument can be made that the behavior of restraining is likely influenced by the same motivational operations that affect other staff behavior. Certainly, the organizational behavior management literature supports this conclusion in that a wide array of behavioral interventions based on functional analyses have been effective at influencing both desirable and undesirable staff practices (Austin, 2000; Johnson, Redmon, & Mawhinney, 2001). It seems, then, that such functional analyses of restraining behavior would likely lead to a more thorough understanding of some of the contributing factors for the use of restraint, and possibly lead to direct interventions that may decrease their use, at least in situations in which it has been unnecessary or unwarranted (Mohr & Anderson, 2001; Ryan, Peterson, Tetreault, & Van der Hagen, 2007). Lennox and colleagues (Houston, 2010; Lennox, 2009, 2010a, 2010b; Lennox, Rourke, & van Herp, 2008) have proposed theoretical accounts of such motivational conditions, including possible positive reinforcement, negative reinforcement, and automatic reinforcement operations. However, more discussion and research in this area is clearly needed.

## REFERENCES

Alvero, A.M. & Austin, J. (2004). The effects of conducting behavioral observations on the behavior of the observer. *Journal of Applied Behavior Analysis, 37,* 457–468.

American Psychological Association. (1994). *Guidelines on Effective Treatment for Persons with Mental Retardation and Developmental Disabilities. A resolution by APA Division 33.* Retrieved from http://www.apa.org/divisions/div33/effectivetreatment.html

Association of Professional Behavior Analysts. (2010). *Position Statement on the Use of Restraint and Seclusion as Interventions for Dangerous and Destructive Behaviors: Supporting Research and Practice Guidelines.* Retrieved from http://www.apbahome.net/Restraint_Seclusion%20.pdf

Austin, J. (2000). Performance analysis and performance diagnostics. In J. Austin & J.E. Carr (Eds.) *Handbook of applied behavior analysis* (pp. 321–349). Reno, NV: Context Press.

Barbetta, P.M., Heron, T.E, & Heward, W.L. (1993). Effects of active student response during error correction on the acquisition, maintenance, and generalization of sight words by student with developmental disabilities. *Journal of Applied Behavior Analysis, 26,* 111–119.

Binder, C. (1996). Behavioral fluency: Evolution of a new paradigm. *The Behavior Analyst, 19,* 163–197.

Binder, C., & Bloom, C. (1989, February). Fluent product knowledge: Application in the financial services industry. *Performance and Instruction, 28*(2), 17–21

Binder, C., & Sweeney, L. (2002, February). Building fluent performance in a customer call center. *Performance Improvement, 41,* 29–37.

Browder, D.M., & Shear, S.M. (1996). Interspersal of known items in a treatment package to teach sight words to students with behavior disorders. *The Journal of Special Education, 29,* 400–413.

Busch, A.D., & Shore, M.F. (2000). Seclusion and restraint: A review of recent literature. *Harvard Review of Psychiatry, 8,* 251–270.

Carpenter, M.D., Hannon, V.R., McCleery, G., & Wanderling, J.A. (1988a). Ethnic differences in seclusion and restraint. *Journal of Nervous and Mental Disease, 176,* 726–731.

Carpenter, M.D., Hannon, V.R., McCleery, G., & Wanderling, J.A. (1988b). Variations in seclusion and restraint practices by hospital location. *Hospital and Community Psychiatry, 39,* 418–423.

Cooper, J.O., Heron, T.E., & Heward, W.L. (1987). *Applied behavior analysis.* Upper Saddle River, NJ: Prentice-Hall.

Couvillon, M., Peterson, R.L., Ryan, J.B., Scheuermann, B., & Stegall, J. (2010). A review of crisis intervention training programs for schools. *Teaching Exceptional Children, 42,* 6–17.

Crenshaw, W.B. & Francis, P.S. (1995). A national survey on seclusion and restraint in state psychiatric hospitals. *Psychiatric Services, 46,* 1026–1031.

Donat, D.C. (1998). Impact of a mandatory behavioral consultation on seclusion/restraint utilization in a psychiatric hospital. *Journal of Behavior Therapy and Experimental Psychiatry, 29,* 13–19.

Doughty, C.J. (September, 2005). Staff training programs for the prevention and management of violence directed at nurses and other healthcare workers in mental health services and emergency departments. *NZHTA Technical Brief, 4*(2).

Farrell, G., & Cubit, K. (2005). Nurses under threat: A comparison of content of 28 aggression management programs. *International Journal of Mental Health Nursing, 14,* 44–53.

Favell, J.E., McGimsey, J.F., & Jones, M.L. (1978). The use of physical restraint in the treatment of self-injury and as positive reinforcement. *Journal of Applied Behavior Analysis, 11,* 225–241.

Forquer, S.L., Earle, K.A., Way, B.B., & Banks, S.M. (1996). Predictors of the use of restraint and seclusion in public psychiatric hospitals. *Administration and Policy in Mental Health, 23,* 527–532.

Forster, P., Cavness, C., & Phelps, M. (1999). Staff training decreases use of seclusion and restraint in an acute psychiatric hospital. *Archives of Psychiatric Nursing, 13,* 269–271.

Hill, J., & Spreat, S. (1987). Staff injury rates associated with the implementation of contingent restraint. *Mental Retardation, 25,* 141–145.

Houston, Z. (May, 2010). Functional analysis of restraint behavior. Presented at the 36th Annual Conference of the Association for Behavior Analysis International, San Antonio, TX.

Jerome, J., Frantino, E.P., & Sturmey, P. (2007). The effects of errorless learning and backward chaining on the acquisition of internet skills in adults with developmental disabilities. *Journal of Applied Behavior Analysis, 40,* 185–189.

Johnson, C.M., Redmon, W.K., & Mawhinney, T.C. (2001). *Handbook of organization performance: Behavior analysis and management.* New York: Haworth Press.

Kellum, K.K., Carr, J.E., & Dozier, C.L. (2001). Response-card instruction and student learning in a college classroom. *Teaching of Psychology, 28,* 101–104.

Koegel, L.K., & Koegel, R.L. (1986). The effects of interspersed maintenance tasks on academic performance in a severe childhood stroke victim. *Journal of Applied Behavior Analysis, 19,* 425–430.

Kuhn, S.A.C., Lerman, D.C., & Vorndran, C.M. (2003). Pyramidal training for families of children with problem behavior. Journal of Applied Behavior Analysis, *36,* 77–88.

Lennox, D.B. (August, 2009). Behavioral approaches to crisis management. Presented at the 2009 National Autism Conference, Hershey, PA.

Lennox, D.B. (May, 2010a). Organizational approaches to restraint reduction. Presented at the 36th Annual Conference of the Association for Behavior Analysis International, San Antonio, TX.

Lennox, D.B. (September, 2010b). *Restraint practices: Understanding motivation behind restraint.* Presented at the annual meeting of the Maine Association of Special Education Directors.

Lennox, D.B., Rourke, D., & van Herp, K. (2008). *Application of behavior analysis procedures to de-escalation situations.* Presented at the 35th Annual Conference of the Association for Behavior Analysis International, Phoenix, AZ.

Luiselli, J.K. (2009). Physical restraint of people with intellectual disability: A review of implementation reduction and elimination procedures. *Journal of Applied Research in Intellectual Disabilities, 22,* 126–134.

Luiselli, J.K., Dunn, E.K., & Pace, G.M. (2005). Antecedent assessment and intervention to reduce physical restraint (protective holding) of children and adolescents with acquired brain injury. *Behavioral Interventions, 20,* 51–65.

Luiselli, J.K., Kane, A., Treml, T., & Young, N. (2000). Behavioral intervention to reduce physical restraint of adolescents with developmental disabilities. *Behavioral Interventions, 15,* 317–330.

Luiselli, J.K., Pace, G.M., & Dunn, G.M. (2006). Effects of behavior-contingent and fixed-time release contingencies on frequency and duration of therapeutic restraint. *Behavior Modification, 30,* 442–445.

Luyben, P.D., Funk, D.M., Morgan, J.K., Clark, K.A., & DeLulio, D.W. (1986). Team sports for the severely retarded: Training a side-of-the-foot soccer pass using a maximum-to-minimum prompt reduction strategy. *Journal of Applied Behavior Analysis, 19,* 431–436.

Martin, G., & Pear, J. (1983). *Behavior modification: What it is and how to do it.* Englewood Cliffs, NJ: Prentice-Hall.

Masker, A. (2001). Reducing physical management and time-outs: One agency's experience. *Residential Group Care Quarterly, 2*(3).

Matson, J.L. & Boisjoli, J.A. (2009). Restraint procedures and challenging behaviours in intellectual disability: An analysis of causative factors. *Journal of Applied Research in Intellectual Disabilities, 22,* 111–117.

McIntyre, L.L., Gresham, F.M., DiGennaro, F.D., & Reed, D.D. (2007). Treatment integrity of school-based interventions with children in the journal of applied behavior analysis 1991-2005. *Journal of Applied Behavior Analysis, 40,* 659–672.

Mohr, W.K. & Anderson, J.A. (2001). Faulty assumptions associated with the use of restraints with children. *Journal of Child and Adolescent Psychiatric Nursing, 14,* 141–151.

Morrison, E.F. & Love, C.C. (2003). An evaluation of four programs for the management of aggression in psychiatric settings. *Archives of Psychiatric Nursing, 17,* 146–155.

Neef, N.A. (1995). Research on training trainers in program implementation: An introduction and future directions. *Journal of Applied Behavior Analysis, 28,* 297–299.

Neef, N.A., Iwata, B.A., & Page, T.J. (1977). The effects of known-item interspersal on acquisition and retention of spelling and sightreading words. *Journal of Applied Behavior Analysis, 10,* 738.

Neef, N.A., Iwata, B.A., & Page, T.J. (1980). The effects of interspersal training versus high-density reinforcement on spelling acquisition and retention. *Journal of Applied Behavior Analysis, 13,* 153–158.

Page, T.J., Iwata, B.A., & Reid, D.H. (1982). Pyramidal training: A large-scale application with institutional staff. *Journal of Applied Behavior Analysis, 15,* 335–351.

Persi, J. & Pasquali, B. (1999). The issue of seclusions and physical restraints: Just how consistent are we? *Child & Youth Care Forum, 28,* 87–102.

QBS Incorporated. (2010). *Safety-Care™ Behavioral Safety Training.* Southborough, MA: QBS, Inc. (SafetyCareTraining. com)

Ray, N.K., & Rappaport, M.E. (1995). Use of restraint and seclusion in psychiatric settings in New York State. *Psychiatric Services, 46,* 1032–1037.

Rowan, V.C., & Pear, J.J. (1985). A comparison of the effects of interspersal and concurrent training sequences on acquisition, retention, and generalization of picture names. *Applied Research in Mental Retardation, 6,* 127–145.

Ryan, J.B. (2012). Regulatory goverance of physical restraint in schools. In Luiselli, J. (Ed.), *The Handbook of High-Risk Challenging Behaviors in People with Intellectual and Developmental Disabilities: Assessment and Intervention.* Baltimore: Paul H. Brookes Publishing Co.

Ryan, J.B. & Peterson, R.L. (2004). Restraint in the schools. *Behavior Disorders, 29,* 154–168.

Ryan, J.B., Peterson, R., Tetreault, G., & Van der Hagen, E. (2007). Reducing seclusion timeout and restraint procedures with at-risk youth. *The Journal of At-Risk Issues, 13,* 7–12.

Shapiro, R.L., Cameron, M.J., & Geary, W. (2005). *Using correspondence training to enhance staff performance of physical crisis intervention techniques in a human service setting.* Presented at 31st Annual Conference of the Association for Behavior Analysis International.

Singh, N.N., Singh, S.D., Davis, C.M., Latham, L.L., & Ayers, J.G. (1999). Reconsidering the use of seclusion and restraint in inpatient child and adults psychiatry. *Journal of Child and Family Studies, 8,* 243–253.

Spreat, S. & Baker-Potts, J. (1983). Patterns of injury in institutionalized mentally retarded residents. *Mental Retardation, 21,* 23–29.

Spreat, S., Lipinski, D.P., Hill, J., & Hagopian, M. (1986). Safety indices associated with the use of contingent restraint procedures. *Applied Research in Mental Retardation, 7,* 475–481.

Tilli, D.M., & Spreat, S. (2009). Restraint safety in a residential setting for persons with intellectual disabilities. *Behavioral Interventions, 24,* 127–136.

Touchette, P.E. (1968). The effects of graduated stimulus change on the acquisition of a simple discrimination in severely retarded boys. *Journal of the Experimental Analysis of Behavior. 11,* 39–48.

U.S. Department of Education. (2010). *Summary of seclusion and restraint statutes, regulations, policies and guidance, by state and territory.* Information as reported to the regional comprehensive centers and gathered from other sources. Retrieved from www.ed.gov/policy/seclusion/seclusion-state-summary.html

U.S. Government Accountability Office. (2009). *Seclusions and restraint: Selected cases of death and abuse at public and private schools and treatment centers.* Washington, DC: Author.

U.S. Government Accounting Office. (1998). *Residential treatment programs: Concerns regarding abuse and death in certain programs for troubled youth.* Washington, DC: Author.

Volkert, V.M., Lerman, D.C., Trosclair, N., Addison, L., & Kodak, T. (2008). An exploratory analysis of task-interspersal procedures while teaching object labels to children with autism. *Journal of Applied Behavior Analysis, 41,* 335–350.

van den Pol, R.A., Reid, D.H., & Fuqua, R.W. (1983). Peer training of safety-related skills to institutional staff: Benefits for trainers and trainees. *Journal of Applied Behavior Analysis, 16,* 139–156.

Vollmer, T.R., Hagopian, L.P., Bailey, J.S., Dorsey, M.F., Hanley, G.P., Lennox, D.B., Riordan, M.M., & Spreat, S. (2010). *The Association for Behavior Analysis International position statement on restraint and seclusion.* Retrieved from www.abainternational.org/ABA/statements/RestraintSeclusion.asp

Way, B.B., & Banks, S.M. (1990). Use of seclusion and restraint in public psychiatric hospitals: Patient characteristics and facility effects. *Hospital and Community Psychiatry, 41,* 75–81.

Williams, D.E. (2009). Restraint safety: An analysis of injuries related to restraint of people with intellectual disabilities. *Journal of Applied Research in Intellectual Disabilities, 22,* 135–139.

Williams, D.E. (2010). Reducing and eliminating restraint of people with developmental disabilities and severe behavior disorders: An overview of recent research. *Research in Developmental Disabilities, 31,* 1142–1148.

# Index